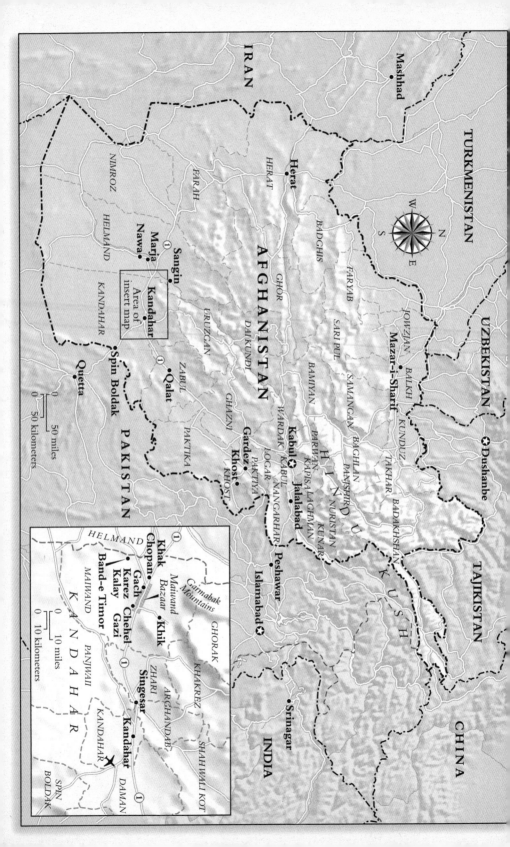

# THE
# TENDER
# SOLDIER

A True Story of War and Sacrifice

\*     \*     \*

Vanessa M. Gezari

Simon & Schuster
*New York  London  Toronto  Sydney  New Delhi*

Simon & Schuster
1230 Avenue of the Americas
New York, NY 10020

First Simon & Schuster hardcover edition August 2013

SIMON & SCHUSTER and colophon are registered trademarks of Simon & Schuster, Inc.

For information about special discounts for bulk purchases, please contact Simon & Schuster Special Sales at 1-866-506-1949 or business@simonandschuster.com.

The Simon & Schuster Speakers Bureau can bring authors to your live event. For more information or to book an event contact the Simon & Schuster Speakers Bureau at 1-866-248-3049 or visit our website at www.simonspeakers.com.

Designed by Aline C. Pace

Map by Paul J. Pugliese

Manufactured in the United States of America

10  9  8  7  6  5  4  3  2  1

Library of Congress Cataloging-in-Publication Data

Gezari, Vanessa M.
     The tender soldier : a true story of war and sacrifice / Vanessa M. Gezari.
       pages   cm
       1.  Afghan War, 2001—Campaigns—Afghanistan—De Maywand Kariz.
2.  Loyd, Paula.    3.  United States. Army. Human Terrain System.
4.  Counterinsurgency—Afghanistan—De Maywand Kariz.    5.  Applied
anthropology—Afghanistan.    6.  Anthropologists—United States—Biography.
7.  Cooper, Clint.    8.  Ayala, Don.    9.  Applied anthropology—United States—
Moral and ethical aspects.    10.  Social sciences—Research—United States—
Moral and ethical aspects.    I.  Title.
DS371.4123.M35  2013
958.104'71—dc23
[B]                                              2013001090

ISBN 978-1-4391-7739-6
ISBN 978-1-4391-7741-9 (ebook)

*For my mother and father*

My story
gets told in various ways: a romance,
a dirty joke, a war, a vacancy.

—JALALUDDIN RUMI

# CONTENTS

Prologue

1

1. Election Day

5

2. What You Don't Know Will Kill You

23

3. The Tender Soldier

47

4. Maiwand

69

5. The Anthropology of Us and Them

101

6. Hearts and Minds

127

7. Crime and Punishment
143

8. Good Intentions
161

9. The Devil You Don't Know
199

Epilogue
221

Acknowledgments
227

Notes
231

Index
329

# Author's Note

This book is based on hundreds of interviews and court, government, and military documents, some obtained under the Freedom of Information Act. I have also drawn on my experience as a reporter in Afghanistan from 2002 to 2004 and during six return trips, several more than a month long, between 2007 and 2010. Much of the recorded speech comes from notes and interview transcripts or from scenes I witnessed, and is marked by double quotes ("..."). Where I have reconstructed scenes based on documents and participants' recollections, dialogue appears in single quotes ('...'). In the interest of maintaining narrative flow, I have sought to minimize complex attribution in the body of the text. Readers can learn more about sources in the Notes section.

# THE
# TENDER
# SOLDIER

# PROLOGUE

Sometimes the events of a single day tell the story of a war. On November 4, 2008, voters in the United States elected Barack Obama president, laying the groundwork for an expanded counterinsurgency campaign in Afghanistan. On the same day, in the tawny flatlands west of Kandahar, a group of American civilians and soldiers set out on a hopeful mission that would change their lives and those of the Afghans they met forever. Among them was a brave and gentle woman with a Wellesley degree, a soldier's devotion to her country, and a fierce curiosity about the world. Theirs was an anthropological undertaking, matching the audacity of Obama, an anthropologist's son.

This book tells the story of what happened that day, and of the conception and rapid early growth of the Human Terrain System, a central tool in what was supposed to be a more culturally conscious way of war. It traces the first four years of this experiment, from its beginnings as a cultural knowledge database to fight homemade bombs in Iraq through its multimillion-dollar expansion. It follows the program through the height of American involvement in Afghanistan in 2010, when one hundred thousand U.S. troops were stationed there along with more than twenty Human Terrain Teams. For much of this period, the project's senior social scientist was an anthropologist-cum-war-theorist raised in a radical squatters community in Marin County, California, and educated at Ivy League schools. She would become the most flamboyant evangelist for an evolving form of battlefield information known as cultural intelligence. Its director was a scrappy and unconventional career soldier who believed the Army could be cured of its ethnocentrism, and that this goal justified almost any means taken to achieve it. Yet he himself embodied a profoundly American worldview: that every problem has a solution, and that Americans can find it.

The Human Terrain System was born in the shadows of a revolution within an Army that had tried to bury the painful lessons of Vietnam. In Iraq and Afghanistan, soldiers revived the low-tech practices of counterinsurgency, emphasizing the value of human contact for intelligence gathering, political persuasion, and targeted killing. The Human Terrain System was the Army's most ambitious attempt in three decades to bring social science knowledge to the battlefield, but it was unwelcome to some American anthropologists, who believed their discipline had too often been hijacked for imperialist ends. They were right, but so was the Army.

In Afghanistan, context makes intelligence make sense. American soldiers could not possibly know where to build a school or vet tips about who was the enemy without knowing which tribe their informant belonged to, who his rivals and relatives were, where he lived, how he had come to live there, and a thousand other details that anthropolo-

2

gists or journalists might collect but that soldiers rarely thought to ask about. Yet here lay a difficulty. Cultural understanding was a tool that could be used for saving or for killing, like the knife that cuts one way in the hands of a surgeon and another in the grip of a murderer. The Human Terrain System wasn't designed to tell the military who to kill. But a child could see that who to kill and who to save were questions that answered each other.

There are two kinds of military cultural knowledge. The first kind gives rise to directives that soldiers in Afghanistan should avoid showing the soles of their feet; that they should use only their right hands for eating; that they should accept tea when it is offered; and that men should refrain from searching women. The other kind of cultural knowledge, sometimes known as cultural intelligence, is what the military needs to make smart decisions about which local leaders to support, who to do business with, where to dig wells and build clinics, who to detain and kill, and when to disengage. Cultural intelligence is the textured sense of a place that helps soldiers understand how tribal systems work; how criminals, drug dealers, and militants are connected; the role of marriage in cementing business relationships and political alliances; and the way money and power move between families and villages. It was important for soldiers to understand Afghan culture so they wouldn't needlessly offend people. But for a force with a mission to strengthen local government and kill and capture terrorists in a place with no working justice mechanisms, it was crucial, too, that Americans make informed decisions about who to protect, which lives to ruin, and which lives to take. They routinely didn't.

The Human Terrain System was developed to help address these problems. What follows is the story of a hopeful moment when America, in the midst of two wars, sought to change the way it fights, and of a remarkable woman and her teammates, who risked everything to save the Army from itself.

# 1. ELECTION DAY

November 4, 2008

In the desert west of Kandahar, the nights were dark and chilly and the stars looked close enough to touch. At midday, the summer sun could kill you, but it was fall now, the dry air smelling of hay and woodsmoke. The Americans had landed three months earlier. They ate precooked food, used portable toilets, and slept in green canvas tents in a gravel lot behind walls that some soldiers judged too low to stop an inventive attacker. Stray cats rubbed up against their legs.

One morning that November, a platoon of soldiers from the 2nd Battalion, 2nd Regiment of the Army's 1st Infantry Division left the base on foot. The autumn sky was clear and bright, and the soldiers thought their mission would be an easy one. As some of the first Americans to patrol Maiwand District, a sandy stretch of farmland deep in the Afghan south, the Third Platoon of Comanche Company was building a detailed map of the settlements at the heart of the area, where most of Maiwand's people lived. On this day they would be photographing the northern quadrant of Chehel Gazi, a village that began about five hundred yards outside the walls of their base.

Three civilians joined the patrol that day. They were part of an experimental Army project called the Human Terrain System, which was designed to help soldiers understand local culture. Before leaving the base, they stood together in a tight circle, holding hands, heads bowed, as they did before every mission.

'God protect us and bless us for this day,' one of the men said.

His name was Clint Cooper, and he was tall and thickly built with a straw-colored goatee and pink, freckled skin. As a younger, leaner man, he'd been roguishly handsome, but war trauma and suburban fatherhood had blunted his features, and now little about him stood out. A former military intelligence soldier and interrogator, he spoke Pashto, one of Afghanistan's two main languages, and he could eavesdrop on Afghans without their having the slightest inkling. On this morning, he and his teammates left the base with the soldiers of Third Platoon. They passed Hesco bags filled with crushed stone, rings of concertina wire, concrete blast walls, and Afghan security guards smiling in borrowed uniforms and baseball caps. Cooper walked toward the rear of the patrol, while his teammate, Don Ayala, strode ahead.

Ayala had a boxer's physique—bulging biceps, meaty forearms, trim waist—and the soulful eyes of a matinee idol. A forty-six-year-old former Army Ranger, he had come to Afghanistan for the first time six years earlier as a contract bodyguard protecting Afghan president Hamid Karzai. Now he scanned the landscape, looking for anything that didn't fit. They'd been warned there might be suicide bombers out here.

As they left the base and walked toward the highway, the land unfolded around them like bleached cloth. They passed a shallow wadi where Afghans burned trash. Women in burqas moved like shadows

6

along the edges of the road, where children scavenged and played. The third member of the Human Terrain Team had a particular affection for these women and children. Paula Loyd walked with Cooper, at the center of the column of soldiers. She was thirty-six, slim and bottle-blond, with a bachelor's degree in anthropology, a master's in diplomacy and conflict resolution, and years of experience in Afghanistan. She had joined the Army after graduating from Wellesley College, and in 2002, her reserve unit had been called up and deployed to Kandahar, the birthplace of the Taliban. She had organized development projects, met Afghan women confined to their homes, watched Afghan girls eagerly returning to school. The people crept into her heart, and the country kept calling her back. She had spent most of her professional life there, working for aid and development organizations and the United Nations. Loyd was an idealist, but she wasn't naïve. She knew the score, knew who had fought on which side in Afghanistan's litany of wars, who was corrupt, which commanders were dealing drugs. Yet she remained optimistic. She was one of the Human Terrain System's best-qualified field social scientists, and on this day she was beat.

She had been up all night working on a report about the governor of Maiwand, a former religious leader who had fought the Soviets years earlier, and she wasn't thrilled about the timing of this patrol. But she and her teammates didn't set the agenda. They were straphangers: if they wanted to get off base, they had to take whatever opportunities came up. Ayala's easy rapport with soldiers meant that he was often the one who got the Human Terrain Team space on patrols. This mission had arisen with little warning, and when he'd mentioned it to Loyd earlier that morning, she had immediately said yes. After hearing Afghans complain about the high price of flour in Maiwand, she and Cooper had decided to create a consumer price index. That morning's patrol to Chehel Gazi would give them a chance to interview shoppers coming and going from the nearby bazaar. Loyd, Cooper, and Ayala had lived and traveled together for months. They had gotten to know each other's rhythms, learned to laugh at each other's jokes even when they weren't funny. But as their boots clicked brightly against the hardtop, Loyd told Cooper that she was irritated with Ayala for not giving them more notice about this patrol.

'You just need to talk to him,' Cooper told her as they walked. 'I'm sure he's open to suggestions.'

'I don't want to hurt his feelings,' Loyd said.

Cooper glanced over at her. He could tell she was tired, but he knew she wanted to be out here. All of them lived for getting off base, especially Loyd. The American soldiers had noticed with surprise that she treated Afghans with genuine warmth, and that Afghans responded in kind. Children flocked to her on patrols, men invited her in to visit with their wives. The soldiers that morning wore digital camo, helmets, and body armor, and carried M4 assault rifles. Cooper and Ayala wore Army uniforms and carried guns, but Loyd did neither. As always, she was unarmed and dressed in civilian clothes: slacks and a long-sleeved shirt under her body armor. She had coiled her shimmering blond hair beneath a military-issue helmet.

They crossed the highway and followed the sloping ground toward the district governor's compound with its walled garden, where the governor worked under police guard. A small stream ran in front of the compound, shaded by mulberry trees and edged on one side by a stand of bamboo. Farther down, men washed in the stream before praying at a little mosque, but here, close to the highway, plastic bags and pomegranate rinds choked the narrow channel. The soldiers fanned out along the lane, some photographing buildings, doorways, and intersections while others formed a human wall to protect them.

Chehel Gazi belonged to the landscape, to the green vineyards and pale dunes rolling away behind it, to the grit and trash of the bazaar on its western edge and the highway that marked its northern bound-ary. Its compounds and courtyards lay behind high, smooth walls that seemed to grow from the yellow mud like ancient earthworks. Only their doors and gates, made of wood or brightly painted metal, marked them as homes. A sand path ran alongside the little stream where the soldiers stood, but it felt more like an alley, edged on one side by compound walls and on the other by the stand of mulberry trees rooted along the banks of the irrigation channel. The village was named for this channel, or more precisely, for its source. Chehel Gazi means "forty meters," the depth at which someone digging a well there would hit an underground aquifer. The village owed its relative prosperity to this water, which fed its vineyards and nourished its people and animals. Its nearness to the road and the bazaar, the economic hub of the district, both enriched it and exposed it to traffic with the outside world, to new ideas, to sin and danger. The bazaar was a gathering place for people from across the south, a place where information was traded and where the usual protections of a closed, communal society did not apply. The Taliban were in the bazaar every day, the district governor had told the Americans. 'Chalgazi Village has Taliban living within it,' a local policeman had told Ayala and the soldiers a week earlier.

It was the morning of November 4, 2008, election day back home, when a citizenry frustrated by seemingly endless violence and spending in Iraq and a lack of focus in Afghanistan would go to the polls to choose a new president. Barack Obama had campaigned on the notion that Afghanistan was the good war, the war the nation needed to fight as opposed to the war it had chosen. If he were elected, America's Afghan campaign would be reconsidered with new optimism and energy. For the first time in years, the nation's attention was turning to a conflict long waged on autopilot, and the soldiers and Human Terrain Team members in Maiwand that morning constituted an advance party. In the minds of some, they were America's last best hope for changing the course of its longest war.

9

For years, soldiers had been arriving in Iraq and Afghanistan with little or no knowledge about the people who lived there. But the longer they stayed on the ground, the more problematic this became. Infantrymen in their teens and twenties had become de facto ambassadors, trying to barter political agreements between tribal leaders and drive a wedge between civilians and an enemy that was all but indistinguishable from them. Shock and awe had given way to the newly rediscovered military strategy known as counterinsurgency, which promised a smarter, more humane way of fighting. The strategy's greatest champion, General David Petraeus, had recently taken charge of Central Command, where he oversaw American military efforts in both Iraq and Afghanistan. Petraeus spoke of Afghanistan's "human terrain" as the decisive battleground for U.S. forces, and by "human terrain," he meant the Afghan people.

The Human Terrain System was designed to plant civilian social scientists, including anthropologists, in frontline military units to act as cultural translators to soldiers, marines, and their commanders. It wasn't just that Americans dealt rudely with Afghans because they didn't know the first thing about their culture. It was that, too often, they detained and killed the wrong people, alienating others and fueling the insurgency. Success hinged on winning hearts and minds, but it also depended on good intelligence, for counterinsurgency was comprised of two distinct and seemingly contradictory kinds of activity. The first involved humanitarian aid and development, psychological operations, and political persuasion to soften local resistance, build relationships, and gather intelligence. The second used that intelligence to guide everything from food handouts to detentions and targeted killings. The Human Terrain System was a soft tool, but it was part of a hard and complicated battle.

The Human Terrain Team and the soldiers split up. Loyd and Cooper lingered near the district headquarters, close to the highway and the bazaar, while Ayala and another group of soldiers kept walking farther along the path edging the stream, stopping at a small footbridge beyond the trees. Ayala sat on the bridge in the sun, bantering with the soldiers and handing out candy to children. There was something intoxicating about this place, so often patrolled that it had come to feel familiar, so close to the base that it almost had to be safe. Water lapped the edges of the channel. Near the bazaar, in an open space at the intersection of two sandy lanes, Loyd and Cooper handed out pens and candy to kids on their way to school.

Their regular translator wasn't with them that day. Instead, they were working with an interpreter the Americans called Jack Bauer after the terrorist-hunting hero of the television show *24*. The soldiers gave funny nicknames to all their interpreters to mask their identities—Rock Star, Tom Cruise, Chuck Norris, even Ron Jeremy after a well-known porn star. Jack Bauer was a twenty-three-year-old Pashtun with a dark pompadour, crooked teeth, and liquid puppy-dog eyes. He often translated for the young captain in charge of Comanche Company, but he had gotten to know Loyd, Ayala, and Cooper because the Human Terrain Team shared a tent with the Afghan interpreters on the small firebase near the district center. The tent was divided by a plywood partition, Americans on one side, Afghans on the other. Sometimes Loyd dropped by the interpreters' side to say hello. Once, she and Ayala invited Jack and some other interpreters to watch *The Da Vinci Code* on someone's laptop. Loyd had asked Jack about his family, what he did before, how long he had been working with the soldiers.

Jack liked this American woman. She was very friendly and kind, equally eager to talk to soldiers, interpreters like him, or Afghans she met on the street. But he didn't entirely understand what she and her teammates were doing out there. They told everyone they were civilians, not soldiers, and Loyd seemed eager to hand out wheat seed to farmers so they wouldn't plant opium poppy. Jack thought that Ayala and Cooper were her bodyguards. He had seen her talking to Afghan soldiers and police during meetings at the district governor's office, and the few times he'd worked with her, he had noticed that she always carried candy, and that kids came running when they saw her. A few days earlier, he had seen some kids swarming around her and spoken up.

'Hey, Paula, this isn't the United States,' he'd told her. 'In this country, it's very dangerous. Actually, this province is very dangerous. Don't give candy to the kids.'

Loyd had stiffened. 'Jack, you're the interpreter,' she had told him. 'You just interpret what I say. You're not my boss.'

'Yes,' he had told her. 'Okay.'

He had thought she was angry with him, but back at the base she'd sought him out, made a point of saying hello, asked if *he* was mad at her. Of course not, he'd told her. Still, those children worried him. She didn't carry a gun. "The enemy will use different weapons in different ways," he would say later. "We can't identify which people is civilian, which people is the Taliban."

Jack's words signaled his mistrust of the situation he'd gotten himself into. He had been raised in Kabul, where young men listened to Bollywood soundtracks, wore tight jeans, and exchanged shy glances with girls. Kandahar was a different story—older, rougher, a universe of men without women—and Maiwand was the countryside. The Afghans he met there were nothing like the people he knew back home. On the rare occasions when Maiwand revealed itself to him, it always managed to remind him how little he knew. The insurgents talked to each other on field radios, and Jack and the other interpreters were given the job of monitoring the conversation and reporting back to the Americans. During patrols, a soldier would hand the interpreters a scanner, and they would listen to insurgents watching them from somewhere nearby. 'We saw the American forces leave their base,' an insurgent would say to one of his comrades on the radio. 'They went through the bazaar. We saw them walking near that small mountain.' The interpreters couldn't see the Taliban, but the Taliban could see them. It was eerie, and there was an element of psychological play to it; the insurgents knew the Americans were listening, knew they would be unnerved by the awareness that they were being watched. Whenever the insurgents wanted to convey something really important they would switch to cell phones, which were harder to monitor. Sometimes Jack heard insurgents talking on the radio about planting bombs near the road, and he and the other interpreters would lean in close and try to figure out where they could possibly be talking about so they could tell the Americans in time.

That morning at the edge of Chehel Gazi, villagers passed the patrol on their way to the bazaar. Jack Bauer stopped a man carrying an armful of bread so that Loyd could ask what he had paid for it. She scribbled something in her notebook. She asked a shopkeeper whether the Afghan police taxed merchants. In a manner of speaking, the man told her. The police sometimes asked for money, or simply took things without paying for them. Cooper stood listening nearby. He watched the soldiers stop a man with a donkey cart and search it thoroughly, carefully, before waving it on.

A young bearded man walked past them. He was thin and slight, dressed in a blue tunic, baggy pants, and a vest, and carrying a metal jug. He stuck his head into a nearby compound with a green metal door, then stepped inside. Some children were playing near the compound, including a boy of about twelve.

'We don't know that guy,' Cooper heard one of the kids say in Pashto. 'What's he doing?' The man with the jug came out and made a sweeping motion with his hand, as if to shoo the children away.

'Hey, Jack, ask that guy if he wants to talk to me,' Loyd said.

'Hey, my boss wants to talk to you for a few minutes,' Jack Bauer called out to the man with the jug. 'Are you ready?'

The man agreed. He even knew a few words of English, enough to say "hello" and "thank you." He appreciated the Americans being there, he told them. He shook Cooper's hand.

'You speak English well,' Cooper told him. 'Where did you learn it?'

'In school.'

'What's in your jug?' Loyd asked.

'Fuel for my water pump,' the man said, reverting to his own language.

He seemed friendly enough, but Cooper thought there was something cocky and tightly wound about him, not dangerous, but not exactly normal, either. The man with the jug reminded him of a particular kind of Afghan who often approached American patrols in Maiwand, striding forward with a sense of purpose, determined to engage the soldiers in a political discussion. These men blamed the Americans for Afghan deaths. Afghans wanted no part of this war, yet they were caught in the middle, driving over bombs and falling under stray gunfire. If the Americans would just go home, the Afghans argued, people could go back to living quietly. When men like this berated the soldiers, Cooper listened patiently, then asked: 'How come you don't blame the Taliban when they commit violence, you only blame us?'

'We can't blame the Taliban,' the men would tell him. 'It's too dangerous.'

The man with the jug wasn't talking about politics, nor had he criticized the Americans. But Cooper sensed something polemical about him just the same.

'How much does petrol cost in Maiwand?' Loyd was asking him.

'It's very expensive,' the Afghan told her. His motorcycle was damaged in the bazaar, and he was carrying the gas to refuel it. That was what Jack Bauer heard, and that was what he translated. What about needing fuel for his water pump? No one asked the man to resolve this discrepancy. Loyd asked about his job. He worked for a local school, he told her, and then a bit later, that he was a shopkeeper from Kandahar. The school should be open for children, he told Loyd.

'Would you like some candy?' she asked him.

'I don't like candy,' the man said. He turned to Jack Bauer. 'Do you smoke?'

'Yes, I smoke,' Jack told him. The stress of working with the Americans only sharpened his cravings. He carried a pack of cheap Pakistani cigarettes in his uniform pocket that day.

'Do you smoke?' the man asked again. Again, Jack told him that he did.

About fifteen minutes passed in this scattershot conversation before the Afghan with the jug of fuel moved away. Cooper has been standing a few feet off, watching and listening, but now he turned to talk to an old man coming from the bazaar. The man had a white beard, and Cooper greeted him with elaborate politeness, asking about his family and where he came from.

He was vaguely aware that the man with the jug had returned and was talking to Loyd again. For a while, another Afghan came up and stood next to the first man. This second Afghan had a brown beard and friendly eyes. Cooper thought he must live in the compound with the green door a few feet from where they were standing, the one the man with the jug had ducked into before Jack had flagged him down. After a few minutes, the friendly-eyed man turned and walked away. Cooper glanced over and saw that the man with the jug had set it on the ground and was gesticulating with his hands. He had now been talking to Loyd for nearly half an hour. The platoon medic, standing a few feet away, noticed that the Afghan was playing with a plastic lighter, turning it over in his hands.

About fifteen feet away, a handful of soldiers formed a loose wall shielding their platoon mates and the Human Terrain Team members from the bazaar. They stopped people and checked them for weap-

15

ons before allowing them past, but now a knot of Afghan men formed around the soldiers, trying to tell them something. The Americans didn't understand. The closest interpreter was Jack Bauer.

'Hey, Jack!' a soldier yelled.

Jack turned to answer, turned away from Loyd and the man with the jug. Suddenly, he felt a rush of air and a blast of heat and saw a bright plume of flame at the edge of his vision. Cooper was still talking to the old man, his back to Loyd, when he heard a gigantic *whoosh*. He turned and saw, where she had stood, a column of flame shooting skyward, so large and furious that he had to step back to avoid being engulfed. The heat was like a solid wall forcing him away. He could see the dark outline of her body in the center of the fire, which burned a hot orange. She was small, slender, stumbling, curling inward. Very softly, behind the crackle and hiss of the flames, he heard her calling his name.

It's strange what you think about at moments like this. Cooper thought about the kids who had been standing around—where were they? He saw that they had disappeared, and he felt relieved that they didn't have to see this. Then he saw the Afghan who had been talking to Loyd, the man with the jug, running away down the lane, flames leaping from his clothes, his metal pitcher bouncing away into the stream. Cooper considered shooting him, but he could see dim shapes farther down. More soldiers waited there, he knew, on the footbridge, where Ayala sat. The man with the jug was running straight toward them. Cooper turned back to Loyd.

From then on, his only thought was how to get to her and put the fire out. He thought, *Stop, drop, and roll.* He wanted to yell these words, and maybe he did, a simple and memorable childhood lesson about what to do in case you catch fire, a phrase he had taught his own kids. He thought he would take off his shirt and throw it over her to smother the flames, so he hurled down his gun and tore off his helmet and body armor, but he had forgotten that he wasn't wearing the regular uniform blouse, big and loose and made of thick fireproof material. The tight-fitting military-issue shirt he had on that day would be useless against the flames.

The platoon leader, a twenty-six-year-old lieutenant named Matthew Pathak, yelled for the soldiers to get Loyd into the stream, but he quickly realized the flames were too high for anyone to get near her, so he filled his helmet with water and shouted at the others to help. Jack Bauer was already standing in the water. When he'd seen the flames, his first thought had been that he was on fire, so he'd run and jumped into the little stream. Now he and Cooper and the soldiers knelt and scooped helmets full of water toward Loyd. They tossed handfuls of dirt and sand to quell the flames. She had been standing hunched over like a bending branch and now she fell. The medic was saying something, drawing closer, reaching for her ankle. Cooper grasped her other leg. With Jack Bauer and another interpreter, the men pulled her across the dirt toward the stream and lowered her into the water. When the flames were extinguished, they lifted her out and gently laid her on the sand.

She was shaking. They cut off her body armor and what was left of her clothes, and she lay there in her underwear in the dirt, small and frail and shockingly exposed. She looked so tiny, Cooper thought. He pulled her watch off her wrist and the melting rubber stretched hot and elastic like Silly Putty. He would remember this later, physical evidence of how fast and completely the world had changed, how things were normal until suddenly they weren't, so that one minute your friend was standing there smiling and talking, and then she was on fire and no one could get to her, and then you had to dip her in a gutter to put the fire out, and now she was lying almost naked in a place where you hardly ever saw a woman outdoors, let alone unclothed. Cooper felt an immense tenderness for her and a growing, directionless rage. Jack Bauer, shocked by her nakedness, unwound his cotton scarf and began to lay it over her body, but the platoon medic told him to stop. Her skin was too hot. The fabric would stick to her. A few feet away, the ground was still burning.

The medic quickly went to work. When they'd pulled her out of the water, he had thought she was dead. Her body had started to freeze up, but now she was telling him she couldn't feel anything in her arms. Cooper was afraid to look at her.

'I'm cold,' she said. 'I'm cold.' And then: 'You guys got the flame out really quick. Does it look bad?'

'It just looks like a bad sunburn,' Cooper told her. He was lying. The only parts of her that weren't burned were her ankles and feet, where her boots had covered her skin. Her face and thighs were a deep reddish pink, and there was faint gray charring on her cheeks, as if someone had rubbed her skin with coal. Maybe it isn't that serious, he thought, God, I hope it isn't. Gently, he lifted off her helmet and found her hair wet and dirty but otherwise untouched. Loyd took meticulous care of her hair, lugging footlockers of products into the desert and brushing it until it shone.

'Your hair looks perfect,' he told her. 'You're about to go through a very difficult struggle. You can ask God for help.' Cooper was a lifelong Mormon, but Loyd had told him she wasn't sure she believed in God.

'I was mad at Don,' she murmured with the ghost of a smile. 'I hope it didn't ruin our prayer.'

She was talking about the surprise of the patrol, her tiredness, and her momentary frustration with Ayala, and she was teasing, Cooper realized. She was still there. But she started shaking again. She could smell gasoline, she told him. She couldn't get the taste of it out of her mouth.

'I'm cold,' she said. 'I'm freezing.'

'Don't worry. You're always cold.'

\*     \*     \*

Down the lane, Ayala saw a bright flash, but he didn't see much else. He was too far off, and the trees edging the stream and the uneven line of compound walls blocked his view. The kids who had gathered around him screamed and ran, dropping the candy he had given them. A young soldier named Justin Skotnicki heard cries from down the path, and then the smell hit him. He had been to the scene of road-side bombings, and he instantly recognized it: the smell of someone burning.

Ayala ran. He pulled out his pistol. It must have been a suicide attack, he thought. He hadn't heard an explosion, but he had been through this before, and he assumed the silence was auditory exclusion, a stress response that causes momentary hearing loss. As he moved along the lane between the stream and the compound walls, a man fell toward him, the sleeves of his tunic on fire. The man was striking his flaming clothes with his hands and running fast and haphazardly down the lane, his eyes wild with fear.

Ayala thought the man was a victim, a bystander, perhaps, caught up in the attack. Then he heard someone yell: 'Stop him! Shoot him!'

Ayala gripped his pistol, raised it. He looked up and saw people moving. He knew Cooper and Loyd were back there. He saw flames up ahead, saw a dark shape rolling inside the fire. He didn't know who or what it was. He didn't shoot. Instead, he stuck out his arm and clothes-lined the running man. His fist hit the Afghan in the throat and the Afghan dropped to the ground.

Ayala knelt and grabbed hold of him, pinning him down. He was close now, close enough to notice the man's long shirt, light beard, and cropped hair, the tattoos on his arms. He looked to be in his mid-twenties and he couldn't have weighed more than 160 pounds, but he was wiry and he struggled like he was pumped with adrenaline or high on drugs, kicking, shoving, writhing, his eyes desperate. Two soldiers helped pin him down, one of them grabbing his legs. The Afghan kicked and bit

19

and grabbed the muzzle of a private's gun. It took three of them to sub-due him. Finally, Ayala raised his pistol and the Afghan subsided. Ayala could feel the captive's warm, skinny body against his own. He smelled the other man's sweat.

'Get the flex cuffs!' Ayala yelled. 'Cuff this guy!'

A sergeant came up and helped one of the soldiers slip a plastic tie around the man's wrists and pull it tight. Ayala squatted next to the detainee, his knee on the Afghan's throat. He ran his hands over the man's body, feeling for weapons. He scanned the path for more attackers.

He thought that only a few minutes passed there on the path, but it might have been longer. Time was elastic, impossible to measure. He heard shots and didn't know where they were coming from, didn't know who stood at the end of the lane, who was watching through the trees. Someone shouted at the soldiers to get in position and men dashed past, but Ayala stayed where he was, guarding the captive. He wanted to see what was happening to Loyd and Cooper, but no one else was around to take his place. Pathak, the platoon leader, came over to talk to the staff sergeant who had supplied the flex cuffs. They were discussing what to do with the prisoner. Ayala heard them say something about handing him over to the local police.

He still didn't know what had happened, but now he was starting to panic. Something deeply fucked-up had occurred and he was stuck here, away from his teammates, too far from the action to be of any use. The cuffed Afghan half lay, half sat against the mud wall of one of the compounds edging the stream, his legs extended across the path, writhing and kicking though his hands were bound. The man was not his responsibility, Ayala thought. The soldiers should have been watching him. But Ayala was the biggest man on hand, and the platoon leader knew he wouldn't let the Afghan escape.

Just then, an Afghan in a military uniform ran up. It was Jack

Bauer. 'You motherfucker!' Jack was yelling at the man on the ground in sharply accented English. 'Motherfucker!'

He started kicking the handcuffed Afghan in the face. Before Ayala could react, Jack had kicked the man into the stream, jumped into the water, and begun pounding him with his fists.

'What are you doing?' Ayala yelled at Jack. 'What's going on?' Later, Jack would remember Ayala scolding him, saying something like: 'Hey, Jack! You don't know about our culture. You can't just kick people in the face—it's not allowed.' But at this moment, Jack Bauer was out of breath, shaken, and terrified. He tried to speak, but his tongue refused to take the shapes required by the English language.

'Slow down,' Ayala told him. 'What's up?'

'He burned Paula!' Jack yelled, grabbing her name from the air.

Ayala hauled the cuffed Afghan out of the stream and threw him hard against the wall. 'I don't know what you're talking about,' he told Jack. He turned to some soldiers standing nearby: 'What's going on over there?'

'Paula's burned,' Specialist Skotnicki told him. 'They'll be evacuating her soon. It looks like she's going to be okay. You can go see her if you want.'

Ayala didn't say anything, but Skotnicki saw his face twist. Ayala was thinking about the conversation he'd overheard between the lieutenant and the sergeant about turning the man over to the local police. The police out here were compromised, he knew. A few days earlier, they had told Cooper they were scared to patrol without American escorts. They didn't even get paid most of the time, which meant they were for sale. If they gave the captive to the police, Ayala thought, he would be free in matter of days, weeks at most.

The handcuffed Afghan lay panting in the dirt and now Jack Bauer was speaking to him, softly and angrily, in his own language: 'What's going on? Why did you burn that girl?'

21

'I'm crazy,' the man on the ground muttered. 'I'm crazy. Don't speak to me. I'm crazy.'

Shaken, Ayala moved to stand over the Afghan captive. He turned to another interpreter, the one the Americans called Tom Cruise, who was standing nearby. 'Ask him why he did this,' Ayala said.

Tom Cruise asked, but the man just lay there. The interpreter asked again. Silence. And a third time. 'Why don't you answer the question?' Tom Cruise yelled.

Finally, the Afghan spoke. 'I'm crazy,' he said. 'I cannot control myself. Sometimes I'm walking naked in the night.'

Ayala's mind was working. He looked at the man on the ground. The Afghan lay in the fetal position, his head facing east toward the wall, his feet toward the water. His clothes were wet and dirty from the stream and the struggle. His hands were still cuffed behind his back.

Ayala turned to Jack Bauer. He had something to say to the man on the ground. 'Tell this guy he's the fucking devil,' Ayala said.

He pulled out his pistol and pressed the muzzle against the handcuffed man's temple. He pushed the man's head toward the ground. He squeezed the trigger.

## 2. WHAT YOU DON'T
## KNOW WILL KILL YOU

The path that brought Loyd, Ayala, and Cooper to Maiwand wound through decades of lost knowledge. In the thirty-three years since the last Americans had been airlifted out of Saigon, most of the Army had turned its back on the failures of Vietnam and vowed never to fight another war like it. The United States had broken the Soviet Union and chased Iraq out of Kuwait without major ground combat. Technology increasingly allowed the Army to fight from a distance, and the Pentagon poured money into computerized battlefield sensors, satellite systems, and unmanned drones. The United States had become the world's foremost military power. The Army wasn't a finely tuned instrument, but it could crush any force that challenged it.

The roots of the Human Terrain System are ambiguous and contested, stained with bad blood and accusations of impure motives, its origin myths embellished by ambitious and therefore potentially unreliable narrators who, nevertheless, each holds a piece of the story. Its elements evolved simultaneously and organically from various corners of the defense establishment and flourished in the atmosphere of ferment that grew out of the Army's realization that it was losing the war in Iraq. To understand how that came to be, you have to go back in time.

Between the disaster of Vietnam and the attacks of September 11, small wars went on, but even when American interests were at stake, Americans often weren't the ones fighting them. In Afghanistan in the 1980s, the CIA funneled billions of dollars in weapons to Afghan mujaheddin attacking the Soviets and their Afghan proxies. Technology didn't defeat the Soviets, though Stinger missiles helped. In the end it was men—bearded fighters with rifles, trusted networks of local contacts, and an uncanny sense of the landscape—who drove the Soviets out and laid the foundation for America's Cold War victory.

In Somalia and Haiti, the conventional Army collaborated with the Marines and Special Forces, but some soldiers realized they didn't have the cultural knowledge and language skills they needed. Troops returning from the strange, uneven battlefields of the 1990s told their colleagues that the military had to change. "What we need is cultural intelligence," retired Marine General Anthony Zinni, who had served in Vietnam and Somalia, said in 1994. "What makes them tick? Who makes the decisions? What is it about their society that's so remarkably different in their values, in the way they think, compared to my values and the way I think in my western, white-man mentality?"

For the most part, the defense establishment didn't listen. Instead, it focused on technology at the expense of history, viewing irregular battles as a distraction from the conventional war that might always be imminent. The Pentagon and the congressional representatives who ensured its funding had plenty of reasons to be more interested in fast planes and fancy weapons systems than the inchoate stuff of language and culture. But at the Foreign Military Studies Office, a small organization at Fort Leavenworth, Kansas, that for more than two decades has served as an in-house think tank for the Army, a handful of scholars had long viewed the service's wholesale embrace of technology as a dangerous mistake. Long before anyone envisioned an American war in Afghanistan, Lester Grau, a Vietnam veteran and Russia specialist at the Foreign Military Studies Office, was researching Soviet combat tactics and the tactics employed by U.S.-backed Afghan mujaheddin against their Soviet enemies. Grau's work was prescient, but much of the wisdom supplied by the Foreign Military Studies Office died on the pages of military journals before it reached the battlefield. By the time the United States invaded Afghanistan in 2001, some former anti-Soviet resistance fighters had become key American enemies, but American infantrymen were innocent of the past. History would only be revived later, in the panic that followed rising insurgencies in Afghanistan and Iraq. Today, Grau's books of battlefield case studies from the Soviet-Afghan War are required reading for American small-unit and non-commissioned officers deploying to Afghanistan.

Among the misapprehensions Grau and his colleagues sought to dispel in the years before the American invasion of Afghanistan was what Jacob Kipp, a Russia historian and former director of the Foreign Military Studies Office, called the "myth of technology." In the late summer of 2001, Kipp and Grau tried to warn the Army that in future wars, technology would be at best a distraction, at worst a fatal obstacle. No longer would American soldiers see the enemy's tanks ranged on a hillside and know exactly where he stood. The enemy would fight and disappear into an urban landscape, and it wasn't just urban terrain that would challenge the military, but "the social nature of cities." Then came the September 11 attacks, and America went to war in Afghanistan with aerial bombings directed by a handful of elite ground troops and CIA paramilitaries. The Americans' chief allies were Afghan militia leaders who wielded considerable power but whose fighters were known to have raped, looted, and slaughtered civilians during the factional battles of the 1990s. In the months after the American invasion, some Afghans wondered openly when these men would be charged with war crimes. Instead, they were rewarded with top jobs in the new government.

The murderous lawlessness of the Afghan civil war had prepared the ground for the Taliban's ascendance. The Taliban had ruled brutally, massacring ethnic minorities, torching farmland, destroying the nation's cultural heritage, and terrorizing everyone with repressive edicts and abundant punishment. Now the Americans had arrived, and Afghans hoped things might change. But in the fall of 2001, Afghans allied with U.S. forces shot and suffocated to death hundreds of Taliban prisoners in shipping containers, drove them into the desert, and dumped the bodies in a mass grave. Years of uninterrupted war had made killing a reflexive act for some Afghans, and they played American forces like the box accordions to which they sang sad love songs at parties. Old tribal structures had been ravaged by war, and those who seemed to be in charge often weren't. American air strikes and other high-tech weaponry became tools in grudge matches between rivals whose enmity had nothing to do with the Taliban or Al Qaeda.

The Taliban were excluded from the United Nations–sponsored Bonn Conference in 2001. The United States and its Afghan allies viewed them as enemies to be captured or killed, not political players with whom they would ultimately have to reconcile. Victory in Afghanistan had seemed quick and easy, but the war would be very long. Elsewhere, another conflict was already brewing. The invasion of Iraq in early 2003 looked like a stunning military success. But within months of Saddam Hussein's toppling, buried bombs—known in military jargon as improvised explosive devices, or IEDs—ripped into Humvees. The earliest ones were low-tech in the extreme, made from explosives looted from ammunition dumps and activated by doorbell buzzers. They tore legs and arms off soldiers, sank metal deep in brain tissue, slashed femoral arteries. By the fall of 2003, the number of IED attacks in Iraq had risen to one hundred a month. By February 2004, it neared one hundred a week.

The Army sent thousands of jammers to Iraq and Afghanistan to interrupt the radio signals emitted by remote detonation devices and deployed blimps with closed-circuit cameras to monitor roads. Beating IEDs became the Defense Department's second-highest priority after capturing Osama bin Laden. Yet for all the money and talk, the men who made and planted the bombs continued to elude the Pentagon. In an experiment designed by the Pentagon's joint staff, spy aircraft, unmanned drones, and a turboprop plane with ground-penetrating radar circled over a twenty-kilometer stretch of road north of Baghdad for ten weeks, looking for bombs. But sandstorms and blowing trash got in the way of the cameras, and smart insurgents planted bombs on days when bad weather grounded the planes. Eight drones crashed; the radar on one of the surveillance planes failed. One day in November, nearly all the surveillance assets focused on a small section of the road where everything seemed normal. Two hours later, a bomb exploded there, killing one soldier and severing another's leg. The cameras had missed it entirely.

In a roundabout way, this high-tech experiment fed curiosity within the Pentagon about insurgent social networks, a decidedly low-tech line of thinking that the Army had mostly failed to explore. Analysts found they could use surveillance video to trace cars and people arriving at a bomb site before an explosion or leaving afterward. When the images were comprehensive enough, they could figure out which building a bomber had emerged from or which house he went home to. The next logical consideration was what he might be doing after he went inside that house and closed the door, when the camera couldn't see him anymore. Who was this man? Where had he grown up? Who did he love, and who loved him? And most of all, what had made him detonate that bomb?

This kind of thinking was unfamiliar to the conventional Army. Getting inside someone's head required knowing something about him, but language ability and cultural knowledge were low on the list of requirements for deploying soldiers. By 2004, some senior military officers were beginning to talk about this openly. Retired Army Major General Robert H. Scales wrote that year that success in a place like Iraq required "intimate knowledge of the enemy's motivation, intent, will, tactical method, and cultural environment," which American soldiers invariably lacked. Intelligence was, in Scales's view, the weakest link. Few young soldiers knew how to gather cultural intelligence or understood why it was important. Most had never left the United States and spoke no foreign language except Spanish. "Ninety-nine percent have never spoken to another person in their lives who doesn't think exactly like they do," the commander of the U.S. Army Intelligence Center would tell an audience of culturally astute soldiers, social scientists, and defense contractors years later. "They come to me, and in 16 weeks, I'm supposed to make them an intelligence analyst. Culture is incredibly important to that, and they have no background whatsoever."

The Pentagon's joint staff assigned one of its biggest brains to fight the IED epidemic. Dr. Hriar Cabayan was a science and technology adviser in the Office of the Secretary of Defense. Slight and animated with an irreverent manner, he had been trained as a physicist and worked at Lawrence Livermore National Laboratory for more than two decades. Known to his colleagues as Doc, Cabayan knew more about the people America was fighting among than most others at the Pentagon because he had not led an isolated life. Born in Armenia, he had been raised in Syria, where he was educated by Jesuit nuns before coming to the United States.

In the winter of 2004, Cabayan met with an Army lieutenant colonel who had just returned from a tour in Diyala Province, north of Baghdad. Cabayan asked the officer what tool he most wished he'd had in Iraq. Lieutenant Colonel Bill Adamson said that he had needed a way to store everything he'd learned about tribal structure and local culture, about the sheiks and other Iraqis he'd gotten to know during his tour, so he could pass it along to the next guy. At the time, the only way information made it from one unit to another was by word of mouth, or through emails the previous commander had left behind that the new commander had no time to read. When one military unit went home, local knowledge went with it. Cabayan was working on the problem with another physicist. Neither of them knew much about the social sciences, so Cabayan asked around. Someone mentioned an anthropologist working for the Navy. "I called her up," Cabayan told me. "Montgomery McFate. She was an obscure anthropologist at the Office of Naval Research. Nobody paid attention to her."

McFate drove over to the Pentagon. When she walked into Cabayan's office, he took one look at her and thought, This is going to be a short conversation. An anthropologist, as far as he knew, was someone with unkempt hair and no sense of style. McFate had on lipstick and wore her hair pixie-short and carefully coiffed. She must be a bureaucrat, Cabayan thought, but within ten minutes, she'd won him over. McFate didn't look the way Cabayan had expected an anthropologist to look, and she didn't think like most anthropologists, either. She had gone to Harvard Law School, married an Army officer, and held a string of research and policy fellowships. Before joining the Office of Naval Research, she had worked as a contract researcher for the CIA.

Cabayan enlisted McFate to work on a project that would later be called Cultural Preparation of the Environment. It was a piece of technology: an ethnographic database that could be loaded onto a laptop and used by soldiers in the field. They began to build a prototype, concentrating on Diyala Province, where Adamson had served. McFate and her colleagues put out a call for information to all the intelligence agencies in the U.S. government, asking about society and politics in Diyala. "About tribes alone, we got back fifteen totally different answers," McFate told me later. The military was gathering intelligence, but it was "mainly on bad people, places, and things." Like the Army, intelligence agencies in the aftermath of September 11 had turned their attention to targeting the enemy, paying far less attention to the demographics, politics, economies, and cultures through which he moved.

Cultural Preparation of the Environment was an open-source intelligence tool designed to reduce violence by understanding the sea in which the enemy swam. McFate had been intrigued by the common ground between anthropology and intelligence since she was researching her doctoral dissertation about British soldiers and Irish Republican Army fighters and realized that anything she wrote about how either side operated could help its adversary. It struck her then that as an anthropologist interested in war, her work could be read by "anyone, anywhere and used for their purposes," she told me. Since Vietnam, many anthropologists had grown highly suspicious of the U.S. military's adventures in far-flung places, whose people were often the subject of ethnographic study. But McFate viewed these concerns as naïve. "If you really want to control or constrain the ability of people to use anthropological materials for the purposes of war, you should not write" ethnographic studies, she told me. "And you certainly shouldn't publish" them.

McFate lost no time advancing her view that the military needed anthropology in the worst way. She organized a conference on the national security benefits of knowing your enemy and wrote a string of military journal articles in which she emphasized the role of anthropology in the colonial conquests of the nineteenth century and its necessity for contemporary military commanders. The U.S. military and policy community's ethnocentrism had led to miscalculations in Vietnam, the

Soviet-Afghan War, the Iraqi invasion of Kuwait, and Iran, McFate argued. In Iraq and Afghanistan, cultural misunderstandings had proved absurdly simple and deadly. Coalition forces arrested Iraqis for having weapons, but they didn't understand that most Iraqis had weapons. They detained hundreds of people because they couldn't make sense of kinship systems, and lost track of detainees because they misunderstood Arabic naming conventions. Shia Muslims who flew black flags for religious reasons were viewed as enemies by marines, who associated white flags with surrender and black flags with its opposite. At checkpoints, the American hand signal for "stop"—arm extended, palm out—meant "welcome" to Iraqis, who hit the gas and got shot. "Across the board, the national security structure needs to be infused with anthropology, a discipline invented to support warfighting in the tribal zone," McFate wrote. She was briefing military officials in Tampa one day in 2005 when a colonel in battlefield camouflage walked in and sat at the back of the room. When it was over, McFate asked him what he was doing there. "I think I'm in the wrong briefing," he said, "but it sounded interesting, so I decided to stay."

The colonel was Steve Fondacaro, an iconoclastic, wiry Army Ranger with close-cropped gray hair and the tenaciousness of a terrier, who had lately become convinced that the United States was its own worst enemy in Iraq. Fondacaro was determined to do whatever it took to defeat the arrogance and bureaucratic inertia that were suffocating the Army he loved, an Army that had defined him since West Point and given him thirty years of workaholic bliss. But he had another problem, one he couldn't do anything about. Most soldiers are required to leave the Army after three decades of service. Fondacaro was staring down the barrel of forced retirement.

Born in New York to a mother of Puerto Rican descent and an Italian-American father, Fondacaro had grown up all over the country but mainly in Fresno, California. When he was born, his family had lived on 114th Street in East Harlem; but his father, a physical therapist, was soon drafted to fight in Korea, and the family moved to follow him. The elder Fondacaro spent twenty-eight years in the Army, retiring as a colonel. Steve Fondacaro was the middle child of three boys and the only one to reach a normal adult height. His brothers, Phil and Sal Fondacaro, are diastrophic dwarfs who played Ewoks in *Return of the Jedi*. But for as long as he could remember, Steve Fondacaro had wanted to go to West Point, and to war.

He entered the academy in 1972, toward the end of the Vietnam War, when public opposition to the military reached an all-time high. But Fondacaro had no reservations. He suspected that his antiwar peers knew less about the conflict in Vietnam than he did, having grown up in a military family, and he knew that to be young and hip and make conversation at a bar in those days you had to bad-mouth Nixon. "That's where I first began to understand how little research anybody does," he told me. "Wisdom is defined, in my view, as in the Chinese proverb: a wise man is a man who is fully aware of how much he does not know."

At West Point, Fondacaro particularly enjoyed his classes in military history and Sosh, the academy's independent-minded social sciences department. The department has long served as an intellectual incubator for officers willing to dispute the official line, and since the 1980s, it has been a particularly important site of debate over the Army's role in Vietnam. As a result, Sosh recurs in the intellectual genealogies of today's leading counterinsurgency advocates, many of whom have taught there. Fondacaro graduated from West Point in 1976, along with Stanley McChrystal, Raymond Odierno, David Rodriguez, and William Caldwell IV, all of whom would go on to hold command positions in Iraq or Afghanistan. David Howell Petraeus, whom everyone called "Peaches," finished two years earlier. Instead of a fancy engineering specialization, Fondacaro chose the infantry. "It's the most enriching life experience," he told me. "Nothing else appealed to me other than being in combat."

He went to Ranger school, then trained for two years as a platoon leader in Panama before joining the 1st Ranger Battalion. He made captain and was sent to Korea for what he thought would be a year of company command, but when he got off the plane, a general commandeered him to serve in a staff job normally given to a higher-ranking officer. There Fondacaro helped organize logistics for Team Spirit, a massive yearly U.S.–South Korean military training exercise. He eventually got his company command, at a post along the demilitarized zone, where he says he led combat patrols to stop North Korean infiltrators on sabotage missions. During this period, he met Insuk Kim, the Korean woman he would marry and with whom he would have two children.

By his own account, Fondacaro was a bit too sharp and outspoken for his own good. He pissed people off by being chosen, as a junior captain, for staff jobs that would ordinarily have gone to officers above him. His extended tour in Korea also meant that he missed the chance to jump into Grenada with his fellow Rangers in Operation Urgent Fury, one of the Cold War's most celebrated combat missions. "The more experienced you get in Korea, the more they want to send you back to Korea," Fondacaro told me. He spent thirteen years there, returning to the States intermittently for advanced courses at several Army schools and a two-year Pentagon tour in the Special Technical Operations Division, a largely "black," or classified, organization.

Fondacaro's immersion in Korea made him intimately familiar with the history of American policy failures in Asia. He began to understand why some people viewed the United States as the world's leading hypocrite, a nation that preached democratic principles while supporting leaders like Ferdinand Marcos and Ngo Dinh Diem. He knew that Ho Chi Minh had begged the United States for support in freeing his people from the domination of the French, borrowing words from the Declaration of Independence to express Vietnamese aspirations for self-rule, and that American leaders had turned away. Like his Korean comrades, Fondacaro grew frustrated by the persistent shortsightedness of American foreign policy. "How is it that we get driven to a last-minute, midnight decision with two lieutenant colonels in the Pentagon that say, 'Hey, 38th Parallel looks good to me, Joe,' and we decide the fate of a nation?" Fondacaro asked me during one of our conversations. "This is our legacy."

When Fondacaro returned to the States as a colonel in 2001, he was asked to conduct an Army-wide study to figure out what the capabilities of the twenty-first-century soldier should be. Later, he would view this as a sort of military ethnography, but he wasn't thinking about anthropology then, not yet. He sent teams to survey, interview, and conduct focus groups with soldiers and officers around the world. The results convinced him of what he called the Army's "tribal nature." It was a sprawling organization atomized into cliques whose members identified primarily as logisticians or supply officers or engineers rather than as combat soldiers, but asymmetrical warfare was making those divisions obsolete. "Those days when you're a logistics guy or you're a transportation guy and all you do is move ammo from the rear, those days are over, because you can be attacked anywhere along the way," he told me. "It's a 360-degree battle. That requires a different kind of soldier." The future soldier he envisioned would operate more like a Special Forces commando than a member of the conventional Army. Like the Marine Corps creed—"every Marine a rifleman"—this new brand of fighter should embody a "warrior ethos," Fondacaro argued. Every soldier, no matter his job description, would need combat and small-unit leadership skills.

Then–Army Chief of Staff General Eric Shinseki grew interested in the study and urged Fondacaro on, enlisting him as an informal adviser. But Shinseki was on the wrong side of power. He had testified before Congress that several hundred thousand troops would be needed for peacekeeping and reconstruction in post-invasion Iraq, angering then–Secretary of Defense Donald Rumsfeld, who favored a much smaller force. Shinseki was more clear-eyed than his boss, but he was marginalized for disputing the official line, and he quietly retired in the summer of 2003. Fondacaro considered Shinseki his strongest supporter. He blamed his failure to make general on Shinseki's fall, but the great majority of Army colonels never earn a star. After Army politics frustrated his attempts to land a job he coveted in Afghanistan, Fondacaro was sent to serve his last tour at a little-known organization called the Army Capabilities Integration Center, or ARCIC, under the Training and Doctrine Command. "Don't ask me what they do," Fondacaro told me. "I gave it the best I could for a year, but it was a waste of time."

Then, just as he was about to leave the Army, Fondacaro was offered a job he really wanted. An acquaintance from his Ranger days, then-Colonel Joe Votel, had been tapped to head a new Army task force with a mission to target the homemade bombs that were killing soldiers in Iraq and Afghanistan. Votel asked Fondacaro to lead a small group of Special Operations and other forces helping combat troops in Iraq. Fondacaro was in his thirtieth year of service, but he got an extension and headed to Baghdad. Part of his job there was to field-test the seemingly endless stream of gadgets and prototypes that defense contractors were developing to counter roadside bombs. They ranged from the useless to the bizarre. One device purported to find buried bombs and defuse them electromagnetically. The machine became so highly charged that it had to be neutralized by soldiers walking up behind it with a giant wooden probe. You guys are on so much dope that I can't help you, Fondacaro thought when he saw it. This was the job he held when McFate met him at the briefing in Tampa. Eventually the database project she was working on, Cultural Preparation of the

Environment, found its way to Fondacaro's testing unit in Baghdad. As he listened to the contractors pitch it, he knew it wouldn't work. 'This is a piece of crap,' he told them.

In Fondacaro's view, the creators of Cultural Preparation of the Environment had missed the point. They had built a laptop stocked with cultural and demographic information for a commander who already had more gadgets than he knew what to do with—a busy officer swimming in data, but with no one to help him interpret it. The creators of Cultural Preparation of the Environment seemed to think that the commander could have a conversation with the database as if it were a human being on his staff, but that was impossible, and anyway, he wouldn't know which questions to ask. "That's when the light went on for me," Fondacaro recalled. What a field commander needed were "social scientists on his staff, belonging to him. Not a dial-a-social-scientist with a fifteen-thousand-mile screwdriver from Brown University on Saturdays. He needed somebody embedded with him, part of his mission, understanding what he and his staff were going through day to day, totally integrated into his decision-making process so that the solutions offered were relevant to the situation he faced." That Arab brides painted their hands with henna before marriage might be of interest to a social scientist, but that marriages in many Arab communities were accompanied by celebratory gunfire was of critical importance to commanders in Iraq. "Do you think that's something the commander maybe needs to know, so that the Apache helicopters flying over at the time the celebratory gunfire comes up don't roll in on a marriage ceremony and kill everyone because they thought they were being fired upon, so that instead of one thousand insurgents, you now have five thousand or maybe ten thousand insurgents?" Fondacaro asked me.

By 2005, things were changing in the Army and in America. With violence intensifying in Iraq, President George W. Bush, who had declared his disdain for nation building, embraced it as the only way to avert disaster. Given the paltriness of America's civilian diplomatic and development corps, no entity but the military could undertake such a giant task. That year, "stability operations" became one of the military's core missions. It was a profound shift, particularly for an Army whose recent engagements had been shaped by the Powell Doctrine's emphasis on overwhelming force and a clear exit strategy. In the short term, stability operations would provide security, "restore essential services, and meet humanitarian needs," but their long-term aims were much broader: "to help develop indigenous capacity for securing essential services, a viable market economy, rule of law, democratic institutions, and a robust civil society." The military's expanded mission meant new intelligence requirements for all the services. Commanders were instructed to draft requirements for "numbers of personnel with appropriate language and cultural skills and proficiency levels." Intelligence products had to bring together information from traditional sources as well as the social sciences, "including from sociological, anthropological, cultural, economic, political science, and historical sources within the public and private sector."

That year, Maxie McFarland, a retired Army colonel and deputy chief of staff for intelligence at the Army's Training and Doctrine Command, published an article calling for more cultural training for soldiers. Even by the low standards of military prose, his appeal was written robotically, as if culture and the people who shape and inhabit it were not human but mechanized. Cultural knowledge had taken a long time to register as important in an Army made up of engineers and systems thinkers, in part because it had seemed incomprehensibly vague, impossible to master. In McFarland's prose, it became a solid thing with hard edges, a tool of military art like a shovel or a gun.

McFarland had worked on the counter-IED task force with Fondacaro and Votel. At the Training and Doctrine Command, his oversight included the Foreign Military Studies Office, the Army think tank that had tried for so long to help the service better understand its enemies. McFarland heard about the ethnographic database project, Cultural Preparation of the Environment, and asked Kipp to look into it, so Kipp sent Lester Grau, the Soviet historian, to one of the regular project briefings, which were attended via video teleconference by a growing number of people in the defense establishment. 'This dog won't hunt,' Kipp remembers Grau telling him. Grau's concerns mirrored Fondacaro's. Cultural Preparation of the Environment would also require soldiers to collect and record reams of data, which they had no time to do.

Nevertheless, Kipp saw enough potential in the project to want to keep track of it. He asked a young Foreign Military Studies Office staffer named Don Smith to sit in on the regular video teleconferences. Smith was an ambitious, fast-talking Army reserve captain with a background in management consulting. After graduating from the Citadel and deploying to Iraq with the 101st Airborne Division during Desert Storm, he had left the Army for business school, but the September 11 attacks had brought him back. Smith told Kipp that while Cultural Preparation of the Environment was far from perfect, elements could be taken from it and put together to build a working cultural knowledge program. Smith would become the Human Terrain System's first program manager. He told me that he came up with the idea for the program at his kitchen table, and he wasn't the only one with a catchy creation story. McFate talked about scribbling the concept on a cocktail napkin at a bar with her husband. Fondacaro claimed that he was the one who had pushed to send civilian social scientists into the field with soldiers.

McFate had written about the Army's need for a social science entity that could be sent to the battlefield alongside soldiers, but the Foreign Military Studies Office was already exploring similar possibilities. After the fall of the Soviet Union, the office had developed or contributed to two undertakings that foreshadowed the Human Terrain System. Both projects were fascinating and largely unknown outside the small circle of military people, academics, and intelligence types who took part in them.

The first was the World Basic Information Library, a government-friendly database of open-source information to which Army reservists, including some with academic backgrounds, contributed research. The Library got its start in the 1990s, when some in the Foreign Military Studies Office and elsewhere realized that the nonmilitary skills of reservists could be used to vastly increase the military's store of open-source intelligence. The project wasn't designed for the battlefield; instead, it would rely on reservists at their kitchen tables to create a database about remote parts of the world in which the government and military increasingly operated. The reservists would dig up interesting unclassified documents and archive them. Many of these documents were so-called gray literature—public information that isn't widely available, like scientific journal articles or the annual reports sent to shareholders. They might include street maps or detailed analyses of a foreign city's transport infrastructure. Subjects of interest to the Library ranged from anthropology and culture to economics, politics, drug trafficking, and technology.

After the September 11 attacks, a retired Army lieutenant colonel at the Foreign Military Studies Office recruited some dozen reservists who had been contributing to the Library to join an "open source intelligence team" supporting homeland defense. The team included people who spoke three or four foreign languages, amateur pilots, a journalist, and a guy who lived and worked on the Mexican border. The group became so successful that some in the Army wanted to expand it, but the idea never got off the ground, in part because the demands of two wars soon drained the supply of qualified reservists. A few years later, when the Foreign Military Studies Office's Soviet expert Lester Grau went on a fact-finding trip to Iraq, a female Arabic-speaking Air Force reservist from the Library served as his translator. Grau was initially taken aback to be traveling to Iraq with a young woman; in a heavily male-dominated society, he thought she would get in his way. But the reservist proved a great asset, especially in speaking with Iraqi women. When they returned, Grau and his traveling companion worked with a team of Arabic-speaking analysts at the Foreign Military Studies Office on a paper for the Center for Army Lessons Learned. Another reservist from the Library network was a medical officer who would serve on the first-ever Human Terrain Team in Afghanistan.

Since 2005, the Foreign Military Studies Office had also been funding the Bowman Expeditions, a grand undertaking that proposed to send professional geographers and graduate students from the United States to study every country in the world, at an annual cost of $125 million. Named for the geographer Isaiah Bowman, who had advised President Woodrow Wilson during World War I, the project was the brainchild of Jerome E. Dobson, a University of Kansas geography professor and head of the American Geographical Society, who had worked twenty-six years at the U.S. Department of Energy's Oak Ridge National Laboratory in Tennessee. Dobson viewed geography as a key source of intelligence that the U.S. government and military had been ignoring for decades. During World War II, a third of America's academic geographers had been summoned to serve in government agencies that were essential to war-related work, principally the Office of Strategic Services, the precursor to today's CIA. Now the United States was a superpower "crippled by abysmal ignorance of its vast global domain," Dobson wrote. "Ignorance of foreign places and people guides U.S. policies toward them and their policies toward us." In 2006, Dobson and other members of the American Geographical Society met for nearly two hours with General David Petraeus at Fort Leavenworth. Petraeus had long "recognized the need for better understanding of cultural landscapes," Dobson wrote after the meeting. "At the conclusion of our visit, he said he had a new appreciation for geography as a source of such understanding." With the Bowman Expeditions, Dobson sought to restore geography to the influential position in U.S. policy making that it had occupied in the early part of the twentieth century, before the discipline fell out of favor and the Vietnam War opened a schism between academia and the U.S. military and intelligence communities.

By 2006, Don Smith had met with then–Colonel John W. "Mick" Nicholson, who commanded a brigade of the 10th Mountain Division, and pitched the idea of embedding a team of cultural analysts in his unit. Nicholson, whose brigade was headed to eastern Afghanistan, made the first official request for a Human Terrain Team, known in military speak as an Operational Needs Statement. That summer, Smith and others at the Foreign Military Studies Office were recruiting reservists to staff a prototype field team. They were also looking for money: tens of millions of dollars to cover start-up costs.

That fall, the men of the Foreign Military Studies Office publicly described the components of a potential "human terrain team" in greater detail than anyone had before. The proposed five-member teams would include "experienced cultural advisors familiar with the area in which the commanders will be operating" and a "qualified cultural anthropologist or sociologist competent with Geographic Imaging Software and fluent enough in the local language to perform field research." The program would put special emphasis on finding social scientists who had lived, studied, or taught in the region to which they would be deployed. Each team would also include a research manager with a "military background in tactical intelligence" who would "integrate the human terrain research plan with the unit intelligence collection effort"; and a "human terrain analyst," also with a military intelligence background, who was a "trained debriefer."

The idea of installing a team of cultural experts in a military unit resonated within an Army that was doing some serious soul-searching.

In the years when the Human Terrain System was being developed, Petraeus, then a three-star general who had led the 101st Airborne Division in Mosul and supervised the training of Iraqi security forces, was stationed at Fort Leavenworth, where he ran the Combined Arms Center. Petraeus saw the move from commanding a division in Iraq to the prairies of Kansas as a disappointment and a potential career setback. It turned out to be anything but. Between 2005, when he arrived at Leavenworth, and 2007, when he took command of American forces in Iraq, Petraeus oversaw the drafting of the Army's first revision of counterinsurgency doctrine in more than twenty years. For an organization accustomed to shock and awe, the *U.S. Army/Marine Corps Counterinsurgency Field Manual* was counterintuitive in the extreme. It argued that in this new, old kind of war, political advances were far more important than military victories. "Sometimes, the more force is used, the less effective it is," the manual advised. "Sometimes, doing nothing is the best reaction. . . . Some of the best weapons for counterinsurgents do not shoot. . . . Tactical success guarantees nothing." The manual brought together military intellectuals and civilian academics like Harvard's Sarah Sewall, who called it a "radical" document that inverted decades of conventional military emphasis on force protection by suggesting that soldiers and marines had to assume greater risks to succeed in places like Iraq and Afghanistan. "In this context, killing the civilian is no longer just collateral damage," Sewall wrote in the manual's introduction. "The costs of killing noncombatants finally register on the ledger."

The manual was a barn burner. Released online in December 2006, it was downloaded more than 1.5 million times. It laid out a plan for winning over Iraqis and Afghans, but by speaking in humble, measured tones, it also sought to marshal the support of America's powerful intellectual elite, the journalists, academics, social scientists, and think tankers whose backing would be necessary to the success of any long-running and politically costly campaign. This would turn out to be a winning strategy, and the counterinsurgency set would use it repeatedly in the years to come. The manual's wildly positive reception in the press signaled a desire, particularly among American liberals, to walk back from the Bush administration's aggressive wartime rhetoric and to quiet lingering misgivings over the conflict in Iraq and, to a lesser degree, the war in Afghanistan. For while many Americans agreed that Islamic militants deserved whatever pain the U.S. military might inflict on them, the growing global perception of the United States as an arrogant occupier rankled. Americans saw themselves, or wanted to see themselves, differently: as a nation sacrificing young lives and billions of dollars to defend its ideals and better the world. Counterinsurgency had reemerged in part because the military had realized that American arrogance, real and imagined, was fueling uprisings. What the manual downplayed was that counterinsurgency wasn't a bloodless way of war. It meant winning over those who were susceptible to being won over and removing America's most determined enemies from the battlefield. And for the strategy to work, every piece of it had to be executed well. Bad cultural knowledge would lead to bad intelligence. Bad intelligence could mean detaining or killing the wrong people. Pretty soon, the Army would be back where it started.

The field manual, known in Army speak as FM 3-24, was a committee effort. Montgomery McFate's articles on adversary cultural knowledge and the use of anthropology in war had drawn the attention of prominent military thinkers, and she was tapped to cowrite a section on cultural knowledge in counterinsurgency. At first, her contribution was to be marginal, a brief appendix. But at a meeting with the manual's authors, Petraeus declared that the section on culture should be moved to the heart of the manual. He considered cultural knowledge an obvious and central intelligence requirement for counterinsurgency. "If you don't get it about this stuff, you don't get it about counterinsurgency," he would tell me later. "Not understanding the human terrain has the same effect on your operations that not understanding the physical terrain has on conventional military operations. If you don't really appreciate the physical terrain and its impact on your operations, you don't succeed. If you don't understand the human terrain in the conduct of population-centric counterinsurgency operations, you don't succeed." McFate's contribution to the manual turned out to be substantial: sixteen pages at the heart of the chapter on intelligence.

The University of Chicago Press published the field manual in 2007. That February, the first-ever Human Terrain Team arrived in Khost, a green and prosperous province along the Afghan-Pakistani border with an active local insurgency led by Jalaluddin Haqqani, a onetime CIA favorite and hardened war veteran from the days of the anti-Soviet resistance, who was now giving the Americans hell. That first team had come together in a rush. In 2006, Smith left the Human Terrain System and Fondacaro, back from Iraq and retired from the Army, took over as program manager. He secured $20 million from the counter-IED task force to build five experimental Human Terrain Teams, and recruited some of the first field team members, who joined at least two others brought in earlier by Smith and his colleagues. Nicholson's brigade, which had originally requested a team, was on its way back to the States, but Fondacaro's old friend Votel had moved into a command position with the 82nd Airborne Division, which was sending a brigade to Khost. The first Human Terrain Team joined them.

If the Human Terrain System had been looking to plant its flag in a place of long-standing significance to the insurgency, it couldn't have chosen better than Khost. It was there, in the fertile bowl-shaped plateau and the mountains along the Pakistani border, that Osama bin Laden had built roads and caves to support U.S.-backed anti-Soviet resistance fighters in the 1980s. In 1986, bin Laden had established his first terrorist training camp for Arab volunteers there, arming them with weapons supplied by the CIA. Years later, he would issue a fatwa from Khost calling on Muslims to kill Americans all over the world. In 1998, after twin bombings of the U.S. embassies in Kenya and Tanzania killed 224 people, the Clinton administration fired American cruise missiles at bin Laden's Khost training camps. At least twenty-one presumed jihadist volunteers died, but the tall, wily Saudi leader lived to fight another day, and the camps were rebuilt. Some of the September 11 hijackers trained in Khost. The Human Terrain System denied that it was an intelligence program, but its first team was not sent to the quiet fringes of the fight. If the insurgency could have been said to have a heartland, Khost was it.

The members of AF1, as the team was known, possessed a rare set of specialized skills. Their leader was a former Special Forces officer, and the team's social scientist, who asked reporters to identify her only as Tracy, was a West Point graduate who had studied anthropology and described herself as a "high risk ethnographer." The brigade commander, Colonel Martin "Marty" Schweitzer, threw his support behind the team. In one community, Tracy pointed out that the Haqqani network was gaining strength because an uncommonly large number of widows depended on their sons for support. With few jobs available, many young men were forced to join the insurgency to earn money. On the advice of the Human Terrain Team, soldiers started a job-training program that put the widows to work and cut the insurgents' supply of recruits. Tracy and her teammates advised commanders on the need to unite the Zadran, a large and influential tribe in eastern Afghanistan. The more atomized the Zadran were, the more likely its members would be to fight each other instead of acting as the single, stalwart force that the Americans needed against the insurgents, Tracy argued. It was a good idea, but one that would be forever complicated by the fact that Haqqani, the leader of the anti-American insurgency in Khost, was himself a Zadran. The Human Terrain Team connected soldiers with local leaders and even convinced the Army to refurbish a mosque on the American base, a project that was credited with cutting insurgent rocket attacks. For Tracy and many soldiers who worked with her, the payoff for this kind of knowledge was uncomplicatedly positive. 'It may be one less trigger that has to be pulled here,' Tracy told a reporter. 'It's how we gain ground, not tangible ground, but cognitive ground.'

Tracy's contributions were quickly felt. She was 'taking the population and dissecting it,' an officer who worked with her said, giving soldiers 'data points' that helped them resolve local disputes and identify problems before they turned violent. Within months of her arrival, Tracy was hailed in the press as the 'key ingredient' in the U.S. military's evolving counterinsurgency strategy: 'a uniformed anthropologist toting a gun.' Colonel Schweitzer would become one of the Human Terrain System's biggest supporters. He believed that AF1 had made American soldiers and Afghans safer and sped the work of connecting Afghans to their government. When Schweitzer had arrived in Khost, only nineteen of eighty-six districts supported the Afghan government. By the end of his deployment, he estimated that seventy-two of them did. He credited Tracy and her team with reducing his unit's combat operations in Khost by 60 to 70 percent.

In attributing a measure of his brigade's success to the work of the Human Terrain Team, Schweitzer helped lay the groundwork for the project's hysterical growth spurt. By the fall of 2007, the Defense Department had authorized a $40 million expansion of the Human Terrain System that would raise the number of field teams in Iraq and Afghanistan from six to twenty-six. Where those teams would come from and how they would be trained quickly enough to meet the Army's needs was left to Fondacaro and his bosses at the Army's Training and Doctrine Command to figure out.

# 3. THE TENDER SOLDIER

I n September 2008, Paula Loyd boarded a Chinook helicopter packed with soldiers for a flight over the deserts and mountains of southern Afghanistan. The back of the chopper yawned open to the sky, and men in flight suits with machine guns guarded the doors and windows. They sped over the wall of Kandahar Airfield, leaving behind the giant sewage tanks and spinning missile detectors that dotted the perimeter of the base like cast iron pinwheels. They flew over glimmering irrigation ditches cutting the flat brown land, over thick green fields and gardens and mud compounds and little outbuildings with holes in the walls, where farmers hung grapes to dry in the warm wind. The land unfurled beneath them, grapevines growing over dirt berms, the fish-scale shine of rivers that had once been wider and wetter. After a while, the green gave way to sand flats and dunes tufted with desert grass that rolled on, undulant and hypnotic, until jagged mountains rose to the north. As the helicopter lowered, a single black peak reared up like a fang against the sky.

This landscape thrilled Loyd, but she came from somewhere else. She had spent her early childhood in Alamo Heights, a small city within the municipal boundaries of San Antonio, Texas, where her parents designed pension and profit-sharing plans and owned rental properties. Loyd was an only child, and although she was named after her father, Paul Loyd, who had trained bomber pilots in World War II, she gained an early reputation as the family peacemaker. Her much older half brother had children her age, and when they fought over toys, Loyd gave them her toys to settle the argument. But her generosity came at a price. When her nieces and nephews headed home after a day's play, they took her toys with them.

Loyd's mother sent her to a Montessori school, but her mind wandered. She craved structure. Later, she would struggle with math. She imagined each number as a character with a distinct personality. Large numbers were families, and when she looked at an equation, she saw not a string of integers but a group of beings in conversation with one another, their interaction mediated by pluses and minuses. Math homework took hours. She grew so distracted by the story the numbers were telling that she forgot to solve the problem.

She was quirky and bright, a ravenous reader who adored Star Wars action figures and animals, even the Persian cat that made her sneeze. Loyd's oldest friend, Susanna Barton, was drawn to this delicate, strikingly beautiful girl with long, sandy-blond hair, always neatly braided. Loyd was different from Barton, and from any other child Barton knew. She made an effort to engage with people Barton generally had no time for, like Barton's annoying little brother. When Barton's grandmother came to visit, Loyd took an interest in her cooking and listened attentively to her stories. At eight or nine, Loyd and Barton started an animal rescue group, dutifully filling out paperwork to incorporate it as a nonprofit. Loyd declared herself a vegetarian a few years later, but not before asking her mother to fix her a "last supper" of the pork chops she loved.

Loyd's childhood home in Alamo Heights had a broad winding staircase, bright green and blue carpeting, and a turkey-shaped phone that gobbled instead of rang. Barton and Loyd played there often, knocking a ball back and forth across the Ping-Pong table and splashing around in the swimming pool with its concrete formations, waterfall, and slide. In his workroom, Loyd's father painted miniature model soldiers two or three inches tall. The family ate in a formal dining room, where they had grown-up conversations about current events, and where Loyd was sometimes allowed to drink nonalcoholic beer or a small glass of wine.

In fifth grade, a new girl joined them. Gretchen Wiker was a recent transplant from Germany, a self-described "nerdy girl" with the wrong clothes who still wore her hair in braids when everyone else had moved on to more sophisticated styles. Loyd immediately befriended her. "She looked past things that other people couldn't look past," Wiker told me. "She was friends with people other people weren't friends with." Once, they mixed all the spices, hot sauces, and vinegars in the kitchen and competed to see who could drink more (Loyd won). Out of nowhere, Loyd decided to give Wiker a facial and makeover and loan her the Esprit argyle sweater Wiker had coveted all through sixth grade. Loyd and her mother were always careening into airports at the last minute, overloaded with luggage, almost missing their flights. One Halloween, Wiker recalled, she and Loyd planned to hand out candy, but they quickly ran out, so they hunted around for packets of hot chocolate and quarters to give to trick-or-treaters. Wiker ate her first artichoke at the Loyds' dining table and smoked her first cigarette with Loyd behind a nearby supermarket. For Wiker and other girls who knew her then, Loyd's friendship had a magical quality, as if you were stepping into an alternate world every time you hung out with her.

49

In some ways, Loyd was a typical preteen girl, susceptible to perms, dangly earrings, and the charms of punk boys. Without her mother's permission, she started cutting her hair with a razor, dying it colors, and outlining her lips with black liner. When Loyd was about thirteen, her parents divorced. Shortly thereafter, she begged her mother to take her to a place where people who looked like her—pale skin, blond hair— were outnumbered by people who didn't. She wanted to see how people would treat her if she were in the minority. "I told her, 'You're a minority already. You're an Anglo in Texas,'" her mother, Patty Ward, recalled. Loyd just laughed. It was an unusual request from a child, and Ward had no urgent desire to leave Texas. But all these years, she had been encouraging her daughter to explore.

Patty Ward was effortlessly friendly. During her lunchtime walks around San Antonio, she fell into conversation with strangers and invited them back to the house for dinner. This was the early 1980s, when you could still get away with that kind of thing, and Ward called it taking in strays. Once, it was two Swedish girls who taught English and were traveling across the country by bus. Over dinner, they talked about socialized medicine with Loyd, who was young but irrepressibly curious. "She's basically always been an anthropologist," Ward told me. Another time, three young people walked up to Ward on the street and asked if she knew of a place they could stay while they visited the Alamo. Ward and her husband owned some rental properties around town, and one of the apartments happened to be vacant and unfurnished. The kids unrolled their sleeping bags on the floor, and Ward invited them to dinner, where one of the young men, a Rhodes scholar, talked to Loyd about geology and South Africa, where he had grown up. Some nights, Ward woke Loyd and her friends and took them outside to see a lunar eclipse or a rare star. Together, Loyd and her mother traveled the West in a motor home. One hot day in Mesa Verde, Colorado, Loyd lay inside the metal shell with the air-conditioning on, deep in a book. It was Ward who made her get out and walk through the ancient settlements, their walls covered in pictographs.

The family owned property in St. Thomas, and Ward and Loyd moved there just as Loyd was starting high school. But after two years, Loyd began to worry that the island school wasn't challenging enough. She spent her junior and senior years at Choate Rosemary Hall, a Connecticut boarding school with rolling lawns and white-columned buildings, where Loyd, in her combat boots and faux-fur leopard-print jacket, stood out among the teenagers in Polo shirts and pearls. "She was this sort of punk-rock girl," one of her fellow students, Rafe Sagarin, told me. "She had half her head shaved and she wore funky thrift-store clothes." He eyed her for months before working up the nerve to talk to her.

They dated for most of her junior year, bonding over the Cramps, the Dead Kennedys, and Minor Threat, taking long walks in the woods, and engaging in vigorous intellectual debates. Loyd admired Ayn Rand and Donald Trump. Sagarin thought Trump was a fool, but Loyd appreciated the billionaire's straightforwardness, his willingness to say what he believed in, even if what he believed in was making a lot of money. "She felt that there were a lot of people just aping values they heard somewhere else, from their parents or teachers," Sagarin told me. "She wanted to figure out what a person really stood for." When he visited her family in St. Thomas over spring break, Loyd's broad range of acquaintances impressed him. "There were Rastas she knew, and someone selling smoothies on the street, and old hippie expats," he recalled. Her teachers noted her hunger for ideas and her gentleness, but there was something fierce about her, too. In a photograph Sagarin took of her that year, she wore faded jeans and her hair was cut short and jagged. She squatted next to a stone statue of a lion and she was imitating the lion, her fingers curved in an approximation of a claw, her mouth open in a roar.

At Wellesley, Loyd ran along the Charles River, slight but strong, driven by a sinuous determination. The small women's college, set among woods and rolling green hills outside Boston, has a history of educating bold, socially and politically active women. Secretary of State Hillary Rodham Clinton is among its alumnae, and while Loyd was at Wellesley, the student newspaper carried frequent stories about the brilliant young lawyer who had recently become First Lady. In college, Loyd befriended a woman she had known glancingly at Choate who was different from her in almost every way. In high school, Stefanie Johnson had been a scholarship kid from Harlem and Loyd her dorm prefect, a couple of years older, friendly but inaccessible. At Wellesley, they rowed crew together, rising at 4:30 a.m. for practice. Loyd ran along the river in her Tevas and pushed Johnson to work harder in the gym. But during van rides to their boathouse in Boston, a few teammates said things that made Johnson seethe. She viewed the comments as racist and classist, but the rest of the team's silence bothered her even more. Loyd tried to talk her down. "Paula was the type of person who always saw the good in people and would try to reconcile," Johnson told me later. Johnson decided to quit, so Loyd stood beside her, and together they tried to explain to their teammates why discrimination was wrong, silence insidious.

In photos from this period, Loyd's hair is cut radically short. In jeans and a blouse, talking with friends at a house party or smiling in a bar, she exudes a new kind of grown-up confidence. She and Johnson worked together at a student-run coffee shop where people drew pictures and wrote poetry on the walls. Loyd mixed homemade honey-walnut cream cheese and helped Johnson with her Spanish homework. They talked endlessly about friends, family, and relationships. "She dated a lot and broke a lot of hearts," Johnson told me. "People just fell in love with Paula. It was hard not to." By this time, Loyd had become captivated by anthropology. For one of her classes, she was assigned to conduct an ethnography of a Boston neighborhood. Her teacher, Sally Engle Merry, asked students to learn about the neighborhood's ethnic composition and describe the social and economic issues affecting its people. This was not easy for college students. They had to walk the streets and brave the awkwardness of talking to strangers. But Loyd was her mother's daughter, and she did this with ease. She impressed Merry as an ideal anthropologist-in-training: outgoing, poised, independent, and genuinely interested in what other people were thinking.

At Wellesley, Loyd championed human rights and equality. Her much older half brother, Paul Loyd, Jr., by now a wealthy Texas oil-man, grew accustomed to their arguments. He saw himself as a prag-matist, while Loyd was more like Don Quixote, always off on a worthy but possibly hopeless crusade. "Paula would say, 'It's right, it's moral, it's what we should be doing,' and she'd go ahead," Paul Loyd told me. He and others were shocked when, upon graduating from Wellesley, she joined the Army. Loyd's decision also surprised Johnson, who remem-bers talking with her about it at the time. "She made it sound like there was a place in the military even for people like her, who loved peace and didn't like war," Johnson told me.

A possible clue lay in an ambitious academic project Loyd had un-dertaken before leaving Wellesley, where she had been one of a very small number of students selected to write an honors thesis in anthro-pology. Her paper clocked in at 181 pages, and it hinted at questions about the military and the lives of people in conflict zones that would absorb her for years to come. Loyd's thesis was a sensitive and meticu-lously researched account of the growth of underground resistance in the gay bar scene in San Antonio, which was home to three major mili-tary bases. Drawing on Marxist and feminist theory, Loyd wrote that she was seeking a "subtle and nuanced account of the various ways subordinate people subvert domination." While some social scientists focused on armed peasant uprisings, Loyd was more interested in "small acts of everyday resistance." "I have found that subordinate groups use the forms of resistance most readily available to them," she wrote. "Yet, resistance is also structured according to the social networks it makes use of." Bars were natural gathering places for working-class gay people, often in rough parts of town that lay beyond the easy reaches of civilian and military authority. Their patrons committed small but crucial acts of rebellion against San Antonio's dominant heterosexual order and the newspapers, churches, police, and military authorities that enforced it. Loyd wrote that she was interested in "the numerous gray areas between overt rebellion and abject submission."

Loyd had always identified with the underdog, always craved a challenge. With her college degree, she could have become an Army officer. Instead, she enlisted. Some acquaintances wondered at this, but it was a choice anthropologists would have recognized. Loyd thrived as an outsider; morally and politically, her sympathies lay with the grunts. The Army gave her an aptitude test that showed she was mechanically inclined. Loyd's maternal grandfather had been a mechanic, and her mother had always been good at fixing things. When Loyd turned sixteen, Ward had taught her how to change a car tire, and Loyd had helped her mother and stepfather rebuild their house in St. Thomas after two hurricanes. Now the Army trained Loyd as a heavy-wheel vehicle mechanic. Soldiers with this job description fix trucks weighing more than five tons; they must be able to lift more than one hundred pounds on occasion and more than fifty pounds frequently. Loyd stood five foot six and weighed 120 pounds at most, but she routinely scored in the men's range on fitness tests. Her commanders marveled at the contrast between her flaxen delicacy and her physical toughness, this tiny woman who could take on a roaring deuce and a half. She was sent to Korea, where she lived for a time on a remote outpost ringed with barbed wire. She was attached to a Patriot missile unit, which had little need for a truck mechanic, so Loyd expected to spend much of her deployment pulling guard duty. She told her half brother these things in a card she sent him, decorated with a cutout in the shape of a dove. It was the kind of card a peacenik would buy, but the scrawl inside belonged to a soldier.

After four years, she switched to the reserves, moved to Washington, D.C., and began work at Georgetown University on a master's degree in diplomacy and conflict resolution. In the rarefied atmosphere that nurtures America's policy-making elite, Loyd and her fellow students discussed the relative influence of coercive military instruments and diplomatic efforts in Bosnia, but she also drove a UPS truck part-time. Then came the attacks of September 11, 2001, and her reserve unit was called up. By now, she had given up fixing trucks in favor of civil affairs, a job that put her at the intersection of military force and humanitarian aid. Civil affairs units are made up of reservists with special skills. Originally part of the Army's Special Operations Command, they work with psychological operations soldiers to bridge the divide between combat forces and local civilians and governments. They hand out food, water, and blankets, talk to local leaders, and pay local laborers to build bridges and clinics. They are the closest thing the Army has to professional nation builders.

Kandahar is a desert city: hot days, cool nights, fine dust that coats your skin and sticks in the roots of your hair. A year after the fall of the Taliban, it hung suspended between a violent past and an unimaginable future, alive with political intrigue that remained largely incomprehensible to the American troops stationed there. Old rivals plotted one another's demise, bearded American Special Forces soldiers rode around in pickups trading cash for dubious information, and the shops in the bazaar sold fat yellow raisins alongside candy with Osama bin Laden's face on the box.

Loyd was assigned to the 450th Civil Affairs Battalion, an airborne unit. She had made staff sergeant by then, and she was the noncommissioned officer in charge of a small team. She and her fellow soldiers lived in a rudimentary canvas-and-plywood tent at Kandahar Airfield, where they slept on cots. They spent about eight months there, visiting villages, assessing water and health facilities, asking people what crops they grew, and doling out aid and school supplies. If a school had been damaged by fighting, Loyd and her teammates would try to repair it. Sometimes they got money from the United States Agency for International Development to dig a well, and Loyd would negotiate with local laborers to do the work. Alert to the potential for corruption, she was especially careful to ensure a wide field of bidders, "not just the local friend of the mayor or the governor," her teammate Mike Rathje told me. She and her fellow soldiers helped repair a radio station in Kandahar and traveled to the Kajaki Dam in Helmand to learn about problems with the power grid.

Because of her line of work, Loyd was one of only a handful of Americans who spent time listening to Afghans, and she began to get a feel for the place, its people, the way power worked, the structure of tribes. Women were confined to their homes, unable to speak their minds. 'We are screaming into the silence,' one woman told her. In her Wellesley thesis, Loyd had written about an anthropological study of Bedouin women in Egypt who were simultaneously resisting government efforts to assimilate them and rebelling against the Bedouin men who ran their community. "They banded together to hide information from the men, helped each other resist arranged marriages they did not want," Loyd wrote. "At the same time, younger women fought against older women to wear makeup and lingerie, items bought from Egyptian society. They would also side with young men against older Bedouins, when arguing for the freedom to choose romantic marriages instead of having an arranged marriage." Many of the same complexities defined Afghan society, and Loyd was primed to see what other Americans missed. At ribbon-cuttings for American-funded schools, she tried to convince Afghans to educate their girls. Male doctors were not allowed to treat women in these conservative areas, but in a country with the world's second-highest maternal mortality rate, Loyd found that even men had an interest in improving women's health. If they wanted more female doctors, she told them, they would have to send their daughters to school.

It was so uncommon in southern Afghanistan to see a woman walking around in uniform that Afghan men sometimes asked Loyd's translator whether she was male or female. But they weren't hostile. They treated her with deference because she was a foreigner and a guest, and as an American woman, she occupied a powerful middle ground. 'The fact that I'm a woman doesn't mean I need to be in a burka and they can't deal with me,' she told a reporter in 2003. 'They take me for who I am, they accept me for who I am. And they're willing to work with me.' Loyd tied her hair back and covered it with a cloth Safari-style hat, but she still stuck out. One day, when she was driving one of the team's pickup trucks, a group of Afghan women pulled up their burqas and gave the Americans a thumbs-up signal. "I was astounded," Rathje, her teammate, told me. "I had not seen that the whole time I was there."

Rathje wondered at Loyd's energy and persistence. He never saw her get discouraged, as he sometimes did. Once during their time in Kandahar, they met a group of young Afghan girls. Loyd smiled and joked with the kids, but Rathje found it hard to look at them. "I saw someone who looked like my daughter with no future, and it would make me sad," he told me. "She was really more jubilant about that than I was, more hopeful, maybe."

'Their fathers love them,' Loyd told him.

'Yeah, they do,' he agreed. But he remembered their visits to hand out aid to young widows who had been married to much older men and left penniless, whose children had no shoes in the middle of winter.

Loyd and her teammates helped lay the ground for one of Afghanistan's first Provincial Reconstruction Teams. Known as PRTs, the teams are made up of rings of combat forces protecting a core of civilian governance and development workers from the State Department, the United States Agency for International Development, and the Department of Agriculture. In those early years, PRTs represented an institutionalized blending of security forces and development personnel not seen since Vietnam. The aim was to extend the nascent Afghan government's reach to unruly provinces, where local thugs and insurgents were seizing power. The U.S. military announced the new concept with fanfare, but the very idea of pairing development workers with soldiers enraged many in the international aid community. Organizations like the International Committee of the Red Cross and CARE viewed the civil-military teams as a risk to aid workers, who depended on their neutrality to move safely around the country. Using government and military-sponsored aid and development to win Afghan allegiance muddied the waters, these groups argued, making it impossible for independent aid workers to convince people they were apolitical. Moreover, these new arrivals often didn't know enough about the communities they were serving to do meaningful development. They chose projects the people didn't need, put them in the wrong places, wasted money because they didn't know the going rates. Loyd understood these concerns, but she was that rare American who had the foresight to pay the Afghan police in her area directly instead of funneling the money through their commanders, knowing that if she trusted the hierarchy, the men on the bottom would probably never see their salaries. Loyd also knew that the battlefield was changing and that Afghan insurgents increasingly viewed even aid workers as political actors. In southern Afghanistan in 2003, a Red Cross staff member was pulled from his truck and executed. The Taliban commander who ordered his killing had been unmoved by his organization's commitment to neutrality. To the insurgents, he was an emissary for Western imperialism.

When her tour in Kandahar ended, Loyd returned to Georgetown and finished her degree, graduating with honors. The School of Foreign Service aims to train practitioners, not scholars, and this suited Loyd's goals. She didn't want a career in academia, at least not then. She wanted to go back to Afghanistan. Soon she was in Kabul, working for a nongovernmental group called the International Organization for Migration. One winter day, she attended a briefing on the upcoming expansion of NATO forces in Afghanistan. The American officer delivering the talk had gray-blue eyes, a square jaw, and a lean, muscular build, but a scar near the outer edge of his left eye hinted at an alluring vulnerability. His name was Frank Muggeo, and he was one of the Army's emissaries to the aid and development world. Loyd was sitting near the front, and Muggeo noticed her immediately. He was in a tough spot, trying to bring together soldiers and humanitarian experts when the simple fact that he was an American Special Forces officer caused many aid and development workers to view him uncomplicatedly as a trained killer. He and Loyd chatted afterward, and he sensed her optimism. She wanted to believe that things could be different, that an expanded NATO presence would better Afghan lives. Muggeo had just arrived in Afghanistan. He had no idea who was who. Loyd knew everyone.

Muggeo and Loyd met at NATO headquarters in Kabul and talked about work and their lives. She was dazzling, he thought. She was a good-looking woman in Afghanistan, which counted for a lot, but there was more to it than that. He was just stumbling around, but she really knew the place, the way things worked. She'd come from a comfortable background, had a good education, more than a lot of people got, yet she'd chosen to spend her time in this shithole where they needed everything. He learned of a time when she was in the Army, when an Afghan had brought his nephew to an American base for treatment. The boy had been shot. It wasn't Loyd's job, but somehow she'd managed to get him on a plane to the big American base north of Kabul, where doctors had treated him. Muggeo noticed that out of respect for Afghan culture, she always wore long sleeves and coiled her hair in a bun. The only time he saw her wear it any other way was when she used the treadmill at the NATO gym. He learned that she was never on time, that she loved to sleep late.

In late 2004, Loyd got a job with the United States Agency for International Development, or USAID. She was assigned to the Provincial Reconstruction Team in Zabul, a southern province between the Pakistani border and the southern desert, and one of the poorest places in Afghanistan. The capital, Qalat, flashes past on the Kabul to Kandahar highway in an eyeblink, a string of dingy bazaar stalls listing in the wind like a clothesline heavy with soiled shirts. Away from the snowbanks and mud pits of town, craggy mountains crest over winding dry riverbeds and men walk the old goat paths known only to locals.

The Provincial Reconstruction Team in Qalat was housed in a large walled compound built by the Soviets in the 1980s. When I visited four years after Loyd's stint there, infantrymen slept on cots in crumbling concrete buildings and civilians from the State and Agriculture Departments lived in dormitorylike barracks toward the back of the property, their rooms decorated with cheap rugs and photos from home. It was January, frigid and gloomy, and the soldiers hewed to the routine of each day—shower, chow hall, work, gym, email, *Friday Night Lights*—as if it were the only thing that kept them in this world.

Even in a place as battered as Afghanistan, Zabul was a tough case. Poverty, disease, and war had broken the traditional structures of cooperation between villagers, and now fighting was like drought, a regrettable but unavoidable aspect of being alive. Land was valuable and disputes had to be settled some way, slights avenged, crimes atoned for. This was where Loyd had spent a year of her life, working with Afghan officials and American soldiers to bring development to people forgotten by their own government. Zabul was considered so backward that Afghans from other provinces could hardly be persuaded to work there. Teachers and officials brought in from Kabul left again as quickly as they could, and anyone from Zabul who managed to get a decent education immediately headed to a big city where prospects were brighter. The provincial governor, Delbar Arman, was one of President Karzai's longest-serving officials. He and Loyd became friends during her time there.

Arman was a muscular man with a neatly trimmed beard and a steady gaze. On the afternoon I met him, he wore a cardigan sweater and a pin-striped blazer over his traditional tunic. In the large, chilly receiving room of his compound near the American base, he sat between a giant Afghan flag and a plastic apple tree shimmering with green leaves and pink fruit. A regal emerald-and-purple jacket hung from his shoulders, but if Arman's clothes suggested power, his pale, pinched face signaled a lingering anxiety. His wife and children were in Kabul, and he rarely left his compound for fear of being killed. Every day in Zabul tested him. Trained as an engineer, he had fought the Soviets under Gulbuddin Hekmatyar, once an American ally, now one of America's bitterest enemies. He had battled the Taliban, fled to Pakistan, returned, sparred with a rival commander, been jailed by his former friends. He had helped deliver the eastern provinces for Karzai during the first post-Taliban presidential election. In return, the president had appointed him to the National Security Council and, later, sent him here.

The job was both an honor and a curse. By the time Arman arrived to govern Zabul in 2004, the insurgents had stitched themselves into the countryside like knots in a rug. The province's few buildings, roads, and schools were crumbling, and elders covered their faces when they came to meet the governor because they didn't want the Taliban to recognize them. Arman had met Loyd that first winter, in the cold and snow, on a trip to one of Zabul's outlying districts. A small group of Americans traveled with him, and Loyd was among them. The governor was busy talking to villagers, leading a shura. At some point, he realized that he hadn't seen Loyd for a while. Some woman was sick, the villagers told him. The American woman had gone to visit her. Loyd had left the group and walked to an Afghan home more than a kilometer away. The next thing Arman knew, they were bringing the Afghan woman to him on a bed.

'Governor,' Loyd told him, 'we want to take her to Qalat so she can get medical care.'

The woman was pregnant and she might not survive in this faraway village in winter. They loaded her onto a helicopter whose rear door stood open, snow and wind blowing in. Loyd covered the woman with her jacket to keep her warm. She positioned herself between the wind and the woman, kneeling uncomfortably in the middle of the helicopter all the way back to Qalat. The governor watched in amazement. Why did this American woman care so much about his people?

In Qalat, the woman did not get better. 'I want to take her to Kandahar,' Loyd told the governor, 'where there is a better hospital.'

Loyd left with the woman and a day and a night passed. The next morning, before dawn, the governor woke to a knock at his door. He was alarmed: who could be knocking at this hour, the sun not even up? He opened the door and Loyd was standing there in the shadows.

'I came back, governor,' she told him. 'I am very happy. That woman is healed and she had her baby.'

Arman took Loyd's hand and told her: 'You are my sister.'

He noticed that she was delicate and thin. He learned that she was a vegetarian, and this struck him as funny. Vegetarians are almost unheard-of in Afghanistan. He thought she must be weak, but he saw how hard she worked. Ten hours, twelve hours a day. He began to invite her regularly to dinner, instructing his cooks to find vegetables in the market for her. During one of these visits, the American soldiers escorting her realized they hadn't seen her in a while. They tore the building apart, only to find Loyd napping comfortably on a couch in the governor's office.

During her year in Zabul, Loyd established a women's tree-planting cooperative and coordinated the delivery of rice and other aid to snowed-in Afghans in the mountains. She helped return the bodies of development contractors killed in Taliban attacks to their families. When townspeople showed up at the American base to report strange women moving around the province without male escorts, it was Loyd who helped track down the group of clueless female Korean missionaries. She invited them to spend the night at the American compound, joined them for Bible study, and spirited them out of the province the next morning under police guard.

In 2005, Loyd took a job in Kabul with the United Nations Assistance Mission in Afghanistan, helping international military forces and nongovernmental organizations work together for the good of Afghans. The tension between these two groups was palpable, and led to all kinds of squabbling. Nongovernmental organizations grew outraged when military forces drove vehicles painted white, which aid workers considered a safe, neutral color and claimed as their own. Soldiers, meanwhile, argued that white was the stock color of some armored SUVs—nothing they could do about it. Loyd was a "very good moderator," a friend who worked with her recalled. She planned conferences for soldiers and civilians working together in PRTs, trained incoming Americans from the State Department and USAID, and traveled to Germany and Norway to prep NATO soldiers headed for Afghanistan.

She loved the job, but life in Kabul had grown risky. Drinking Heineken on the roof of her house at 2 a.m., she and a friend watched tracer fire in the distance. One day, Loyd was in a downtown building when a large bomb exploded nearby, shattering windows and knocking her down. Shaken, she called Muggeo in Baghdad. She had always known Afghanistan could be dangerous, but this was the first time its violence had touched her directly. She took comfort in her wide group of friends and in her work. Her concerns were fundamentally humanitarian, but military officers liked and trusted her because she was knowledgeable and she spoke their language. An Air Force officer who took command of the Provincial Reconstruction Team in Zabul after Loyd left found that she was one of the few people in Afghanistan with whom he could talk openly. He knew a lot about blowing things up from forty thousand feet, but now he had to charm local Afghan leaders and craft a meaningful development strategy. Loyd had no problem telling him he was full of shit, but she was also adamantly in his corner. During a visit to the Afghan capital, he asked her to accompany him and another officer to a lavish brunch at one of Kabul's elegant new hotels. The men were armed, but the hotel forbade weapons. Before they reached the door, Loyd buried their guns in her purse and breezed past the metal detectors, flashing the Afghan guards a wide, innocent smile.

In 2006, Loyd spoke on a panel at the Woodrow Wilson Center in Washington, D.C., about challenges to military and civilian cooperation in war and crisis zones. The moderator noted that this debate was often polarized, with the military and those who supported them on one side and aid workers claiming neutrality on the other. But in Afghanistan, Loyd told the audience, military forces, the United Nations, nongovernmental organizations, and aid workers had transcended traditional divides. The old polarities no longer accurately described a battlefield where soldiers spent more time meeting with elders than shooting insurgents, and where Afghan and foreign aid workers were routinely kidnapped and executed. "We have realized that we have to cooperate," Loyd said. "It could be because people are dying on all sides. Maybe in some ways that brings us all together."

Loyd was two days shy of her thirty-fourth birthday. She wore grown-up clothes—white blouse, dark blazer, pearls—but there was something girlish about the rhythms of her speech, her heavy bangs, and the long bright ponytail hanging down her back. She was not opposed to the war, but neither was she blind to the shortcomings of the U.S. military. She described an unplanned visit by American soldiers to a U.S.-funded school construction site, a visit that the local organization building the school had pleaded with its American partners not to make. "They came in with Humvees, they blocked up the streets, they engendered some ill will among the community," she said. The organization building the school started getting death threats and had to slow down its work. This cultural tone deafness showed up elsewhere, too. Every American unit and every national force in NATO wanted to show that it had accomplished something, even when building a new school or government office wasn't what Afghans most needed. Those projects looked good on paper, Loyd told the audience. They carried your flag and commanders liked them, but in the end, they didn't help. Even more troubling, the U.S. military had shown itself incapable of sustaining long-term relationships with local officials and tribal leaders. Those connections, carefully nurtured over months, were continually broken when one group of soldiers left and another arrived. Patterns of behavior, information about arguments between families, the way a village economy functioned—all of it was lost because no one had come up with a way to capture and preserve it. The outgoing unit told new soldiers where they were most likely to get blown up, but failed to pass on important details about local leaders, who could stop the insurgents from planting bombs in the first place.

"Military forces don't always have a good understanding of the tribal politics of the area in which they work," Loyd told the audience at the Wilson Center. "Sometimes they can inadvertently worsen the situation by supporting one tribal group versus another." During her time in Zabul, she had worked with an American Special Forces unit that drew all its interpreters from a single tribe. Those translators brought their worldview, shaped by their tribal affiliation, to every meeting, every conversation. The soldiers started arresting Afghans based on tribal disputes, not because they were insurgents or terrorists. But advising soldiers otherwise produced uneven results. "Sometimes they listen to us," Loyd said. "Sometimes they don't. Sometimes their short-term objectives mean that they're not really interested in this."

As the panel drew to a close, a State Department official in the audience posed a question about America's civil-military coordination efforts: "How long will this take?"

"For Afghanistan, the current wisdom is fifteen to twenty years," Loyd told him, smiling sweetly. "And I think that if we draw down too many troops, and if we cut the budget too much, or if we don't spend it in a wise way, then we're going to have to go back in, twenty or thirty years from now, again."

Millions of Afghans had returned to Kabul since the American invasion, choking it with traffic that generated clouds of smog, and Loyd's lungs had begun to bother her. She reluctantly moved back to the States in 2007 to recover her health, planning to return to Afghanistan as soon as she could. She had been offered a good job at Research Triangle Institute International, a nonprofit in Raleigh, North Carolina, that advises businesses and governments. She bought a house, fenced in half the yard for the Afghan dogs she had adopted, and reconnected with Muggeo, the Special Forces officer she'd gotten to know in Kabul.

They'd dated on and off, but work had kept them apart. Now she visited him at Fort Benning, Georgia, where he headed the Army Marksmanship Unit. When they spent weekends together, he rose early and made coffee. 'I know you wanted some alone time,' she would tell him when she woke several hours later. He was a committed carnivore, but for her sake he devoted half his grill to portobello mushrooms. He took her riding on his Harley and they talked about the future. They were good together, but she wanted kids and he didn't. At the end of one visit, they decided to split up. Loyd flew back to North Carolina. Weeks passed. Then a text message appeared on his phone: 'Can we talk?' After that, they were together even when they were apart.

Still, Loyd was restless. Her life in North Carolina felt so ordinary, too ordinary. She traveled to Pakistan and Beirut for work, but spent most days in a clean, modern office. One night, she complained about it to her mother.

'You'd rather be sitting on a rug talking to elders and drinking tea, wouldn't you?' her mother asked.

A few months later, Loyd was on a military helicopter thundering over southern Afghanistan.

# 4. MAIWAND

The Chinook touched down amid a swirl of dirt and stones, and Loyd walked down the ramp into the middle of the desert. She wore military-issue body armor, a helmet, and sunglasses, and all around her lay the vast, yellow plain. Forward Operating Base Ramrod wasn't much then. The Americans were building it from nothing. Afghan contractors had trucked fist-sized rocks into the helicopter landing zone to hold the fine dust in place and stop it from turning to mudslick when the rains came, but the rest of the base remained a powdery moonscape. The soldiers had pitched a few tents and strung desert camo nets to blunt the sun. It got up near 120 degrees some days, the heat so oppressive that soldiers building the base had been ordered to return to the big airfield in Kandahar every few days to avoid getting sick. The battalion intelligence section consisted of a single wooden bench.

Loyd's teammate, Clint Cooper, scanned the horizon: peaks knifing the sky, dun-colored ground. It reminded him of the Indian reservation where he'd lived as a boy. The landscape of Cooper's childhood held a powerful place in his memory, and in the American imagination. His family had lived on Navajo Nation land in Arizona, where his father worked as a schoolteacher for the Bureau of Indian Affairs. Monument Valley was a favorite backdrop for John Wayne films and, as a boy, Cooper had seen truckloads of uniformed cavalry soldiers on their way to movie sets and watched Westerns on old-style reels at the reservation school where his father taught. They would set up chairs in the gym and make popcorn, and the Indian kids would cheer on the cavalry that rescued white settlers from their native attackers. Cooper liked playing with his Indian friends, going to their school dances and eating lamb stew and fry bread. His mother headed a Mormon relief society, and she used to take him to visit Navajo families in traditional mud houses with dirt floors, where, while the woman talked, Cooper herded goats and sheep with the Indian boys. But he was one of only a few white kids on the reservation, and it was impossible to forget that he was different. He had chaps, a cap gun, and a wooden stick horse. When they played cowboys and Indians, he always got to be John Wayne.

When Cooper was about fifteen, his father got a job doing administrative work at day-care centers for the children of U.S. service members stationed overseas, and the family moved to a small village in Germany. Cooper learned the language and stayed on for two years after high school to complete a Mormon mission. He returned to Utah, where his family had settled, joined the Army National Guard as a German linguist and counterintelligence specialist, and studied criminal justice at Weber State University. In 2000, he and his wife, Kathy, started a side business buying saltwater taffy in bulk, then repackaging and selling it, and the following year, Cooper left active duty to devote himself full-time to the candy business, keeping only his weekend commitment to the National Guard. But the economy turned and the taffy enterprise stalled. By September 11, 2001, he was a sergeant first class, one of a small group of noncommissioned officers with foreign language skills and intelligence experience. Instead of Afghanistan, they sent him to Bosnia.

By then, Bosnia wasn't much of a war. Cooper and his fellow intelligence officers wore civilian clothes, left the base whenever they chose, and spent hours talking to people in coffee shops, trying to intercept threats to NATO peacekeepers. Along the way, they learned about Islamic militant groups that recruited young Bosnians and funneled fighters from the Middle East through Muslim Bosnia into Europe. They monitored local politics and even helped with war crimes investigations, interviewing victims and locating mass graves. Slobodan Milošević was on trial in The Hague, and Cooper and his teammates passed their findings up the chain of command.

Growing up in Germany, Cooper could walk out behind his house and see craters left over from the aerial bombardments of World War II. In Bosnia, he saw decomposed bodies at mass grave sites, but listening to the stories of war crimes victims was what really got to him. One man told Cooper he had been forced at gunpoint to rape his daughters. As Cooper listened, he looked into the man's eyes and felt himself teetering on the brink of something, as if he, too, were enduring this horror. In an area between Serb and Muslim territory, he lay awake at night listening to land mines explode as the freezing ground tightened around them. He learned not to step off paved roads and well-worn paths. Years later, back home, Cooper's wife and kids would step down from the porch and walk unthinkingly across the lawn to the family minivan while he took a different route: porch steps, paved walk, driveway. The mines had followed him home.

He returned from Bosnia in 2003, as the Army was mobilizing for Iraq. The National Security Agency was looking for linguists who spoke

Pashto and Dari, Afghanistan's two main languages, and Cooper signed up. They sent him to the Defense Language Institute in Monterey, California, where he and his classmates pored over a Pashto dictionary written by a nineteenth-century British cavalry officer and listened to local-language radio broadcasts on the BBC and Voice of America. That year, doing push-ups at the gym, he fell violently ill. Doctors found a tumor on one of his auditory nerves. The Army medically discharged him. It was 2004, and with a military intelligence background, a security clearance, and a year of intensive Pashto behind him, Cooper was a defense contractor's dream. Lockheed Martin hired him to work as an interrogator for the U.S. military in a secret facility attached to Kandahar Airfield. He would spend fourteen months there questioning prisoners, mainly Afghans brought in by the American Special Forces.

Paula Loyd had inhabited the same geography early in the Afghan war, but her work had been different. She had gotten to know the area around Kandahar well enough to understand what development projects Afghans needed most, what kind of humanitarian aid would best contribute to their security—in short, how the U.S. military could use money and persuasion instead of bullets to fight the insurgency. But if Loyd's work in Afghanistan told one strand of the story of American involvement there, Cooper's told another. Loyd had worked on the soft side of the war, while Cooper had lived along its hard edge. He was not a trigger puller, but he pried intelligence from detainees and suspected militants who, having no recourse to a working justice system, were generally desperate to free themselves any way they could.

Cooper and the other interrogators lived in a mud-walled compound at the edge of Kandahar Airfield and worked in a wooden shed. The prisoners lived within the compound walls in open-air barbed-wire structures with tentlike roofs. In winter, the pens were enclosed in plastic and heat was piped in. High-profile and underaged detainees were separated from the rest and kept in an old maintenance hangar known as the Barn. When Cooper arrived, the Kandahar facility housed several hundred prisoners, but partway through his deployment, the military decided that all detainees would be moved to Bagram Air Base in the north, where the military had recently doubled the size of its detention facility. This changed the nature of Cooper's job. In his first months in Kandahar, he had interrogated the same detainee as many as a dozen times over an extended period. In the latter half of his deployment, the Kandahar facility never housed more than ten or twenty prisoners at a time, each one staying only a couple of days at most. Instead of getting to know a small handful of captives, Cooper quickly assessed them, trying to figure out whether they should be released or sent to Bagram for further investigation. At his desk, beneath a whiteboard listing the names and numbers of detainees, a small, tan mouse emerged from the wall every morning and tried to steal his breakfast. Cooper began leaving it a piece of cake every day. He took pictures of the mouse and emailed them to his kids.

His language skills were more than sufficient to exchange greetings and elicit biographical information, and they improved with near-constant questioning. But he still worked often with an interpreter to make sure he wasn't missing something important. The stakes were high, and he didn't want to mess with people's lives. As in Bosnia, he felt something for Afghans, something troubling and hard to articulate that blurred the line between him and them. Most of the detainees were low-level Taliban: Afghan Pashtuns, lots of Pakistanis, a couple of Chechens. "And honestly, a lot of them weren't Taliban," he would tell me later. With the Taliban out of power and Afghanistan relatively stable, waves of Afghan refugees were returning from Pakistan and Iran. Land disputes broke out between new arrivals and squatters who had taken up residence in their absence. Afghans had few ways to settle such arguments. One of the most effective was to call the Americans and tell them that the person occupying your land—or the person who wanted to reclaim it—was Taliban.

Cooper learned that the insurgents moved in groups, depending on locals to supply and shelter them. Villagers helped the militants, bound triply by their code of hospitality, their fear of marauding gunmen, and their conservative religious and political sensibilities. The U.S. military viewed these people as Taliban supporters, but that was an oversimplification. Even the fighters were more complex than they looked. During Cooper's time there, he visited a village where a boy of about twelve had fired at a coalition helicopter. The helicopter's 30 mm cannon had decimated the insurgents below, and when Cooper and the soldiers arrived, the boy's legs had been blown off. Cooper talked to him as he lay on a stretcher. He questioned the boy and everyone else in the hope of saving soldiers' lives. But as he looked at the child lying there wounded, he felt acutely the strain of occupying two contradictory positions at once. He was an American trying to protect his comrades, but he was also a father with protective instincts for a kid who had been indoctrinated, given an AK-47, and told to shoot at helicopters. Cooper spoke the language and had begun to understand how the war looked to Afghans. The longer he stayed, the harder it became not to empathize with both sides.

As an interrogator, Cooper worked subtly. By his account, he wasn't a screamer; he didn't rage or pound his fists on the table. Instead, he used what he knew about Afghan culture to come in close. Once, the Special Forces had captured a Taliban commander, a big man with money and power. The insurgent had lunged at his captors and they had beaten him into submission; now he sat at one end of a cargo container and Cooper stood at the other end, poised to step out if the captive got wild again. That must have been devastating for a man of your stature, Cooper told the Afghan in Pashto, to be humiliated when you were captured like that, in front of your family, your friends. He started talking about the man's daughters, and the commander burst into tears and began to tell Cooper what he wanted to know. "You do things—not torture, but you play with people," Cooper would tell me later. He didn't doubt the worthiness of his mission, but he was emotionally astute enough to feel unsettled about this kind of button pushing, about using language and culture, the signposts of fellow feeling, to snoop around inside people's heads and hearts.

His most complicated experiences as an interrogator often involved children, maybe because he missed his own kids. Years later, he would tell me about a boy of ten or eleven whom the Special Forces had found in a known Taliban hideout up in the mountains. Cooper guessed that the insurgents had abandoned him in their rush to escape. The boy was emaciated, and an interpreter judged by his accent that he came from a southern coastal region of Pakistan. When Cooper asked the boy about his family, he reeled off the names of Indian movie stars. Although they offered him a latrine, he would defecate in the corner of his cell. He was slow, they realized, perhaps mentally handicapped. When Cooper asked what he had eaten in the mountains, the boy replied: 'Semen.' It occurred to them that he might have been kept as a sex slave. It was the middle of winter, and the boy was so weak that Cooper feared he would die of malnourishment and cold if they released him. If they kept him, he would be branded an insurgent, but he would get medicine and food. After a few months, he might be strong enough to make his way home. So they declared him Taliban and held him in Kandahar in the hope that he would survive.

During his time as an interrogator, Cooper worked with a female lieutenant. She was a public relations officer, and one day she went out to a village to hand out coloring books. On the way back, her Humvee hit a buried bomb. Afterward, Cooper went to look at what was left. The Humvee's front seat was gone. The lieutenant had been sitting behind the driver. He saw the book she had been reading, a bookmark where she'd left off, her half-empty can of Diet Coke. Afghan police caught the guy who had planted the bomb and beat him until he was bloody and blue, his buttocks and legs covered with bruises. He lay shaking and crying in the corner of his cell. Cooper went in to question him. The dead lieutenant had been beautiful and brave and American. Her remains would now be shipped home to her family in a box. Yet Cooper was horrified to find that he also empathized with her attacker, a man he would have preferred to dismiss as scum. This quivering heap of flesh had been paid two hundred dollars to put the bomb in the ground. He said he had done it to support his family. He didn't care where the money came from—he would probably have taken two hundred dollars from the Americans to inform on insurgents planting IEDs. Where was the radical Taliban they were always hearing about, the bloodthirsty enemy who lurked behind these pathetic henchmen? "These are the Taliban," Cooper would tell me, shaking his head. "These are the religious radicals. They're just a bunch of opportunists is what they are." Cooper believed absolutely that some people needed to die, but which people, and for what crimes? The war's ideological groundwork was beginning to give way. "The percentage of bad Taliban, what is that? Five, ten percent maybe? The rest were just trying to survive," he would tell me later. "Where is the evil? This war is just crazy. There's no good or bad."

For a kid raised on cowboys and Indians, Kandahar was a letdown of existential proportions. Cooper returned from Afghanistan a changed man. Once gentle and uncommonly patient, he was now distant and quick to anger. He raged when a cop pulled him over, dressed down his boss, caught himself mentally preparing to destroy his adversary in an argument. His wife, Kathy, felt as if she had been married to two different men: Clint before and Clint after. They moved to Sierra Vista, Arizona, at the edge of Fort Huachuca, where Cooper had been hired to train teams collecting HUMINT, or human intelligence. Coyotes howled at night, rattlesnakes slid into their son's sandbox, and migrants sneaking across the border died by the hundreds, littering the Sonoran desert with sweat-stained clothes and empty water jugs. Cooper turned inward until he had no friends outside work and Kathy. He didn't want to know people and he didn't want them to know him. Panic attacks seized him in church. He would sweat, his hands would shake, he would weep. He started seeing a counselor, who suggested that revisiting the scene of his earlier trauma in a different capacity and replacing bad memories with good ones could help him heal.

Good experiences, good memories—that was what Cooper had been looking for when he applied to join the Human Terrain System. He was convinced there was more to Afghanistan than the filthy, bruised men he'd questioned. There were good people, too, and the Army wasn't reaching them. Once during his time in Kandahar, he had accompanied the Special Forces to a village, where soldiers herded the men into a shallow streambed and kept them there all day for a security screening. The soldiers' behavior wasn't criminal, but it wasn't smart, either, and it certainly wasn't in keeping with the elaborate social customs of Afghans. The next day, the soldiers returned to the village and handed out coloring books and pencils. Man, Cooper thought, we're just clueless. The Human Terrain System was designed to address the stupidities that made Afghans hate the Americans who were trying to help them. Sometime early in 2008, he read a news article about it and applied. The project hired him immediately.

Seven months later, he was in Afghanistan, sweating beneath a field pack and body armor, fine dust scouring his regulation sunglasses. He and his teammates stumbled over stones and through shifting sand toward the Tactical Operations Center at the heart of the base. Someone directed them to a tent with a few cots, where Loyd curled up in her dust-covered clothes, stuffed a sleeping bag under her head, and fell asleep. Don Ayala threw down his gear and went outside to look around.

Ayala had missed this place. He had lived the war's early optimism, back before so much went wrong, and he remembered the thrill he'd felt flying to Kabul for the first time in 2002. At home, his life had grown comfortably routine. He had worked in telecommunications, occasionally moonlighting as a private bodyguard to earn extra money. After a shattering divorce, he had started a promising new relationship; he and his girlfriend, Andi Santwier, had recently bought a house together in a Los Angeles suburb. But the September 11 attacks had stirred an old restlessness. When a friend had urged him to send his résumé to the State Department, he'd quickly complied. A few weeks later, he'd been hired as part of an elite bodyguard team protecting Hamid Karzai, the new Afghan president, on whose survival the success of America's Afghan campaign depended. For a longtime soldier committed to his country, there was no more important job.

Ayala and the other bodyguards lived in tents on the grounds of the presidential palace. It was winter and cold, snow and mud thick on the ground, and they burned wood in stoves at night. There were no showers or permanent toilets, but they had their own cooks and cleaning crew and Ayala was paid sixteen thousand dollars a month, more than three times what he'd made at home. Back then, Kabul was so quiet that Ayala and the other Americans didn't even wear body armor. Maybe a bulletproof vest if they were going to Ghazni or Gardez, but nothing around the capital. Fighters loyal to the Afghan militia leader Gulbuddin Hekmatyar occasionally fired rockets at the palace, but they always landed outside its walls. The Taliban had mostly fled. As far as Ayala could tell, the main threat to Karzai in those days came from within, from ethnic Tajiks in his government and their loyalists, who resented the president's rapid rise.

Karzai was a royalist from Kandahar, the son of a tribal leader and former Afghan parliamentarian. A relentless diplomat who had been trying for years to broker truces between his country's fractious militia leaders, he had risen to the presidency in no small part through his assiduously cultivated contacts in Washington. Karzai embraced the cooperative, multiethnic vision that prevailed after the Taliban's fall, but he had a long and complex history with the Tajiks in his government, especially his defense minister, Mohammad Fahim. In the 1990s, after the Soviets withdrew from Afghanistan, Karzai had served as deputy foreign minister in the Kabul government led by Burhanuddin Rabbani and dominated by the famed Panjshiri militia leader Ahmed Shah Massoud. Fahim had been Massoud's security chief, and in 1994, Fahim had heard that Karzai was working for Pakistani intelligence. He'd had Karzai arrested and roughly interrogated. Karzai had escaped, but the incident sent him into exile in Pakistan and convinced him to back the Taliban, whose commanders he knew from his days fighting the Soviets. Karzai donated fifty thousand dollars to the conservative student militia and supplied them with weapons. A few years later, a critical event reordered his loyalties. In 1999, appalled by the brutal consequences of Taliban rule, Karzai tried to organize a traditional tribal council and invited the Taliban leader, Mullah Omar. Instead of agreeing to talk, the Taliban assassinated Karzai's father as he walked home from a mosque in Quetta, Pakistan. After that, Karzai reached out to Massoud, but it was too late. Arab bombers posing as journalists assassinated Afghanistan's most celebrated resistance leader two days before the September 11 attacks. By early 2002, Karzai and Fahim were working together, but Faulkner's famous observation was nowhere truer than in Afghanistan. The past wasn't dead. It wasn't even past.

The men on the Karzai Protective Detail believed in the president; they wanted him to succeed. It didn't hurt that the United States government lionized him as if he were some kind of philosopher king, but for Ayala the key thing was the way Karzai treated Afghans. He noticed how kindly the president spoke to everyone, especially women and children, and he saw firsthand what this leader was doing for his country. Ayala accompanied the president as he celebrated the openings of girls' schools and watched a game of Buzkashi, a wild, ancient sport played on horseback with the carcass of a headless goat. He went with Karzai to inaugurate medical clinics and mosques, and to visit the Salang Tunnel connecting Kabul to the north. At a school, he and the president watched students raise kites that snapped in the wind and fluttered like birds' wings against the sky, a tangible expression of the hope everyone seemed to feel. On Christmas, Karzai served his bodyguards dinner in the palace and thanked them for leaving their families to protect him. Ayala would sit outside the president's office, guarding his door during days of endless meetings. American military commanders and Afghan officials streamed in; Karzai's chief of staff, diplomats from countries whose support he couldn't do without, journalists and visiting celebrities who had no idea what he was up against. Karzai greeted them all graciously. Sometimes, between meetings, the president would ask for a few minutes alone. He would sit by himself, staring out the window. Ayala thought about what must be going on in his head. Nearly every evening, he and other bodyguards would escort the president past a garden of carefully tended rosebushes to visit the old Afghan king, Mohammad Zahir Shah, a dignified man in his eighties who lived in a small palace inside the presidential compound.

Eventually, Ayala would lead one of two close protection teams guarding Karzai. A natural mentor, he counseled the president's Afghan bodyguards and bonded with the other Americans, many of whom were ex–Special Forces like him. But Ayala wasn't your typical heavy. He painted, for one thing. He and Santwier would soon move to New Orleans, where Ayala hoped to open an art gallery with the money he was saving. He wrote poetry on his bedroom wall in Kabul, and the other bodyguards made good-natured fun of him. They called him

"Don Juan" because when they drank together after work, he would listen selflessly while female friends talked about their lives. He listened as if he were some kind of shrink, and this amazed his fellow bodyguards, who talked to women in bars for the same reason most men talk to women in bars. They called him the "Minister of Hugs and Kisses" because he was the only one among them who would put his antipathy to male-on-male affection aside long enough to engage in the Afghan male practice of embracing and cheek kissing on meeting. When a friend back home offered to send him a care package, he asked for pens and notebooks to hand out to kids.

He left Afghanistan in 2004 and spent much of the next four years in and out of Iraq, where most recently he had been mentoring a team of Iraqi bodyguards protecting Prime Minister Nouri al-Maliki. But that job had ended abruptly when Maliki dismissed the American security advisers in early 2008, choosing to rely entirely on his own people. The Human Terrain System recruiter had called when Ayala was looking for work. He would be trained in Iraqi, Afghan, and Islamic culture, the job description said. He would learn local languages. He flew home from Baghdad and arrived at the Human Terrain System training facility in Leavenworth, Kansas, less than a week later. At first, the project wanted to send him to Iraq. They assigned him to classes in Arabic language and Iraqi culture. He had been craving something like this, a new challenge, but the instruction wasn't as challenging as he'd hoped. He and the other trainees were taught military rank structure, as familiar to ex-soldiers as the alphabet and as alien to many social scientists as the language of an uncontacted tribe. One goal of the Human Terrain System was to help the military understand the web of relationships that connected Afghans or Iraqis living in a particular area so they could figure out how power and influence worked. As a research manager, Ayala was taught to use social network mapping software to link villagers by ethnic group, tribe, and political affiliation. For a class project, he used the software to trace connections between President Karzai and powerful people in his government. It reminded him of the Kevin Bacon game.

The Human Terrain System's mission appealed to Ayala. He knew the military needed something like this. After training him for Iraq, the program had sent him to Afghanistan, in part because he had lobbied to go there. He liked the place and the people, always had, but there was something else. The leader of this particular Human Terrain Team, a barrel-chested former Marine infantry officer named Mike Warren, was one of the few men in the program under whose leadership Ayala had felt comfortable deploying. Warren had worked for Blackwater and other private security firms before joining the Human Terrain System. He had come to know Afghanistan in the early years after the invasion, when it was a macho fantasyland of muddy pickup trucks, guns, and no rules. Back then Warren had supervised Afghan security guards protecting laborers building the Kabul to Kandahar highway, the most important American-funded reconstruction project in the country. Warren at least knew what he was getting into in Maiwand, but Ayala suspected that many of the civilians he'd met in training would be unable to work or even survive in a combat zone. There was a reason that people like Ayala had trained the way they had, a reason for Ranger school, where they woke you up every half hour and made you sit on watch half the night, then woke you again before dawn to do pull-ups, eat on a three-minute clock, run drills, suffer through classes, and take tests until they saw who could handle it and who would break. What the Army needed, Ayala thought, were sharp observers who understood the mission and had enough of the human touch to talk convincingly to locals. Ayala was no anthropologist, but you didn't have to be an anthropologist to turn a would-be enemy into an ally; he himself had plenty of experience talking drunken men out of stupid bar fights. He felt lucky that Paula Loyd wasn't one of the fakes. She was an Army vet, after all. She was cordial, focused, and soft-spoken, but there was a stubbornness about her. She knew what she was talking about and she would tell you what she thought, even if you didn't like it. She was in excellent physical shape and had village savvy in spades. Her boyfriend, Frank Muggeo, had met Ayala before they left Kansas, and maybe it was the unspoken bond of the Special Forces, but Muggeo immediately trusted him. 'Make sure you stay next to Don,' Muggeo had told Loyd. Ayala felt a special responsibility to protect her.

Loyd and her teammates had landed in Maiwand at a moment of renewed hope for the Afghan war. The apparent success of the surge in Iraq had vaulted Petraeus to a supervisory role in America's two Middle Eastern conflicts, and in the fall of 2008, he and his bosses in Washington surveyed the military's Afghan project and found it wanting. They urged the recently appointed NATO commander in Afghanistan, General David McKiernan, to adopt a strategy that focused less on killing insurgents and more on protecting the Afghan people. But McKiernan was an old-school commander, and he lacked sufficient forces for counterinsurgency. While he continued to pursue a conventional mission, the political winds were shifting in Washington. "We can't kill our way to victory," Admiral Mike Mullen, chairman of the Joint Chiefs of Staff, told Congress just days before Loyd and her teammates landed in Kandahar.

Loyd was one of two social scientists assigned to the seven-member Human Terrain Team known as AF4, the fourth team to be sent to Afghanistan and the first to venture into the deep south, where the Taliban were strongest. The team was attached to an Army unit, known as Task Force 2-2, that constituted the first significant deployment of American troops in this stretch of desert since the beginning of the war. The brigade's other battalions were stationed in and around Kunar, a mountainous province in northeastern Afghanistan where thick forests encouraged gunfights, but the 2-2 had been split off and sent to

Maiwand by presidential order after the Canadians stationed around Kandahar had threatened to withdraw if they didn't get reinforcements. The 2–2 was an anomaly: an American unit under Canadian command, sent to a dangerous place to sustain a fraying international partnership.

At first, the Americans thought Maiwand was tame. The land stretched flat and silent into the distance, but the silence was a trick. The place had a history of resisting invaders. East of the half-built American bases and north of the paved highway, on an open plain ringed by mountains, Afghan fighters had overwhelmed the British in one of the most stunning military defeats of the Victorian era. This was the age of the Great Game, when Afghanistan lay restless and mercurial between Russia and British India, and both empires sought to dominate it. The plain was not then, and is not now, an advantageous place to fight. One British officer called it "a military rat-trap." On a blistering summer day in 1880, the British forces—overburdened with baggage and servants and poorly prepared for the heat of the march—dug in near the center of Maiwand at a place called Kushk-i-Nakhud. They hoped to block the advance of an Afghan prince, Ayub Khan, who had marched across the Helmand River from the west to take Kandahar. Local volunteers had joined Ayub's forces, tribal fighters and ordinary people armed with swords, spears, and old muskets copied from European designs. There were *ghazis*, too, "killers of infidels," who wore white robes that resembled shrouds and signified their willingness to die.

By the day of the battle, the Afghans significantly outnumbered their British opponents. They hid in shallow wadis, surprising the British and outflanking them. But the British hammered them with artillery until, exhausted by the heat and eager to evacuate their wounded, the Afghans wavered. At that critical moment, an Afghan woman named Malalai stood and urged the fighters forward. She was the daughter of a shepherd from a nearby village, and when the Afghan standard-bearer fell, Malalai lifted her veil as a flag and led the column forward. The Afghans rolled over the British line like a wave, decimating the soldiers at close range with swords and knives.

A century later, a pious peasant arrived in Maiwand. His name was Muhammad Omar, and he was the son of a religious teacher who had died when Omar was a boy. As a young man, Omar studied at a religious school in Kandahar, and in the village of Singesar in Maiwand, he led prayers and opened a small madrassa. Between 1989 and 1992, he fought the Russians and the Soviet-installed Afghan regime of President Mohammad Najibullah. He was wounded several times, and lost his right eye. When Najibullah's government fell, Afghan militia commanders turned their guns on each other. Local big men kidnapped women and children as consorts and hung chains across roads, stopping cars and collecting tolls. In the spring of 1994, one story goes, Omar's neighbors told him that a local commander had kidnapped two teenaged girls. The commander had the girls' heads shaved and took them to an armed outpost where they were gang-raped. Omar gathered about thirty men and set out to free them. With only sixteen rifles between them, they rescued the girls, hanged the commander from the barrel of a tank, and made off with his guns. A few months later in Kandahar, two commanders fought over a boy they both wanted to sodomize, killing bystanders in the bazaar. Omar and his fighters intervened and freed the boy, and people started asking them for protection from the warlords and help resolving disputes. The Taliban movement was born.

The American-led war had been going on for seven years by the time Loyd and her teammates arrived, but in Maiwand it was still year one, only much worse. In the beginning, there had been a sense of possibility, a feeling that something might change. But in the early years after the American invasion, Afghans in Maiwand had been exposed all over again to the depravities from which they had begged the Taliban to save them. In 2001, the American-supported governor of Kandahar was Gul Agha Sherzai, a thuggish personality with reported ties to the drug trade. Sherzai's chief factotum was a glib, unctuous man named Khalid Pashtoon, whose fluent English and intimacy with the governor made him one of Kandahar's most powerful people. American Special Forces listened to Pashtoon because he was one of the few Afghans they understood. But many powerful Afghans and their allies saw the invasion as an opportunity to get rich, and they found ways to make money off people living in the countryside around Kandahar, especially those whose tribes they opposed. Maiwand was one of their favorite targets. After the invasion, well-connected Afghan strongmen harassed people and shook them down. The people had no recourse. The Taliban had promised to get rid of the warlords, and for a time, they had. Now, the Americans had revived them.

With the Taliban gone and the soil parched, many farmers in Maiwand and the other districts around Kandahar planted poppy. After the harvest, commanders raided people's homes and seized their stores of raw opium. Some farmers were given a choice: split the drugs with their pursuers, or they would be sent to the U.S. detention facility at Guantanamo Bay, Cuba. This was no idle threat; everyone knew that the raiders had the ear of the Americans. Afghans connected to the Kandahar government also ran a kidnapping scheme, picking people up on fake charges, holding them in private prisons, and extorting huge ransoms. In the early years of the war, Hajji Ehsan, the Maiwand District representative on the Kandahar Provincial Council, told me that he himself had paid thousands of dollars to buy the freedom of two men from Maiwand being held in one of these private prisons. The corruption and venality of the U.S.-backed government made people crave the stern order of the Taliban. As the months and years passed and the Taliban began to trickle back in from Pakistan, people in Maiwand did little to oppose them.

Maiwand's value to the insurgents and their business partners lay primarily in the ribbon of asphalt running through it. The road and its tributaries cut east to west, from the Pakistani border through Kandahar and Helmand, where more than half of Afghanistan's opium is harvested, and on to Herat at the edge of Iran. It was part of the ring road that connected Afghanistan's major cities, and it had been repaved after the invasion with American tax dollars. The U.S. military called it Highway 1. Whoever controlled this road could move drugs, weapons, and smuggled goods to markets all across southern Afghanistan and into Iran and Pakistan. Whoever controlled it could extort money from truckers ferrying supplies to U.S. and NATO bases. Near the center of Maiwand, gas stations lined the road. Bazaar stalls selling puffed corn, meat, tea, and lumber clustered up to the asphalt, and little boys yelled, "Fuck you!" at passing NATO convoys. It was so quiet—more truck stop than town, an in-between place that looked like nothing on a map—that in the early years of the war, the Americans and their international allies had paid it scant attention, and that was just what the people moving men, guns, cash, and drugs between Pakistan and Helmand wanted. They didn't want to get into a shoot-out, not here where the ground was flat and the dunes stretched into the distance.

The soldiers of the 2–2 landed in Maiwand in mid-August 2008. As the first American unit deployed there, they knew very little about the place, its politics, or its people. They had ten months to learn, and to execute a mission the military called "clear, hold and build," the bone structure of counterinsurgency. When the battalion was fully deployed, some nine hundred soldiers would live on three bases around a district roughly the size of Rhode Island. They would map the place from scratch, seeking to make sense of this parallel world where they hoped to survive long enough to get home to beer, girls, and mom and dad. They would meet with local elders, befriend farmers, walk all day, and sleep on rocky ground far from their bases. They would quickly expel the insurgents, win local trust, and build roads and schools. That was the vision, at least. The reality was something else. The flat earth over which they sometimes walked but mostly drove concealed a murderous subterranean landscape of bombs—metal cooking pots filled with fertilizer, nails, and ball bearings and wired to rudimentary fuses. Every day, it seemed, someone got hit and the wrecker went out to recover a twisted, charred hunk of metal. A Humvee blew up, killing a soldier and severely burning a young lieutenant. For a time that fall, more buried bombs were found in Maiwand than anywhere else in Iraq or Afghanistan.

The soldiers rarely saw these attacks coming. With each one, they grew angrier, more suspicious. They retreated behind the walls of their bases where the bombs couldn't reach them. Their mission was to win Afghans away from the insurgency, to strengthen the local government, but they quickly found that it was impossible to know who was friendly and who wanted them dead. They passed their days in frustrating conversations with Afghans, conversations that led nowhere. A man cleaned his teeth with a stick as the soldiers passed, eyeing them sideways, spitting in the sand. Was he a Taliban spotter, or just some guy? What was the default setting for dealing with Afghans, the soldiers wondered, and what was America doing out here anyway—was this a war or an aid mission? It wasn't so much that counterinsurgency was impossible or that these kinds of wars were inherently unwinnable. What was impossible, or very nearly, were the emotional demands that counterinsurgency made on the individual American soldier who had neither been adequately trained nor sufficiently prepared for what he was asked to do.

The Human Terrain System had been created to deconstruct places like Maiwand, to determine what political and social networks, what tribes and subtribes, what economic interests held them together. But Maiwand was so far from being controlled by U.S. forces that Ayala began to feel that the Human Terrain Team's presence there was premature. The territory was still in the throes of serious combat; maybe this wasn't the time for civilians to be wandering around asking questions. And yet, the whole point of the program was to understand the ground for soldiers before they screwed things up, favoring one tribe over another for a road contract, arresting a man on the false accusation of a local rival. Ayala and the Human Terrain Team's leader, Mike Warren, discussed the risks over cigars in the evenings, but they were warriors who enjoyed a challenge. Paula Loyd didn't share Ayala's doubts, at least not that her teammates could tell. But she was franker with a close friend, a development worker with whom she spoke often on the phone that fall. "She didn't necessarily feel that the protection was as good as it should have been," Loyd's friend recalled.

Loyd also harbored doubts about the validity of the data she and her teammates were gathering. Interviewing Afghans through an interpreter, surrounded by armed soldiers, was far from ideal, and she knew it. But whatever her reservations, she persevered. She wanted to teach farmers about drip irrigation, a less wasteful alternative to flooding their fields. Don't treat the locals badly, Loyd and her teammates counseled the soldiers. You're just going to make enemies. Get to know them. Be patient. The soldiers listened, trying to get their heads around this. Gentleness, patience, respect—when your buddies were getting slaughtered, anything would be easier.

Paula Loyd's fellow social scientist on AF4 was Tim Gusinov, a stubby, crude-humored Russian who had been a student at a Soviet military academy when his country invaded Afghanistan in 1979. Trained as an Afghan area specialist and Persian linguist, Gusinov had served two tours with the Red Army in Afghanistan in the 1980s, advising Soviet-backed Afghan troops and acting as an interpreter and cultural adviser to Spetsnaz, the Soviet special forces, whose job, he would tell me later, involved "mostly killing people." In the 1990s, with his country in turmoil, Gusinov moved to the United States and found work as a Russian translator. After the Afghan invasion, he parlayed his knowledge of Dari into a job as a contract linguist with the military. He quickly determined that the Americans on the big base where he was stationed might as well have been on the moon. One officer, a devout Christian, was convinced that Afghans worshipped demons. When a Human Terrain System recruiter called, Gusinov eagerly signed on. "I saw such great potential in that," he told me.

In Maiwand, Gusinov affixed himself to the hip of the 2–2's commander, a wry, forty-year-old lieutenant colonel named Dan Hurlbut. Observing that the Americans were sometimes poorly served by their Afghan translators, Gusinov often acted as Hurlbut's interpreter during meetings with the Maiwand District governor, a onetime anti-Soviet resistance fighter. The Americans loved watching the Russian talk to his former enemy. "He's like a rock star," Hurlbut would gush when I met him. "He knows the culture, he can get in with them, and they don't hear the accent like we do." Of course the Afghans heard Gusinov's accent, nor was the significance of the U.S. military's decision to hire a former Soviet officer lost on them. But Gusinov's Russian-tinged Dari and his long experience in the country also opened doors. He could tell where explosives were buried because the stone piles insurgents used to warn civilians resembled those the mujaheddin had used years earlier. He was so skilled at engaging Afghans in casual conversation that an American officer praised him for "getting more information accidentally" than the unit's military intelligence team gathered on purpose. Indeed, Gusinov had been trained by the Soviets to gather intelligence, and he was good at it. "It goes with the language, it goes with my ability to open something in Afghans, it goes with my skills to push the right buttons," he told me. "Even cultural knowledge can be intel."

Since they'd met in Kansas, Loyd and Gusinov's relationship had been strained. She seemed to prefer her own company, Gusinov told me, but it was no surprise that his casual mention of his visits to Afghan hookers as a young Soviet soldier appalled her. In Maiwand, they almost never worked together. Gusinov thought it was no place for a woman, that her very presence was liable to outrage locals, though that wasn't the impression her other teammates got. Moreover, Loyd's and Gusinov's philosophies clashed. While she focused on development projects in the firm belief that they could contribute meaningfully to security, Gusinov grew frustrated with the Americans' unwillingness to play tribes off against each other, a tactic that had served the Soviets well. His attention was drawn to the edges of the district, where insurgents moved freely. In Band-i-Timur, an opium-growing region south of the highway, a small field hospital treated wounded Taliban fighters, and American soldiers found loads of hidden weapons and drug-processing facilities there. In the Garmabak pass, a mountainous cut-through to the north, they discovered mortars and recoilless rifles, medical supplies, a base camp with sleeping quarters, and ID cards from Iraq's Green Zone and Kandahar Airfield. Gusinov asked the commander pointedly why he wasn't targeting the areas that were most valuable to the insurgency.

Part of the Human Terrain Team's job was to advise the soldiers on culturally acceptable behavior and basic good manners. When the Maiwand District governor quoted from the Koran, Gusinov told the soldiers not to smile. Instead, they should put their right hands on their hearts and say: "Thank you for sharing the wisdom of the Holy Book with us." Loyd, Ayala, and Cooper accompanied soldiers to an Afghan family compound, where the whole patrol swarmed inside. The soldiers should be more respectful and considerate, the team suggested. Instead of packing the compound, just one or two soldiers should venture inside, and the Americans should watch where they stepped so as not to trample fields and vegetable patches.

Loyd, Ayala, and Cooper lived together, ate together, prayed before each mission together. Nearly every day that October, they drove out in armored vehicles or walked with a platoon to a nearby village, where they interviewed farmers, merchants, mechanics, and police. Back on base in the afternoons, they would talk about what they had seen before heading to showers and chow. Loyd structured their areas of inquiry. She was the primary interviewer and she and her teammates sat up late writing field reports, which were sent to the battalion commander, his company commanders, the unit's operations and intelligence officers, and back to the Human Terrain System's headquarters in Kansas. Eighteen-hour workdays were routine, one day bleeding into another. They were contractors and well paid compared to soldiers. With his hazard differential, Ayala was making nearly a thousand dollars a day; Loyd, Gusinov, and the team leader, Mike Warren, were paid more. Their bases were nascent and rough, the countryside hazardous, and Ayala had never worked this hard. As a bodyguard, he would come back after a day's mission, hang up his gear, and take a break. In Maiwand, there were no breaks. He and Cooper usually turned in by midnight, but Loyd didn't even make it to bed some nights. She liked working into the early morning, when the command center on the little firebase was empty. She told her teammates she could concentrate better with no one around to bother her. Ayala worried that she wasn't getting enough sleep. He ordered her to nap. Some days, she turned in after the team's 8 a.m. meeting and slept until early afternoon, waking in time to join a 3 p.m. patrol.

They were getting out so often and writing so many reports that Ayala had no time to enter the information they gathered into the mapping software he had been trained to use back in Kansas. If he'd tried to use it, he would probably have found it a waste of time. The software was cumbersome and couldn't connect to the rest of the military computer system. Understanding the links between Afghans was also proving much harder than he had expected. People in Maiwand were standoffish, and Ayala and his teammates were never sure who was telling the truth. It would take more time and many repeat visits to get deep, to ask people who their relatives were, who they knew, who they hated, and to believe what they told you. They moved between Comanche and Darkhorse Companies, between the firebase near the center of the district and Ramrod, the desert outpost. If soldiers were raiding a compound to detain insurgents, Ayala would politely decline to join them. But if they were just getting to know a village and stopping to talk to people along the way, he would ask if the team could go along.

While the soldiers worked, Ayala, Cooper, and Loyd interviewed villagers. Sometimes Loyd asked Cooper to tell people that he was her husband, a nod to the area's conservative sensibilities. But Afghans were generally eager to talk to her. A woman gave Loyd her baby to hold, and children followed her around. Sometimes the kids were useful. On one mission, Loyd asked a man his name, and when he gave it, a small girl standing next to him said: 'That's not your name.' The man told the girl to get lost. It was one more indication of how much remained hidden.

Nevertheless, Loyd and her teammates learned quite a bit about Maiwand in their first few weeks. Afghan police stationed along the highway were shaking down motorists, charging as much as fifty Afghanis, about a dollar, for a passenger car or pickup, and up to eight hundred Afghanis, or sixteen dollars, for a heavy truck with cargo. One day in October, Ayala and Cooper visited an Afghan police station. While Ayala and the soldiers talked to the police chief's assistant, Cooper wandered off to find some of his men, who told him they hadn't been paid in months and rarely left their headquarters. The chief's assistant told the Americans that locals supported them, but the Human Terrain Team members knew that the opposite was true. Their interviews in seven villages in Maiwand had shown that Afghans viewed the cops primarily as thieves. The chief's assistant named a local Taliban leader and mentioned the village from which he operated. Ayala wrote this down: the Taliban commander's name and the name of the village.

'What is the plan to get the Taliban out of the villages?' a lieutenant asked.

'Too many Taliban to arrest,' the chief's assistant replied.

Ayala and his teammates were not supposed to be gathering intelligence about the enemy, but reading their reports it becomes clear how difficult, even impossible, it was to separate traditional threat-centered intelligence from anything else. Sometimes they could see it coming. When Loyd's interpreter overheard a man say that he had seen Taliban fighters at a local restaurant, it was the platoon leader who interviewed him to get more information. But much of the time, the enemy slipped into the Human Terrain Team's interviews like water between rocks. Afghans knew what the Americans were after, even these other Americans who wore camouflage body armor but said they were not soldiers; who talked about helping people and understanding people and then climbed into vehicles with the rest of the soldiers and drove away. A widow told Loyd how much she hated 'the motherfucking Taliban.' 'They have informers everywhere,' the woman said. She was so worried about the insurgents that she woke up two or three times each night and climbed onto her roof to see if anyone was around. The woman told Loyd about one of her neighbors, who had tried to stop the insurgents from planting a bomb in the road nearby. The fighters threatened to kill the man's whole family if he didn't cooperate. The woman's sons were farm laborers and she needed food. She offered to work with the Americans. Loyd wrote all this down, noting that the woman and other "targets of opportunity/people in need of assistance" should be given flour, beans, oil, and sugar.

Loyd paid close attention to the tribal tensions that inflected life in Maiwand. She suggested mapping tribal affiliations down to individual compounds to better understand the human and political landscape.

When people told her about their time as refugees in Pakistan, she proposed gathering more information about refugees to shed light on the mix of tribes in the area. When a group of men offered fresh bread to soldiers, she noted that discreet return visits from the Americans would help strengthen their relationship with the Afghans and "encourage the family to share information." "Requests to share information should be presented delicately and with an acknowledgement that it was dangerous for the family to share this kind of information with U.S. Forces," she wrote.

The people of Maiwand lived in peril. The Taliban were a permanent condition there, as unavoidable as the sun or the absence of rain. They were everywhere; they saw and heard everything. Some Afghans privately supported the Karzai government, but they knew the government was too weak to protect them, that even perceived loyalty to the government could get them killed. That October, insurgents stopped a bus on the highway in Maiwand. After a purported Taliban trial, a half dozen bodies were found mutilated and beheaded in the sand near the road. The insurgents claimed the passengers were Afghan soldiers on their way to fight in Helmand; local officials said they were poor civilians headed to Iran to find work. As it turned out, the insurgents were closer to the truth. The men on the bus were Afghan police recruits bound for Herat. An Afghan told the Human Terrain Team that buried bombs were the biggest problem for people in his village. The road was so dangerous that no one walked far, and they couldn't send their children to school or to the clinic in the bazaar. The man seemed eager to talk, but he didn't own a cell phone and had no way of quietly contacting the Americans, so the Human Terrain Team advised the soldiers to set up a joint checkpoint with Afghan security forces. The Taliban might punish a villager for walking to the American base, but not for being stopped at a checkpoint.

Insurgents taxed villagers and common bandits waited at a known holdup point along the highway, where they kidnapped drivers and threatened to kill them if their families didn't pay. The Human Terrain Team met a family whose fifteen-year-old son had been kidnapped, who'd had to sell their car and tractor to raise the six-thousand-dollar ransom. Corrupt cops and thieving private security gangs didn't help, and Afghans were scared of the Americans, too. A man begged the soldiers not to shoot at his sons on their way home from work. A local mullah told them that he didn't use his kerosene lamp at night because he worried that American planes would bomb his house. People needed fuel for generators to irrigate their fields, and the Human Terrain Team recommended installing a hand pump for drinking water, solar lights, a windmill to generate power. They encouraged soldiers to build trust with locals, urging them to "remember we are competing against the Taliban and they had a head start." Villagers in Maiwand were poor and would accept help from anybody, the Human Terrain Team members pointed out. In reality, though, the Americans seemed woefully ill-equipped to confront the degree of damage that Afghans had endured. When a man who had lost his foot to a land mine complained to the soldiers, a medic gave him aspirin.

That October, Loyd was working on a document that sought to spell out the difference between the village *malik*, whom she described as "a wealthy landowner," and the *mesheran*, or elders. She sketched the relations between two large tribes in the area, the Noorzai and the Achekzai. In one draft, she included an injunction to the Americans against choosing a single "go to guy." "Patrols should keep in mind that Afghans have a collective decision making process," she wrote. While Americans liked to rely on a single trusted informant, this could be misleading in a place where every story had a dozen competing versions. Like the interpreters Loyd had watched years earlier in Zabul, who had translated everything through the lens of their own tribal and political allegiances, Afghans

96

in Maiwand knew that whoever controlled the narrative would benefit. Part of her job was to make the Americans understand that stories in Afghanistan were not simple collections of facts but tools in an old and well-developed game of one-upmanship. Often, they were the only tools Afghans had. Stories could deflect attention from weakness or guilt. They could be told for money, to take a life or to spare one. Perhaps most important, they were a defense mechanism, a way of preserving cultural cohesion against the damaging influence of the outside world.

The soldiers didn't listen, and neither did the rest of the Human Terrain Team. Over Loyd's protests, her teammates organized a meeting between the battalion commander and America's main "go to guy" in the south, Ahmed Wali Karzai. Ahmed Wali was President Hamid Karzai's half brother, and he ruled Kandahar like a king. He was said to be on the CIA's payroll and suspected of links to the drug trade, but he had real and deep-rooted power in Kandahar, and when the Americans wanted something, he obliged. Ayala, Gusinov, and Mike Warren, the team leader, saw the meeting with Karzai as a coup, but Loyd refused to go along. She thought Wali Karzai was "'basically . . . a criminal,'" Cooper would tell me later. The president's brother had killed someone she knew, Loyd told Cooper, and she adamantly opposed the Human Terrain Team supporting or acknowledging him in any way. "She was a little bit idealistic about that," Gusinov would tell me later. "She forgot the principle: 'He's a son of a bitch, but he's our son of a bitch.'"

At the heart of Maiwand stood the bazaar, a collection of stalls lining the highway. It was the main shopping center between Kandahar city and Sangin, across the Helmand border, and it buzzed with frenetic energy. The bazaar was dangerous, but it was also a trove of information about local politics, economics, and corruption. Loyd and Cooper learned about a shopkeepers' organization, a sort of guild that provided informal security to merchants. They were intrigued, of course—what drove Afghans to band together and come up with their own security arrangements? Could the Americans nurture something similar elsewhere? The bazaar might be risky, but it was too important to avoid.

At least three times, Loyd, Ayala, and Cooper wandered amid the close stalls in the company of soldiers, buying small rugs and brooms. They bought sugar and tea, dried apricots, roasted peanuts, corn chips, sweetened almonds, white radishes, and fresh bread to supplement their field rations. Cooper bought two sickles, an excuse to talk to the man who sold them. Later, he would take a picture of himself holding the sickles and load it onto Loyd's laptop so that the first thing she saw when she opened her computer was Cooper grimacing like a madman behind crossed blades. Kids in the bazaar sometimes threw rocks at the soldiers, and Ayala was the one to notice when the crowd around Loyd grew uncomfortably large. He could feel something radiating from people as the Americans passed, hostility edging into hatred. No one wanted to talk to them, at least not in public, but Ayala was determined to break through. Once, when he didn't like the way a shopkeeper was looking at him, he walked over and shook the man's hand. The Afghan challenged Ayala to arm-wrestle. He was bigger than Ayala, but Ayala beat him. Let's try again, the Afghan suggested. By the time it was over, the Afghan was smiling. Shoppers complained that wheat flour and other staples were exorbitant in Maiwand. People were struggling to get enough to eat. A local official charged every shopkeeper 150 Afghanis a month, about three dollars, but look, the merchants said, the sewers are not cleaned out, the school is closed. Loyd and Cooper wondered where the money was going.

Loyd's field notes were infused with the doubt of someone well acquainted with Afghanistan. "He said there were no other elders (did he just not want to name them?)," she wrote that fall. "The Malik system seem [*sic*] to be working in his village (bears further investigation— probably force of personality to some extent). There is no single Noorzai

98

leader in Maiwand; each village chooses a Malik (Does Malik vary from tribe to tribe?)." Loyd understood the nature of covert rebellion as well as anyone; it worked the same way whether Afghans were opposing the Taliban or the Americans. People might be "very cautious about expressing their resistance openly when they perceive the power of the dominant group to be very strong," Loyd had written in her Wellesley thesis years earlier. But "[a]way from public scrutiny, when they are among their own, the peasants carry on an entirely different dialogue." Between what people said and what they really thought lay a category of behavior that Loyd had described as "partially veiled and partially open." This type of activity unfolded in public, but took "disguised or anonymous forms," its revolutionary intent "veiled within multiple levels of meaning." People talked in jokes, metaphors, folktales, songs, and codes. "In this way," Loyd had written, "subversive meanings may be denied if necessary."

One Human Terrain draft report that fall recorded a conversation between the team and a group of Afghans. The Taliban planted mines at night, the Afghans said, but the village elders didn't know who was actually laying the bombs in the roads. They welcomed the Americans to their village, as long as they came to talk and didn't kick down doors.

'How do you define security?' Cooper asked.

'Peace, so the children can grow up without war,' one of the Afghans said. 'There has been too much war.'

"We felt these people would have talked a lot more given more time," Loyd wrote. "They were just starting to open up."

# 5. THE ANTHROPOLOGY OF US AND THEM

For a very long time, war and anthropological fieldwork have been intertwined. T. E. Lawrence's success during the Arab Revolt is legendary, and it is easy to see why. He had studied history at Oxford, hiked across the deserts and mountains of the Middle East, spent years on an archeological dig in Syria, and served with the British Army in Cairo, and he used everything he knew about Arab culture to influence the Hejaz in Britain's interest. "The beginning and ending of the secret of handling Arabs is unremitting study of them," the man known as Lawrence of Arabia wrote in 1917.

The anthropologist who helped create the Human Terrain System was born Montgomery Carlough in 1966, but you had to go back before that to understand who she was. Her life story was so colorful that it was easy to get caught up in the details, to lose sight of how she, of all people, had landed at the center of a bold attempt to transform the Army into an organ of cultural knowledge and sensitivity. Her personal history could be distracting, but ignoring it wasn't an option. It held clues to why the Human Terrain System evolved as it did. She was born of contradictions: California beatnik counterculture, a familial fascination with the primitive "other," and a quiet but persistent strain of military DNA that was as mainline American as it got. She embodied at once the forces that drove the military and anthropologists apart and the desires and imperatives that have historically drawn them together.

The story of Montgomery McFate, née Carlough, began far from the American heartland, where she would live for a time as the Human Terrain System's senior social scientist. Her mother had been the half-Mexican granddaughter of a man who lost everything in the Mexican Revolution. Unable to care for his many daughters, he had sent them to family scattered around Latin America, and three, including McFate's grandmother, Mequilita, to a distant relative in New Orleans. Mequilita Ramirez was an exotic beauty. "My grandmother really looked very Indian, very South American Indian," McFate told me. "If you look at pictures of her, she definitely does not look at all Caucasian."

Mequilita Ramirez's line of descent slowly whitened. She married a much older man who played coronet in Marine Corps bandmaster John Philip Sousa's orchestra, according to family lore. Their daughter, Frances Poynter, had dark skin, long black hair, and prominent cheekbones, which made her look vaguely Mediterranean, but still more Caucasian than her mother. She grew up in New Orleans, where she worked as a telephone operator and a window display designer for department stores. McFate didn't know much about this period of her mother's life, except that Poynter was warm, outgoing, and free-spirited, that she enjoyed the companionship of black musicians and felt at home in the jazz scene.

Sometime around 1950, Frances Poynter and her husband, Cecil

Westerberg, made their way to the San Francisco Bay area. They bought property near the Mount Tamalpais ridgeline in Muir Woods and opened a small business—McFate thought it might have been a restaurant. At some point, Westerberg, who went by the nickname Barney, got arrested for dealing marijuana. As part of his rehabilitation, he learned to carve wood. "He basically changed his name and created an entire fictive biography for himself," McFate told me. Instead of Cecil Westerberg, he became Barney West.

West told people that he had served in the merchant marine and been shipwrecked on a Polynesian or Micronesian island. During his time on the island, he said, the natives had taught him how to carve wood. This was in the early 1960s, a decade after the publication of Thor Heyerdahl's *Kon-Tiki*, when Elvis Presley starred in *Blue Hawaii* and Hula-Hoops and tiki bars were the rage. In McFate's view, America's cultural obsession with Polynesia stretched back even further, to Margaret Mead's *Coming of Age in Samoa*. "The cultural eye," McFate told me, "was focused on Polynesia."

Poynter and West moved to Sausalito, a city just north across the bay from San Francisco, and started a little woodworking shop called Tiki Junction, where West carved giant, iconic tikis that he sold to Trader Vic's, a Polynesian-themed restaurant chain; McFate's mother painted the carvings. West, a handsome, muscular man with a handlebar moustache, relied on his story of shipwreck and native tutelage to give the carvings authenticity, and to patrons of Trader Vic's, mai tais in hand, they were indistinguishable from the real thing. He had found a way to turn mid-twentieth-century America's fascination with the primitive to profit, but the cultural artifacts he supplied were "all fake," McFate told me. "It was all made by Barney, painted by my mom."

McFate's mother and West eventually divorced, and in 1957, Frances Poynter bought a surplus wooden Navy barge for a dollar. The barges had been used to tow ammunition to Hawaii during the war;

now they were being torn apart for scrap. Poynter docked her barge in Richardson Bay, in a nascent houseboat community known as Gate 5. She divided it into apartments, renting out two and living in the third. Most of the walls in McFate's childhood home were made from driftwood that her mother had collected from the beach after storms. Frances Poynter knew nothing about fireplace construction, but she built a fireplace out of river rocks and a giant industrial smokestack. McFate found it kind of beautiful, but also deeply weird, like the sailboat some friends of her mother's built with a telephone pole for a mast and a barrel from a fun-house ride for a table. Gate 5 residents shared a profound confidence in their ability to remake their environment, even when they lacked the most basic technical training.

Poynter met McFate's father, Martin Carlough, at a festival in Golden Gate Park. A handsome former marine and itinerant carpenter nine years younger, Carlough was also a diagnosed schizophrenic who lived on the streets and self-medicated with PCP, LSD, and belladonna. He spent most of McFate's childhood in and out of mental hospitals, where, like Barney West years earlier, he underwent electroshock therapy. The treatment ruined his mind, and he became a kind of zombie with damaged, clawlike hands. McFate remembers him as a "terrifying presence," very tall with a shaved head and a pink denim jacket that said on the back, in rhinestone letters, "I am God." When she was six or seven, he killed her cat by breaking its neck and throwing it off the deck of the barge. "Just run-of-the-mill family horror," she told me, with a little laugh.

Although McFate's parents were married briefly, her father didn't live with them. He would come by the barge to ask her mother for money or food. For a time, he lived in a cave nearby, in a dugout beneath a dock that he lined with tinfoil and cardboard. When McFate was about ten, he jumped off the Golden Gate Bridge, and her mother had to go down to the morgue and identify his body. Frances Poynter's lover, a local shipyard owner, became McFate's primary father figure. Though he was wealthy, he lived in a broken-down house and wore overalls. He let her smoke his pipe and told her she could have as much homemade liquor as she wanted, so long as she poured it over ice cream; she perused his collection of *Playboys* with interest. The houseboat community was ungoverned and chaotic, she told me, "the opposite from what you would find on an Army base, where there's a lot of social-norming going on, a lot of social control that is exerted just within the community." Craving order, McFate begged her mother to let her join the Girl Scouts, but Poynter objected. She advised her daughter never to join anything.

In addition to drawing rent from the barge apartments, McFate's mother molded Easter Island–style heads from cement and sold them. For a while, she made what McFate described as "these Egyptian sort of plaque-looking things" that were plaster and painted. The fabrication of anthropological artifacts—culture as curio—was a family obsession, but the cement heads proved less profitable than West's tikis, and McFate and her mother subsisted mostly on beans and rice. When McFate was eleven or twelve, one of her mother's friends tried to convince Poynter to apply for food stamps. She refused. "She would not take anything from the government," McFate told me. "I remember getting mad at her about it. 'Would you prefer that we don't have enough to eat? You're going to turn down charity on principle, and who's going to benefit from that? I'm hungry.'" Her mother was stubborn, McFate said, unwilling to compromise her principles for practical good. To McFate, this seemed ridiculous, even immoral. The important thing was to stay alive.

McFate's mother had a complex relationship to authority and to the antiauthoritarian culture that surrounded her. Apolitical and deeply suspicious of government, she nevertheless viewed hippies with disdain. Poynter was one of the few houseboat dwellers in Gate 5 with a legal lease, one of the few who paid for electricity instead of snaking a cable up the street and siphoning it off the lines at the Mohawk gas station. Yet several times, including one Christmas Eve, building inspectors posted "Condemned" notices on the barge. "She was very aware of how tenuous her hold on the property was and how on the margins we were," McFate recalled. When Marin County judged the community of houseboat dwellers and squatters at Gate 5 a giant floating health hazard—the boats were pumping raw sewage into the bay—Poynter supported efforts to bring the place up to code. And when a development company announced its intention to turn Gate 5 into an upscale yacht harbor, Poynter, by most conventional definitions a radical, came to be viewed by her neighbors as something of a stooge.

The developers declared that people like Poynter, who had legal leases, could stay; everyone else had to get out. But they didn't understand "the context they were operating in," McFate told me, "ironically, much like the military in Afghanistan. So their solution was, 'We're just going to start building.'" The developers brought in a pile driver and went to work. At night, some Gate 5 insurgents blocked in the pile driver with a big ammunition barge. The resistance boat, known as the Red Barge, became a floating rebel campground. When the Marin County sheriff's department came down to remove the holdouts, a maritime battle ensued, with Gate 5 residents storming the authorities in rowboats and the cops fighting back with high-pressure fire hoses.

The standoff began when McFate was about eleven years old and carried on intermittently for years. The developers hired Samoan security guards, enormous men who camped on the back of her mother's barge, and this surreal battle with its shifting cast of outlandish characters became the defining experience of McFate's young life. At times, it frightened her. A man known as Teepee Tom, who lived in a deerskin lean-to that he'd mounted on Styrofoam blocks so it would float, fired his rifle through her bedroom window (the bullet lodged harmlessly in a broken upright piano). But the war also intrigued her. "People really drew sides," she told me; it was absorbing to watch. Meanwhile, a private drama played out on the barge, where Poynter drank cheap vodka and drifted in and out of a desultory maternal role. Many days, McFate didn't want to go home, not knowing what she would find: "Would my mother have actually cooked dinner or would she be basically passed out in vomit?" McFate spent hours in the evenings at a bus stop on Bridgeway, a big road in Sausalito, doing her homework beneath a streetlight like a child in one of the underelectrified villages of the developing world. Passing cops sometimes mistook her for a child prostitute.

By middle school, McFate was beginning to be aware of a different, more stable and predictable world beyond Gate 5. She befriended a classmate who lived in Marin City, a predominantly black community that had been built to house shipyard workers during World War II. The housing projects of Marin City were beautiful to McFate. She envied her friend's comparative wealth and, even more, his family's conventionality. He had a father who lived at home, where pink lacy curtains covered the windows. As a target of schoolyard mockery a few years earlier, McFate had realized with surprise that not everybody's father jumps off the Golden Gate Bridge. It took her slightly longer to figure out that her friend from Marin City wasn't part of a privileged black class that ruled America. The knowledge that there were other worlds and, indeed, that multiple realities existed beyond the borders of her own perception, soon became one of McFate's chief consolations. Understanding—even empathy—was, for her, a defensive posture, one that followed her into adulthood. If you believe that war is inevitable, she told me, "you will never be surprised by it. If you think it's inevitable, you can take some kind of activity to stop it or mediate it or moderate it. But if you think that war isn't part of human nature, you're constantly going to be surprised and disappointed by human beings."

The writer Cintra Wilson, McFate's oldest and closest friend, grew up in a houseboat community near Gate 5 that was comparatively gentrified. In her novel *Colors Insulting to Nature*, Wilson introduces the character Lorna Wax, based loosely on McFate, by noting that she "had an unconventional childhood. She lived in Sausalito, in a cluster of ramshackle houseboats made locally famous by a legion of hippie squatters who fought off gentrification (and subsequent eviction) in the 1970s by staging a riot. Long-haired men shouting in rubber dinghies were teargassed on the news; braless mothers hit police with oars. Finally, after months of bloody foreheads and pro-bono legal wrangling, the houseboat community was written off as an intractable nuisance by the city and left to fester. Dead, rusty cars filled the unpaved parking lot; children with dirty mouths and no pants ran barefoot on splintering gangplanks."

Wilson described the houseboat communities of their childhood to me as a "social experiment," of which Gate 5 was the most extreme iteration. "We were essentially raised by pirates," she told me. In the houseboat community where Wilson lived for a time with a jazz musician mother and a father who taught art at Chico State, the men banded together to bring the houseboats up to code, while at Gate 5, the county's request that people install sewage pumps sparked riots. Wilson recalled visiting McFate on her mother's barge, with its wide-plank floors and weird art. The two became friends in elementary school, but went to different middle schools. When they met up again at Tamalpais High, McFate picked a fight with Wilson. "She was just sort of a terror," Wilson told me. "She was the first punk rocker Marin County had ever seen."

McFate dressed almost entirely in black, and she hardly fit in at tony Tamalpais. But she was good at school, and its uncomplicated logic—the more she studied, the better she did—was a welcome respite from the unpredictability of the rest of her life. As far back as high

THE ANTHROPOLOGY OF US AND THEM

school, Wilson told me, McFate seemed to have an understanding of what Wilson called "mortal consequences." McFate wasn't giggly and silly like other teenaged girls. "She might have done dumb things, but it was more like clinical experiments, like 'I am making a conscious experiment right now,'" Wilson told me. "She never lost control." Having grown up in an environment with few rules, McFate found "safety in discipline," Wilson told me. "She had no structure, so she had to impose it on herself. In a different life, I think she would have had a brilliant military career." As a teenager, McFate had a recurring dream in which she was a soldier leaving a village where she had fought, passing a fountain filled with dead leaves. She "would be overcome with these tremendous feelings of having been through this ordeal and people having died," Wilson recalled. The dream "seemed to inform her character in some way."

McFate started working when she was fifteen, giving her mother most of the money she earned. She frequented punk clubs in San Francisco, staying out all night, "and having sex with boys and girls," she told me. One of her friends at the time, a girl named Elizabeth, came from a home as offbeat and dysfunctional as McFate's. Elizabeth's mother was a filmmaker who never had any food in the house except vitamins, grapefruit, and, in the freezer, LSD. Two strippers were always sunbathing naked on the roof. Elizabeth moved into the Golden Eagle Hotel, where she succumbed to heroin addiction and hepatitis and eventually sank into a coma. She was the first in a series of friends McFate would lose to drugs, suicide, crime, and accidents. One was shot in the head; another died of a brain aneurism. Two boyfriends in a row committed suicide. McFate realized that she and her friends were behaving self-destructively. Even if they hadn't exactly wanted to die, they had "allowed death to happen to them. There was no brake mechanism on their train, and so once they started down the hill, they were not going to stop until they crashed into something." Her well-honed survival instincts kicked in. She called her boyfriend and told him she wouldn't be seeing him again. Soon afterward, he died of a heroin overdose.

As a teenager, McFate told me, fighting to stay alive was harder than dying. Dying was like "lazily slipping into the mud." Nihilism was "the disease that was floating around. It was very easy to catch." But McFate has always viewed herself as fundamentally optimistic. "I could always see that there was, not necessarily a pot of gold at the end of the rainbow, but at least there was something at the end of the rainbow," she told me. "It might be a lump of coal, but you could always hope, and that's what Nietzsche says is the definition of happiness, right? Or actually, the definition of sadness is the opposite of hope, or the absence of hope."

Actually, Nietzsche famously wrote that hope is "the worst of all evils, because it prolongs the torments of Man." But McFate's intellectual dance with Nietzsche was real and influential. When she talked about choosing life over death, she might have been quoting from *Twilight of the Idols*, in which Nietzsche wrote that "[s]aying Yes to life even in its strangest and hardest problems" elevates man, "[n]ot in order to be liberated from terror and pity . . . but in order to be *oneself* the eternal joy of becoming, beyond all terror and pity." Moral dogmatism was "naïve," Nietzsche wrote, for "[r]eality shows us an enchanting wealth of types, the abundance of a lavish play and change of forms." Accordingly, the philosopher and his fellow "immoralists" have "made room in our hearts for every kind of understanding, comprehending and approving. We do not easily negate; we make it a point of honor to be *affirmers*." Like McFate, for whom the realization that different perspectives could be equally valid was a source of comfort amid chaos, Nietzsche asked his readers to transcend good and evil, leaving behind "the illusion of moral judgment." Even war, that most terrible of things to the Western humanist thinker and the typical American anthropolo-

110

gist, had for Nietzsche its benefits. "One has renounced the *great* life when one renounces war," he wrote. "[E]ven in a wound there is the power to heal."

McFate's determination to survive drew her to zombie movies, especially those with stories of siege and endurance. In *Night of the Living Dead*, humans holed up in an abandoned house are besieged by zombies that feed on human flesh, "and you can be besieged by anyone," McFate told me. "The undead are just a metaphor for the forces in your life or in the world that are attempting to harm or cannibalize you, and the siege is a metaphor for resistance and triumph." In graduate school, McFate and her roommate, Brian, nursed various obsessions. For a while, they were fascinated by the Russian poet Marina Tsvetaeva. Another time it was Jeeves and Wooster, and they were reading P. G. Wodehouse to each other in the kitchen. For a time, their interest centered on the Donner Party, the group of nineteenth-century pioneers snowed under in the Sierra Nevada mountains, some of whom resorted to cannibalism to stay alive. They read books about the disastrous expedition and watched movies about it. "Brian would always say, 'I think you definitely would be the last survivor. You'd have no problem eating human flesh,'" McFate told me, laughing. "And I was like, 'You know, actually, it's perfectly true.'"

✳   ✳   ✳

McFate spent two years in community college before transferring to the University of California, Berkeley, in 1985. On her first day of classes, her mother suffered a fatal stroke, and McFate inherited the houseboat and responsibility for its tenants. She finished the semester, dropped out of school, and moved back to Sausalito to settle her mother's affairs. In 1987, after living briefly with a boyfriend in Las Vegas, she returned to Berkeley as a social sciences major. She created her own academic program, taking classes on German cinema, modern poetry, the anthropology of death, and women in literature. She walked around campus in a fur-collared horsehide jacket, black jeans, and lace-up boots, her hair in dreadlocks.

Berkeley had a democratic education program that allowed students to design their own classes. McFate and a friend created one called "Punks on Film," which began with the roots of punk and ended with its commodification when a faux-punk band called Pain appeared on an episode of the TV series *CHiPs*. McFate's interest in what she called "the commodification or fetishization of the body" led her to write her senior thesis on Nazi aesthetics. She wanted to explore how certain images—like a close-up shot of a soldier's helmet and jawline in Leni Riefenstahl's *Triumph des Willens*—take on symbolic importance. "I was really interested in the way that propaganda worked," McFate told me. The morality of the Nazis intrigued McFate less than the symbols by which they perpetuated power. "To me, the interesting question was, 'How did they do it and what was the effect?' In what way does art—if you think it's art—in what way does imagery become a manifestation of power?"

Like the adolescent who had watched with fascination as her houseboat neighbors fought the law, the adult McFate had an uncanny ability to distance herself from the moral concerns of war and view the thing coldly. She also shared her mother's impatience with lazy hippie leftism. Liberal Berkeley kids partying on their parents' dime annoyed her. After graduation, she spent part of her mother's life insurance settlement traveling with a friend. In Northern Ireland, she visited the Milltown Cemetery on Falls Road, where IRA volunteer Bobby Sands and other hunger strikers are buried. She had viewed the Irish Republican Army as terrorists, and was surprised and intrigued to learn that people in Belfast saw things differently. To them, Britain was an occupier and the republicans were legitimate defenders of their territory. An old man gave her a tour of the cemetery, and in the Sinn Féin bookstore she bought a book published by the republican National Graves Association that gave a detailed account of how the movement memorialized death. She was taken aback by the IRA's political and cultural cohesion. "You think, Okay, these people are a bunch of terrorists," she told me, "and then you go there and you find out, well, they've got an incredible body of literature, an incredible body of music, and they've got all these incredibly complex rituals associated with death."

McFate, too, was intrigued by death's rituals. Back home, she got a job at Chapel of the Chimes, a historic Oakland funeral home, and returned to KALX, the Berkeley radio station, where as a student she had hosted a show. She applied to a handful of graduate programs in anthropology. Having grown up poor, she was petrified of going into debt. She chose Yale because it offered her the most generous financial aid package.

Yale turned out to be a good fit for McFate in other ways, too. Since 1949, the university has been home to the Human Relations Area Files, a database of cultural and ethnographic information used by social scientists and members of the U.S. military and intelligence communities in times of war. One of McFate's advisers was John Middleton, a British-born Africanist who had served in World War II and studied at Oxford under E. E. Evans-Pritchard. Known as a "traveler, raconteur, casual pistol-shot . . . and determined drinker," Evans-Pritchard had been deeply embedded in the colonial politics of his day. He led Anuak tribes against the Italians on the Ethiopian border during World War II at Britain's behest, and his 1949 book on Libya, *The Sanusi of Cyrenaica*, helped convince the United Nations to endorse the head of the Sanusi order as Libya's king. "It helped of course that most of my research was carried out in a country, the Sudan, at that time ruled by the British and with a government and its officers friendly disposed to anthropological research," Evans-Pritchard wrote near the end of his life.

This was the tradition in which McFate was trained. Yet even at

Yale, anthropology's late-twentieth-century self-consciousness and its desire to distance itself from its colonial past determined which texts were considered important and which weren't. McFate and her fellow students learned to connect anthropologists of the British colonial era to the imperial project and, in doing so, to criticize their own discipline. Like everyone else, McFate wrote papers arguing that structural functionalism was invalid because it objectified and dehumanized the subjects of anthropological observation. But the pragmatist in her rejected this argument. Instead, a key question of the colonial era absorbed her: what utility did this early anthropology have for the British? "Why weren't we reading Sir Richard Burton? In many ways, he was one of the first anthropologists," McFate told me. "Of course, he was a spy and he was working for the British Empire. But he was an astute observer of life around him."

McFate was still thinking about what she had seen in Belfast. For her PhD dissertation, she wanted to explore the link between the Irish Republicans' "heavy narrative about the blood and the soil" and the way the IRA legitimated political violence. But when she proposed this as a dissertation topic, fellow students and professors at Yale told her she belonged in the political science department, because war was political, not cultural. "We say in anthropology that the utensils you use to eat your food, the sexual practices that are common in your culture, the way you rear your children, and the art you produce is a matter of culture," McFate told me. "But somehow, violence—violence in pursuit of political power or economic resources—is somehow not cultural? Like, everything's cultural except war? Because as an anthropologist, we can't study war—*why is that?*"

She ultimately prevailed, conducting her fieldwork in Belfast and London. Her first draft, she told me, was distinctly pro-IRA, written in the voice of "an angry Berkeley undergraduate," criticizing the British for advancing their colonial ambitions in Ireland. But when a friend at Sandhurst, the British military academy, asked to read it, McFate quailed. On closer examination, she decided it was biased and immature. She threw it out and started over.

Her dissertation is remarkable for its engaging tone, its clinical detachment from the human costs of fighting, and its affirmation of the durability and inexorability of war. It marked the beginning of a process, through which McFate would come to see anthropology as a "natural" practice for soldiers, and to view war itself as a kind of anthropology. She was drawn to the paradoxical relationship between empathy and killing: that you had to know your enemy to fight him effectively, but that knowing him also made you love him. In her dissertation, she asked whether "good anthropology" might lead to "better killing." It was a dangerous question but, for her, a necessary one.

Even before McFate finished her dissertation, she had grown tired of anthropology. "I wanted to do something in the world, not just write about it," she told me. She was interested in international law and the laws of war, so she applied to Harvard Law School and almost quit her anthropology program when she got in. At an adviser's urging, she finished her dissertation and started at Harvard the following fall. During her final year there, a friend introduced her to a young Army officer named Sean Sapone, who wanted to study anthropology. They corresponded, and over Valentine's Day weekend in 1997, Sapone came up to Cambridge and they met in person. "We just really hit it off," McFate said. One night they were having dinner and she told him she had an intuition that they were going to get married. "He put his fork down and he said, 'Okay,' just like that," McFate told me. By the end of the weekend, they were engaged. They married ten months later.

Sapone deployed to Germany and McFate (whose original married name was Montgomery Sapone) graduated and took a job as a litigation associate at the San Francisco offices of Baker & McKenzie, where she had interned in law school. She needed the money to pay off student loans, and at the time, she told me, she thought that tax litigation was "absolutely the most interesting thing in the world." But her interest waned, and she soon quit and moved to Germany to join Sapone. His unit, the Air Defense Artillery, struck her as "a narrow, cliquish tribe," and she judged the Army a throwback: "It was like time stopped in 1957." Friendships between officers' wives were governed by their husbands' rank. One wife tried to convert her to fundamentalist Christianity over coffee. A colonel asked if she was pregnant yet. "I totally failed as an Army wife," McFate told me. When she fumed over the colonel's assumption that she would immediately start popping out babies, Sapone urged her to remember that the officer's experience had shaped his worldview. 'You —anthropologist—can't be offended by that,' McFate recalled Sapone telling her. 'You've lived in Berlin, you've lived in London, you've lived in Las Vegas, you've lived in Northern Ireland, but you've never lived in the middle of the country.'

While Sapone worked, McFate learned to cook Vietnamese food and published her law school thesis on mercenaries and the laws of war. Somewhere along the way, the couple changed their last name to McFate, Sean Sapone's mother's maiden name. Montgomery McFate worked for her mother-in-law's company for a time. Her job involved Internet research and gathering information about "a lot of different public policy issues," she said, but this period of her life would later return to haunt her. McFate's mother-in-law was accused of being a corporate spy who infiltrated citizen activist groups at the behest of the gun lobby. McFate allegedly helped by collecting and analyzing intelligence and providing "confidential litigation support research." When Sean left the Army, they moved to Washington, D.C., where McFate took a contract job with the CIA, traveling to Europe to conduct research on Muslim minorities. She was not a clandestine agent, but neither did she tell her interview subjects that she worked for an intelligence agency. She moved on to the RAND Corporation, and in 2003, to the Office of Naval Research, which had supported the anthropologists Margaret Mead and Ruth Benedict half a century earlier. McFate started to wonder in earnest how anthropology might contribute to the needs of a military she had grown to respect.

In Washington, she began a concerted networking campaign. She met a Navy anthropologist and a former British intelligence officer, both of whom would become players in the cultural knowledge boom of the next few years. She sought out officials working on low-intensity conflict in the Pentagon and introduced herself to rising counterinsurgency star David Kilcullen. She and her husband hosted dinner parties at their apartment in the capital's Adams Morgan neighborhood, inviting ambassadors, generals, and military intellectuals. McFate eventually started a blog called "I Luv a Man in Uniform," where, under the pseudonym "Pentagon Diva," she composed tongue-in-cheek paeans to the sex appeal of military thinkers like H. R. McMaster.

During a conversation with the commander of the Marine Corps Warfighting Laboratory, McFate suggested that cultural misunderstandings had caused difficulties for marines in Iraq. 'I don't have any facts about that,' she recalled the general telling her. 'I'd like you to do a study.' She started interviewing marines, and later soldiers and sailors, returning from Iraq. Somewhere along the way, she heard Hriar Cabayan's name and wrote it down, but she never got around to calling him. One day, out of nowhere, he called her. He was looking for an anthropologist. Could she come to the Pentagon?

\*     \*     \*

McFate and Cabayan weren't the only ones thinking about anthropology's utility for counterinsurgency and intelligence gathering. Around the time they began working together on Cultural Preparation of the Environment, the military and intelligence communities were eyeing the social sciences with an intensity not seen in thirty years. In 2005, the CIA posted an employment ad on the website of the American Anthropological Association, seeking someone to help its analysts understand terrorist groups and social and cultural responses to disease, migration, and other crises. That the CIA would try to hire anthropologists—and that the American Anthropological Association would allow the agency to advertise on its website—outraged some anthropologists. One of them, David Price, suggested that the association was ignoring "the CIA's history of torture, terror and covert global support for anti-democratic movements." In 2006, Roberto J. González, an associate professor at San José State University, asked the association to publicly oppose the use of anthropological knowledge in torture. News of the Abu Ghraib scandal was still fresh, and González's effort was inspired by reports that Army interrogators had relied on anthropologist Raphael Patai's 1973 book, *The Arab Mind*, to identify cultural taboos that could be exploited during interrogation.

Anthropologists tend to be overwhelmingly politically liberal, and few supported the administration of George W. Bush or the wars in Iraq and Afghanistan. Yet more than politics was at work here. To many anthropologists, using cultural insights to wage war was like using a screwdriver to pry open a door: it indicated the commission of a crime. Beginning in 2007, a small group of anthropologists carried on a vigorous argument with McFate and other champions of anthropology as a tool for counterinsurgency. McFate's critics advanced three main arguments. The first was that deploying social scientists to war zones, particularly to gather military intelligence, could endanger the people being studied and lead all anthropologists to be viewed as spies. The second was that, on principle, anthropology should not be used to subjugate unruly people while expanding American power. The last, and in some ways the most compelling, was that anthropology is not predictive and does not yield the kind of data useful for military operations. Instead, it produces stories about stories that are as ambiguous as they are illuminating. The anthropologist Kerry Fosher, who works for the Marine Corps, described the disconnect between most anthropologists and the defense establishment as "profound." She compared the defense and intelligence communities to an organization that calls in a group of physicists and asks them to determine how fast the sun orbits the earth, or that summons a group of doctors to save a dying patient, with the stipulation that they must use only leeches and mercury. "The questions they are asking and the data they want are fundamentally at odds with reality," Fosher told me.

That the U.S. military was rediscovering anthropology as if for the first time inspired cynicism in many anthropologists, who remembered the past all too well. "Of all the modern social sciences, anthropology is the one historically most closely tied to colonialism," wrote Edward Said, "since it has often been the case that since the mid-nineteenth century anthropologists and ethnologists were also advisors to colonial rulers on the manners and mores of the native people to be ruled." Colonel Creighton, the ethnographer and spymaster who grooms Kipling's Kim for his role in the nineteenth-century Great Game, tells the boy: "There is no sin so great as ignorance." One day, he will pay Kim for "knowledge of what is behind those hills—for a picture of a river and a little news of what the people say in the villages there." Claude Lévi-Strauss wrote that anthropology "is the outcome of a historical process which has made the larger part of mankind subservient to the other, and during which millions of innocent human beings have had their resources plundered and their institutions and beliefs destroyed, whilst they themselves were ruthlessly killed, thrown into bondage, and contaminated by diseases they were unable to resist. Anthropology is the daughter to this era of violence: its capacity to assess more objectively

the facts pertaining to the human condition reflects, on the epistemo-
logical level, a state of affairs in which one part of mankind treated the
other as an object."

Around the time that McFate and others were developing the
Human Terrain System, the Australian counterinsurgency expert David
Kilcullen began working for the State Department and as an adviser to
General Petraeus in Iraq. Kilcullen had studied political anthropology
and done his doctoral research on Muslim and Timorese insurgents
in Indonesia as an officer in the Australian army. In 2006, he wrote a
tip list that was widely read by U.S. officers deploying to Iraq and Afghanistan. The list was a self-conscious allusion to a similar document
composed nearly one hundred years earlier by T. E. Lawrence, Britain's
celebrated ethnographer-spy.

Kilcullen's list raised the question McFate had stumbled on years
earlier in writing her dissertation: what was the difference between ethnography and intelligence? Was there a difference? "Know the people, the topography, economy, history, religion and culture," Kilcullen
wrote. "Know every village, road, field, population group, tribal leader
and ancient grievance." T. E. Lawrence had wanted to influence the
Arabs' behavior, and he knew that he would be most successful by making them forget he was British, or that he was even there. "Remain in
touch with your leader as constantly and unobtrusively as you can,"
Lawrence wrote. "Live with him, that at meal times and at audiences
you may be naturally with him in his tent. Formal visits to give advice
are not so good as the constant dropping of ideas in casual talk." For
the British military adviser, "complete success" came "when the Arabs
forget your strangeness and speak naturally before you, counting you as
one of themselves."

When the anthropologist Clifford Geertz and his wife arrived in a
Balinese village in the late 1950s to begin fieldwork, they at first "wandered around, uncertain, wistful, eager to please." Villagers pretended

to ignore them but were in fact watching them closely. The anthropologists were outsiders; if their study was to be fruitful, they had to find a way in. Their point of entry came when police raided an illegal cockfight that the Geertzes and all the other villagers had gone to see. The Balinese scattered and the anthropologists fled with them. Because they had not laid claim to their status as distinguished foreign researchers, but instead had acted like ordinary Balinese, the village opened to them. Their near arrest became the key to achieving what anthropologists call "rapport." "It led to a sudden and unusually complete acceptance into a society extremely difficult for outsiders to penetrate," Geertz wrote. This looks like Lawrence's moment of success, too, when "the Arabs forget your strangeness and speak naturally before you." But Geertz's aim and the ultimate product of his study were different: not to advance national security goals but to explore the Balinese cockfight as a "combination emotional explosion, status war and philosophical drama of central significance to the society whose inner nature I desired to understand."

In the United States, anthropology's tortured relationship with intelligence and war lay at the heart of the nation's expansion. The nineteenth-century Bureau of Ethnology sent social scientists into Indian country with military forces to document native cultures that were being constrained and transformed by war. Early American military leaders also sought to learn about the Indians, and to fight like them. But the settlers took far more than they gave. Under the management of the U.S. government, Indian cultures would be all but extinguished.

In 1919, the celebrated German-American anthropologist Franz Boas alleged that four American anthropologists had used their discipline as a cover for spying during World War I. He called them out for having "done the greatest possible disservice to scientific inquiry," noting that because of them, "every nation will look with distrust upon the visiting foreign investigator who wants to do honest work, suspecting sinister designs." But Boas was out of step with the mood of his time. The American Anthropological Association, known as the AAA, quickly and publicly censured him, and two of his best-known students, Margaret Mead and Ruth Benedict, became key contributors to American policy and planning during World War II. In 1941, the AAA passed a resolution placing "itself and its resources and the specialized skills of its members at the disposal of the country for the successful prosecution of the war." More than half the anthropologists in America at the time are thought to have worked on the war effort, while many of the rest contributed part-time. They wrote handbooks for soldiers explaining the "habits and customs" of faraway peoples and suggesting "policies to enlist the active coöperation of local or native populations." They worked in military intelligence and at internment camps for Japanese-Americans, censored foreign mail, analyzed the impact of Allied bombings on enemy military and civilian populations, and spied for the Office of Strategic Services, or OSS, a precursor to the CIA. Although some anthropologists expressed doubts—"Now that we have techniques, are we in cold blood, going to treat people as things?" Gregory Bateson wrote in 1941—these were quickly assuaged; Bateson himself went to work for the OSS.

Vietnam changed everything. Anthropology, which twenty years earlier had volunteered itself in the service of a wartime nation, became intensely suspicious of American imperialism, for while World War II had been a "good" war, Vietnam was considered a bad one. In 1965, Project Camelot, a U.S. Army–funded social science research program designed to explore the likelihood of insurrection and revolt in various Latin American countries, drew international attention to the clumsiness of American foreign policy and the growing rift between the U.S government and social scientists increasingly outraged over Vietnam. The creators of Camelot set out to develop "a general social systems model" that could "predict and influence politically significant aspects of social change in the developing nations of the world." What they really wanted was to win the Cold War, and that meant tamping down leftist insurgencies, a task that would be much easier if the Army could predict where such uprisings might occur.

The Special Operations Research Office of American University, known as SORO, enlisted social scientists to conduct field research paid for by the Defense Department. But before the project even got off the ground, an assistant professor of anthropology named Hugo G. Nutini traveled to Chile, where he met with a high-level university administrator to expound on the benefits of participating in Project Camelot. What Nutini presumably didn't know was that a Norwegian social scientist named Johan Galtung, who was working in Chile, had already drawn the attention of Chilean academics to Camelot's "imperialist features." If the U.S. military wanted social scientists to help it understand when the United States might usefully intervene in the political affairs of Latin American nations, Galtung wondered, why didn't they also ask when it might be appropriate for Latin American countries to intervene in the affairs of the United States? A leftist Chilean newspaper denounced Camelot as a thinly veiled attempt at U.S. espionage. The American ambassador to Chile cabled his outrage at the project's having been undertaken without his knowledge or participation, the Defense Department swiftly canceled the initiative, and congressional hearings ensued. A key lesson of Camelot—that competition between the State and Defense Departments can lead to foreign policy disasters—would have to be learned all over again in Iraq and Afghanistan.

"The story of Project Camelot was not a confrontation of good versus evil," the sociologist Irving Louis Horowitz wrote in 1967, yet it has often been presented that way. Camelot—admittedly suspect, ethically problematic, and potentially a cover for spying—appears never to have achieved any of its goals. Perhaps its most significant negative outcome for social scientists was that, for a time, it made working in

Chile and other Latin American countries more difficult. At least one PhD student doing fieldwork in Chile had his research confiscated, and Camelot became a running joke among Latin Americans. For Horowitz, one of the noteworthy things about Camelot was the idealism that drove its participants. They were united, he wrote, by "a profound conviction of the perfectibility of mankind." They sought to "create a social science of contemporary relevance," and even if they were uncomfortable with military sponsorship, they felt that "the Army had to be educated." This was exactly the rationale articulated by McFate and Fondacaro in building the Human Terrain System forty years later. But Horowitz's contention decades earlier that the U.S. military could not be viewed purely as an instrument for social good remains pertinent. As Horowitz wrote, the assumption "that people in power need only be shown the truth in order to do the right thing is unacceptable."

The blowup that ended Camelot did little to resolve Horowitz's central and most lasting question: "Just what are the limits and obligations, no less than the rights, to investigate the viscera of another society on behalf of a government foreign to that society?" A few years later, in 1970, a group of students opposed to the Vietnam War published documents lifted from the files of an anthropologist at a California university that detailed the involvement of a number of anthropologists and other social scientists in U.S.-funded counterinsurgency research in Thailand. Social scientists had been asked to supply "up-to-date information" on the "location of tribal villages, the number and ethnic identity of the inhabitants, [and] their migratory history." The Thai and U.S. governments specifically wanted information that anthropologists might not normally have collected, at least not in a systematic way: map coordinates for villages; names of village leaders; how long they had lived there; the names, occupations, and racial affiliation of residents; and whether they had weapons. The purloined documents revealed that the U.S. government was "less interested in the economic, social, or political causes of discontent than in techniques of neutralizing individual or collective protest," the anthropologists Eric Wolf and Joseph Jorgensen wrote. "The days of naïve anthropology are over. It is no longer adequate to collect information about little known and powerless people; one needs to know also the uses to which that knowledge can be put." Anthropology had to "disengage itself from its connection with colonial aims or it will become intellectually trivial," they wrote. "The future of anthropology, its *credibility*, depends upon sustaining the dialectic between knowledge and experience. Anthropologists must be willing to testify in behalf of the oppressed peoples of the world, including those whom we professionally define as primitives and peasants."

From its conception until at least the mid-twentieth century, anthropology had considered itself a scientific discipline based on objective observation. McFate had studied anthropology at a university where many senior professors "really believed that anthropology was a science," she told me. As a scientist, she wasn't "supposed to be making moral arguments." Yet McFate's view made her an outlier. The dominant trend in late-twentieth-century anthropology has been toward a subjectivity that is morally and often politically responsive to the people observed.

In 2007, the American Anthropological Association declared its opposition to the Human Terrain System, calling the program "an unacceptable application of anthropological expertise." Paula Loyd's college anthropology professor, Sally Engle Merry, served on the executive board that helped draft the statement. Indeed, Loyd had harbored no illusions about how her former teacher would view her work with the Human Terrain System. 'I don't think Sally Merry would approve of this,' she had told her old college friend Stefanie Johnson before leaving for Afghanistan in the late summer of 2008. In fact, Merry remembered her former student fondly, and her views on the use of cultural knowledge in war were more nuanced than Loyd might have guessed.

"It's a really hard question," Merry told me. "I'm not a fan of war, and I don't think war as a way to produce peace makes much sense. But I also think the military is in a very difficult box, and people are trying to do the right thing. I just wish we could find a way to use the knowledge anthropology can produce to bring these wars to an end."

McFate's house in Weston, Missouri, was full of Orientalist art. A painting of a camel train moving across the desert hung near an image of a pale-skinned European who had "gone native" by donning a robe and Arab headdress. Some anthropologists privately wondered if McFate had simply stopped paying attention to developments in anthropology after the early twentieth century, but McFate had always been a pragmatist. Since childhood, she had been looking for a way to survive. In the military cultural knowledge boom of the early years of the twenty-first century, she found one.

## 6. HEARTS AND MINDS

Back in Maiwand, Don Ayala had just put a bullet in the head of the handcuffed Afghan who had set Paula Loyd on fire. Specialist Justin Skotnicki heard the shot. He looked and then he couldn't look. He turned away. 'Oh fuck!' he said. 'Fuck, fuck, fuck!'

A few steps down the path, the platoon leader turned. He saw Ayala standing with his pistol in his hand, saw the Afghan slumped in the dirt, blood pouring from his head.

'Are you serious?' Lieutenant Pathak yelled.

Ayala looked squarely at him. 'Yes, I am.'

'I have to confiscate your weapons.'

Ayala handed Pathak his rifle and pistol and headed down the path toward where Cooper still knelt on the ground beside Loyd. Cooper hadn't moved this whole time, not even when he heard a scattering of gunfire behind him, Afghan police firing off rounds to clear the highway. Not when he heard the single gunshot from down the path in the shadow under the trees.

The medic was applying clear gel to Loyd's burned skin. Ayala saw her lying there and felt a stab in his gut as he took in her raw, pink skin, her nose melted to a nub, her lips and eyebrows gone. She lay there shaking as the medic leaned over her. 'I'm cold,' she said. 'I'm cold.'

Ayala walked over and stood behind Cooper, talking low so only his teammate could hear him. 'I just shot the guy,' Ayala said. 'I killed him. They took my gun.'

Cooper reached back and squeezed Ayala's calf in what he meant as a reassuring gesture. He rose unsteadily, turned, and embraced Ayala. 'You did the right thing,' Cooper told him, but Ayala felt a rush of protectiveness for this big mess of a man, broken and desolate as a child.

'Paula's doing great,' Ayala heard the medic say, and the words jolted him. 'Okay, all right, Paula, you're looking good,' Ayala said. 'You're fine.'

He and Cooper stepped apart and began gathering up her helmet and body armor.

'Clint, don't leave me,' she murmured, shivering as the medic tried to soothe her. An Afghan police truck pulled up with an old mattress in back and the men lifted her onto it. Cooper climbed up after her and Ayala was about to follow, but the soldiers told him to stay where he was. He watched them drive away.

Back at the base, they laid her on a cot in the aid station, and she started talking again. 'How does it look?' she asked the young medic who had been treating her. 'Don't hold back. Just be honest with me.'

'I can't tell,' he told her haltingly. 'I don't know.'

What he and the other medics knew was that third-degree burns covered 60 to 70 percent of her body—her face, neck, arms, and legs.

'Call Frank,' she said. 'I want to talk to Frank.'

She started giving Cooper instructions. He could hardly move fast enough. Her cell phone was in the pocket of her backpack. Muggeo's number was in the contact list. She calculated the time difference between Afghanistan and St. Thomas, where her mother lived. Muggeo was in Georgia. 'Call him first,' she told Cooper. 'I don't want to worry my mom. And make sure the colonel gets my report. I don't want to have stayed up all night typing for nothing. Jeez, I hope this doesn't affect my typing ability.'

Her hands were a mess. The medics wrapped each finger separately in burn pads so her skin wouldn't stick and tear. They gave her an IV, pumped her full of antibiotics and pain relievers, and loaded her onto a helicopter. The belly of the Chinook was lined with rudimentary seats, baggage stacked down the middle, and they laid her stretcher on the floor. She was covered in burn blankets and lotion, and Cooper knelt beside her. As the helicopter spun up, he leaned in close. The rotors and the wind were so loud that he had to yell to make himself heard: 'They're taking us to FOB Bastion'—a British base in Helmand with a good field hospital. He wasn't sure she heard him, or that she understood, but he wanted her to know she wasn't alone, so he stroked her hair, the only part of her that felt safe to touch.

The flight was mercifully short. An Army burn specialist from Germany happened to be at Bastion, and while he examined Loyd, medics swabbed the dirt and rocks from Cooper's knees. His pants were torn and stained with his own blood from where he had dived forward to pull Loyd into the water. His uniform stank of gas, smoke, and sweat. He searched her phone for Muggeo's number.

At 2 a.m. at Fort Benning, the phone rang. Muggeo answered it, but heard only silence. He turned over and drifted off until it rang again. 'Paula? What happened? Is everything okay?'

'Frank, it's Clint. Paula's been hurt. She's alive.'

The connection was unsteady and long pauses separated his words.

Muggeo listened, his brain dim with sleep. She'd been burned, Cooper told him. Muggeo tried to take this in. If anyone knew her way around southern Afghanistan it was Loyd, and if anything were to happen to her, it wouldn't have been this, an attack that fell outside every known pattern of the insurgency.

'We're evacuating her,' Cooper told him. 'She wants you to call her mother, but don't call her too early. Don't wake her up.'

'Tell her I'll be there for her,' Muggeo said, and hung up.

They put Loyd on a flight to Germany, and in the air Cooper slipped a jade pendant from her neck. It had been a gift from Muggeo, and Cooper knew it was important to her. Now he feared it would get lost with all this moving around, all these people touching her. At the Army hospital in Landstuhl, someone gave him clean clothes and sent him to a quaint rooming house for the relatives of wounded soldiers, where an old woman cooked him pancakes and he started speaking German without thinking about it. The contrast between this house and the place he had just left was almost too much for him. He lay exhausted on the bed, leaden with guilt.

They flew on to Texas, and in the solid roar of the engine over the Atlantic, Loyd lay immobilized on a stretcher, wrapped in gauze. Goggles covered her eyes and she was tiny and unrecognizable but for the exposed flesh around her chest and shoulder where her body armor had covered her skin. They touched down at Brooke Army Medical Center in San Antonio, where Loyd's mother waited, a chaplain by her side.

Cooper was afraid to see Muggeo. He had let Loyd down, had allowed this terrible thing to happen to her, and he half expected Muggeo to punch him. Instead, Muggeo invited him out to a steak house for dinner, joking lamely but good-naturedly that Paula wouldn't approve—there wasn't much for a vegetarian to like about a steak house. The next morning in the hospital elevator, Cooper reached into his pocket and pulled out the jade pendant. Muggeo's eyes reddened as he reached for it.

White bandages hid Loyd's body. She couldn't talk, but she recognized them when they came in and tears welled in her eyes. Cooper could barely look at her. Pull yourself together, he thought. He brought his face close to hers, whispering so only she could hear him. 'You've got to get better,' he told her. 'We need you for this project.'

\*       \*       \*

Back in Maiwand, Ayala sat cross-legged against a wall in the shade. The soldiers didn't know if he was nuts or what, so they put a guard on him. When Ayala got up to stretch his legs, the soldier told him to sit down.

'Are you here to watch me?' Ayala asked.

'What do you think?'

Ayala sat down. He caught sight of Jack Bauer. 'Hey, Jack,' Ayala called. 'Give me a cigarette.'

Jack handed him the pack. The interpreter was shaken and confused, first by the attack on Loyd and then by Ayala's execution of the captive. Ayala who, a few minutes earlier, had ordered Jack to stop kicking the very same man because it was culturally inappropriate. Ayala must have loved Loyd, Jack thought.

'Why you killed that person?' he asked.

Ayala lit up and inhaled deeply. When he heard what had happened to Loyd, he told Jack, he'd lost control. He didn't know what was going to happen next. Ayala looked at the interpreter. 'Do you know what's going to happen to me?'

After a while, an officer came over. They were taking Ayala back to the base. Ayala rose and dusted himself off. 'Hey, take care, Jack,' he said. 'See you.'

Jack stood there watching him go.

They took Ayala to Ramrod, the desert base where he, Loyd, and Cooper had landed a few weeks earlier. He sat in the command center waiting for someone to tell him what was going on. A few soldiers came up. 'Everything's going to be okay,' one told him. 'Are you all right?' someone else said. 'Sorry about Paula.'

Ayala had been a soldier. He wanted someone to look him in the eye and tell him what was going to happen to him, whatever it was, but no one would. Finally, he asked the unit's senior enlisted man what he should expect. The command sergeant major said he didn't know.

At last, two young soldiers took him to the landing zone. They boarded a Chinook like the one Ayala and his teammates had flown in on. The copters usually carried scores of soldiers, but on this day Ayala and his escorts had the aircraft to themselves. They flew fast and low over desert and farmland, the late-afternoon light turning the land-scape a glittering gold, and landed at Kandahar Airfield at sunset. Mike Warren, the team leader, stood waiting as the helicopter lowered onto the tarmac. As he watched armed escorts lead Ayala off, he noticed something different about his friend. Ayala always stood exceptionally straight. Now his shoulders slumped and he walked with a shambling aimlessness, as if he were lost.

Military police cuffed Ayala and took him to a truck. Warren tried to get close enough to talk to him, but the police wouldn't let him. They took Ayala for a physical exam, then to a holding cell that had once been a bathroom: sewage pipes cemented into the floor, a lingering stench. The two soldiers who had flown with him took turns standing guard outside. They didn't talk to him much, and studiously avoided discussing what had happened that day. What little they said concerned football, women, and things they'd done in the Army.

That evening, Army investigators showed up and questioned Ayala until midnight. He refused to write a statement without a lawyer, but he had nothing to hide, so he answered their questions. 'I was thinking I saw Paula and thought fuck this guy,' Ayala told them. An investigator asked how he'd felt after the shooting. Ayala said he was angry at the Afghan and worried about Loyd. "He had no remorse about shooting the man because he deserved to die for what he did," an investigator wrote.

After three days, they cuffed Ayala and shackled his legs. Four airmen escorted him north to the American base at Bagram. Once there, they put him in a six- by ten-foot cell designed to house prisoners overnight. When he had to use the bathroom, they marched him to the portable toilets in leg shackles. When he showered, his guards made everyone else clear out and wait for him to finish.

He spent three weeks there. As in Kandahar, two soldiers sat beyond the barred door of his cell, watching him sleep, eat, and read. Sometimes he talked to them, drawing them out as he had the young soldiers in Maiwand. They told him about their fifteen-month tours, how they would come home after a couple of those and find their wives had left them for someone else. This was why so many soldiers were committing suicide, Ayala thought. They had been sent to do jobs they hadn't been trained to do in a war they didn't understand. To pass the time, he read *Roberts Ridge* and *Lone Survivor*, stories about heroic battles waged by Navy SEALs in the Afghan mountains. In these books, as never in the real war, a reassuring morality guided the cosmos, a sharp and unmistakable line separated good from evil. When one of Ayala's guards finished John McCain's memoir, *Faith of My Fathers*, he handed it through the bars, and Ayala read about McCain's time as a prisoner of war in North Vietnam, how political considerations there had hamstrung servicemen, how Navy pilots had been forbidden to fire on North Vietnamese surface-to-air missiles unless they were fired on first. How similar that war had been to this one, Ayala thought. American soldiers in Afghanistan watched their buddies get killed and were ordered not to shoot back unless they were sure the area was clear of civilians. Ayala himself had delivered those lessons to the soldiers of the 2–2. But now he saw things differently. The Taliban were the enemy, but the Taliban were also the people they were trying to help. It was an impossible conflict—impossible and unwinnable.

He had killed the Afghan captive at a politically sensitive moment. U.S. and NATO forces had been firing from the air on Taliban fighters and people they believed were Taliban since the beginning of the war, but their intelligence was often flawed, and many civilians had been killed in the strikes. Anger over those killings had crested the month before Ayala and his teammates arrived in Kandahar. In August 2008, a coalition air strike in the western village of Azizabad killed some ninety unarmed men, women, and children. The military at first denied that its bombs had killed any civilians, but a U.N. investigation and cell phone video confirmed the deaths. It made Afghans wonder, as they always did when things like this happened, whether the war was worth its human cost, and the Karzai government made a lot of noise about whether it could continue to support NATO. Then–Secretary of Defense Robert Gates flew to Kabul to apologize, and the NATO commander in Afghanistan, General McKiernan, declared reducing civilian casualties "of paramount importance." That fall, McKiernan ordered soldiers to "demonstrate proportionality, requisite restraint, and the utmost discrimination" in their use of firepower. When infantrymen read that, some started to wonder if they would be punished simply for firing their guns.

The Azizabad bombing was one more event driving the shift toward counterinsurgency that would occur, at least temporarily, under Barack Obama and the generals he would choose to run the war. Civilian casualties played into the hands of insurgents, who accused the Americans and their international allies of a brutal occupation. Karzai used the civilian deaths to distance himself from U.S. and NATO policy and win political support at home. He cried on TV as he spoke of children maimed by coalition bombs, and he accused the foreigners of arrogantly failing to cooperate with his government. On November 3, the day before Paula Loyd had been attacked, U.S. aircraft had bombed a wedding party north of Kandahar, killing thirty-seven civilians, including twenty-three children. At a news conference later that week, Karzai said that ending civilian casualties would be his first demand for Obama, the U.S. president-elect.

Ayala knew that as a civilian contractor working for a new, experimental program, he was of little value to the Army. He had killed a cuffed detainee, a crime that fit neatly into the prevailing Afghan narrative of an arrogant foreign occupation that valued Afghan lives cheaply. If the Americans were looking for someone to hold up to their Afghan partners as a symbol of the military's ability to police itself, he would do just fine. That Ayala's victim had attacked and severely wounded an American—that many Afghans would have considered death an appropriate penalty for setting a woman on fire—did not change the laws of war. With Loyd's Afghan assailant dead, U.S. forces might never know what had motivated him, and this was exactly the kind of question Ayala and his teammates had been sent to Maiwand to answer. Ayala knew that he would be accused of betraying his mission. He knew that people would blame him for killing a man who, had he been convinced to talk, might have helped the Americans fight the insurgency. But he had seen that kind of information misused or ignored too many times to put much stock in the notion that it would do any good, and here, his real-world experience ran up hard against the idealistic goals of the Human Terrain System. What was anybody going to do with that information? Ayala wondered. How many Americans had died in Afghanistan, were still dying, and what good had information done them? A few months earlier, more than one thousand men had escaped from the main prison in Kandahar, about four hundred of them insurgents.

The jailbreak had been carefully planned and masterfully executed, almost certainly with help from inside. Now they were going to hand Loyd's attacker to the Afghan police, to the Afghan prison system? No, Ayala had thought in those fateful seconds before he pulled the trigger. Not on my watch.

Americans had to take responsibility when they killed innocent people, Ayala thought; that went without saying. But they also had to take responsibility for the young men and women they sent to war. The nation owed its soldiers the right to self-defense, the right to defend their comrades, and the right to know what they were doing out there. He was thinking about the way counterinsurgency required soldiers to act like police or development workers. But rushing aid and development into Maiwand was getting soldiers killed, and just as important, it was failing. The U.S. military was building a new office for the district governor, but the current governor would soon be gone, and his successor would prefer the old office with its mature garden of trees and flowers. He would continue to work there, only visiting the new building for meetings with the Americans. Meanwhile, a series of U.S. military units would busy themselves installing plumbing and electricity in the new building and buying fancy furniture that remained encased in plastic. Soon, bored Afghan police would be chipping holes in the new plaster walls and shitting in the unplumbed toilets, and the governor and his administrators would start asking the Americans for satellite TVs. American commanders seemed more interested in winning awards and promotions back home, Ayala thought, than in what would become of Afghans after they left.

Alone in his cell, Ayala thought about his time as Karzai's bodyguard. Back in the early years of the war, he had accompanied Karzai to open a girls' school and a hospital in Ghazni. Now both had been shuttered, and the Taliban ran a shadow court there. How had this happened? Ayala wondered. Who had fallen asleep on duty? It was perhaps the critical question of the war, and the question of responsibility lay beneath it. Who fell asleep—was it us, or was it them? The United States had lost interest in Afghanistan, but Afghan leaders, too, had failed to seize the most powerful moment of possibility their country had seen in decades. In Maiwand and Kandahar, Ayala had seen how local big men kept American money for themselves, using it to buy weapons, armored cars, and property in Dubai. The fledgling political system that America had helped build in Afghanistan was a cruel joke. "It's not what you can do for the people," Ayala would tell me. "It's what can you guys do for me as a leader, how can I get power and fame?" Afghan politicians made sure everyone in their family and tribe got paid. The powerful grew stronger while the weak stayed weak, if they survived at all.

Ayala believed that the work he'd done in Iraq and Afghanistan had made a difference. That, along with the money, was why he had signed up to guard Karzai and Maliki. It was why he had gone to work for the Human Terrain System. He'd wanted to change the way the Army dealt with Afghan civilians. He had kept himself from shooting Salam as he ran, when he heard someone yelling those words—*Stop him! Shoot him!*—but there on the path, with the Afghan in handcuffs, his judgment had betrayed him. He knew what he'd done was technically wrong, but it hadn't felt wrong, still didn't. He had come to Afghanistan to make a difference. Over time, he would feel that the real difference he'd made in the war—maybe the only difference one man could make—was having killed the man who had attacked Paula Loyd. Everyone was always talking about information operations, the fight to control the narrative, the battle for hearts and minds. "Fuck this Muslim shit," he would tell me later. "You want to be part of the information operation? Well, this is a message sent. This is a message sent to the Taliban."

Ayala was known among friends and acquaintances for his calm good humor. He had trained men who would guard American diplomats in war zones, teaching them about the use-of-force continuum, the idea that the force used to counter a threat should be proportional and that only a grave threat could justify a lethal response. He'd taught them to make sure there were no allies or civilians in their line of fire, that they had a clear shot. He knew that in a counterinsurgency, shooting the wrong man could be worse than failing to shoot the right one. If he of all people had killed an Afghan detainee, what could Americans expect of an eighteen-year-old kid going to war for the first time?

About a week after Ayala arrived in Bagram, his military lawyer asked a magistrate on the air base to release him to the custody of the Human Terrain Team stationed there. But military prosecutors argued that with his combat training, Ayala could easily escape to Kabul, just forty-five minutes away by road. The magistrate agreed. Ayala would remain in the cramped holding cell until they could figure out whether he would be tried by the Army under the Uniform Code of Military Justice or back home in federal court. Members of the Bagram Human Terrain Team visited often, bringing warm socks, long-sleeved shirts, magazines, and sometimes barbecued ribs or a cup of coffee from the Green Bean, a Starbucks look-alike on base. Soldiers brought him cigarettes, and even though he didn't smoke, he would say he needed one just so they would take him outside in the sun. He would be shackled and cold, but at least he got out of his cell. Mike Warren flew up from Kandahar. Outraged at how the Army was treating his friend, he drove to Kabul and tried to get a message to Karzai. This man protected you, Warren wanted to tell the president. This man is not the enemy. He passed the message to a Karzai bodyguard and left. He never found out if it reached the president.

About two weeks after Ayala's arrest, the U.S. government charged him with second-degree murder under the Military Extraterritorial Jurisdiction Act, a statute designed to handle crimes committed by U.S. contractors accompanying the military overseas. It was the same law used to charge Blackwater security guards who opened fire in a Baghdad square in 2007, killing fourteen Iraqi civilians and wounding twenty others. Ayala would be tried in federal court. Strategic Analysis, the defense contractor that had employed him during his stint with the Human Terrain System, promptly fired him.

In late November, military police escorted him by plane to Kuwait and handed him off to soldiers from the Army's Criminal Investigation Division. Federal marshals arrived the next day to take him back to Washington, D.C. They flew on a commercial plane, where the marshals cuffed his wrists and covered his hands with a jacket so as not to alarm the other passengers.

They landed early on a Sunday morning, and at the federal holding facility in Virginia, they put him in solitary. Ayala didn't know how long he would be there, but he knew a thing or two about the prison system, enough to know that he wanted to be in the general population. He would stay in solitary, the guards told him, because of the severity of the charge against him.

He went to court the next morning dressed in an orange prison jumpsuit. His longtime girlfriend, Andi Santwier, watched from the gallery, along with her parents, who had flown in from California. She signed over their house in New Orleans as collateral for his bond. If Ayala ran, the government could sell the house and take two hundred thousand dollars.

When he got out that afternoon, he and Santwier and her parents walked across the street to the Westin hotel and sat at the bar. Ayala downed a scotch and then ordered a Sazerac, a New Orleans cocktail with rye whiskey, bitters, and absinthe that reminded him of home. They spent the night with Santwier's relatives in Washington. Ayala and Santwier talked, but he doesn't remember what they said to each other. He was exhausted, his body worn. He had lost twelve pounds since he killed the Afghan.

\* \* \*

At Brooke Army Medical Center in Texas, Paula Loyd had been struggling to survive. Ward and Muggeo spent hours at her bedside and friends streamed in to see her. Someone brought Star Wars books and Muggeo read them aloud to her, stumbling over the names of imaginary planets. He touched her foot, which hadn't been burned, squeezing her big toe in a silent greeting. Her body battled infections, and those who loved her fully believed that she would recover, but even they sometimes found it hard to look beyond what they saw in front of them. Layers of gauze hid her body and head. She had been talking when she arrived, but the doctors pumped her full of sedatives and drugs to numb the pain. After that, she was rarely lucid. Muggeo wanted to *do* something. When he heard she'd been hurt, he'd called in every last favor to make sure she got the best care. "I'm not a doctor," he would tell me later, "but I can be an asshole." Now he ducked into the hallway to take calls from Fort Benning, trying to stay busy and sane. He wasn't religious, but he prayed every day. He knew that whatever happened, everything about their lives would be different.

Doctors harvested healthy skin from her back, stomach, and scalp and grafted it onto her arms, legs, hands, and neck, but she contracted pneumonia and needed a ventilator to breathe. On January 7, nine weeks after the attack, she died of complications from her burns: cardiovascular decompression, respiratory distress, and sepsis. The Bexar County medical examiner's office declared the cause of death "complications from conflagration." The manner of death was listed as homicide.

Texas law requires next of kin to identify a body that arrives from a hospital before cremation, but some sights can permanently disorder your mind, and the undertaker judged that Loyd's body was one of them. When Ward got to the funeral home, she told him she could

140

identify her daughter by the tiny dragon tattoo on Loyd's ankle. But the undertaker advised her not to look at her daughter's remains. He pushed a paper toward Ward, who signed it.

The next day in Maiwand, a man on a motorcycle blew himself up in the bazaar, killing two American soldiers and sixteen Afghans, including an interpreter, and ripping open Jack Bauer's stomach. Jack would spend the next six months in the hospital with a colostomy bag. It was the worst attack yet on the Americans in Maiwand, and after it happened, the soldiers of Comanche Company steered clear of the bazaar. The company commander decided it wasn't worth the risk.

# 7. Crime and Punishment

The federal public defender came to see Don Ayala the day he landed in prison. Michael Nachmanoff had a throaty voice, a second-degree black belt in karate, and a keen ear for dramatic stories. The son of a distinguished Foreign Service officer, he had spent part of his childhood in London, where he'd watched Shakespeare plays incessantly and longed for a career on the stage. The courtroom had claimed him instead. He was fresh off a Supreme Court victory, and he knew the prosecutors and judges of the Eastern District of Virginia better than anyone else. Courtroom narratives didn't get more dramatic than Ayala's case, and Nachmanoff wanted to be personally involved. It was perhaps the most compelling human story he'd heard in his career as a defense lawyer.

The Justice Department had initially charged Ayala with second-degree murder. If convicted, he could have faced life in prison. In early

2009, he pleaded guilty to the lesser charge of voluntary manslaughter to escape the possibility of a life sentence and to get the thing over with as quickly as possible. A guilty plea meant acknowledging wrongdoing; Ayala knew he had broken the law, but "wrongdoing" wasn't what he would have called it. Nevertheless, the plea significantly lessened the possibility of a long jail term. He flew back to New Orleans, a convicted felon, to await his sentencing.

Victory in a legal case depends on which side tells the better story, and Nachmanoff had quickly discerned the nuance that made Ayala's story so compelling. Ayala's temperament was the opposite of what many people would have expected from a private security contractor freelancing in the lucrative world of wartime executive protection. He was no undisciplined cowboy. Instead, Nachmanoff thought, he had the biography of an old-school American hero who had been drawn back into service after September 11, protected senior American officials, and risked his life to guard the internationally anointed leaders of post-invasion Iraq and Afghanistan. He had killed an Afghan whose hands were cuffed behind his back, but that Afghan had just set fire to Ayala's teammate, a gentle young American woman. "Anyone possessing a shred of compassion would feel rage at the sight of this," Ayala's former Special Forces team commander wrote to the judge. "In this situation all sense of fairness is shattered, the rules of combat are broken." In fact, the black plastic flex cuffs that had restrained the Afghan constituted the entirety of Ayala's legal problem. Had he shot the man while he was running the case would probably never have come before a judge. Ayala's Afghan victim had a name—Abdul Salam—and like Ayala, he had a history. But Nachmanoff's strategy was masterful. In addition to telling his client's life story in as much sympathetic detail as possible, he would do all he could to make the flex cuffs and the Afghan who had worn them disappear.

Nachmanoff and his legal team collected forty-eight letters from people who knew Ayala, including veterans, police, business owners, even a corrections officer. The wife of one of Ayala's fellow Karzai bodyguards wrote that after her husband had died of a heart attack in Afghanistan, Ayala had volunteered to escort his remains home and helped arrange his funeral. When Ayala learned that she'd pawned her jewelry to avoid being evicted, he'd sent money for rent and food. People wrote about how Ayala had opened his house in New Orleans's Garden District to police and federal agents during Hurricane Katrina, offering them cold drinks, hot meals, and the first showers they'd had in days. A combat medic who had served with him in the Special Forces remembered Ayala as the guy who checked on everyone else, who gave you his water if you ran out and his last packet of instant coffee on a cold night. Yet Ayala was more than just a reliable friend. He had integrity, grit. Though he had known the medic for years, Ayala had refused to recommend him as a candidate for a State Department bodyguard detail because the man hadn't performed well enough on the practical exercises.

A childhood friend wrote that in forty-five years, he had never seen Ayala lose his temper. Friends told stories of his refusal to tangle with French Quarter drunks or racist guests at family gatherings, preferring civil conversation to a fight. Late one rainy night, a New Orleans police officer wrote, he had seen Ayala intervene to protect women at a bus stop from a large, threatening man. When Ayala asked the man to stop bothering the women, the man lunged at him. Instead of fighting back, Ayala "took a defensive stance and kept the man at a distance by shoving him away" until the police could get close enough to help.

The most powerful letter came from Paula Loyd's mother, who recalled Loyd's emails home about the villages they had visited in Maiwand and the people they had talked to, about their attempts to better Afghan lives and to convince Afghans that America was looking out for them. "It is one of those horrible realities of life," Patty Ward wrote, that a young woman "who was very highly regarded by many governments who worked with her, a talented, optimistic, extremely well-educated negotiator, who left a void that is impossible to fill, should be victimized by someone who had not the slightest notion of the terribleness of the act he was performing." When Ayala learned that Loyd had been burned, he must have thought of all that he knew about her—the good she had done and would have continued to do on America's behalf, her contributions to a more humane approach to conflict, the pleasure of her company, "the glory of her smile"—and responded instinctively. It made perfect sense to Ward. While she waited for the plane carrying her wounded daughter, a hospital chaplain had asked if Loyd's attacker had been "dispatched." On hearing that he had, the chaplain had bowed his head and thanked the Lord. Standing next to him, Ward had murmured: 'Thank you, Don.'

A person who commits the crime of voluntary manslaughter knows what he is doing, even if he acts out of passion. In the statement of fact that Ayala signed as a condition of his guilty plea, the prosecution and defense agreed that he had killed Abdul Salam intentionally "upon heat of passion and without malice," and that his act "did not result from accident, mistake or other innocent reason." And yet, not wanting to leave any room for doubt, Nachmanoff added another element to his defense. In preparation for his sentencing, Ayala spent two ten-hour days at his home in New Orleans talking with a human development and trauma specialist named Dr. Charles Figley. Figley taught at Tulane University's Graduate School of Social Work and headed its Traumatology Institute and Psychosocial Stress Research Program. He had edited a book on combat trauma and advised the Navy and Marine Corps on combat stress–related injuries. Figley prepared a report based on his conversations with Ayala. It was filed under seal, and it became a linchpin of the defense strategy. In it, Figley sought to show that Ayala's repeated exposure to violence

146

over many years had led to a psychic breakdown that had caused him to kill Abdul Salam.

In the upstairs study of his Garden District home, with his three Rhodesian ridgebacks dozing at his feet, Ayala had told Figley about his childhood in Whittier, a middle-class suburb east of Los Angeles. He was the third of five children born to a government meat inspector and a teacher's aide, themselves the descendants of Mexican immigrants who had sweated in slaughterhouses, meatpacking plants, and factories for a shot at the American dream. Ayala and his brothers played baseball, football, and basketball and shared a single bedroom, roughhousing like a pack of young dogs. They rushed through chores so they could play war in the backyard, hurling lemons plucked from a tree as grenades.

It was an idyllic childhood. But in junior high, some kids pushed Ayala up against a locker and asked what neighborhood he came from. The school had kids from all over, and they were just beginning to understand the geography that would define them. Ayala was thirteen, thin and small, but he had grown up with brothers and he knew how to fight. He and his friends banded together, joining a neighborhood gang called Sunrise. Long before Ayala gained a reputation as a peacemaker, fighting had been the way he survived. He fought in school and on his own time, in organized bouts or just because. He fought at a roller rink, at a movie theater, on a busy street. Sometimes the gangs would organize baseball or football games that devolved into fistfights. He grew into Sunrise organically, until he was so far gone that his older brothers grew afraid to acknowledge him in the hallways at school. Meanwhile, his neighborhood roughened. There were drive-by shootings. Ayala pitched all through Little League and into high school and quarterbacked the football team. He was regarded as a leader in sports and on the streets, where he was sharp and watchful, a good fighter. He also liked to draw, and he was good at it. He became a sought-after tattoo artist, using ink-dipped needles filched from his friends' mothers' sewing baskets and sterilized with a lighted match.

He started getting thrown out of school for fighting. He didn't come home for days, and the more his mother nagged and yelled, the further he receded. His father set up chairs on the back lawn, sat him down, told him there would be consequences. His mother kicked him out of the house. He lived with classmates and their families. One friend, depressed and deep in drugs, tied a sheet around his neck and jumped out a window. Ayala, then seventeen, came home and found him. When the holidays rolled around, he would leave the home of whichever friend he was staying with so the family could celebrate together. He went to the movies or walked the streets alone.

The gang brought pain, but it also gave him power. Ayala's high school principal sought him out to help negotiate a truce between rival gangs. He started dating an older girl from the neighborhood and soon she was pregnant. Ayala's father sat him down in the backyard again. You did this, his father told him. You need to be responsible. You don't bring kids into the world and not care for them. When the baby was born, Ayala would stuff diapers and wipes in his pockets and carry his infant son out to the corner to hang with his friends.

He wanted to quit school and join the military, but he wasn't old enough and his mother wouldn't sign the papers for him. She told him to wait until he was eighteen. After high school, he enrolled at a local community college, where he played baseball and dreamed of the majors. Then one winter Saturday night he was driving around with some guys from Sunrise when they heard that a friend had been shot while ordering tacos from a fast-food truck. They rushed to help him, but on the way they ran into a carload of guys from a rival gang and got into a shoot-out, driving fast as they fired. When they saw lights and heard sirens, they turned a series of corners and tossed the guns beneath roadside ivy bushes one by one. With the cops behind them, they ran a red light and T-boned a truck. The police cuffed them all and hauled them to jail. They charged Ayala and his friends with assault with a deadly weapon, but they didn't find the guns.

In jail, a group of rival gang members beat Ayala so severely that he woke up chained to a hospital bed. He looked in the mirror and didn't recognize himself. He was disappointed that his gang friends hadn't stepped in to protect him. He was disappointed in himself. When he got out, he had lost his spot on the community college baseball team, and he never went back. Instead, he went straight to the Army recruiter's office. He was assigned to the 82nd Airborne Division and that spring, he boarded a plane for Georgia to start basic training. It was his first flight, and he had never been so happy.

After what he'd lived on the streets, basic training felt easy. He liked the structure and the whiff of adventure, and most of all he liked being away, far from the darkness, the drugs and suicides. He quickly established himself in his platoon as a scrappy fighter. One night when they were all trying to sleep, a big black guy from Boston ordered a meek white kid to shine his shoes. The smaller soldier told the big man to leave him alone, but the guy wouldn't stop. Finally, Ayala couldn't take it. 'Listen, why don't you go back to your bunk, go shine your own shoes,' he said. 'We're trying to get some rest here.'

'What are you going to do?' the big guy said.

Pretty soon Ayala was out of bed and had the other recruit under a bunk, smashing his head against the bed frame. Drill sergeants came in and everyone spent the next two hours outside, in push-up positions, in their underwear.

In spite of the discipline or maybe because of it, Ayala excelled at basic training as he never had in high school. He racked up high scores on physical fitness and qualification tests. He learned to parachute out of helicopters. In airborne school, someone pulled him and a handful of other young soldiers aside and offered them slots in a Ranger battalion if they could survive the training. The Ranger Indoctrination Program started with forty-seven men. By the end, only thirteen were left, and Ayala was one of them. He was assigned to the Second Ranger Battalion in Fort Lewis, Washington.

In the fall of 1983, at the height of the Cold War, Ayala's unit was sent to Grenada to stop the Soviet Union from gaining a new strategic foothold in the Caribbean. A coup had unseated the Grenadian prime minister, the left-wing military had seized power, and the Rangers were ordered to take control of the island's main airport. As they neared the landing strip, rounds hit the bellies of their aircraft. The pilots flew off and doubled back, and someone told the Rangers to get ready to jump. They parachuted in from five hundred feet, lower than Ayala had ever practiced. They landed on the runway and fought their way to the control tower.

The next day, they flew to a different part of the island to rescue a group of stranded American medical students—the "hostages" everyone back home was talking about. On the way, Ayala's helicopter was shot down and crashed in a cove. No one was seriously hurt, but they had to destroy the chopper in place and board another. They found the students huddled together in a room, loaded them onto helicopters, and flew them to the airfield. That night, their mission complete, they turned in their ammunition and grenades and celebrated as they waited to fly home. But the next morning, the officers passed out the ammunition again. Several hundred soldiers from the leftist Grenadian military were dug into a training base on the other side of the island. The Rangers were going to confront them.

Ayala and the other men boarded Black Hawk helicopters. As they skimmed over the treetops, one copter took fire and crashed into another. A third chopper struck the first two, and in the tangle, several

Rangers were chopped to bits. Eight or nine Rangers, including Ayala, were ordered to collect the wounded and the dead. He had been trained never to leave a fellow soldier behind, but he'd assumed that the bodies would be whole. They worked with medics, building piles of remains that would be loaded into body bags. One of the dead men had gone through the Ranger Indoctrination Program with Ayala. Another had been celebrating with him the night before. They had found some wine and Cuban cigars at the airfield, and the man had raised a toast. Less than twenty-four hours later, Ayala gathered up what was left of him. When he and his fellow soldiers got back to Fort Lewis, people greeted them with banners and marquees that said "Job well done, Rangers!" and "Welcome Home!" Operation Urgent Fury was Ayala's first lesson in the difference between a war's ground truth and the way people saw it back home. He felt proud and tried not to think about the body parts strewn amid the trees.

He left Fort Lewis the following year and moved back to Southern California, where he joined the 12th Special Forces Group in Los Alamitos as a weapons sergeant, deploying briefly to Honduras and Panama. It was a reserve unit, so Ayala returned to civilian life. He got a job delivering wrought iron fences, went to school at night, and eventually built a career in telecommunications. He married and had two more sons. But he missed the Army, so he reenlisted in the 1990s, joining a Special Operations team training drug enforcement agents. He and his wife divorced, and Ayala needed cash for alimony and child support. A Special Forces buddy had started a company that offered bodyguards for hire, and Ayala started working for him on the side. When the mayor of Moscow came to Los Angeles, Ayala and a team of contract security guards protected him, along with astronaut Buzz Aldrin and TV and radio host Larry King. Then came September 11 and the invasion of Afghanistan. In 2002, the same friend told Ayala that the State Department was looking for bodyguards to work overseas. Ayala applied and a few days later, the phone rang. It was DynCorp, the private security company hired to protect Hamid Karzai, the new president of Afghanistan.

He spent about fifteen months guarding Karzai, but in early 2004, he was lured to Iraq by a job protecting American officials in the Coalition Provisional Authority at a salary of twenty-eight thousand dollars a month, nearly twice what he had been paid in Afghanistan. At first, he lucked into protecting a high-level American diplomat in Irbil, the relatively peaceful capital of Iraqi Kurdistan, where the green hills and waterfalls reminded him of California wine country. But soon he was back in Baghdad, escorting American executives up and down Route Irish, as coalition forces called the road from the airport into town. Every day, they passed burning vehicles on the roadside, some belonging to other, less fortunate protection details. They were ambushed and trapped by attackers who pulled ahead and to either side of them, blocking the road and forcing them to stop. Men dropped grenades from bridges as Ayala's convoy sped below, and gunmen fired as they passed, or launched "rolling ambushes," in which cars hurtled down highway on-ramps, pulled alongside convoys, fired, and exited at the next opportunity, disappearing into the labyrinth of the city. Ayala and his team lived in a fortresslike compound near the airport. At night they would sit on the roof drinking cold beer and watching insurgent rockets and mortars arc overhead, aiming for the American soldiers at Camp Victory.

The skills and techniques of a bodyguard are not those of a soldier. Soldiers are trained for offensive action, while bodyguards call themselves "bullet catchers" because they step into danger on purpose. Being big and tough is helpful in close protection, but mental acuity matters more. The job rewarded the alertness that had distinguished Ayala as far back as his gang days, a sensitivity to the tension running through a crowd, a feeling for what was coming before it happened. Bodyguards are taught to scan their surroundings for color, contrast, and movement. Look for patterns, they're told, and don't just look, *see*. Pay attention to hands, not faces. Concentrate on midsections, where guns and bombs hide beneath layers of cloth. If something happens, a bodyguard's first thought isn't to take out the assailant. He puts himself between the attacker and the principal, brings the principal to the ground if necessary, and gets him out of there.

On the morning of Ayala's sentencing, a sunny day in May 2009, I drove to the federal courthouse in Alexandria, Virginia. Ayala and his family stood out front dressed in dark, tailored clothes. His girlfriend, Andi Santwier, was petite and blond, with waxen skin and a torch singer's raspy voice. She wore a dark suit and big sunglasses that hid her eyes, but the tightness around her mouth suggested the intensity of her effort to hold herself together. They looked like mourners at a graveside as they shook hands with well-wishers. The brick courthouse stood across the street from a manicured park where office workers ate lunch on benches in warm weather. I crossed the park slowly. Ayala stood with his back to me, but he was easy to pick out, a man in a dark suit with the bearing of a Secret Service agent. We had never met in person, but when I drew within twenty feet of him, Ayala turned and looked back over his shoulder, staring directly at me. He reached to shake my hand, greeted me by name. This was the uncanny sense of peripheral vision—an awareness not just of what lay in front of him, but of who stood behind him—that had made him such a gifted bodyguard. During a visit to Maiwand earlier that spring, I had wondered aloud whether Ayala might have been angry with himself for failing to protect Loyd. His former team leader, Mike Warren, had nodded curtly. When Ayala shot Abdul Salam, Warren told me, he had really been shooting himself.

Ayala and his supporters filed into the courthouse a little before

9 a.m. When his case was called, he left Santwier's side and moved to the defense table. His lawyer, Michael Nachmanoff, outlined the aspects of the case that the defense and prosecution agreed on: that Paula Loyd's death was a "tragedy." That she had endured "unimaginable suffering" and death as a result of Abdul Salam's attack. "We also agree that Mr. Salam deserves no sympathy," Nachmanoff told the judge. Ayala's victim had "committed an unspeakable act against an unarmed woman who had dedicated years of her life to helping the Afghan people."

Federal sentencing guidelines set a range of sanctions for every crime, from probation to prison time. The actual sentence can vary based on a defendant's criminal history and other factors, but the judge usually chooses a sentence somewhere within the guideline range. For manslaughter, the guidelines recommended six to eight years in prison. Nachmanoff was asking the judge not to imprison Ayala at all, but to sentence him to probation, an outcome that even the public defender viewed as unlikely. Still, it was worth a try. A judge is not bound by the sentencing guidelines if he believes the appropriate sentence lies outside them, and Nachmanoff would argue that if ever a case warranted a departure from the guidelines, Ayala's was it. Most voluntary manslaughter cases involve fights: drunken barroom brawls, a husband coming home to find his wife in the arms of another man. Crimes of passion constitute the legal "heartland" of manslaughter, but Ayala's offense fell well outside this familiar territory. He had killed Abdul Salam on a distant battlefield at a moment of perceived imminent danger to himself, his teammates, and the soldiers. The struggle to subdue the Afghan had been "very violent," a soldier had told Army investigators, and the detainee, though physically slight, had fought hard, even trying to grab one of the soldiers' guns. They'd had reason to think that the assault on Loyd might be part of a more complex attack, and in that context, the defense argued, Salam could be seen to pose a continuing threat, even with his hands cuffed behind his back.

A victim's behavior—his role in provoking the attack that kills him—is an important factor in manslaughter sentencing. In Abdul Salam, Ayala had encountered "the kind of provocation that I think this court has never seen and I hope will never see again," Nachmanoff told the judge. Paula Loyd had been unarmed, asking questions and taking notes, when Salam doused her with gas and set her on fire. Her assault was "a terrorist act," for which the Taliban had claimed responsibility, Nachmanoff said. Ayala, on the other hand, was not just an accomplished and law-abiding American, but an "outstanding individual, a hero . . . who's dedicated his adult life to public service and protecting others." If Ayala's friends and relatives were surprised that he had killed the Afghan, the soldiers of the 2–2 were no less so. Ayala routinely scolded them for "morbid jokes" and "frequently encouraged us to be very gentle" with Afghans, Lieutenant Pathak, the platoon leader, had told Army investigators.

Anyone would have been angry at what Salam had done, Nachmanoff told the judge. But anger didn't fully explain what had happened or why. What did explain it, according to the defense, was an error of judgment resulting from nearly lifelong exposure to violence and combat trauma. A manslaughter sentence can be reduced if the defendant can prove he was "suffering from a diminished capacity," and this was where Charles Figley, the trauma specialist, came in. When Ayala had shot Salam, Figley surmised, he had been suffering from "a significantly reduced mental capacity" brought on by battle fatigue and trauma. In a life of combat, Ayala had been shot at eight times and physically assaulted three times, Figley wrote. He had cleared and secured homes or other buildings on eighteen occasions, twice helped to clear makeshift bombs, and witnessed two explosions. On five occasions, he had known someone who was injured. He had seen the dead bodies of enemy fighters, soldiers, civilians, and children more than a dozen times, and handled the bodies of dead American soldiers twice. He had experienced "intense fear" in combat on five occasions, and twice thought he would not survive. These experiences, Figley wrote, had significantly impaired his judgment. The accumulated weight of them had made it impossible for him to understand, in that moment in Maiwand, that his behavior was wrong and to stop himself. The attack on Paula Loyd had led to a convergence that had "awakened" Ayala's "previously dormant combat stress injuries," Nachmanoff argued, causing him to shoot Salam.

Ayala had already been severely punished, Nachmanoff told the judge. As a felon, he would be forbidden to carry a gun or get a security clearance, making work as a battle zone contractor impossible. Then, turning to the rows of chairs behind him, Nachmanoff asked Ayala's supporters to stand. As if choreographed, the somberly dressed men and women who filled the visitor's gallery rose to their feet in a single motion. Patty Ward was there, pale in a ruffled shirt and black jacket, and Loyd's half brother, Paul. Nearly everyone in the courtroom stood. "He's affected many, many people in his life in a positive way," Nachmanoff told the judge. "The government wants the court to impose a punishment now based on one moment, one act."

Assistant U.S. Attorney Michael Rich rose to address the court. He was in an unenviable position. Early on, the government's case had seemed admirably straightforward: it was advocating on behalf of a handcuffed victim and defending the laws of war. But this simple and compelling narrative had lost much of its potency since the defense had filed photos of Ayala handing out stuffed animals to Afghan children, the letter from Paula Loyd's mother endorsing Ayala's execution of her daughter's killer, and a moving sentencing documentary in which Loyd's boyfriend, Frank Muggeo, had said that punishing Ayala would amount to a terrorist victory. Rich was a veteran himself—a retired Marine general who had led the Corps's Judge Advocate Division before becoming a federal prosecutor. He had taken his LSATs in Da Nang, Vietnam, the year before Michael Nachmanoff was born. Now he found himself arguing for the punishment of a man he seemed unwilling to blame.

"Ms. Loyd and her friends and supporters and family deserve all of our sympathy," Rich told the judge. "Abdul Salam, the nominal victim in this case, the person whose despicable act set these terrible events in motion, deserves none, and neither does the defendant, Your Honor, which I hasten to add is not to say that we don't empathize with what the defendant did. He did what he thought he had to do. Whether it was morally or philosophically right is for each of us who know the facts of this case to individually decide for ourselves. Whatever the answer to that question is, Your Honor, what he did, most assuredly, was not legally right."

Here Rich ceded the battle for the better narrative, retaining only the cold comfort of the law. It was not an auspicious strategy. Figley's report was "a bunch of psychiatric mumbo jumbo," Rich told the court. Ayala was having it both ways: "He can't be a hero on the one hand and somehow be mentally deficient on the other. It simply doesn't wash." But in the next breath, he found himself almost defending Ayala for shooting the Afghan out of "passion born of friendship and respect for Ms. Loyd, passion born of abhorrence of what Salam had done to her, passion exercised in the heat of the moment."

Rich was not arguing for six to eight years' imprisonment. He agreed that Ayala's crime merited a more lenient sentence. Yet he was defending one of the most basic rules of combat: that capturing forces are forbidden to shoot prisoners. Ayala was not some green young soldier. He had years of training and experience, Rich told the court, and he knew better. When he killed the handcuffed detainee, he had threatened to erase much of what had been drilled into the heads of the impressionable young soldiers he'd been accompanying. A tough sentence would make the point that prisoners could not be killed with impunity, that no matter how angry you got, killing a captive was wrong.

In the legalistic realm of his written filing, Rich had pursued Ayala with greater verve than he now seemed able to muster in a courtroom filled with Paula Loyd's relatives. "The facts and circumstances of this case are not complex," the prosecutor had written. "It was an execution." He went on to highlight the fact on which the battle of narratives turned, the fact that Nachmanoff had so successfully exploited and that, had Ayala's crime occurred on an American street and not an Afghan one, would have been impossible to obscure. "We know much about Paula Loyd and the defendant," Rich had written, "but very little about Salam."

In the emotionally charged courtroom that day, Salam remained a cipher. Had he been American, or even a citizen of some more developed and less frightening country, a country where America was not at war, his crime would have been no less heinous, but neither would he have been such a complete blank. Indeed, if Salam had been described to the judge as anything other than simply a "terrorist," he would not have been entirely deprived of sympathy by the government prosecuting his murder. In constructing Ayala's defense, Nachmanoff had tried to show that people are complex, that every act grows from a dizzying web of antecedents, and that punishment should be based on a life's entirety rather than a single instant. He had urged the judge not to punish Ayala "based on one moment, one act." But it was impossible to overlook the fact that, in this Virginia courtroom, Abdul Salam's life had been reduced to one moment, one act.

Only a couple of small gestures by the government even hinted at the fact that Salam's backstory was entirely absent from consideration.

"All we know about Ayala's victim, Abdul Salam, is that he was a 'frequent stranger' in the village where he died," Rich wrote in his sentencing memo. "We know nothing at all about what caused him to torch Paula Loyd. But we do know that when Ayala executed him, he was no longer a threat to Ayala, or his other teammate or the soldiers who were with them. In fact, Salam was his prisoner. That is what makes this a serious offense."

A few days before the sentencing, the government had entered fifteen photographs into evidence. They were pictures that agents from the Army's Criminal Investigation Division had taken when they traveled to Maiwand the day after the killing. In some, Lieutenant Pathak, the platoon leader, restaged Ayala's killing of the Afghan. A soldier playing Salam lay on the dirt path with his hands behind his back, while Pathak, pretending to be Ayala, knelt behind him with his knee in the man's ribs. One photograph showed Salam's forearm bearing a rudimentary tattoo of his name, which means "Servant of Peace." In another picture, Salam's dead body lay on the path, his feet toward the river. A stain darkened the sand beneath him, and a body bag waited a few feet off. The most disturbing picture was taken at close range. In it, Salam's body was unnaturally twisted, his head bent away from the camera. He had been turned on his side to reveal that his hands were still bound behind his back. He was small and thin and his tunic was hiked up to reveal the pale skin above his hip. The ground beneath his legs was wet from the stream, where Jack Bauer had wrestled with him. Blood ran from his head, small black rivers in thick dust.

When Rich finished speaking, Judge Claude Hilton looked up from the papers scattered across his desk. He asked if Ayala had anything to say. Ayala walked to the podium and stood there, solid as a wall in his dark suit.

"The day of November 4, 2008, I wish it never occurred," he said, his voice soft and gravelly. "I'm standing here in a not so very favorable position, but whatever is imposed on me, I will continue to serve honorably and professionally. Thank you."

In the gallery, Santwier sat next to her father, a criminal defense lawyer who had devoted many hours to Ayala's case. Loyd's half brother and his wife held hands as Judge Hilton began to speak. Although the guidelines called for a sentence of six to eight years, the judge said, the facts of the case called for less. Salam's attack on Loyd had provoked his killing, "and would provide provocation for anyone who was present there at the time." Ayala had a sterling record of military service and had led a productive life. "You can't forget that this didn't occur here on the streets," Hilton said. "This occurred in a hostile area, maybe not right in the middle of a battlefield but certainly in the middle of a war. Considering all those things, it will be the sentence of the court, Mr. Ayala, that you be placed on probation for a period of five years—"

He wasn't going to prison. Gasps and sobs drowned out the judge's words. Loyd's mother hunched forward, leaning against her husband, her shoulders shaking, and Loyd's half brother and sister-in-law cried in each other's arms. The judge was saying that Ayala would have to pay a $12,500 fine, that he wouldn't be allowed to work in security or protective services, that he would have to undergo whatever mental health counseling his probation officer required, but Ayala was already standing and hugging his lawyer and Santwier, and everyone spilled out into the hallway, where Patty Ward threw her arms around Loyd's half brother and someone picked Santwier up and swung her around until a bailiff came out and said, "Can you hold it down? The judge is still on the bench."

# 8. Good Intentions

n the months after Paula Loyd was attacked, I retraced her steps. I flew to Zabul, the poor province in southeastern Afghanistan where she had worked for USAID, and to Kabul, where, one evening, I mentioned her name to a member of Afghanistan's Independent Human Rights Commission. He had known Loyd but hadn't heard of her death, and when I told him what had happened he sat still and stared at the floor. After a while he rose and walked to his computer to search his email inbox for her last note to him. I switched off my audio recorder, feeling like a voyeur.

By early 2009, the Human Terrain System was showing signs of strain. Paula Loyd had been the third Human Terrain social scientist killed in the field in eight months. The previous May, a brilliant thirty-one-year-old former Marshall Scholar named Michael Bhatia had died when a roadside bomb exploded near his Humvee. It had happened in Sabari, whose gentle green hills and winding lanes conjure a nineteenth-century landscape painting and mask its status as one of the most violent places in Khost, the eastern Afghan province where the first-ever Human Terrain Team had seen such success. A month later, Nicole Suveges, a thirty-eight-year-old graduate student at Johns Hopkins, was killed when a bomb exploded during a meeting she was attending in Baghdad's Sadr City. By the fall of 2008, reports of trouble on the teams were multiplying. It emerged that among the Human Terrain social scientists deployed to Iraq were several who knew nothing about Iraqi culture, who had done their field research in Latin America or with Native Americans or among Dumpster divers, ravers, punk rockers, and Goth kids. In Afghanistan, a Human Terrain Team leader and other male team members mocked a female teammate, writing the Spanish words "Mata La Vaca," or "Kill the Cow," on a whiteboard in the team's office at Bagram Air Base. The woman interpreted these words as a death threat and accused her team leader of sexual harassment. A military investigation found that she was not alone. Men on the team had displayed pictures of naked women around the office and several other female team members had been subject to insults, ethnic slurs, and unfair work assignments. The military asked that the team leader and another male team member never again be deployed with their unit, the 101st Airborne Division Special Troops Battalion, but the men kept working for the Human Terrain System. Meanwhile, the United States was planning to send more troops to Afghanistan and the Army wanted more Human Terrain Teams. In early 2009, shortly after Loyd's death, the Pentagon more than doubled its requirement for field teams in Afghanistan.

Paula Loyd, Don Ayala, and Clint Cooper had trained in Kansas before their deployment, so in February 2009, I flew out to Leavenworth. The training consisted of four to five months of classroom work that included basic social science and research methods, military rank structure, and courses on culture and history tailored to Iraq or Afghanistan. There was also a period of several weeks known as "immersion," when trainees bound for Afghanistan spent time at the University of Nebraska in Omaha, studying Dari and talking with Afghan-Americans, while those headed for Iraq undertook a special course at the University of Kansas.

The program's administrators told me that the most interesting part of the training cycle would be the final week, when proto–Human Terrain Team members took part in a practical exercise to test what they had learned. The exercise was called Weston Resolve, named for the town of Weston, Missouri, near Leavenworth, where some of it took place. The Human Terrain System's press handler, former Army intelligence officer Lieutenant George Mace, described Weston Resolve to me as "a practicum in doing ethnography in any kind of village." Mace was a veteran of the first Human Terrain Team in Iraq, and when I phoned him from my rental car after landing in Kansas City, he quickly directed me to the National Public Radio station on my FM dial. Reporters visiting from Washington were under no circumstances to be subjected to Middle America's standard menu of conservative talk, Christian preaching, and country music, at least not when they were writing about a project that billed itself as a politically liberal fringe movement within the Army. My minder that week in Kansas was Major Robert Holbert, an Army reservist and former high school social studies teacher who had served on the first Human Terrain Team in Afghanistan, and who embodied the offbeat, left-leaning vibe the program sought to project. A convert to Islam with a shaved head, Holbert drove a Saab and listened to the Sex Pistols.

Human Terrain System training took place in the basement of a brick mini-mall in downtown Leavenworth called the Landing. It stood a couple of blocks from the railroad tracks and the Missouri River, which lunged along thick and sullen behind a stand of trees. The old federal prison and the sprawling Army garrison that anchor the town lay about a mile to the northwest. Fort Leavenworth is home to mid-career master's programs for officers; it is where the nation's biggest service contemplates its past and tries to get ahead of its future. The Human Terrain System laid claim to this spirit of military intellectualism, but if the rolling lawns of the base conjured a gracious university, the Landing had the dismal, downtrodden feel of an underfunded community college. Trainees shuffled between classes in a warren of bare rooms whose windows, if they had any, looked out on a parking lot.

The trainees I met that week were to leave for Iraq or Afghanistan within a few months. They included a former soldier who spoke Dari; a female information operations expert who had advised the military in Iraq and at the Pentagon; a middle-aged Lebanese-American woman who spoke Arabic; a cultural anthropologist and self-published novelist who had done fieldwork among male prostitutes, homeless alcoholics, and drug users; a quiet, levelheaded Army captain with a law degree; and a flamenco guitarist with a PhD in theology who had done counterterrorism work for the FBI that she declined to describe in detail. Weston Resolve was an elaborate game that began with the imagined secession from the United States of a big swath of territory between the Dakotas and Missouri. In keeping with this fictional turn of events, separatist groups and criminal elements were supposedly making trouble in eastern Kansas, burglarizing a pharmacy in Leavenworth, among other misdeeds. The United States government feared that crime syndicates and terrorists would commandeer this unstable new quadrant of the heartland for their own ends, and they sought to bring the revolt under control. The trainees' job was to figure out as unobtrusively as possible what kind of people lived along the Kansas-Missouri border and to gather information about their customs, values, and beliefs. They would deliver their findings in the form of a military briefing to retired officers and National Guardsmen hired to play the role of battlefield commanders.

The exercise began early on an icy morning in a parking lot a few blocks from the Landing. I followed the trainees around as they interviewed a young woman making smoothies at a local gym, a man on an exercise bike, mall walkers, college students, and people eating lunch at the food court on the nearby military base. The trainees asked people about their greatest successes and failures, whether it was appropriate in their culture for a little girl to talk to an older man she didn't know, and what they had worried about most in the last month.

"I've lived in Leavenworth my whole life and it's very trashy," the girl behind the smoothie counter told them. "That's my personal opinion."

"What's the most offensive thing you've seen someone do in public?" one of the trainees asked.

"Shoot someone," the girl said.

"What's the worst thing a friend can do?"

"Go behind my back and cheat with my boyfriend that I'd had for two years."

The Human Terrain System had been sold to the Army as a means of providing cultural knowledge to battlefield commanders. But as I watched the trainees interview residents near the Kansas-Missouri border, it became clear that whatever information they would be providing did not stem from any special knowledge of Iraqi or Afghan culture. Practitioners like Loyd, a former soldier with extensive experience in nongovernmental organizations and significant time on the ground in Afghanistan, were rare. I met only a few trainees with comparable experience during my visits to Leavenworth and my time with Human Terrain Teams in Afghanistan. Instead of offering cultural expertise, the Human Terrain System was training recruits to parachute into places they'd never been, gather information as quickly as possible, and translate it into something that might be useful to a military commander. One of the few Human Terrain social scientists I met with relevant experience, a PhD candidate in anthropology who had done his dissertation fieldwork in Afghanistan, would describe his Human Terrain work as "windshield ethnography."

Clint Cooper and Don Ayala had found their training in Kansas disappointing, as had nearly every other Human Terrain Team member I would speak with. Ayala in particular told me that the courses were ill-conceived and flimsy, but the quality of his fellow trainees discouraged him most. Thrown together at the Landing were former intelligence officers, defense industry contractors, social scientists of various and often conflicting persuasions, military reservists, and immigrants with language skills. They would have been an awkward group under any circumstances, but Ayala was appalled by their lack of discipline. People ate and answered cell phones during class, coming and leaving as they pleased, sniping and complaining as if they were still in high school. Almost anything could lead to an overheated argument, particularly the question of whether the Human Terrain Teams would be gathering intelligence. If someone mentioned the word *intel*, a social scientist would say, 'We're not supposed to be doing intel!' and an ex-military guy would say, 'What's the big deal?' and someone else would say, 'Okay, well, then, we'll just call it information.'

To Ayala, these disputes were as baffling as they were irritating. Like many former soldiers, he viewed the anthropologists' concerns as narrow and irrelevant. If they could help Iraqis and Afghans, what were they waiting for? At the same time, he understood that his job was to take photographs, collect demographic information, log villagers' concerns, count their livestock, research their water sources, and bring all that back to the military unit to which he was attached. The military could use the information any way it wanted—for development projects or to find and destroy the enemy. People who didn't get that had obviously never been to Iraq or Afghanistan and had no concept of what they'd signed up for. The project's determination not to use the word *intelligence* struck him as an unvarnished attempt to appease the academic community from which it hoped to recruit, a community that had already grown suspicious of the enterprise. The Human Terrain System's administrators masked the realities of deployment because they didn't want to scare social scientists, Ayala told me, but their coyness had consequences. Bhatia and Suveges had been killed while Ayala was in training. He had attended their memorial services in Leavenworth before heading to Afghanistan himself. He came to believe that the program's murkiness about its goals was part of the problem. "This is what was getting people killed out there," he would tell me later. "Bottom line, you can't sugarcoat anything. This is a combat zone."

The project's nebulousness of purpose wasn't something people talked about loudly or often, but the suspicion that it played a role in the injuries and deaths of Human Terrain Team members never went away. Everyone said that those deaths were unavoidable, that this was war and in war people got killed. But it didn't help that teammates often shared little beyond a very general understanding of what they were doing and why. In the words of one former Human Terrain Team member, they specialized in "that touchy-feely thing that no one understood." Some thought they were part of a humanitarian aid mission. Others thought they were there to tell the commander why local people supported the insurgency. Still others saw it as a chance to play spy. Philosophical disagreements split the teams, making a difficult job even harder. Human Terrain Team members were going into active conflict zones to do things that variously resembled ethnographic research, intelligence gathering, psychological operations, and humanitarian aid. Holbert, who worked in the training directorate when Loyd and her teammates were preparing to deploy, agreed with Ayala. "If you go into a totally unknown area with an unclear mission, bad things are going to happen," Holbert told me.

The deaths of Bhatia and Suveges made Ayala angry. In 2008 and for several years afterward, trainees got no operational security training in Kansas, no survival skills beyond a brief medical course, no firearms training. "As a member of a 5-person HTS team, you will be safely attached to a brigade combat team," read a cheerful 2008 recruitment brochure from BAE Systems, the big defense contractor that hired Human Terrain Team members. But what could being "safely attached" to a United States military unit in Afghanistan possibly mean? Some military units gave their Human Terrain Team members guns, but often the civilians had little or no idea how to use them. When Ayala completed his training, he told me, the Human Terrain System gave him a certificate saying that he had completed five days of weapons training. Everyone else in his class—about sixty-five people—got the same piece of paper. He knew how to shoot, of course he did, but that wasn't the point. "The only range I saw during the training course was a driving range at a golf course," he told me later.

I had expected to find wide-eyed hopefulness and team spirit at the Landing. Instead, trainees indiscreetly alerted me to who was disliked and disrespected. On my first morning there, the cultural anthropologist in the group I was observing told me he didn't want anyone to know who he was. When I reminded him that I was a reporter and pointed out that the information he had already given me—including his surname and the name of a university where he had taught—would likely identify him, he grew agitated. "I'm an anthropologist," he told me. "I have a lot of anthropologist friends, and I don't want to get a bunch of emails telling me I'm the scum of the earth for joining this program." When we met again many months later in Afghanistan, he would tell me that he had always been "well to the right" of his colleagues, and that he felt the United

States' invasion of Afghanistan had been justified. But like so many others, he had his own reasons for being there. "I'm not interested in doing anything to defend this program," he told me. "This program deserves to go down in flames. But it's an opportunity to do something good now."

Maybe because of the recent deaths, including Loyd's, the Landing in February 2009 had a tense, fevered quality. It was deep winter and cold, and when my days of interviews ended I drove the arrow-straight farm roads with relief, taking in the flat yellow fields, the freight trains chugging past heaped with coal, the chilly emptiness of the landscape.

*       *       *

In March 2009, I flew to Kandahar to embed with AF4, the Human Terrain Team to which Loyd, Ayala, and Cooper had belonged. The team had been reconstituted since Loyd's attack. A sixty-four-year-old psychologist from Texas had taken her place, a middle-aged former marine had filled Ayala's spot, and a young man with a master's degree in Central Asian studies had replaced Cooper. Unlike their predecessors, none of them had ever been to Afghanistan.

I wanted to believe in the Human Terrain System's capacity to make the U.S. military smarter, but the more time I spent with the team, the more confused I became. The psychologist, a tall man with wire-rimmed glasses named Karl Slaikeu, was a can-do type who had apparently figured out how to solve Maiwand's security problems before ever setting foot in Afghanistan. One afternoon, I watched as he tried to convince two Canadian soldiers and a USAID officer who had been in Afghanistan far longer than he had that he understood the place better than they did. Later, I asked one of the Canadians what he thought of the Human Terrain Team members. "I don't know where they got these guys," the Canadian soldier told me, shaking his head.

Slaikeu had been issued an assault rifle but neither the Human Terrain System nor the Army had trained him to use it. He'd gone out and shot on a range near his home in Texas, and one of his teammates had taken him to shoot on a military range in Afghanistan. The former marine who had replaced Ayala went by the nickname Banger. He wore a thick beard, carried copious ammunition, and sometimes advised Slaikeu not to chamber a round when we traveled in armored vehicles for fear the bespectacled social scientist's gun might fire by mistake when we went over a bump.

Early in my visit, when I was just getting to know the Human Terrain Team members, I accompanied Banger and some soldiers to a barbecue at a nearby Afghan army base. I liked Banger. He was refreshingly unpretentious. He had grown up on a farm in Iowa, and his understanding of rural, agrarian culture gave him a winning ease with the Afghan farmers he met on patrols. The Americans had organized the barbecue to celebrate the Persian New Year, Nowruz, and to boost the morale of the local Afghan army unit they were mentoring. They brought boxes of burgers, Rice Krispies treats, soda, and Gatorade, but the Afghans had other ideas. They invited the Americans to join them on a patch of gravel near the kitchen, where the cooks were about to slaughter a goat for lunch. Banger and I went along to watch.

We were deep in the Afghan south, but I noticed that many Afghan soldiers at the base were Tajiks from the north. The commander came from Logar, near Kabul. This was not unusual; the Afghan army has had much greater success recruiting Tajiks than it has Pashtuns. As we stood there, two Afghans dressed in Army fatigue pants and plain T-shirts grabbed a goat that had been loping around the yard, bound its feet with a thick yellow hose, and pushed it to the ground. One man held the goat's feet while the other laid his hands on its head and moved two fingers along its throat. The goat bleated softly. The man at the animal's head brought a blade to its neck, and with a quick, heavy thrust, sliced its windpipe in half. Blood poured onto the ground. When the wound had run dry, the two men dragged the goat to a piece of burlap, where one of them nicked the animal's skin along its back leg and put his mouth against the opening. He blew until the goat's body swelled like a beach ball, then sliced its inflated skin down the middle. He began to methodically skin the animal, slicing the connective tissue so the skin and flesh separated easily. Banger and I watched in fascination.

The men who slaughtered and skinned the goat were dressed like the other soldiers, but they had smooth brown faces and the Asiatic features of Hazaras, an Afghan ethnic group concentrated in the center of the country. Hazaras have long occupied the lowest rung in Afghanistan's ethnic hierarchy, so it was no surprise that these men had the job of butchering an animal and cooking for the other soldiers. In Kabul, Hazara men haul carts like oxen and many Hazara women work as cooks and housemaids. I said something about this to Banger.

"What?" he said.

"Hazaras always get the worst jobs."

"Huh?"

It took me a few seconds to realize that he had no idea what I was talking about.

"Look at those men," I told him, motioning toward the cooks. "Do you see any difference between them and the others?"

He thought about it. "I guess," he said.

Afghan tribal structures are complex and fragmented, but the fact that there are three major ethnic groups who control various regions of the country and don't always get along is about as basic as Afghan cultural knowledge gets. That Hazaras make up an often oppressed minority is not difficult to understand if you have spent five minutes observing the country. Not knowing this is like not knowing that the Afghan mujaheddin fought the Soviets in the 1980s, that Afghan village women generally don't socialize with men outside their families, or that most Taliban are Pashtun. It would have been one thing if Banger had been an ordinary soldier. But soldiers and officers often described him and his teammates to me as "cultural experts." Banger had never before been to Afghanistan, but he had worked at the Army Culture Center and sat through five months of Human Terrain System training. I wondered how he had come so far without knowing what a Hazara was. A year later, after a lengthy deployment in southern Afghanistan, Banger emailed me: "You should interview me now! I have learned a great deal. I can also differentiate between Hazara and Pashto." He was learning on the ground, just as soldiers did.

A more culturally knowledgeable member of AF4 was the thirty-one-year-old who had been hired to replace Clint Cooper. He spoke some Pashto and asked that I identify him only by his nickname, "Spen," an Afghan approximation of "whitey." I had been warned by other members of the team that Spen was a disgruntled naysayer and that I shouldn't put much stock in what he told me. But as we walked the uneven gravel that covered the desert ground at Ramrod, Spen told me of his initial hope for the Human Terrain System and his subsequent disappointment. By far the most serious problem, in his view, was the utter lack of specific cultural knowledge or expertise among Human Terrain Team members.

What about you? I asked.

Spen turned to me sharply. "This is my first time to actually live in Afghanistan, and I don't really even live in Afghanistan," he said. "I live on an American base with lots of young men from all over the United States, a lot of wonderful young men, but I don't live with Afghans. I hang out with the interpreters, who aren't even local. They're actually all from Kabul." He traveled to Afghanistan two or three times a week when he went out on patrols with the soldiers around Maiwand. "I go to Afghanistan for half the day and I come back," he told me. "Other people have claimed I'm an expert after I've told them I'm not. The whole notion of being an expert I find very entertaining, because I think that's part of the problem of the U.S. situation in Afghanistan: we're being misled by a lot of self-proclaimed experts." Unconventional approaches were one thing, and maybe a good thing, but expertise was something else. "People are being misled about what this program brings to the table, and I personally think that needs to be corrected," Spen told me. "A soldier doesn't want to be out in the field and think that he's got a rifle that can shoot a thousand yards and then find out it can actually shoot five hundred." He was right about the lack of expertise, but the Army mostly didn't know the difference. For many young soldiers I met, cultural finesse still amounted to the response of a turret gunner one day on patrol in Maiwand, when an approaching car failed to heed the Americans' signals to slow down. The gunner remembered the Pashto word for *stop*.

"*Wadarega,* motherfucker!" he bellowed, pointing his .50-caliber machine gun at the Afghan driver's head.

That spring, the Human Terrain System was riven by an administrative change that surprised and angered many field team members. Previously, they had worked on contract. They were not technically part of the Army, nor were they employed directly by the Defense Department. Instead, they worked for private defense companies with varying pay scales and benefits. Like the original members of AF4, many were paid very well, easily earning between $250,000 and $350,000 for a year of training and deployment. But in early 2009, the Human Terrain System ran up against a new Status of Forces Agreement between the U.S. military and the government of Iraq that did away with legal immunity for foreign contractors. Under the new agreement, contractors working for U.S. forces in Iraq would be subject to Iraqi law. An official from the Army's Training and Doctrine Command emailed Human Terrain Team members and gave them a choice. They could sign on as Department of the Army civilian employees, a change that would cut their pay by as much as half; or they could quit. They had just ten days to decide. Morale among Human Terrain Team members, already low, plunged deeper. Many had already deployed to dangerous places and were counting on generous salaries. Some were just in it for the money. About a third of the project's field team members quit in disgust. The rest stayed on, but stayed mad. They had a lot of complaints, and they talked to anyone who would listen.

\*   \*   \*

In the spring of 2009, the Obama administration announced a new approach to the war in Afghanistan. The insurgency was spreading unchecked, and beating it back would require big changes. Obama had already agreed to send 21,000 more troops, bringing the total number of American forces in Afghanistan to more than 60,000; he also promised to send more qualified civilians, whose expertise was urgently needed on everything from economics and the rule of law to agriculture and development. Training for Afghan security forces would be expanded, and the Afghan government would be encouraged to reintegrate low-level Taliban. Ties between the drug trade, the insurgency, and highly placed Afghan officials would be ferreted out and cut. The United States would make a better case for the war at home, expand its diplomatic efforts abroad, and engage more frankly with Afghans and Pakistanis in the hope of winning their trust. The Obama administration called it an "integrated civilian-military counterinsurgency strategy." It came too late.

In the first few years after the invasion, many Afghans welcomed the presence of international forces in their country. The Taliban had grown corrupt and widely detested; the militia leaders who opposed them were remembered for brutalizing civilians during the factional battles of the civil war. The economy was a disaster, and millions of

Afghans had fled the country to avoid destitution and oppression. An invasion is rarely something to celebrate, but the Taliban's expulsion promised an end to Afghanistan's isolation and fed hopes that the country could reinvent itself as a functioning member of the global community. In those years, Afghanistan opened itself readily to foreigners, but the wounds of September 11 were still fresh, and most American soldiers treated Afghans with disdain. In a place of ritualized politeness, the Americans' aggressive behavior was particularly distasteful, but there was more. Because American soldiers didn't know Afghanistan's history or understand its culture, they were often misled by informants with an axe to grind, which caused them to hunt, jail, and kill the wrong people. With the Taliban in hiding and a newly installed, progressive, Western-friendly Afghan government seeking to influence villagers who had been ruling themselves for as long as they could remember, the United States chalked up the war as a win and turned its attention to Iraq. As one year slipped into the next, Afghan farmers seeded their fields with opium, the early optimism that had briefly buoyed the government gave way to corruption, and the insurgency grew. By 2009, even pro-Western Afghans had come to view the United States and its allies with skepticism. The war had been so poorly managed that it was hard to know whether any strategy at this late stage could save the Americans and the Afghans from themselves.

That summer, then–Secretary of Defense Robert Gates fired the commander of NATO forces in Afghanistan, General McKiernan, making him the first general to be removed from command of a theater of combat since 1951. McKiernan was said to be too plodding and conventional to undertake the new strategy, but he and his predecessors had never enjoyed much latitude for bold moves in Afghanistan. General Stanley McChrystal, then director of the Pentagon's joint staff and a veteran of the Special Operations Forces, took McKiernan's place. McChrystal had spent two years supervising kill-and-capture teams targeting high-level insurgents in Iraq. In his assessment of the Afghan war that summer, he proved willing to tell unpleasant truths. "[M]any indicators suggest the overall situation is deteriorating," he wrote. The insurgency was "resilient and growing," fed by "a crisis of confidence among Afghans . . . that undermines our credibility and emboldens the insurgents." A perception that the United States was not committed to the long fight left Afghans disinclined to side with the international community against the insurgents. "The key take away from this assessment," McChrystal wrote, "is the urgent need for a significant change to our strategy and the way we think and operate."

McChrystal observed that U.S. and NATO troops were ill-equipped to wage counterinsurgency. "Pre-occupied with protection of our own forces, we have operated in a manner that distances us—physically and psychologically—from the people we seek to protect," he wrote. "The insurgents cannot defeat us militarily, but we can defeat ourselves." Members of NATO's International Security Assistance Force, known as ISAF, didn't understand local languages and cultures. "The complex social landscape of Afghanistan is in many ways much more difficult to understand than Afghanistan's enemies," McChrystal wrote. "Insurgent groups have been the focus of U.S. and allied intelligence for many years; however, ISAF has not sufficiently studied Afghanistan's peoples, whose needs, identities and grievances vary from province to province and from valley to valley. This complex environment is challenging to understand, particularly for foreigners. For this strategy to succeed, ISAF leaders must redouble efforts to understand the social and political dynamics of . . . all regions of the country and take action that meets the needs of the people, and insist that [Afghan] officials do the same." Noting that key ISAF officers should be trained in local languages and serve long enough tours to make use of what they had learned, McChrystal issued an injunction to the forces under his command that would have been unthinkable in the early years of the war, when the stated mission of the U.S. military was simply to kill and capture members of the Taliban and Al Qaeda: "All ISAF personnel must show respect for local cultures and customs and demonstrate intellectual curiosity about the people of Afghanistan."

That summer, ten thousand American marines landed in Helmand, the first wave of a troop surge that would build through mid-2010. A small number of British forces had been struggling and losing ground for years in the rural southwestern province, where the insurgency had dug in and metastasized. A new Human Terrain Team, known as AF6, was sent to work with the marines at their main base, a sprawling desert outpost called Camp Leatherneck. The team's leader was Steve Lacy, a thoughtful, serious Army officer and lawyer I'd met during my visit to Leavenworth. With him were Cas Dunlap, an information operations specialist, and the former FBI analyst, flamenco guitarist, and theology PhD, AnnaMaria Cardinalli. I wrote to ask Lacy if I could visit and spend a few weeks with his team. He agreed.

Camp Leatherneck occupied an expanse of fine sand and rock that Afghans call the Desert of Death. Windstorms blew dust everywhere, under the flaps of tents, even between your teeth. Young men wrestled like gladiators on the rocky ground outside the gym, and in the Marine female officers' tent, competition for bottom bunks was fierce. One night, an officer scolded me for borrowing her ladder to climb up to my déclassé top bunk. The Taliban were out there, but in here, life sucked. The base was crawling with officers, all trying to out-politic or out-asshole one another. The atmosphere grated on everyone's nerves, and the guys on little exposed firebases in the countryside felt lucky to be away from it. The Human Terrain Team worked in a small, dark tent near the command center, sharing space with members of the Marines' fledgling Female Engagement Team. A group of translators sat nearby, crafting propaganda broadcasts for the American-run radio station on base, and the profane tirades of a senior officer could be heard through a makeshift wall. The tent was dusty and cramped, but the members of AF6 felt lucky to have desks. In the early months of their deployment, Lacy and his teammates had worked in their living quarters or in Internet cafés on Leatherneck and Camp Bastion, the British base nearby.

AF6 had been sent to Helmand too early. The team landed at Leatherneck at 3 a.m. in late April 2009, more than a month before the main Marine force arrived. Cardinalli immediately headed to Kandahar, temporarily joining the Human Terrain Team in Maiwand, where her then-fiancé, whom she'd met during training in Kansas, was also stationed. Dunlap flew north to Bagram, where she found two Human Terrain Teams whose members spent most of their time walking the kilometer that separated their offices so they could talk to each other. Dunlap was eager to get out and work with Afghans and help soldiers; she had suffered through training, but the possibilities of the job excited her. "I knew that if I got hold of some work, if I ever got a hold of that piece of meat, I would just gnaw it to the bone," she told me. She found no opportunities in Bagram.

A month later, Lacy summoned them both back to Helmand, where the Marines were settling in and exciting research possibilities were beginning to open up. But right away, more problems arose. The Marine colonel supervising the Human Terrain Team didn't know what the team was supposed to do, but to be fair, neither did anyone else. Lacy and his teammates were figuring it out as they went along. AF6 had begun with four members, but one had immediately quit and returned to the States, and of the three who remained, two were women. The Marines disliked the idea of sending civilian women out on patrols in their new area. Unable to conduct the village and area assessments they had anticipated, Cardinalli and Dunlap headed to Lashkar Gah, Helmand's capital, where the British forces weren't afraid to work with them. There, Cardinalli put together a report on homosexual behavior among Pashtun men, while Dunlap made herself useful advising British soldiers about the nuances of Taliban night letters. Night letters were threatening missives left in villages overnight for Afghans to find in the morning. The Taliban used them to intimidate Afghans so they wouldn't cooperate with NATO and the Afghan government. They worked because they belonged to the place; they had long been a tool of revolutionary forces in Afghanistan and Iran. They also testified to the insurgents' eerie intimacy with the villages and the countryside. In the morning, no one knew whether the letters had been left by an outsider or whether the author was one of their own.

A few days after I arrived at Leatherneck, I joined Cardinalli and a Marine unit known as Fox Company for an early-morning patrol to a cluster of compounds just outside the gates of the base. Cardinalli had olive skin, glasses, and long dark hair, which on this day she hid beneath a khaki bandana. She had grown up in New Mexico, where she told me she had been something of a prodigy, finishing high school at thirteen and recording her first album at fifteen. At Notre Dame, she had written a PhD dissertation linking the musical and liturgical traditions of the Penitentes, a Catholic lay confraternity in northern New Mexico, to those of Christians, Muslims, and Jews in medieval Spain. When hijacked planes hit New York and Washington on September 11, 2001, Cardinalli had wanted to help. But given her background in music and theology, a practical role in the Global War on Terror wasn't immediately apparent. Nevertheless, she got to thinking about the connection between her research on the Penitentes and intelligence work. In her dissertation, she had written that the "secrecy" of the Penitentes made their communities difficult for an outsider to penetrate. Later, she would describe her dissertation research as "directly relevant to current intelligence and counterterrorism issues" and say that while working on it, she had "employed a variety of techniques typical of intelligence, investigative, and ethnographic work." She connected her research on the Penitentes to penitential themes in Shiite Islam and served as an intelligence analyst, deploying briefly to Iraq. "Being an activist type, I had a lot of preconceptions about how the military operated," she told me. Yet she was touched by the work U.S. soldiers were doing to improve Iraqi lives.

Cardinalli was now in the final days of an abbreviated tour as AF6's social scientist, and that morning's patrol would be her last. It had grown out of a medical mission a few weeks earlier, when Cardinalli had accompanied female marines and a female Navy doctor on a visit to the small group of houses that the Marines called Settlement 1. She had gone along on the medical mission because it offered a rare opportunity to interview Afghans in the desert around Leatherneck where few people lived. When the Navy doctor had finished talking to an Afghan family and doling out pills, Cardinalli had gotten to pose a few questions of her own, though the Afghans were not as forthcoming as she'd hoped. But the thing that struck Cardinalli most forcefully was the Navy doctor's lack of bedside manner. The Afghans had seemed to grow visibly angry when they were handed small packets of six or eight pills. The Marines didn't give out large quantities of medicine for good reason; they were doing all they could to prevent overdoses. But this concern struck Cardinalli as unimportant compared to the possibility that Afghans might view Americans as "stingy." When the military doctor told people she could only give them a small number of pills, her words "were inevitably perceived by the local residents to be a lie," Cardinalli wrote later. Afghans "view American forces to be resource-rich and . . . it is inconceivable that our supply would be so limited. Instead, local residents are forced to view the Americans with the anger of unfulfilled expectations and question the team's motives for intruding upon their homes in order to provide something of such little benefit." Cardinalli wanted to make things right with the people of Settlement 1. She wanted to show them that Americans were not just rich, but generous.

Cardinalli planned to conduct a follow-up medical mission of her own. She had filled a camouflage backpack with over-the-counter cold medicine, ankle braces, Carmex lip balm, motion sickness tablets, and pain relievers. She had gathered these medicines from boxes of donations outside the chaplain's offices around base or bought them at the PX. She had no medical training beyond a brief combat first aid course, and when she told me about the mission, I wondered what the Afghans in Settlement 1 would do with all these pills and potions with their incomprehensible English instructions.

The officer in charge of Fox Company was a thirty-eight-year-old captain named Bob McCarthy. He wore his uniform open to reveal a triangle of chest and walked with a swagger. The Marines planned to hand out child-sized Crocs, knapsacks, notebooks, cooking oil, beans, and tea. Before we set out, McCarthy told Cardinalli to make sure she took time to thoroughly explain the medicines to Afghans she met. But he also cautioned that the patrol would be short—a little over two hours. Some of us climbed into a Max Pro, a giant armored vehicle, while the rest of the marines piled into Humvees. We drove about two miles over soft dunes studded with volcanic stones and climbed down near a scattering of compounds. Cardinalli and Flo, an Afghan-American interpreter from Los Angeles, pulled out a cardboard box full of book bags and school supplies. It said "The Church of JESUS CHRIST of Latter Day Saints" on the side.

"I would just watch the box," McCarthy told them. Cardinalli stuffed it back into the truck.

She and Flo made their way to the nearest compound, where an Afghan dog, long-legged and rangy, barked at them. The man of the house had a tanned, open face, a clean beard, and dark hair under a white turban. He later told me he was from Nad Ali, a place in Helmand that had seen a lot of fighting. He had bought the house and land where he and his family lived for ten thousand Afghanis, about $200. They had been there about three years, and he worked as a laborer, building mud houses. He invited us inside. Cardinalli and Flo had been here before with the female medical team. The Afghan led them through a hallway into a clean, sunlit room with mats on the floor and sleeping mattresses piled high. The walls were adorned with some of the family's prized possessions: embroidered cloths, silver serving spoons, a plastic fork, a scrub brush, a clock, and a headless doll.

Cardinalli and Flo arranged themselves on the floor across from a woman in a red sequined dress and matching headscarf. The woman had curly dark hair and black eyes, and her forehead was tattooed with blue ink. She wore thick sets of red and gold bangles, and her feet were dirty and calloused. She held a baby with a blue pacifier on her lap and eight other children of varying ages clustered around her. They were Kuchis, nomadic herders whose regular migrations had been disrupted by war and drought. Many Kuchis were now settled, but putting down roots had made their traditional herding impossible. Some had been industrious enough to farm or find work in villages, making bricks, doing manual labor, or driving taxis. Others, like the residents of Settlement 1, were desperately poor.

Cardinalli opened her bag of medicines. The Afghan man immediately assumed she was a doctor—the Marines had, after all, brought a doctor to visit his family before. He asked Cardinalli to feel his wife's stomach, which had been hurting since she had given birth to her latest set of twins. She had borne ten children in all, the man told us, and her stomach tissue had stretched. It hurt when she did chores around the house. They'd been told that she needed an operation, but they couldn't afford it.

"Tell him that I'm not a doctor, but I'm a medic, a nurse," Cardinalli told Flo. She wasn't a medic or a nurse. She and her teammates had taken an emergency first aid course before deployment, learning to clear an airway, bandage a bullet wound, and apply a tourniquet.

"Obviously I can't do an operation," Cardinalli continued, "but what I can give her is things that can help relieve the pain." She dug into her backpack and pulled out a container of Icy Hot, a cream for arthritis and joint pain. She handed it to the Afghan man. "If the tissue hurts—when it's hurting—rub this cream on," Cardinalli said. "It'll feel hot at first, but then it will help the tissue. It'll ease the pain on the inside."

The man took the cream. The woman asked for food for her baby. Cardinalli offered them a handful of honey sticks and four strawberry protein bars from the chow hall on base, suggesting they dissolve the bars in milk. The woman said she was always in pain. Cardinalli handed her some pink tablets, a generic form of Pepto-Bismol. Flo dug into her bag and pulled out a pile of scarves. She handed them to the woman and her daughters.

Cardinalli scanned the room, gazing at the embroidery on the wall. "Her work is very beautiful," she told the man. "Americans would pay good money for it." She began asking questions. Where did they get their news? From Lashkar Gah, the man said. Did the woman listen to the radio? Yes, the man told her. What kind of programs did she like? Programs for women, songs with a fast beat for women to dance to. Cardinalli dutifully recorded his answers in her notebook. The woman said nothing.

When they were done, the man walked us to the door. Outside, the marines were ornery. One of the kids had been goading the dog to bite them.

"Next time that fucking dog gets near, we're going to kill his fucking dog," a twenty-one-year-old lance corporal from Texas said.

An Afghan man in a tunic and vest appeared and led us to the next compound, which lay about five hundred yards away. I asked the man what he thought about the Americans.

"It depends which Americans," he said. "Some are tough and aggressive with us and as Pashtuns we feel kind of threatened by them."

"Tell him we're not here to threaten," Cardinalli put in. "We're here to help."

At the next house, children swarmed the marines. "You guys are a lot better than those other fucking brats," the lance corporal from Texas said.

This place was poorer than the other compound, and more ragged. Eight children crowded the room where we sat. One little girl had tangled, matted hair and glassy eyes. A boy tried to grab my water bottle. The patriarch was big and unkempt, with a loud voice and a gray beard. He wore a dirty green tunic unbuttoned at the top, a white turban, and old black shoes.

"Did you guys bring me dollars?" he asked Cardinalli and Flo once they were inside. "It doesn't matter if you speak Farsi or Pashto, I just need the medicine," he told them. "Every time I stand up I get dizzy."

"When you stand up and get dizzy, that's because your blood doesn't have enough water, it doesn't have enough fluid, so it doesn't reach your head in time," Cardinalli told him confidently.

I had no idea what she was talking about, and the big man wasn't listening. He asked again for medicine. The kids moved around uneasily in the shadows, where a thin, dark-haired woman sat. She had a shrill voice and a crescent tattooed on her forehead; more blue ink patterned her lower lip and chin. Cardinalli was asking the man about his ailments. She gave him two packages of cough drops, a bag of vitamin C tablets, and a tin of Carmex.

"That's all I get?" he asked.

The woman wanted skin lotion. Cardinalli told her to rub Carmex on her face. Flo handed out Sprite, Snapple, and grapefruit juice from the base cafeteria. Cardinalli wanted to know if they had trouble sleeping. She was holding a package of motion sickness pills. They had no problem sleeping, the man said. Cardinalli handed the woman a knee strap and an elbow band for athletic injuries.

The man wanted more. Cardinalli handed over all that was left of her plastic bag full of medicines, hurriedly explaining that he shouldn't eat a cold pack meant for icing athletic injuries. When there was nothing more to give, they remembered the book bags and shoes in the Humvees outside. The man wanted those, too. He walked them out. A few cornstalks grew in front of the house. Cardinalli asked what he did for work.

"I don't do anything," the man said. "No food, no water. We just grow a few things here."

"Does he have any other training or education?" she asked Flo.

The man ignored the question. "Tell these Americans not to destroy our country," he told Flo.

The man's children had streamed out with us, and now I watched them grab the schoolbags and shoes.

"Some people really get the idea about self-sustainment," Cardinalli said, "and some don't." She turned to the Afghan man. "What do the ladies do mostly during the day?" she asked hopefully. "How do they spend the day?"

"There's nothing to do," the man said.

"Do they have any hobbies or talents, like sewing?"

He waved the question away. When he was gone, I told Cardinalli what he had said about the Americans destroying his country.

"They live in the security that we provide. They moved here because of us," Cardinalli said testily. "So we're destroying their country!" We climbed back into the Max Pro. "It just sucks the life out of you, doesn't it?" Cardinalli asked me. "You end up kind of—sad."

She was not wrong about the complicated, parasitic relationship between the Afghans of Settlement 1 and the foreign troops who had taken up residence in Helmand. A trickle of mostly transitory Afghans—nomads, internally displaced people, returning refugees—had settled on the unwelcoming dirt around the American and British bases. Some undoubtedly hoped to benefit from their newfound proximity to foreigners, but the nature of that benefit was mixed. On the way back to Leatherneck, we stopped at a compound next to a stand of green vegetation. The plants were rooted in blackish mud, and a cornfield stretched along one side of the property. It was the only cultivated area in a sea of desert.

"This is the compound that flourishes from shit runoff," someone announced. I looked around and saw a dark stream. The Afghans were growing vegetables in the sewage runoff from the nearby military bases.

"We've told him about the health risks," one of the marines said. "He moved here because of it. Says it's good fertilizer."

On the way back to the base, I asked a sergeant whether he thought giving out Crocs, notebooks, beans, and tea could sway local opinion about the Americans.

"Some of them like us, some of them don't," he told me. "I really don't know if we've had much effect changing people's minds."

He was right. When Lacy and I stopped by Fox Company's tent the following afternoon, we learned that a military convoy had hit a buried bomb just south of the second compound Cardinalli had visited; the marines had found two other explosives buried in the road nearby. It was likely that the old man in the compound had seen the insurgents burying the bomb near his house, or at least heard about it. He had taken everything Cardinalli had to give, but he had said nothing to warn the Americans.

A fresh Human Terrain Team showed up at Leatherneck a few days later. AF7 was bound for Camp Dwyer, another base in Helmand. One morning, I found the new arrivals seated in a semicircle around Dunlap, who was briefing them about the area. The team's two social scientists, a fresh-faced young woman and a slight man in a black mock turtleneck, leaned in. A female Army major sat next to a young man in a T-shirt. The team leader, a silver-haired retired Marine officer, stood listening. Dunlap was telling them about the pro-NATO night letters she'd written for the British psychological operations guys.

"What are night letters?" one of the new team members asked.

Patiently, Dunlap explained.

The social scientist in the turtleneck spoke up. "Why don't they just put it in the mailbox," he asked, "rather than hang it up somewhere and see if they see it?"

Dunlap paused, unsure how to respond. "It's traditional," she finally said. "It's like a proclamation. This is the way they pass messages to the community."

AF7 had arrived at the beginning of a long-awaited troop surge in one of the most important parts of the country for the U.S. military, and they didn't know that mailboxes were all but obsolete in Afghanistan. Cardinalli had handed out Icy Hot to a woman with a medical condition that stemmed from having given birth to ten children in a country with dismal health care and a soaring maternal mortality rate. Was this really the best we could do?

*     *     *

Counterinsurgency was the fad of the moment, and it was all about protecting the Afghan people. But the Marines had landed in Helmand eager for a fight. In the summer and fall of 2009, the brass at Leatherneck obsessively planned the invasion of Marja, which some were calling the next Falluja. Meanwhile, a group of marines in the verdant, sandy Helmand River valley were learning plenty about local culture. Their commander, Lieutenant Colonel Bill McCollough, had served in Iraq's Anbar Province, where Sunnis had risen up against Al Qaeda. Before coming to Afghanistan, he and his men had spent three months boning up on Islam, Afghan culture, and Pashtunwali, the traditional code of the Afghan south. Eighty of McCollough's marines had studied Pashto, the main language spoken in Helmand, and they could be found practicing with Afghan petitioners who approached the gates of their small firebases. After landing in the farming district of Nawa in June 2009, they had beaten back the Taliban and transformed a deserted bazaar into a busy shopping center. They patrolled on foot day and night, sometimes sleeping in cornfields; helped resolve local disputes; and threw money at bridge repairs and irrigation projects that the Afghans badly needed. Along the way, they got to know the place well. The company I visited lived on a small stretch of rocky dirt near the bazaar, where they slept on cots in the dust or in tents open to the night air. They bought chicken, rice, and onions from local shopkeepers and cooked over campfires.

Marines are perhaps best known for killing, but McCollough's battalion exemplified the service's long-standing interest in cultural intelligence. An expeditionary force, amphibious and adaptable, Marines have a history of engagement in small wars. They landed 180 times in thirty-seven countries between 1800 and 1934, supporting "native troops" and taking on routine police and judicial functions until they could be turned over to the "native agencies to which they properly belong." A Marine Corps intelligence officer had to know the enemy leaders in his area and track their movements, but he was also expected to understand the vagaries of local politics, the workings of the economy, social mores, and "the attitude and activities of the civil population and political leaders insofar as those elements may affect the accomplishment of the mission." That is a much broader definition of intelligence than the one traditionally favored by the Army, where some believe that "intelligence" refers solely to information used to target the enemy.

A few months before my visit to Helmand, Marine Corps Major

Ben Connable had written that the Human Terrain System was a flimsy and transitory undertaking that devoured scarce resources yet was ill-equipped to meet the military's crying long-term need for better cultural intelligence. In Quantico, Virginia, the Marine Corps's Center for Advanced Operational Culture Learning was housed in trailers next to the railroad tracks. For Connable, the trailers symbolized the military's fleeting interest in initiatives that should have been ensconced in brick and cement. The military was engaged in a heady romance with all things culture-related, but what would happen when the moment passed and the money dried up? The Human Terrain System was a contractor-heavy, boutique operation that relied on field teams' ostensible separation from the intelligence cycle to recruit civilian social scientists; conceptually and practically, it was unsustainable. An Arabic speaker, Connable had served in Iraq and seen firsthand the consequences of Americans' paltry understanding of the people they were trying to win over. But he believed servicemen and -women were smart and capable enough to learn this stuff on their own. They didn't need to outsource it to civilians. The military ought to take the problem seriously enough to invest in a durable, long-term solution, he argued. The Human Terrain System was just an expensive distraction.

Connable had a point, but the main problem with the Human Terrain System was much more basic: about half the Human Terrain Team members I met over eighteen months in Afghanistan should never have been there. AF6 managed some modest accomplishments, but none of the Human Terrain Team members at Camp Leatherneck had the kind of expertise that field commanders told me they were looking for. Indeed, none of the members of that team had ever been to Afghanistan before their Human Terrain deployment. Because the marines in charge at Leatherneck didn't know what the Human Terrain Team was meant to accomplish, the team members did whatever they could, and whatever came up. Dunlap, the Human Terrain analyst, wrote night letters for the British psyops team because that was where she felt most able to contribute and where her contributions were most appreciated. Cardinalli's report on homosexuality among Pashtun men was used by a Marine intelligence sergeant to shame a young man he was questioning. Major Steve Lacy, the leader of AF6, found that the only way he could gain traction within the Marine command culture in Helmand was by meeting the operational needs of the 2nd Marine Expeditionary Brigade, which in the fall of 2009 was primarily concerned with the impending invasion of Marja, the small farming community that had become a getaway zone for insurgents fleeing other parts of the province.

That fall, a Marine officer asked Lacy to begin collecting cultural information and "open source intelligence" in preparation for the invasion of Marja. In a September 30 field report, Lacy detailed his interview with an Afghan police sergeant and landowner from the northern area of Marja, who identified the location of his home there and of a onetime police checkpoint, both of which had been taken over by insurgents. The Afghan marked the areas inhabited by several Pashtun subtribes, but he also supplied the name of the Taliban commander who had moved into his house and allegedly turned it into a bomb factory. The report included grid coordinates for important places in Marja, including the home of a local leader who had been killed by the Taliban; the home of an elder that had been occupied by the Taliban; a gas station used by insurgents "for refueling and as a gathering place"; and a Taliban checkpoint on the road to Lashkar Gah, "where the Taliban are reported to collect taxes from local residents." The source supplied the radio call sign for a Taliban commander who controlled most of eastern Marja and pointed out a minefield and a bridge rigged with explosives that the insurgents planned to use against ISAF forces. He also described the location of an insurgent campsite, a cemetery, a cell phone tower, several mosques, a school, and a number of key traffic intersections. This was not the sort of cultural information the Human Terrain System had told commanders and the public it would be gathering; it sounded more like the Phoenix Program in Vietnam than a gentle effort to learn about local people. But this was exactly the kind of information the Marines wanted. "They have a hard time, any of these guys, distinguishing sociocultural information from intel," Lacy told me. "To them, it's all the same stuff, and in a way, it is. Quite frankly, intelligence, by doctrine, is not supposed to be just classified stuff."

By late 2009, the American Anthropological Association had conducted its own study of the Human Terrain System and concluded, correctly, that the teams were not doing anthropology. The distinction was important, but it didn't entirely solve the anthropologists' problem. Anthropology remained poorly understood by the military, the intelligence community, and the public. Too many people still thought of the Human Terrain System as "that military-anthropology program," and too many press accounts still described it that way. The program had encouraged this confusion, even fed on it. In doing so, one anthropologist told me, the Human Terrain System had "set the relationship between anthropology and the government back forty years."

What most people didn't know was that a number of anthropologists in good standing with the American Anthropological Association worked for the U.S. military and other defense and security organizations in jobs that they and their colleagues deemed ethically defensible. It wasn't working for the military or the government that caused trouble, these anthropologists contended; it was *what* you did. Rob Albro, an anthropologist at American University and one of the Human Terrain System's chief critics, acknowledged a reality that some anthropologists ignored. "The military has been given a lot of shit work for which it is not prepared," he told me. "They've been given it because they are a large logistic organization. None other exists on the planet, so they get it. It's stability operations, it's nation building, it's development, it's humanitarian relief. Should they be doing these things? My feeling is, no. Are they doing these things? Of course. We have to take seriously the idea that we can, in small but significant ways, help them to do that better." Teaching culture to soldiers and marines before they deployed was one thing—and possibly a necessary thing. Conducting in-house studies of corporate culture at a big national nuclear lab was another. And deploying to an active war zone with soldiers, in uniform and often armed, to interview local people and gather intelligence, was something else again.

The Human Terrain System lied to the public and to its own employees and contract staff about the nature of its work in Afghanistan. The program did many things there, but intelligence gathering was certainly one of them. Not just, on occasion, the old-school, find-the-enemy kind of intelligence, but—in what were perhaps the program's finest moments—the cultural, demographic, and political context that could transform inscrutable Afghanistan into a place with an intact social structure and clear mechanisms for conveying power, much like anywhere else. There were bright spots, but in the end, the Human Terrain System would prove less controversial for what it did than for its sheer incompetence. Within a few months of my visit to Helmand, a Human Terrain Team member was fired after refusing to turn off her reading light during a night mission, attempting to reprimand a marine for what she viewed as inappropriate treatment of a troublesome Afghan, and spending three hours getting her hair braided in an Afghan compound while marines stood guard outside. One of her teammates, a Vietnam veteran, was sent home after he pulled a knife on a British soldier in a tent the men were sharing. By February 2010, the Marine colonel who supervised the Human Terrain Team at Leatherneck wrote in an email to a program official that the program's effort in Helmand "is a mess and I think the guys in Kabul are full of crap. If

I were king for the day, then I would start firing people at the top. . . . I am still an advocate for HTT but my patience is wearing thin. If HTT fails in Helmand, then I am not sure the program should continue to exist at all."

✳    ✳    ✳

War is a form of hysteria to which no industry is more susceptible than defense contracting. Suddenly there is money for everything, but political will is fickle, Congress mercurial, and manufacturers and program developers must move fast before the funding dries up. The moment calls for speed, and speed calls for cutting corners.

The Human Terrain System had grown too fast. In early 2007, Steve Fondacaro had accompanied the first team to Afghanistan. Soon after, the military wanted twenty-six teams instead of the original five. "We thought we had five teams and two years to build them, and it turned out we had to build twenty-six teams immediately," McFate told me. "It was kind of catastrophic." Recruitment was shoddy, and there were no systems in place to handle training and deploying so many teams. She and Fondacaro argued over how to proceed. 'Look, this is expanding too fast,' McFate says she told him. 'We need to slow it down.' They had been asked to provide Human Terrain Teams "that are going to be functional," she told me, yet too many basic questions about how the teams should be trained and how they would operate in the field remained unanswered. But the massive, heavy gears of the Pentagon had already begun to turn. Soldiers were dying, and the Army wanted what it wanted, and wanted it now.

In 2006, before the first Human Terrain Team shipped out for Afghanistan, the men of the Foreign Military Studies Office had described the proposed teams in detail. Years later, two things about that debut article in *Military Review* stand out. The first is its frankness about

193

the close connection between the Human Terrain System and military intelligence, a connection that program officials repeatedly denied. The second is its precision about the area-specific qualifications that Human Terrain Team members would purportedly possess. As the people who ultimately ran the Human Terrain System would find out, only a handful of people with detailed sociocultural knowledge of Iraq and Afghanistan existed in the United States. Many had already taken other, better-paying jobs in the defense industry, and a significant number of social scientists, particularly anthropologists, refused to work in an active war zone for the U.S. military. Jacob Kipp, the former director of the Foreign Military Studies Office, had been one of the article's authors. At the time, he told me, he had been thinking primarily about the Army's needs in Iraq. He knew several qualified reservists who spoke Arabic; he knew hardly any who spoke Pashto. And therein lay a revelation. The article was not shy about the need for intelligence skills on Human Terrain Teams because, at the time, its authors intended to staff the Human Terrain Teams not with civilian social scientists but with military reservists, for whom involvement in the intelligence cycle would be no big deal. But using reservists ultimately proved impossible. Once the Human Terrain idea gained currency, the ranks of qualified reservists couldn't keep pace with the Army's demand for teams. "Once we began to sell it, it got very popular," Kipp told me, "and we had to look at another way of finding people to do it."

I met colonels and generals who talked about the Human Terrain System as if it were the best thing that had ever happened to the Army. They included Colonel Martin Schweitzer, who had been so thrilled with the accomplishments of the first Human Terrain Team, and Colonel Mike Howard, one of the most experienced American officers I met in Afghanistan. Howard had served three previous tours there, and he had gotten to know the eastern part of the country well. During his fourth rotation in late 2009, the Human Terrain Team attached to his brigade in Khost had mutinied, refusing to work for a team leader they considered incompetent. Howard had to personally phone Fondacaro back in the States to get the team leader fired and bring in a replacement. Nevertheless, Howard was a big supporter of the teams. "My only criticism is there's not enough of them," he told me. Mike Flynn, a sharp, contrarian general who served as the chief of NATO intelligence under McChrystal and Petraeus, shared Howard's view. In January 2010, Flynn published a paper calling for "sweeping changes to the way the intelligence community thinks about itself—from a focus on the enemy to a focus on the people of Afghanistan." Because the U.S. military had directed most of its intelligence efforts at insurgents, the intelligence community "still finds itself unable to answer fundamental questions about the environment in which we operate and the people we are trying to protect and persuade," Flynn and his coauthors wrote. "This problem or its consequences exist at every level of the U.S. intelligence hierarchy, and pivotal information is not making it to those who need it." More than eight years into the war, the intelligence community remained "[i]gnorant of local economics and landowners, hazy about who the powerbrokers are and how they might be influenced, incurious about the correlations between various development projects and the levels of cooperation among villagers, and disengaged from people in the best position to find answers—whether aid workers or Afghan soldiers."

Human Terrain Teams could help solve these problems, Flynn believed. He called them an "extraordinary capability." "Whoever had that idea was a genius," he told me. What made the teams so valuable was precisely the fact that many of their members weren't "intel people," by which Flynn meant collectors or analysts who had spent their whole lives narrowly focusing on the enemy. "They're different and they're willing to take the risk," Flynn told me. "And these are people that absolutely have much better things to do, but they decided that they want to serve."

Did the people staffing Human Terrain Teams have much better things to do? Some did and some didn't. Some were bright, driven, talented people who contributed useful insights, but an equal or larger number of unqualified people threatened to turn the whole effort into a joke. If McFate knew that the pace of the Human Terrain System's growth was catastrophic, why didn't she and Fondacaro tell the Defense Department it couldn't be done at that speed? McFate and Fondacaro had told me that their recruitment process was crippled by an overly generous contract with BAE Systems, which got paid to find and hire potential Human Terrain Team members—a contract that was already in place when they started building the program. BAE kept sending the Human Terrain System unqualified candidates, including an eighty-two-year-old man and a woman who had been charged with vehicular manslaughter, but there were no accountability mechanisms in the contract when such problems arose. Convinced that the project's failures stemmed from weak hiring practices, McFate and Fondacaro had tried unsuccessfully to detach the Human Terrain System from the Army's Training and Doctrine Command, which had signed the contract with BAE. Yet all the while, they kept promoting the program as if nothing were wrong. Why had they kept insisting that they could produce the capability they had promised, when they knew they couldn't?

"Steve has the attitude that 'I can take this idea and make it real, and nothing will stop me,'" McFate told me in the summer of 2010, after Fondacaro had been fired from his job as the Human Terrain System's program manager. "You have to think about his personality. It was fill or kill—thirteen months to do it or it dies. We had some arguments at the time," she said, but in the end, "there was a war on. We felt a moral obligation to do it." And yet McFate wasn't innocent, either. I remembered something her old friend Cintra Wilson had said about her. "When she decides something, it's hard to undo her," Wilson had told me. "Even if she's wrong, it's really hard to explain why she's wrong. Actually, no, it's impossible."

Program development within the Pentagon is an exercise in circularity. An idea needs money to develop into a program, but it can't get money without stating in the strongest possible terms what it hopes to accomplish. Overselling is pretty much required. The ultimate product may not be all that its creators envisioned, but by that time the government has already invested in its development, and everyone has an incentive to keep the money flowing. The Human Terrain System had been described in the pages of military journals and briefed to commanders in glowing, best-case-scenario terms, but it was a human capability, a complex mix of brains and ambition, idealism and greed, idiocy, optimism, and bad judgment. "The problem with the Human Terrain System," Steve Fondacaro told me, "is that we have too many humans."

But the problem with the Human Terrain System was bigger than that. It had everything to do with the contradiction between the United States' self-image as a benevolent superpower and the realities of war and the economy that drives it. "American lives have become intertwined with the fate of government contracts," Irving Louis Horowitz wrote in his 1967 book on the fall of Project Camelot. How much truer those words ring today. In Iraq and Afghanistan, the military had grown interested in the problems and possibilities of nation building. Generals had stepped into the gap left by a weakened civilian diplomatic and development corps that was poorer by far than the Defense Department. The military was America's all-purpose tool: war was America's foreign aid, war was America's international diplomacy. Contractor-run programs to help the armed forces understand their new sphere of influence grew faster than summer weeds.

By 2012, the Human Terrain System had cost U.S. taxpayers more than $600 million. Fondacaro was no longer in charge by then, but in more optimistic times, he had spoken of it as a kind of mini State Department within the Defense Department. In fact, the program was a giant cultural metaphor. If you could have found a way to project on a big screen the nation's mixed feelings about its role as the sole superpower in a post–Cold War world, this was what it would have looked like: American exceptionalism tempered by the political correctness of a postcolonial, globalized age and driven by a ravenous hunger for profit. The Human Terrain System was a cosmic expression of the national zeitgeist, neatly encapsulating both a justification for war and the intoxicating belief that war could be less lethal, more anthropological. We claimed to want to understand the Afghans. What we wanted was to understand ourselves.

# 9. THE DEVIL YOU DON'T KNOW

I t seemed obvious to everyone back home that the Taliban had killed Paula Loyd. Who else could have done it? It was generally believed, moreover, that she had been singled out for this excruciating punishment because she had offended the insurgents' misogynistic sensibilities, because she was a Western woman working openly in a conservative part of the Afghan south. For those who knew and loved her, the complex array of forces that drove her killer might have been unwelcome or impossible to contemplate. Perhaps, too, his motivations would simply have proved uninteresting. The important thing was that she was gone.

But the Human Terrain System had no such excuse. "Paula Loyd, in our estimation based on the facts that we have, because of her success and because of the way she stood out—because she was an unveiled Western woman, blond, pretty, the antithesis of what the Taliban would think is the proper role of women, and she was having such success, she was so well loved, she was getting so much traction in that particular community—was, in our view, what made her specifically targeted," Steve Fondacaro, the Human Terrain System's then–program manager, told me shortly after her death. "They sought to make an example of her. The technique they used to get close to her was very well thought out, very well rehearsed. Carefully rehearsed."

"Who was the guy?" I asked. "Do you know?"

Fondacaro said he didn't. What he knew was that Loyd's killer was not from Maiwand. The insurgency had chosen an outsider to commit the attack on purpose, he told me. That way, if he were killed, locals wouldn't be able to identify him. The leaders of the Human Terrain System knew the killer wasn't from Maiwand because of something that Loyd's teammate Clint Cooper had overheard that day near the bazaar.

"You know there are a lot of kids in Afghanistan," Montgomery McFate told me. "And they were coming up and they were saying, 'Who are you? Who are you? You're not from here, who are you?' And he was kind of trying to move them out and he was saying, 'Go away, go away,' and they would say—"

"'You're not our father. You're not from here,'" Fondacaro put in.

"Yeah," McFate said. "'You can't tell us what to do. You're not our father, you can't tell us what to do.' So we know he wasn't local."

They were not the first or only ones to tell the story this way, but they were wrong. A boy who had been playing in the lane that morning had recognized Loyd's killer. When it was over, the boy told the soldiers he had seen the man around, and that his name was Abdul Salam.

*　　*　　*

Shortly after Loyd's death, I went to Kandahar to learn what I could about her killer. I worked with a tenacious Pashtun journalist named

Muhib Habibi, who came to collect me outside the gates of Kandahar Airfield. Before I arrived, Muhib had asked how tall I was. Now, as I climbed into the Toyota Corolla, he handed me a burqa he had bought in the market. I had never worn a burqa before for any length of time, but I hadn't been to Kandahar in several years, and things had changed. The synthetic blue sack with its woven eye-screen was hot and constricting, but I pulled it on without argument.

Muhib is physically fearless and will go just about anywhere for a story, but he didn't like the idea of taking me to Maiwand. "Getting there is one hundred percent," he told me. "Getting back is fifty-fifty."

Driving to Maiwand without a powerful Afghan escort seemed unwise. But by early 2009, political alliances in and around Kandahar had become so fragmented that only a few prominent Afghans could have guaranteed our protection over two and a half hours of highway that covered the outskirts of the city and the province's western districts. Since those people's allegiances might have endangered the people we would be talking to, we ruled them out. In an earlier era, we might have traveled under the protection of a Taliban commander, but that fall, a few months before I climbed into Muhib's car in Kandahar, a *New York Times* reporter had been kidnapped on his way to interview just such a commander.

The biggest threat on the road to Maiwand was buried bombs, which we might encounter no matter whether we traveled with an Afghan official or in an unmarked taxi. But the drive wouldn't have been the hardest part. Lingering there and talking to people would have been dangerous for Muhib and me, and possibly even more so for the Afghans we were visiting. Even if the insurgents didn't catch up with us, they would certainly notice that we had been to see people and want to know why. Our visit might have consequences we couldn't foresee.

We decided to start in Kandahar, meeting with elders from Maiwand who came to the city regularly on business. At the same time, we would try to make contact with Abdul Salam's family through intermediaries. I would offer to pay their taxi fare to come to the city and meet us.

The neutral place we chose for our meetings with people who might or might not be insurgents was the Kandahar office of the Afghan government reconciliation commission, a modest building behind high walls on a quiet street. Rosebushes grew in the garden and pale, wintry sunlight illuminated the room where we sat on cushions drinking tea. The commission had been set up several years earlier to bring in Taliban who wanted to stop fighting and join the government. In 2007, as many as twenty or thirty insurgents had come to Kandahar seeking amnesty every month, the director, Hajji Agha Lalai Dastagiri, told us. The government had promised to help support former fighters and protect them, but this had proved impossible. By the time we showed up in January 2009, Hajji Lalai, a provincial council member and former mujaheddin commander, was finding it almost impossible to lure anyone away from the insurgency.

The Taliban had grown and changed since I'd lived in Afghanistan as a reporter at the beginning of the war. In late 2001 and early 2002, some midlevel field commanders had cut deals with the new government and melted back into Afghan society. The Americans had killed and detained a handful of deposed Taliban leaders, while others had declared their loyalty to the Karzai government and received amnesty. In the villages, Taliban loyalists kept their mouths shut. And in Kabul, Kylie Minogue blared from car speakers, men shaved their beards and styled their hair with gel, and women walked proudly to new jobs, their headscarves pushed back to reveal several inches of hair, their open-toed high heels caked in mud.

Amid the euphoria, it was easy to forget that many prominent Taliban leaders, including Mullah Omar, were lying low in Pakistan, where they had old and powerful friends. But by 2003, the insurgents were edging back. Using Pakistan as a base, they attacked American forces along Afghanistan's eastern border. In the south, a new, more extreme brand of Taliban were targeting aid workers and sabotaging Western-funded reconstruction projects. Then came the assassinations: a moderate, progovernment mullah here, an earnest, progressive police chief there. One by one, the insurgents picked them off. Afghans had been weakened by decades of war, and few remained unbroken. Now, simply advocating progress was becoming deadly, not just for the outspoken ones, but also for their families.

By the time I visited Kandahar in 2009, the insurgency's tendrils had spread into government and the business community, its attacks motivated as much by economic gain as by political resistance. The insurgency was rooted in Pakistan, and felt largely disconnected from any meaningful Afghan national goals. Foreign fighters and outside moneymen were understandably more interested in promoting jihad and killing Americans than in prospects for meaningful reconciliation, and Afghan lives mattered little to them. To complicate matters, the power of warlord militias, criminals, and drug cartels had surged under the weak and increasingly corrupt Afghan government. Rising lawlessness made it virtually impossible to figure out which crimes were insurgent attacks and which were the work of drug dealers or ordinary bandits. For Afghans, it didn't much matter. They got killed either way.

Hajji Sadoo Khan, an Alokozai tribal elder from Maiwand and a member of the district shura, had agreed to meet us at the reconciliation office. He was an elfin man with a yellowish beard and a high-pitched voice that emanated from somewhere far back in his throat. He wore a brown turban and a khaki military surplus jacket that said "Österreich," the German word for Austria, on the arm. He said he had heard about Salam's attack on the American woman from his brother, who had witnessed it.

Abdul Salam was in his twenties, Sadoo Khan told us. He was a

poor laborer who, like many Afghans his age, had been born in a Pakistani refugee camp and spent part of his boyhood there before moving
with his family to Maiwand. For as long as most people could remember, he had lived with his father near the highway in Chehel Gazi, about
five hundred yards from the lane where he had thrown gasoline on the
American woman and set her on fire. He was married and had recently
become a father.

Salam's family owned a tractor, a rare and valuable piece of equipment in Maiwand. His father, Mohammad Umar, had worked as a day
laborer, making mud bricks and building walls, but now Mohammad
Umar was old. He had bought the tractor with borrowed money, and
his sons—Salam and his brother—used it to make a living. They did
some work for the local district government, bringing gravel to the
district center and tearing up poppy fields as part of a government
drug eradication effort, for which they were paid about five hundred
Afghanis, or ten dollars, per hour. At some point, angered by Salam's
collaboration with the government, the Taliban had captured him and
seized his tractor. Salam had pleaded with them, saying he had only
agreed to work for the government because he needed the money. The
Taliban held Salam and his tractor for several days. Finally, they offered
to let him go, but they kept his tractor, the key to his family's livelihood.
If he wanted it back, they told him, he would have to do something for
them. It wasn't clear whether the Taliban gave him a specific assign-
ment, or just assumed that he would know what "doing something" for
them meant. 'If you don't do this for us, it is easy for us to catch you,'
the insurgents told Salam, and he knew this to be true. Shortly after his
release, he saw the American woman in the market and attacked her.

Another man soon joined us, tucking himself into an armchair
and accepting a cup of tea. His name was Hajji Qala Khan, and he,
too, was an elder from Maiwand and a leader of the district shura, the
council of progovernment elders who worked with the district gover-

nor. Qala Khan looked much younger than Sadoo Khan because his hair and beard were a deep black, but he confided that he had recently married a second wife and had dyed his hair for the occasion. He wore a traditional tunic under a gray pin-striped blazer and dark sunglasses, which he never took off.

Qala Khan was a distant relative of Abdul Salam. When he heard about the attack on the American woman, he had berated Salam's father: 'What bad work you have done!' Qala Khan said he told his kinsman. 'Your son left a bad name for the people of Maiwand, to kill a woman!' Salam's father was distraught. "He just cried and screamed," Qala Khan told me. "He said, 'My son was not doing that. He was compelled to do that.'"

Qala Khan agreed that Salam had been captured by the Taliban, but he could give no details about how or when this had happened, or about the bargain that Salam had supposedly struck with the insurgents. All he knew was that Salam had disappeared for a short time. People guessed that ordinary criminals had seized him, but two nights later, he resurfaced. 'I was arrested by the Taliban and I was beaten and they have tied my hands,' he told people. Neither elder had talked to Salam directly, but both had heard this story. After Salam set the American woman on fire, villagers crowded around the crime scene, trying to figure out what had happened. 'Who did this?' they asked each other. 'This was done by the son of Mohammad Umar,' someone said. 'He was arrested a few days ago by the Taliban.' And people began to talk about how the Taliban had told Salam that if he didn't do something for them, they would kill him.

If people in modern, developed countries use stories to master the violence that occasionally disrupts their carefully ordered lives, imagine the power of stories in a place where the better part of reality is constantly open to interpretation. In Afghanistan, hard facts are exceedingly difficult to come by. Official accounts are not written down and bound into books that say the same thing every time you open them; they are not numbered and placed in investigative files like the one the Army produced on the killing of Abdul Salam. Afghan stories are told around hot coals in wintertime, changing and evolving as each teller elides something or adds something, for stories are not just a way of preserving the past, they are also sources of entertainment and works of art. A storyteller's choice of allegory over literal truth, his decision to exaggerate one detail and change another, are matters of creative agency that Afghan listeners expect. Afghan stories don't just order the world; they remake it.

The villagers who gathered near the bazaar the day Abdul Salam attacked Paula Loyd had a lot to make sense of, because the attack was unusual, perhaps even unprecedented in Afghanistan. On the Indian subcontinent, fire is linked to notions of ritual purification. The immolation of women survives in the old and now outlawed practice of sati, in which a widow throws herself on her husband's funeral pyre to expiate his sins, or because her family or community compel her. Bride burning persists in India, and immolation is a known form of domestic abuse in Pakistan, where dozens of women are also subjected to acid burns each year. But such crimes are less common in Afghanistan. Instead, Afghan women mostly set fire to themselves. Dozens of Afghan women have spoken of trying to burn themselves to death to escape domestic abuse, forced marriages, or the pain of everyday life.

The notion of burning as a form of purification lingered in the legend that sprang up around Paula Loyd's killing. If the ideologically motivated Taliban had viewed this unveiled Western woman as an abomination, perhaps they had also believed that only fire could cleanse Maiwand of her influence. Lighters bearing English lettering—in Salam's case, the word "Health" in green—and jugs of gasoline are not common weapons of the insurgency, but this would not have been the first time insurgents had chosen to attack with whatever lay nearest at hand. In 2006, at a routine community meeting in Kandahar, an Afghan man swung an axe into the head of a Canadian officer, shouting, '*Allah-ho-Akbar.*' The attack was completely unexpected, but soldiers later recalled that children had been escorted away from the gathering a few minutes before the officer was struck, suggesting that someone had known it was coming. In Maiwand, the platoon medic had told Army investigators that he saw Abdul Salam pick up a little boy and carry him inside the compound with the green door before he began talking to Loyd. The medic remembered this detail because the boy wore a skullcap that reminded him of a character from *Fat Albert*. But in this as in so much else, Salam's intentions were not entirely clear. Earlier in the patrol, another Afghan had been trying to hurry the kids along, saying they would bother the Americans. The interpreter, Jack Bauer, had his own reasons for wanting to minimize the number of children hanging around. Even an American staff sergeant had tried to disperse the kids pooling around Loyd's legs, until she told him to let them stay.

But the main problem for the people in Maiwand as they tried to make sense of what had happened was that while Abdul Salam was known as an oddball and an annoyance in the village, he was not known as an insurgent. Like the people in the bazaar, the Maiwand elders were perplexed by Salam's behavior. Salam and his family were ordinary poor people, Qala Khan told us. "They were working all the time. They were not in touch with any politics." Sometimes at night, the Taliban would fire their guns around Salam's neighborhood, and his father, Mohammad Umar, would come to the bazaar the next day and curse the insurgents. 'What's wrong with them?' Mohammad Umar would say. 'We are innocent people!' Qala Khan shook his head as he recounted this. Salam's father, he told me, was "totally against the Taliban."

The Afghans in the bazaar after Paula Loyd's attack were confronted with several pieces of "information" that didn't fit together:

This was done by the son of Mohammad Umar; he was arrested a few days ago by the Taliban; the victim was an American woman and the attack happened in the middle of the bazaar. The story of the stolen tractor and the bargain with the Taliban was a device to force into alignment an array of details that otherwise refused to congeal. Salam had said nothing to anyone, as far as I could tell, about agreeing to "do something" for the Taliban in exchange for the return of his tractor. The only evidence to support this was something else Sadoo Khan told us: that after Salam's death, the Taliban sent a message to Salam's father praising his son for killing the American woman, and returned the tractor to Salam's family.

Something else about the tractor story didn't make sense. If Salam had hoped to get it back so that he could return to work, why had he committed what was essentially a suicide attack? A platoon of soldiers had surrounded Loyd. Salam must have known they would kill him. The elders discussed this among themselves. The path down which Salam fled twisted beneath the trees, they said. Maybe he didn't know that more soldiers waited farther down, near the footbridge. If he had managed to slip into the narrow alleys between the compounds in Chehel Gazi, the Americans might never have caught him.

Sadoo Khan and Qala Khan condemned Salam's crime in the strongest terms. They were at pains to tell me that it was not rooted in or accommodated by Afghan culture. But whatever might once have been called "Afghan culture" had by now been so profoundly altered by violence and the sudden, disjointed modernity that Afghanistan had been thrust into by the war that no one could say with any certainty what it was or wasn't. Suicide attacks, unknown in the early years of the conflict, had grown common. In Kandahar, men sprayed acid at Afghan girls as they walked to school, scarring their faces and marking them forever. Maybe immolating a foreign woman surrounded by soldiers on a sunny morning in the middle of a village had likewise entered the realm of the unremarkable.

The widespread misogyny that Westerners attribute to Afghans is real enough, but it is also true that many Afghans would consider attacking a woman, especially a female visitor, more egregious than attacking a man. There was a place in Maiwand where bandits had always waited to attack caravans, Sadoo Khan told me. Even if several nights passed without any spoils and the bandits were hungry, they would not attack a convoy with a woman in it; they abstained out of respect. "I'm the grandson of Malalai," Sadoo Khan said firmly, speaking of the heroine who had roused the Afghans' fighting spirit when they defeated the British in Maiwand more than one hundred years before. "The grandson of Malalai is not killing a woman."

Like most things in Afghanistan, the mistreatment of women is more complicated than it looks. Afghan boys and young men are also frequently deprived of control over whom they will marry, how and where they will live, and who has access to their bodies. Nevertheless, it is true that many Afghans in the conservative, rural south don't like Americans or other foreigners, particularly women, wandering around their villages. I saw few Afghan women on the streets during my visits to Maiwand, and although I was never singled out for mistreatment there, I heard stories from other foreign women who ventured out in the company of the U.S. Army. A female American lieutenant who approached a patient in the local clinic to inquire about the quality of his care was stunned when he told her that she was the daughter of a whore. The acid attack on schoolgirls in Kandahar occurred shortly after the attack on Paula Loyd, and across the country, girls' schools have been burned and female teachers threatened with death. In at least one case, insurgents even threatened to burn a teacher's daughter if the woman didn't quit her job.

These divergent views on women stem in part from a clash between traditional, indigenous Afghan culture, conservative and patriarchal as it is, and the outsider culture that has grown prevalent since the Soviet invasion, and whose influence on the insurgency has become even more pronounced since 2001. The anti-Soviet war forced millions of Afghans to flee to Pakistan and Iran, where they lived as third-class citizens in refugee camps, subsisting on a steady diet of Islamic extremism that replaced the more moderate strains of Islam traditional in Afghanistan and starved them of any understanding of Afghan culture. The Taliban were the inheritors of this ignorance. Since the American invasion, the Taliban and their fellow travelers had gone back to Pakistan, where they had grown even more radical and alienated from what Afghan culture used to be. In Sadoo Khan's view, there were Afghans who lived "independently" and clung to their culture, and there were others—men he called "slaves"—who, while technically Afghan, knew little about their culture and were being used by more powerful people, often foreigners, for the latter's own purposes. The men who had thrown acid at the girls in Kandahar were slaves, the elders said, like the insurgents in Maiwand who planted bombs in the roads that killed ordinary people. "Who is giving permission for that?" one of the elders asked. "Is Islam giving that? Or the Koran? None of them are allowing this." The old men were not angry that Abdul Salam had been executed. "We are not blaming the Americans for what they have done," Qala Khan said. "We told them, 'You have done good work.' She left her country and she was in Afghanistan. Why? To help us."

The elders had one more piece of information to impart. Salam had a brother, they said, who was mentally unstable. "His brain is not working," one of the elders explained. Salam, on the other hand, had been "a very wise person, a smart person," Qala Khan said. "I never saw him with an AK, a Kalashnikov gun."

\* \* \*

Amir Mohammad worked as a police officer in Maiwand. He was off duty the day we met him at the reconciliation commission, and instead of his uniform, he wore a gray T-shirt, a tunic, a pin-striped vest, and a red and silver skullcap. He said he was about twenty-one and that his family came from Kandahar. He had thick dark hair, hazel eyes, and a steadiness that made me trust him.

Mohammad had been stationed in the district center the morning that Salam attacked Loyd. He hadn't actually witnessed it, but a fellow officer watching from the roof had seen it and cried out, and Mohammad and four other policemen had run into the street. They saw the American woman lying on the ground, smoke still rising from her body. She moaned softly, a low sound that followed the slope of her breathing. From this Mohammad knew she was alive.

Farther down the path, Abdul Salam lay on his stomach in the dirt, and Mohammad recalled that an American soldier was holding the Afghan's hands behind his back. The Americans were shouting to each other up and down the path, while Salam shook on the ground and rolled his head back and forth "just like a crazy person." Mohammad heard him utter the words *"Allah-ho-Akbar"*—God is great. "It looked like he had lost his mind," Mohammad said. Another policeman heard Salam murmur: 'Leave me, I want to go to my mother.'

What had Salam told the interpreters? *I'm crazy. Sometimes I'm walking naked in the night.* He had also said something about having epilepsy, the Afghan interpreter known as Tom Cruise later told Army investigators. Epilepsy. In this part of the world, where mental health treatment means bringing the patient to a shrine to banish the djinns, "epilepsy" is what they call it when the spirits seize you.

Amir Mohammad watched a uniformed American walk close to

where Salam lay. The American raised his gun. He walked around Salam's body and stood in front of him, aimed, pulled the trigger. Salam's face turned in the dirt. The young policeman was astonished. "What we were expecting was that they would hand Salam over to the law," he told me. "The law might execute him, might sentence him. Otherwise, if he is going to be killed on the spot, maybe the woman should have killed him. The woman was still alive at that time."

Another American soldier started talking fast to the man with the pistol. Mohammad knew a bit of English, but he couldn't understand what the soldier said, except one word, repeated over and over: 'Fuck!' the American was saying to the man with the gun. 'Fuck! Fuck!' That must have been Specialist Justin Skotnicki, twenty-two at the time and the only member of his platoon to actually witness the shooting. When I met him several months later, he was still trying to erase it from his memory. "We all know what's the right thing to do, and shooting an unarmed man in zip cuffs is not right by any stretch of the imagination," he told me, "It's one thing when someone's shooting at you, but an unarmed human being getting shot like that—it's not right."

Amir Mohammad and the other Afghan police wanted to take Salam's body into the district center, where they knew that his family would come to collect it, but the Americans wouldn't let them. After a while, the Americans brought the body to the district center themselves and instructed the Afghans to keep it there overnight. They told everyone to stay away from the dead man, even the police.

Burials are a quick business in Afghanistan, and within a few hours of his death, Salam's father and brother had arrived with a group of villagers to collect his body. When the Afghans wouldn't give it to them, Salam's brother yelled and cursed the police. He tried to grab one of their guns, and a policeman hit him. Salam had been mentally ill, his father and brother told the police. His illness must have caused him to lose his mind and attack the American woman.

Qala Khan and Sadoo Khan had told us that Salam's brother was weak in the head. Now Mohammad was suggesting that Salam himself was crazy. Stories told many times have a way of changing like this, almost imperceptibly, but here the difference was crucial. What about Salam's brother, I asked, the one who had screamed at the police and tried to grab one of their guns—did he seem mentally disturbed? Mohammad thought about it. He agreed that Salam's brother had gotten in their faces and used bad words when they wouldn't turn over Salam's body, but he didn't think Salam's brother was insane. "He was fine—normal," Mohammad told me. When one of the Afghan police struck Salam's brother for trying to grab the officer's gun, the police commander rebuked him: 'Don't hit him, just take him away. His brother is dead.'

But there was something else. Salam's father and brother told the police that Salam had attacked the American woman because of his 'mental problem and also the emotion of his heart.' What emotion could that have been? Mohammad now wondered aloud—what about this American woman had so enraged him? Had Salam seen these foreigners before? Had he argued with them, or with this woman in particular? "Were they local people, were they tribes?" Mohammad asked, incredulous. "No. They were strangers."

*The emotion of his heart.* Was Salam really an extremist, an insurgent who had somehow managed to hide this even from his relatives and neighbors? On the day Paula Loyd was attacked, the Taliban had issued a statement saying that children had poured fuel on a female foreign soldier and set her on fire while she was searching homes in Maiwand. "The soldier caught fire immediately after petrol was poured on her and then explosions were set off because of the ammunition on her," the statement said. "As a result the female soldier was killed instantly and a large number of other foreign soldiers were wounded."

The statement was interpreted by many as a Taliban claim of

responsibility, yet nowhere in it did the insurgents claim they had committed the attack, and it was impossible not to wonder why. The Afghan insurgency is prone to exaggerating its accomplishments, claiming that it has killed more soldiers and destroyed more tanks than it actually has, taking credit for assaults it wished it had had the foresight to commit. So why *didn't* the Taliban quickly and publicly claim responsibility for setting Paula Loyd on fire? Instead, the Taliban statement described a spontaneous children's uprising against the infidels, the kind of mystical event that fit neatly into the idea of Maiwand as a site of organic Afghan resistance. And it suggested that "children"—simple beings who could not always be reliably controlled—had done something that a bona fide insurgent would not have done, for this was a strange and unmanly way to attack a foreign woman. Unlike her fellow Human Terrain Team members, Loyd had not been wearing a military uniform. A civilian woman traveling with soldiers might always come under attack if the soldiers were targeted, but I had never heard of a civilian in the company of soldiers being singled out for special violence. And if the Taliban were, as some would certainly argue, too brutal to care about such distinctions, if they *had* carefully planned the attack, why hadn't they sent a suicide bomber packed with explosives into the bazaar, as they would two months later, to exact the greatest possible damage?

I wanted to hear the local Taliban's account of what had happened, so we asked a Taliban field commander in Maiwand. He went by the name Al Fathy, an Arabic nom de guerre, and he, too, was oddly silent on the subject of organizational responsibility. Salam was "a mujahid and the son of a mujahid," Al Fathy told us, using the Arabic term for a holy warrior that has been employed for generations in Afghanistan to describe armed men battling foreign occupation. Far from being mentally ill, Al Fathy said, Salam was "normal" and "perfectly well, and he could not tolerate the presence of infidels in the streets of his hometown. Because of his emotions and his Islamic fervor, and by his choice, he carried out that sacrificial act."

We asked about the tractor. Had the Taliban taken it and threatened to kill Salam if he didn't do something on their behalf?

"The Taliban did not take a tractor from him," Al Fathy said. "We did not even take a rooster from him. He sacrificed himself for the protection of his land from the infidels."

The Maiwand policeman, Amir Mohammad, didn't believe that Salam was crazy. How could a crazy man arrange such an attack, buying the petrol, throwing and igniting it, then running away? Yet like everyone else we spoke to, Mohammad was at a loss to explain what had motivated Salam. The Afghan police investigation had yielded little of interest about him. No one could remember Salam saying anything against the government or in favor of the Taliban. Mohammad had even heard that Salam had worked a few months earlier for a security firm guarding NATO logistics convoys.

Mohammad was sorry that Salam had been killed. If he had been handed over to the police, they might have learned what had driven him: "Why is he doing this? Who is behind him?" Mohammad asked. "We could get more information if he was alive." Salam's family did own a tractor, and on the morning of our conversation, before Mohammad drove to Kandahar to meet us, he had seen Abdul Salam's brother driving the tractor along a streambed in Maiwand. But Mohammad had never heard the story the elders had told, about Salam being kidnapped by the Taliban and his tractor held for ransom.

*     *     *

Agents from the Army's Criminal Investigation Division had arrived in Maiwand the morning after Loyd's attack. They wanted to see Salam's body, but it had already been released to his family. About sixty village elders and residents had come to the district center and asked the Afghan police to give it to them, and the American company commander had finally agreed, hoping to "maintain good relations with the officials he dealt with constantly," the investigators wrote, "and to prevent possible retaliation against US forces for the incident."

The investigators asked to see the crime scene. It was a clear, warm, windless day when Lieutenant Pathak took them out there. The ground was charred black where the fire had burned, but the place where Salam died had been raked clean. Where blood had pooled a day earlier, only sand remained. Looking at the investigators' photographs, you can almost hear the wind in the bamboo and feel the quiet emptiness of the lane, the warmth of the sun, the soft young grass fringing the stream.

Paula Loyd had possessed a rare kind of personal power. "She had a disproportionate effect on a lot of people," Lieutenant Colonel Dan Hurlbut, the battalion commander of the 2–2, told me when I visited Maiwand a few months after her death. For savvy Afghan leaders, her attack had also constituted a political opportunity. The governor of Kandahar went on TV to denounce Salam's crime, and prominent Afghan leaders began talking about collective punishment. General Abdul Razik Sherzai, the brother of the powerful Barakzai tribal leader and former Kandahar governor Gul Agha Sherzai, offered to "whack" Salam's entire family, Hurlbut told me. Even Ahmed Wali Karzai, the Afghan president's brother and the most powerful man in the south, had promised to "get tough." It would have been comforting to think they were motivated by Loyd's service to Afghanistan, but Wali Karzai—the man Loyd had refused to meet because she considered him a criminal—was no friend of hers. "She hated that guy," Hurlbut told me with a chuckle.

The promises to avenge Loyd's burning also indicated something else: that it wasn't an ordinary Taliban hit. People like Sherzai and Wali Karzai didn't generally promise to exact revenge on an insurgent's family—if they could have done that, the Taliban would have been much easier to defeat. Salam was a local man. People knew how to find his relatives. Indeed, the Maiwand shura elders were concerned that his family would be punished for what Salam had done. The elders were contrite, and they had only one request for the Americans. "They asked us, 'Please don't kill the family,'" Hurlbut recalled.

Salam was not a hard-core militant, but someone who "had been mentally challenged for a long time," Hurlbut told me. The insurgents might have planted the idea in his head. They might have drugged him, but even this was unclear. After the attack, Hurlbut's soldiers had overheard insurgents talking about the assault on the radio. 'We did this to him,' they said. 'We got him ready and we told him to attack that person.' But Mike Warren, Loyd's team leader, was skeptical of Taliban involvement. Salam, he told me, had been known around Chehel Gazi as "the village wacko."

"He didn't have Taliban connections," Warren told me. "He was really a guy who had some drug and mental health issues. The local police had had trouble with him before for, basically, erratic behavior." When Afghan leaders asked if the Americans wanted Salam's family dead, Warren told me, "it was like, 'No, this is a tragic accident.'"

"So you saw it as an accident?"

"Do I think it was a preplanned, premeditated attack on Paula? No," Warren said. "For twenty minutes they were having a great conversation, and something flipped in the guy's mind. I think it was the act of an irrational man, who for one reason or the other, something went wrong in his mental psyche and he attacked Paula. He tried to kill her."

I would hear a similar story later from Hajji Ehsan, the Maiwand district representative on the Kandahar Provincial Council. Salam was well known to everyone in Maiwand, Ehsan told us. He sometimes showed up at community meetings and shuras, but people tried to keep him away because he could be disruptive, so he often sat outside. "People were just making a joke of him because he was an abnormal person," Ehsan said. Sometimes they would ask him questions just to see what he would say: 'Salam *jan*, how are you? What did you see and what did you hear?' Salam would say something and people would laugh. He must have been convinced to set the foreign woman on fire without even understanding what he was doing. As Ehsan put it: "Salam was the kind of person who, if someone told him to throw this petrol at the Taliban, he would do that also."

$$* \quad * \quad *$$

Hajji Sadoo Khan, the Maiwand elder, had begged Salam's father and brother to come to Kandahar to meet us, but they refused. The father, Mohammad Umar, was old, weak, and terrified. Was it us the old man feared, foreigners who might lure him into a trap? Or was he scared of what the Taliban might do if anyone learned that he and his son had talked to a foreign journalist?

Through intermediaries, we found a cell phone number for Salam's brother. We reached him briefly, but the brother refused to talk. At last, we got through to Salam's father by phone. Muhib asked the questions, taking notes as he listened.

Abdul Salam had been about twenty-five years old, his father said. He was married with one child. He worked with his brother, driving a tractor on construction jobs and delivering crushed stone to the district center. And since childhood, he had suffered from a mental disorder that seized him occasionally, maybe twice or three times a year.

During those spells, Salam lost control. He had a history of arson. The previous year, in the crowded Maiwand bazaar, he had set fire to his motorbike and then pushed it into the water, likely the same stream where the soldiers had dunked Loyd. When Mohammad Umar asked why he'd done it, Salam had told his father: 'I did not understand what I was doing.'

"What he did with that American lady, I did not like that," Mohammad Umar said. "She did not have any kind of hostility with him, and I have never seen any kind of sign from him that he will do such bad things. But what he did, he was not in a normal condition. A normal person won't do such things. My son did not want to do those things, but the time came that he was not in control. He had changed from normal condition to abnormal."

Mental health care in Maiwand is nonexistent, but even a peasant like Salam's father knew this was not the case everywhere. "The Americans are not mentally ill," the old man said. "They are wiser than us. If someone blames my son for what he did, that is right. I agree with that. But I can prove that my son was mentally ill. Was the American who killed my son mentally ill, too? I blame him. He must not do that. I would bring him into the court."

Mohammad Umar likely meant something more like "judgment"— he would have liked to bring Ayala before a council of elders, before the shura. "They did not give a chance to my son to express his views, why he did such a bad deed," the old man said. He started to cry. "It would be better if they kept him alive in prison, or at least they could hand him over to the Afghan police. They would bring him to court. They did not do that. They killed him."

Salam was not an insurgent, his father said. He was not even a Taliban supporter. "These are all lies," he said. "I am working with the government, Abdul Salam was working with the government, and my son, Abdul Salam's brother, is working with the government. Even today, he is busy with his tractor and working for the government."

What about the story of the kidnapping and the stolen tractor? Had Salam been put up to the attack by the Taliban on the condition of getting his tractor back?

"What you were told, these are lies," Mohammad Umar said. "The truth is that the tractor was captured by the Taliban a year before this attack on the foreign woman." The Taliban had taken the tractor because the family was working for the government, bringing gravel to the district center, where it would be used to level lots and pave roads. Mohammad Umar and his sons had appealed to a local contractor to help them get the tractor back, and eventually the Taliban had handed it over. Abdul Salam and his brother had returned to work. "I wanted my son to help me and live with his young wife and help raise his children," Mohammad Umar said. "That was his ambition, too."

It was unlikely that anyone in the Maiwand shura would have seen fit to punish Ayala for killing Salam, but Mohammad Umar felt differently. He viewed his son's shooting in much the same way the Uniform Code of Military Justice and the American judicial system did.

"That American did an illegal deed," Mohammad Umar said. "When my son was handcuffed, he killed him."

# EPILOGUE

n October 2010, nearly two years after the attack on Paula Loyd, I returned to Maiwand. I landed at Forward Operating Base Ramrod amid news that a group of soldiers recently stationed there had been accused of killing Afghan civilians for sport. They had snapped pictures of themselves with the corpses, and cut off the dead men's fingers as trophies. Things had changed since Loyd, Cooper, and Ayala had arrived there, full of hope for what the Americans could achieve.

In conversation with a young American officer that fall, Abdul Salam's name came up. The Afghan police had recently told the Americans that Salam's brother was planting deadly homemade bombs around the district. The Americans and Afghans were planning to raid his home and arrest him.

The Afghan police commander who had told the Americans about this was named Hajji Ahmadullah, but everyone called him Hajji Lala.

He was built like a troll, brief and squat with a black beard, a gold watch, and rough hair sprouting from his toes. Lala was a powerful man in Maiwand. He was in charge of the police post at the district center, and the Americans held him in high regard.

Abdul Salam's brother was named Omar Bank, Hajji Lala told me. Bank was a committed insurgent, just like Salam. In fact, by Lala's lights, the whole family was a bunch of radical jihadis. Lala had learned of Bank's insurgent activities some time back, when the Americans had seen someone planting a bomb and radioed him to investigate. He had driven to the site and when he got out of his truck, he saw a man running. The police fired at the man, but he got away. They questioned some children who had been standing around. One of the boys identified the fugitive as Bank and said that Bank had given him ten Afghanis, about twenty cents, to go to a shop and buy himself corn chips for a snack. Lala surmised that Bank wanted to get rid of the kids so they wouldn't see him planting the bomb.

The allegation that Bank was Abdul Salam's brother weighed heavily against him. Abdul Salam had been "a Talib," Lala told us without hesitation—"a big person of the Taliban." He entirely rejected the notion that Abdul Salam had been mentally ill, but his argument was a self-fulfilling loop: Abdul Salam was an insurgent because his family were insurgents, and his family had to be insurgents because Salam had been one. "Is his brother also mentally sick?" Lala asked. "Then why does he love bombs and things like that?"

Lala exemplified a certain kind of old-school Afghan official whose survival depends on patronage. He griped that the Americans took his intelligence informants for granted, underpaying them and spending too much money on fuel, roads, and other "useless things." Lala had a better idea. "Give some money to those Taliban," he suggested, "and buy them." Lala had consolidated his power in Maiwand by making himself valuable to the Americans, and he knew that in some corners,

Paula Loyd's killing had not been forgotten. He had met with her the day before she was attacked, he told me. He had been on his way to Kandahar, and they had planned another meeting when he returned. He never saw her again.

A few weeks after I talked to him, Lala and the Americans arrested Bank. He was detained for a time at Kandahar Airfield. But although the Afghan police had told U.S. soldiers that they had multiple tips incriminating him, the Americans couldn't make the charge stick. They had arrested Bank in part because he had tested "weakly positive for explosives," a young American intelligence officer told me later. But the more they learned about him, the clearer it became that the tips that had incriminated him might have stemmed from a personal dispute between Bank and one of the Afghans who had informed on him. "This is just one example of the many situations we have to deal with when working with tips from locals and our Afghan National Security Force counterparts," the intelligence officer told me. "Many times they offer great information that leads to IED finds and legitimate detentions but, on occasion, there are situations such as this where the information just simply doesn't pan out." The Americans turned Bank over to the Afghan intelligence service, which promptly let him go.

The allegation that Bank and Abdul Salam were brothers also turned out to be wrong. It had been based entirely on the single, brief statement of an Afghan informant, the same informant who had reported seeing Bank detonate a bomb that struck an Afghan army patrol. "As best we know, Bank Mohammad has three younger brothers, a younger sister, and lives with his mother and father," the American intelligence officer told me. "None of our information provides any possible connection to Abdul Salam." Abdul Salam had become a symbol. He stood for violence against Americans in Maiwand, and anyone related to him was guilty by association.

No Human Terrain Team was operating in Maiwand when I visited in 2010, but the soldiers had inherited a fair amount of information from their predecessors. Their commander, Lieutenant Colonel Bryan Denny, acknowledged that there was much he didn't know—might never know—about Maiwand. "Who really controls the governance here?" he wondered aloud during one of our conversations. "Where is the shadow government for the Taliban? Who really pulls the strings?" By late 2010, the American objective in Afghanistan was to get out as quickly and cleanly as possible. Denny's job, as he saw it, was to train the local Afghan army unit so his men wouldn't have to come back.

In the United States, the Human Terrain System's administration had been overhauled. In the spring of 2010, the project had come under scrutiny from Congress and the Army, which found that it suffered from inadequate government oversight, an overreliance on unaccountable contractors, and "unprofessional conduct" that included racism and sexual harassment. Human Terrain System workers submitted time cards that exaggerated their hours, yielding annual salaries between $224,000 and $280,000 and allowing workers to take almost six months of paid leave after completing nine-month tours. The government had spent $28 million a year on a contract with a social science research unit, the quality of whose reports was "frequently questioned." It was paying contract instructors $1,200 to $1,500 a day even though they received "extremely negative student feedback."

All this had transpired on Steve Fondacaro's watch, and, faced with a mess it had helped to create, the Army's Training and Doctrine Command cut him loose. Fondacaro had been the right person to start the enterprise, an Army official told me, but the experiment had spun out of control. Fondacaro had always said he didn't want the Human Terrain System to be corrupted by the Army's DNA. "He was right to a degree," the official told me. "But at some point, it has to accept some of the DNA to be recognized as a child." Montgomery McFate quit soon afterward. She seemed exhausted. "I want to retire to obscurity and raise llamas and go surfing," she told me. Instead, she moved to Rhode Island, where she teaches at the Naval War College. The Training and Doctrine Command tapped one of its own to lead the Human Terrain System forward, and the program quietly began turning itself into an institution. By 2013, its sleek new web site described it as a "sociocultural intelligence enabling capability."

Clint Cooper had returned to Afghanistan briefly after Loyd's attack to serve on another Human Terrain Team, but he had left the program in the spring of 2009 and returned to Sierra Vista, Arizona, where he worked for the Army Culture Center, writing handbooks for soldiers about Afghanistan and Pakistan. By 2012, he was traveling often to train deploying soldiers, teaching them basic cultural cues, how to exchange polite greetings, in his words, how to "understand the Afghan frame of mind." As so-called insider attacks by Afghan security forces multiplied, he told soldiers that Afghans had distinct ideas about personal space, honor, and pride. If one of their Afghan counterparts were unhappy, he hoped the Americans would at least see it coming.

Don Ayala had gone home to New Orleans and returned to painting, between regular visits to a court-ordered psychologist and his probation officer. Although he had been sentenced to five years' probation, Nachmanoff convinced the court to release him from the system after only two and a half. In 2012, Ayala and Santwier moved back to Southern California to be close to their families. When I visited, they were still moving in. We ate dinner on a card table in the unfurnished living room, their pack of regal copper-colored ridgebacks snoozing nearby. Since his conviction, Ayala had patched together stints in telecommunications and short-term jobs training close-protection officers, but applying for steady, full-time work terrified him. He hated the idea of being rejected because he was a convicted felon. He thought often of the three lives that had ended that November day.

When Paula Loyd traveled to Afghanistan for the last time, she left behind detailed instructions in case anything should happen to her. She wanted to help bring young Afghan women to the United States to study at Wellesley College, and not just any women, but members of some of Afghanistan's most disadvantaged communities: girls from the southern provinces of Kandahar and Zabul, and ethnic Hazaras. Loyd stipulated that the scholarship recipients had to return to Afghanistan after completing their education, a noble goal but practically difficult for young Afghan women from poor backgrounds who, after four years studying in the United States, might find it almost impossible to go back to the way things were. "Your daughter was a remarkable public servant, and I know her work changed lives and helped us forge a better future for the people of Afghanistan," Secretary of State Hillary Rodham Clinton wrote to Loyd's mother in 2010. "Her spirit will live on in the wonderful work you will do and through her legacy, and in her honor, the women and girls of Afghanistan will know a brighter future."

Finding young Afghan women from disadvantaged backgrounds who spoke enough English to meet Wellesley's entry requirements proved difficult, but in the years since Loyd's death, her mother and stepfather have worked hard to secure her legacy. By 2013, they were helping an Afghan girl attend Choate Rosemary Hall. She plans to apply to Wellesley.

# Acknowledgments

First I thank the Afghans who shared their country and their stories with me. Without their patience and hospitality, this book would have been impossible. For their brains and guts, for protecting me and making me laugh, I am especially grateful to Muhib Habibi, Farouq Samim, Najib Sharifi, Waheedullah Massoud, Danish Karokhel, Bilal Sarwary, and Hassina Sherjan.

The main characters in this book participated actively in its writing. Tremendous thanks to Patty Ward and Frank Muggeo for helping me preserve Paula Loyd's memory; to Don Ayala and Clint Cooper for wanting the story told and trusting me to tell it; to Andi Santwier and Kathy Cooper for their graciousness; to Montgomery McFate, Steve Fondacaro, and Mike Warren for opening the Human Terrain Teams in Afghanistan to my scrutiny; to Michael Nachmanoff for help with the legal parts of the story; and to Rob Albro and Kerry Fosher for their insights about anthropology and its troubled relationship with the military.

I benefitted from the kindness of hundreds of soldiers and marines in Afghanistan who fed and sheltered me, shared jokes, songs, and stories, and sometimes gave up their cots so I wouldn't have to sleep on the ground. They are too numerous to mention, but I am grateful to them all. Thanks to the commanders who hosted me in their battlespace, especially Colonel Mike Howard, Lieutenant Colonel Dan Hurlbut, and Lieutenant Colonel Bryan Denny of the U.S. Army; and Lieutenant Colonel Bill McCollough of the Marine Corps. I am grateful to Generals Mike Flynn and David Petraeus for finding time in the middle of a war to share their thoughts about the role of culture in military intelligence. For their powerful insights and good spirits in challenging circumstances, and for reinforcing my faith in what America could accomplish abroad, I thank Alberto Fernandez, Matt Pottinger, Kirsten Ouimette, Jimmy Story, Trevor Voelkel, Ted Callahan, Alec Metz, Robert Holbert, Steve Lacy, Cas Dunlap, and the Kandahar CAAT of 2010.

Several years ago, I walked into Gail Ross's office convinced that I had the best story of my life. She immediately understood, and her support has never wavered. I am immensely grateful for her guidance and warmth, and for Howard Yoon's editorial skill. I could not have written this book without the intellectual clarity and dedication of my editor, Priscilla Painton. Her curiosity and persistence made me stretch time and again, and she came to believe in this story as passionately as I did. Mike Szczerban offered a critical structural suggestion that transformed this book spectacularly in the eleventh hour; he was also a complete pleasure to work with. My conversations with Elisa Rivlin were among the most challenging and enjoyable aspects of the production cycle. I am grateful to Jonathan Evans and his copy editors for their meticulous attention to the manuscript and for accommodating my many questions, and to Sydney Tanigawa for helping make this book a reality. My heartfelt thanks to everyone at Simon & Schuster, and especially to Jonathan Karp for his inspiring leadership.

Writers need encouragement, genial colleagues, peace and quiet, and enough money to keep the lights on. I am exceedingly grateful for the support of the Fund for Investigative Journalism and the Pulitzer Center on Crisis Reporting, where I have been especially fortunate in the camaraderie of Jon Sawyer and Nathalie Applewhite. In the fall of 2010, the MacDowell Colony invited me to the New Hampshire woods and gave me the keys to a cabin where James Baldwin had once written. I will always be grateful for the peace I found there, and for the brilliant artists and writers I met. Thanks to Sydney Trent at the *Washington Post*, for assigning me the story that evolved into this book; to Colin McMahon of the *Chicago Tribune* for having faith in a young freelancer many years ago in Afghanistan; and to Bill Duryea, Kelley Benham French and my former colleagues at the *St. Petersburg Times* for making me a better storyteller. Sara Breselor's stellar research skills saved me from many errors and significantly deepened some aspects of this story; her dedication and engagement provided a measure of companionship in a largely solitary effort. My deepest thanks to the Knight-Wallace Fellowship at the University of Michigan, especially to Charles Eisendrath and Birgit Rieck, for the lasting gift of time and renewal. I am grateful to Susan Douglas, Tony Collings, and the faculty, staff, and students of the Department of Communication Studies at the University of Michigan, where I've had the pleasure of teaching and learning this past year.

I am lucky to have generous, tough-minded friends who know how to listen. Anjali Kwatra, Nara Schoenberg, Candace Rondeaux, and Delphine Schrank read early versions of this book. Their insights litter its pages and their company on long walks, over many dinners or during afternoons of Lego Ninjago with Calvin and Zephy freed my mind and nourished my soul. Travis Holland and Doug Ollivant also graciously read portions of this book in draft form and offered valuable feedback. For their support and companionship along the way, I also thank Kathleen Flynn, Marc Kaufman, Vicki McClure, Scott Dempsey, Mark Oppenheimer, John Schidlovsky, Anita Huslin, Sam Roe, and the Knight-Wallace Fellowship class of 2012, especially Phillip Morris and Sarah Robbins.

My brother Sam Gezari's visual sensibility shows in every part of this book, from the cover to the typefaces. His affection and support, and his willingness to indulge in marathon games of Words With Friends, have sustained me through long days of writing and revision. When I set off to freelance in India in my twenties, my father, Walter Gezari, tried everything he could think of to talk me out of it and bring me home. Over time he has become my steadfast supporter. This book is dedicated to him and to my mother, Janet Gezari, who has been my most exacting and appreciative reader for as long as I can remember. From the beginning, she encouraged me to travel the world and chart an unconventional path, though I'm sure my long engagement with Afghanistan caused her moments of regret. Her brilliant mind, girlish delight in the physical world, and fierce love for me have been indispensible in writing this book, and in many other aspects of my life.

# NOTES

vii *My story / gets told:* Maulana Jalal al-Din Rumi, "Sometimes I Forget Completely," *The Essential Rumi,* translated by Coleman Barks with John Moyne (San Francisco: HarperCollins, 1995), 47.

*Prologue*

2 *It follows the program through the height of American involvement:* For the number of U.S. troops deployed to Afghanistan here and below, Ian S. Livingston and Michael O'Hanlon, "Brookings Afghanistan Index," May 16, 2012, 4.

*Chapter 1: Election Day*

5 *In the desert west of Kandahar:* This chapter is based on interviews with Don Ayala; Clint Cooper; the Afghan interpreters known as Jack Bauer and Tom Cruise; and soldiers of the 2nd Battalion, 2nd Regiment, of the Army's 1st Infantry Division. I have also drawn on witness statements, diagrams, crime scene photographs, and other documents included in a report on the events of November 4, 2008, prepared by the U.S. Army Criminal Investigation Command and obtained under the Freedom of Information Act. Some documents in the Army file later resurfaced as court records, and in a few instances when the Army redacted pertinent information, I have relied on the more complete version of a document submitted in federal court. I used other court records, as well as photos Ayala and Cooper took

during their time in Maiwand, as secondary sources. Finally, I have relied on my field notes, photographs, and video and audio recordings from visits to Maiwand in March and April 2009 and October 2010, when I slept on the same bases as Loyd and her teammates and walked the patrol route they walked on November 4, 2008.

5 *the soldiers thought their mission would be an easy one:* Clint Cooper described it as a "routine patrol to the Maiwand District Market and the village of Chehel Gazi which was located just south of the market. . . . We walked through the bazaar and set up a perimeter in an open area just inside the village. We were interested in finding out the value of commodities within the bazaar. Several days previous we'd been through the bazaar polling local merchants about the cost of various grains, fuel, bread, as well as other items. We were also trying to map out the local leadership structure as well as to find out more about a coalition of merchants working together within the Bazaar. There were dozens of children walking through the area on their way to school and we were handing out pens to the older kids and candy to the smaller children. Villagers would be roughly screened by soldiers at the perimeter and Paula and I would talk to them. People were very friendly and nothing seemed out of the ordinary." Cooper statement, U.S. Army Report of Investigation 08-CID369–43873–5H1.

6 *On this day they would be photographing:* "We were mapping out north Chehel Gazi, doing the entire town in sections." Specialist Justin Skotnicki, interview by author, March 24, 2009. In his statement to Army investigators, the platoon leader, Lieutenant Matthew Pathak, described the work of the soldiers and Human Terrain Team members that day as "intel gathering efforts." Statement of Lieutenant Matthew Pathak, November 4, 2008, filed in federal court, 1:08-cr-00474-CMH, May 1, 2009.

6 *'God protect us and bless us for this day':* Don Ayala remembered the words of their prayer on November 4, 2008, this way. Clint Cooper recalled: "We'd pray for safety and protection and that we would know what to do and what to say and be able to determine what the people were in need of—that we'd be well accepted." Ayala, interview by author, August 19, 2009, and Cooper, interview by author, April 22, 2010.

6 *His name was Clint Cooper:* Cooper is six foot two. Physical descriptions of him, Ayala, and Loyd are drawn in part from photographs taken during their time in Maiwand.

6 *They'd been warned:* Cooper told me: "[W]e had seen intel reports of suicide bombers and things like that in our area, so we always knew that was a possibility." Cooper, interview by author, April 22, 2010.

7 *She had been up all night:* "Paula stayed up writing the report . . . I think it was an all-nighter." Cooper, interview by author, April 22, 2010.

7 *After hearing Afghans complain:* "Patrol Report: Today We Went to the Bazaar," draft report, November 1, 2008, and Cooper, interview by author, April 22, 2010.

8 *Loyd told Cooper that she was irritated:* Cooper, interview by author, April 22, 2010.

8 *The American soldiers had noticed:* An Army medic in Maiwand told me: "She was pretty much interested in doing her job and [in] these people, local nationals. I got another word for them: terrorists. Don't write that. She loved going out on patrol."

8 *As always, she was unarmed:* Every photo I have seen of Loyd during her time in Maiwand shows her in civilian clothes and unarmed, though she did wear a Kevlar vest and a helmet. That she wasn't wearing a uniform on November 4, Army medics, interview by author, March 24, 2009, and Cooper's and Ayala's statements to Army investigators.

8 *others formed a human wall to protect them:* "She was talking with some kids when I set up my security watching the road to the north." Statement of Specialist Chad Schadewald, November 4, 2008, filed in federal court, May 1, 2009.

9 *Chehel Gazi means "forty meters":* Hajji Sadoo Khan and Hajji Qala Khan, interview by author, January 19, 2009.

9 *The Taliban were in the bazaar every day:* Don Ayala, Clint Cooper, Timothy Gusinov, and Mike Warren, "HTT Patrol Report: Maiwand District Governor Meeting," October 25, 2008.

9 *'Chalgazi Village has Taliban':* Ayala and Cooper, "HTT Patrol Report: 'Hotel' Police Station," October 26, 2008.

9 *Afghanistan was the good war:* For Obama's 2008 campaign position on Afghanistan, see "Obama's Remarks on Iraq and Afghanistan," *New York Times,* July 15, 2008, and Don Gonyea, "Is Obama in an 'Afghan Box'?" NPR, September 29, 2009.

10 *General David Petraeus, had recently taken charge:* Petraeus was named head of U.S. Central Command in April 2008, though he did not officially take command there until October 2008. Thom Shanker, "Petraeus Steps Into New Role as Head of Central Command," *New York Times,* October 31, 2008.

10 *"human terrain" as the decisive battleground:* For Petraeus's use of this term *human terrain* in 2008 and following, see General David H. Petraeus, "Multi-National Force-Iraq Commander's Counterinsurgency Guidance," *Military Review,* Sept–Oct 2008, 3. For his use of the term in relation to Afghanistan, see Petraeus's remarks at the 2009 Munich Security Conference, http://www.securityconference.de/1/activities/munich-security-conference/msc-2009/speeches/general-david-h-petraeus/, accessed March 1, 2013.

11 *Their regular translator wasn't with them:* Cooper, interview by author, April 22, 2010, and Ayala, interview by author, January 4, 2013.

11 *The soldiers gave funny nicknames:* "My unit called me Jack because they told me, 'If I called your real name, that all people from Kandahar knows about yourself, you're Afghani, or your name is —, everybody easily can memorize that name." Jack Bauer, interview by author, September 23, 2010.

11 *Jack Bauer was a twenty-three-year-old Pashtun:* Details about Jack Bauer and his relationship with the soldiers and Human Terrain Team members below are from Jack Bauer, interview by author, September 23, 2010.

11 *Jack thought that Ayala and Cooper were her bodyguards:* Jack Bauer wasn't alone in this. The platoon leader, Lieutenant Pathak, believed that Ayala's job "was to secure the HTT," Pathak wrote in his statement to Army investigators.

12 *He had been raised in Kabul:* Jack Bauer was originally from Kapisa in the center of the country. He had been orphaned as a boy and raised by his grandparents in Kabul. After high school, he'd sold DVDs and carpets to diplomats and soldiers at the NATO headquarters in the capital. He liked the soldiers he met, and he knew that Afghan interpreters made good money, so he started taking private English classes and applied for a job with Mission Essential Personnel, or MEP, the Ohio-based contractor that hired nearly all interpreters for U.S. forces in Afghanistan at the time. When the call came, his new boss asked if he would go to Kandahar. Jack knew it was the most dangerous part of the country, but he needed the money; he and his brothers had their grandparents to support. The job would pay $700 a month, a generous sum for a striving Kabul boy. He lied to his grandparents, telling them he was going to Mazar-i-Sharif, a more peaceable city in the north. In mid-August, he and a dozen other Afghan interpreters were flown to Kandahar Airfield. They gave him an American uniform, body armor, and a helmet and flew him to Maiwand the same night. At first he was terrified, but he liked the soldiers and grew accustomed to the work. By the time I met him, Jack's two brothers were also working as interpreters with American forces. "All my family is educated people," he told me. "Most of the Afghanistan people don't like the Talibans, *because they have a different culture.* They say the woman can't be educated. In my idea, that's wrong. The womans can working with the boys, too." Emphasis is mine.

13 *A young bearded man walked past:* Descriptions of the man are from interviews with Jack Bauer, Cooper, and Ayala, as well as statements from soldiers to Army investigators and photos filed in federal court.

13 *'We don't know that guy':* Cooper, interview by author, April 22, 2010. That Salam entered a house nearby, came out, and "directed some of the kids to move away from Ms. LOYD and picked up a little boy and put him in the house he just came out of," statement of a soldier to Army investigators. Cooper told the investigators: "Looking back I now realize that he was trying to shoo the kids away, perhaps in an attempt to clear the area."

13 *'ask that guy if he wants to talk to me':* Jack Bauer, interview by author, September 23, 2010.

14 *He even knew a few words of English:* Details of Loyd's exchange with the man are from interviews with Jack Bauer and Cooper and witness statements in the Army investigative report.

14 *He seemed friendly enough:* Cooper told me: "He seemed a little bit cocky. It's hard to describe. He didn't seem normal to me. He seemed like he came out of his way

to talk to us. I thought that immediately. But that wasn't uncommon . . . for an Afghan to track us down and debate one point or another with us, 'Why are you guys here?' And 'You're just causing trouble.' You know: 'The only reason Taliban cause trouble is because you're here and why don't you and the Taliban take your fight elsewhere?' We'd have that kind of debate with villagers and people all the time." Cooper, interview by author, April 22, 2010.

14 *His motorcycle was damaged:* Jack Bauer, interview by author, September 23, 2010. According to the Army investigation, an interpreter (presumably Jack Bauer) "asked the man why he had 'petrol' in a 'teapot'[*sic*], and the man said it was oil for his motorcycle."

15 *that he was a shopkeeper from Kandahar:* Jack Bauer, interview by author, September 23, 2010, and Jack Bauer statement to Army investigators.

15 *He was vaguely aware that the man with the jug:* The account here and below of the man's behavior is from interviews with Cooper and Jack Bauer, witness statements to Army investigators, and crime scene photos obtained by the author.

15 *The platoon medic, standing a few feet away:* Statement of Specialist Djeens Brun, November 4, 2008, filed in federal court, May 1, 2009.

15 *a handful of soldiers formed a loose wall:* It is important to note that while the platoon was armed and accustomed to providing security for its soldiers, it was not a protective detail for the Human Terrain Team, nor were the soldiers trained as bodyguards. As one soldier recalled in his statement to Army investigators: "I wasn't really paying attention [to Loyd] because I was too busy focusing on the LT, listening to transmissions, writing notes."

16 *Jack turned to answer, turned away from Loyd:* Jack Bauer, interview by author, September 23, 2010.

16 *Cooper was still talking to the old man:* Details here and below are from my interviews with Cooper and Jack Bauer, and witness statements to Army investigators.

17 *yelled for the soldiers to get Loyd into the stream:* "I heard a sudden rush of flame and a number of shouts. Turning around I saw Paula (HTT) engulfed in flames large enough to cause everyone around her to back off 3–5 m. As I was screaming to get her into the creek, I realized the flames were too big for anyone to approach her. Rushing to the creek, I filled my helmet with water, and instructed those nearby to help." Statement of Lieutenant Matthew Pathak, November 4, 2008, filed in federal court, May 1, 2009.

17 *He pulled her watch off her wrist:* Cooper statement to Army investigators and author interviews.

17 *unwound his cotton scarf:* Jack Bauer, interview by author, September 23, 2010.

18 *he had thought she was dead:* Specialist Djeens Brun statements to Army investigators: "[H]er body started to freeze up. [F]or a moment I thought she was died [*sic*]. . . . [S]he lost all feeling in her harms [*sic*] at that moment. [H]er face was completely burn [*sic*]."

18 *'I'm cold,' she said. 'I'm cold':* Dialogue between Cooper and Loyd here and below is from Cooper, interview by author, April 22, 2010, and Cooper's statement to Army investigators.

18 *He was lying:* "I was afraid to look at her," Cooper told Army investigators. "I cut off her helmet and her hair was still intact and I could still recognize her. . . . She asked me how she looked and I lied to her miserably, I told her she looked fine and the burns didn't look severe."

18 *'Don't worry. You're always cold':* Cooper statement to Army investigators.

19 *Ayala saw a bright flash:* This and many details below are from Ayala, interview by author, August 19, 2009, and witness statements to Army investigators.

19 *A young soldier named Justin Skotnicki:* Skotnicki, interview by author, March 24, 2009, and Skotnicki statement (undated) filed in federal court, May 1, 2009.

19 *he heard someone yell: 'Stop him!':* This was a crucial moment. "I didn't know if he was an innocent civilian that got burned," Ayala told me. "I didn't know he was the attacker." Ayala, interview by author, August 19, 2009. That someone yelled, "Stop him," and "Shoot him," ibid., and soldiers' statements to Army investigators. According to the Army investigative report: "Ayala drew his pistol and aimed at the man, but recognized the HTT and Soldiers were behind the man so he didn't fire."

20 *It took three of them to subdue him:* Skotnicki told investigators that the man only quieted after Ayala drew his pistol. "The man managed to slap one soldier in the face and push off soldiers in full kit bearing down on him," Pathak recalled. Asked if the detainee had hurt any soldiers, Pathak replied: "Only their pride." Statements of Pathak and Skotnicki, Army report and court records.

20 *something about handing him over to the local police:* Ayala, interview by author, August 19, 2009.

20 *now he was starting to panic:* "Now, I'm kind of like in a panic mode. I'm kind of worried about who's burned over there. I had a feeling who it was. And I had this antsy feeling about being around this guy." Ayala, interview by author, August 19, 2009.

20 *writhing and kicking though his hands were bound:* Pathak told investigators: "Reports to me later indicated that he wasn't, in fact, subdued, and continued to fight when the flex cuffs were put on him." After he had been cuffed, the detainee was "[j]ust flailing around, trying to get out," the investigators wrote.

20 *The man was not his responsibility:* "I felt that it wasn't my responsibility to have him, being a Human Terrain [team member]. The soldiers or the commander, they should have taken him." Ayala, interview by author, August 19, 2009.

21 *'You motherfucker!':* This is Ayala's memory of what Jack Bauer said. Ayala, interview by author, August 19, 2009. Jack Bauer told me: "I kick his face, like, two or three times." Jack Bauer, interview by author, September 23, 2010. Another soldier told Army investigators: "I saw [the detainee] get punched once in the head and then

thrown in the water. While he was in the water someone jumped down and kicked him in the side of the head."

21 *'You can't just kick people in the face':* "Don has told me, 'Hey, Jack, you don't know about our culture. It's not allowed for you, that you should be kicking somebody's face!'" Jack Bauer, interview by author, September 23, 2010.

21 *Jack Bauer was out of breath:* Jack recalled: "I speaking English, but I was scared from that happening. My tongue is not speaking English. And Don has told me, 'What's up? Can you speak English or not?'" Ibid.

21 *Ayala hauled the cuffed Afghan:* Ayala, interview by author, August 19, 2009.

21 *'Paula's burned':* "I informed Don that Paula was hurt and if he wanted to, he could go see her, because we were going to be getting her out of there pretty quick. He didn't say anything. I could see he was hurt. That's about it." Skotnicki, interview by author, March 24, 2009.

21 *The police out here were compromised:* "I wasn't comfortable with the police's situation," Ayala told me. "They were being paid off by the Taliban, because the central government wasn't paying these guys. And the police feared the Taliban. They would not go into any villages without any U.S support. And I figured he would be released and he's going to get away. The guy who attacked our patrol would have been set free and I was uncomfortable with that." Ayala, interview by author, August 19, 2009.

21 *'Why did you burn that girl?':* Jack Bauer, interview by author, September 23, 2010, and Jack Bauer statement to Army investigators.

22 *'I'm crazy,' he said. 'I cannot control myself':* Tom Cruise, interview by author, March 24, 2009: "He told me, 'I am a crazy man. I cannot control myself. Sometimes I'm walking naked in the night.'" See also Tom Cruise statement to Army investigators: "[The detainee] said at night he walks around the village naked and that he also has epilepsy."

22 *His hands were still cuffed behind his back:* Statement of a staff sergeant, Army report.

22 *'Tell this guy he's the fucking devil':* "I told Jack, 'You tell this guy he's the fucking devil.' 'Cause that's the last words I wanted him to hear. . . . And then I pushed the gun into his head, pushed his head into the ground, and I squeezed." Ayala, interview by author, August 19, 2009. Skotnicki also recalled this: "[Don] wanted [the interpreter] to tell the man that he was the devil: 'Tell him he's the devil.'" Skotnicki, interview by author, March 24, 2009. See also Skotnicki statement to Army investigators.


*Chapter 2: What You Don't Know Will Kill You*

23 *Technology increasingly allowed the Army:* Jacob W. Kipp, historian and former director of the Foreign Military Studies Office, interview by author, July 2, 2010.

24 *"What we need is cultural intelligence":* Major General Anthony C. Zinni, USMC,

"Non-Traditional Military Missions: Their Nature, and the Need for Cultural Awareness and Flexible Thinking," presentation to the Armed Forces Staff College, June 4, 1994, in Joe Strange, *Capital 'W' War: A Case for Strategic Principles of War (Because Wars Are Conflicts of Societies, Not Tactical Exercises Writ Large)* (Quantico, VA: Marine Corps War College, 1998), 267.

24 *Instead, it focused on technology at the expense of history:* Colin S. Gray, "Irregular Enemies and the Essence of Strategy: Can the American Way of War Adapt?" Strategic Studies Institute, March 2006, 32–33. Both this and Zinni's presentation are cited in Christopher J. Lamb, James Douglas Orton, Michael C. Davies, and Theodore T. Pikulsky, "Human Terrain Team Performance: An Explanation, draft" (Washington, DC: The Institute for World Politics Press. Forthcoming 2013), 13–14.

24 *But at the Foreign Military Studies Office:* Kipp, interview by author, July 2, 2010. Founded in 1986 as the Soviet Army Studies Office, the Foreign Military Studies Office had been conceived to educate the Cold War–era U.S. Army about how the Soviets thought and operated on the battlefield. Army veterans who understood the history and culture of the Soviet Union and spoke Russian worked alongside civilian academics, developing a unique intellectual culture. When the Soviet Union fell, the office changed its name and adopted a broader vision, but its hard-won knowledge of Russia and the former Soviet bloc continued to define it. In the 1990s, U.S. soldiers returning from peacekeeping missions in Bosnia complained that they hadn't been adequately prepared for the asymmetrical, urban combat they'd found there. One of them, Maxie McFarland, would later supervise Kipp and others at the Foreign Military Studies Office. Realizing that future conflicts would probably not resemble the Cold War, the Army started using social science variables to analyze operational environments, but its focus remained on technology. "I perpetually argued that it was dangerous because it didn't take culture into account," Kipp told me. "But in the 1990s, culture wasn't seen as important. We had all the people looking at advanced technology and they were saying, 'We'll have perfect transparency on the battlefield. . . . We don't have to worry about this.'" For more on the Foreign Military Studies Office, see "Foreign Military Studies Office: About Us," http://fmso.leavenworth.army.mil/About-Us.html, accessed June 26, 2012.

25 *Long before anyone envisioned an American war in Afghanistan:* Lester Grau, interview by author, July 28, 2010. Grau joined the Foreign Military Studies Office in 1989 and published his first paper on the Soviet-Afghan War in 1995. "I got into Afghanistan back when nobody could care less," he told me. "We were never going to Afghanistan." Kipp recalled: "We had to struggle to get Les to have the time to do the three books" on the Soviets in Afghanistan. The powers that be argued it was a useless project for three reasons: "'You want to do a book about the Soviet-Afghan War; the Soviets don't exist. It's about counterinsurgency; we're not going to do that. And we're never going to Afghanistan.'" Kipp, interview by author, July 2, 2010.

25 *Today, Grau's books of battlefield case studies:* Grau's *The Bear Went Over the Mountain: Soviet Combat Tactics in Afghanistan* (1996) and *The Other Side of the Mountain:*

NOTES

*Mujahideen Tactics in the Soviet-Afghan War* (1998), the latter written with former Afghan Interior Minister Ali Ahmad Jalali, are included in "Pre-Deployment Afghanistan Reading List," http://usacac.army.mil/cac2/coin/repository/AFG ReadingList.pdf, accessed June 26, 2012.

25 *Among the misapprehensions Grau and his colleagues:* Kipp, interview by author, July 2, 2010. Grau had been chipping away at the notion that technology would guarantee future military success for some time. "Future war may indeed be a computer-driven battle between high-technology systems," he wrote in 1997, but "there are limits to technology. . . . All the answers are not in the application of new technology." Lester Grau, "Bashing the Laser Range Finder with a Rock," *Military Review* (May–June 1997), http://fmso.leavenworth.army.mil/documents/techy.htm, accessed June 26, 2012.

25 *In the late summer of 2001, Kipp and Grau tried to warn the Army:* "The siren song of technology is that it will eliminate the fog and friction of war," Kipp and Grau wrote. "The reality is that the military's application of technology has usually created its own fog and friction. . . . Technology promises much—the paperless office, the perfect intelligence picture, the rapid destruction of enemy forces, the collapse of civilian morale—but it rarely delivers. . . . Cookie-cutter solutions do not work universally in different theaters, on different terrain, or against different forces and cultures. . . . The side with the greater ability to adapt, exercise initiative, and enforce tactical and operational innovations discovered during combat will enjoy success." Kipp and Grau, "The Fog and Friction of Technology," *Military Review* (September–October 2001), http://fmso.leavenworth.army.mil/documents/fog/fog.htm, accessed June 26, 2012.

25 *No longer would American soldiers see the enemy's tanks:* Kipp, interview by author, July 2, 2010. When the Army's high-tech 4th Mechanized Infantry Division arrived in Iraq in 2003, kitted out with every kind of computerized sensor, its equipment found neither enemy tanks nor high levels of detectable radio traffic, Kipp told me: "There's just [the enemy] exercising initiative by an RPG and run, or an IED, and we're blind, and we're stuck." The 4th ID was celebrated at the time as the "only division in the Army fully 'digitized' to carry out computerized warfare." See Michael Killian, "Mechanized Infantry Ships Out," *Chicago Tribune,* March 28, 2003.

25 *The enemy would fight and disappear into an urban landscape:* Kipp, interview by author, July 2, 2010, and Grau and Kipp, "Urban Combat: Confronting the Specter," *Military Review* (July–August 1999), http://fmso.leavenworth.army.mil/documents/urbancombat/urbancombat.htm, accessed June 26, 2012. "'Don't go there' remains the best advice for urban combat," Grau and Kipp wrote. "However, urban sprawl, the high-tech battlefield and the expeditionary role for US Armed Forces make this axiom problematic. . . . An urban combat training center . . . should be developed to teach urban tactics, techniques and procedures. Such a training center would need to incorporate training models that include *social, cultural, ethnic and political dynamics* as well as urban terrain features." Emphasis is mine.

239

26 *The Taliban had ruled brutally, massacring ethnic minorities:* On the Taliban's massacre of Hazaras, see among many others Lawrence Wright, *The Looming Tower* (New York: Vintage, 2007), 304.

26 *But in the fall of 2001, Afghans allied:* "War Crime in Afghanistan," Physicians for Human Rights, http://physiciansforhumanrights.org/issues/mass-atrocities/afghanistan-war-crime, accessed August 10, 2012. See also Scott Horton, "Dasht-e-Leili, Ten Years Later," *Harper's*, December 13, 2011. In Kabul, the bodies of Arabs and Pakistanis were found hanging in a pleasant downtown park, their mouths stuffed with dollars. See Kate Clark, "2001 Ten Years On: How the Taleban Fled Kabul," *Afghanistan Analysts Network*, November 13, 2011, http://www.aan-afghanistan.org/index.asp?id=2237, accessed August 10, 2012.

26 *Old tribal structures had been ravaged by war:* "In Afghanistan, power is rarely transparent," Noah Coburn, an anthropologist who has written about political power in Afghanistan, told me. "This is a very old game in Afghanistan," where there is a pattern of "stronger individuals allowing a weak person to ascend to a position that appears powerful, whereas most of the real power is behind the scenes." This subterfuge shields the genuinely powerful from direct responsibility for what happens under them and protects them from blood feuds, among other benefits. Coburn, interview by author and email correspondence, July 24–25, 2011.

26 *The Taliban were excluded:* "Talking About Talks: Toward a Political Settlement in Afghanistan," International Crisis Group, Asia Report N°221, March 26, 2012, 9.

26 *But within months of Saddam Hussein's toppling, buried bombs:* Rick Atkinson, "Left of Boom: 'The IED Problem Is Getting Out of Control. We've Got to Stop the Bleeding,'" *Washington Post*, September 30, 2007. Radio-controlled IEDs had begun to plague U.S. forces in Afghanistan in 2002, but at that time there were relatively few of them.

27 *The Army sent thousands of jammers to Iraq and Afghanistan:* Atkinson, "Left of Boom: 'The IED Problem Is Getting Out of Control,'" and Rick Atkinson, "Left of Boom: 'There Was a Two-Year Learning Curve . . . and a Lot of People Died in Those Two Years,'" *Washington Post*, October 1, 2007. Atkinson writes that by 2007, more than thirty thousand jammers of various kinds had found their way to Iraq.

27 *Beating IEDs became the Defense Department's second-highest priority:* Atkinson, "Left of Boom: 'The IED Problem Is Getting Out of Control.'"

27 *In an experiment designed by the Pentagon's joint staff:* Hriar Cabayan, interview by author, December 7, 2009, and Atkinson, "Left of Boom: 'There Was a Two-Year Learning Curve.'"

27 *The cameras had missed it entirely:* Cabayan, interview by author, December 7, 2009. The experiment, known as IED Blitz, was "a complete failure," Cabayan told me. "Not a single IED was detected."

27 *Analysts found they could use surveillance video:* Ibid. The technique, known as "backtrack-ing," was another technological fix, but Cabayan called it the "silver lining" of IED Blitz because it pushed him and others to "figure out how to connect IED emplacers within a social network, within the context of a population that is partly support-ing them." It was this kind of thinking that would lead to the creation of Cultural Preparation of the Environment and, by extension, the Human Terrain System.

28 *This kind of thinking was unfamiliar to the conventional Army:* The U.S. military had lost most of what it had learned in Vietnam, Cabayan told me: "The Colin Powell Doctrine, you go in with overwhelming force, you win, and you get out. You don't need culture to do that. So it was all lost. The Army and the Marines had to re-learn something that had gone out of their training."

28 *Retired Army Major General Robert H. Scales wrote:* Major General Robert H. Scales, "Culture-Centric Warfare," *Proceedings,* U.S. Naval Institute, October 2004.

28 *Few young soldiers knew how to gather cultural intelligence:* Remarks by Major General John Custer at the Fourth Annual U.S. Army Culture Education and Training Summit, Tucson, AZ, April 19, 2010. "Everything that you and I grew up with is irrelevant," Custer told his audience. "I'm an anachronism, and many of you are too. . . . The world has changed. Culture . . . will be a critical factor in everything we do, and let's face it, some of our failures in the past have been directly related to our lack of cultural understanding." Custer compared the role of cultural knowl-edge in contemporary counterinsurgency to that of chemical weapons in World War I, nuclear bombs in World War II, and satellites in the Cold War. "We are going to fight in sewers," Custer said. "We are going to fight clans. We are going to fight warrior-based societies forever. That's the way of the world."

28 *Slight and animated with an irreverent manner:* Cabayan, interview by author, December 7, 2009; David Schwoegler, "Pentagon Recognizes Hriar Cabayan's Decade of Service," *Newsline* (Lawrence Livermore National Laboratory) 32, no. 11 (May 7, 2007), 2; and "DOE Pulse: Science and Technology Highlights from the DOE National Laboratories," no. 235, May 21, 2007, http://www.ornl.gov/info/news/pulse/pulse_v235_07.htm, accessed June 27, 2012. Cabayan became an adviser to the joint staff in time to evacuate the Pentagon when a plane struck it on September 11, 2001. Later, he would receive the Joint Distinguished Civilian Service Award, the highest civilian award that the Chairman of the Joint Chiefs can bestow. The secrecy of his weapons work was well known, but he would come to believe that broad sharing of information and open-source intelligence among academics, military officers, and analysts was the only way to save soldiers' lives and succeed in Iraq and Afghanistan.

28 *Born in Armenia, he had been raised in Syria:* Cabayan, interview by author, December 7, 2009: "I am an Armenian and spent a lot of time in the Middle East before I came over. That was when I was young, so I'm very attuned to cultural things." For his time in Syria, see Schwoegler, "Pentagon Recognizes Hriar Cabayan's Decade of Service," 2.

28 *In the winter of 2004, Cabayan met with an Army lieutenant colonel:* Cabayan, interview by author, December 7, 2009. The other physicist was Nancy Chesser, a contractor who worked often with Cabayan. For Cabayan and McFate's first meeting, Cabayan, interview by author, December 7, 2009, and Montgomery McFate, interviews by author, January 28, 2009, and June 30, 2010.

29 *When she walked into Cabayan's office:* Cabayan, interview by author, December 7, 2009. Anthropologists are actually a stylish bunch; Cabayan's assumption betrayed his unfamiliarity with their tribe. For a photo of McFate from that era, see "ONR Conference Makes Case for Study of Cultures," *OrigiNatoR*, December 13, 2004, http://fellowships.aaas.org/PDFs/2004_1210_ORIGConf.pdf, accessed June 28, 2012.

29 *She had gone to Harvard Law School:* McFate, interview by author, June 30, 2010.

29 *Cabayan enlisted McFate to work on a project:* Cabayan, interview by author, December 7, 2009, and McFate, interviews by author, January 28, 2009, and June 30, 2010. See also Montgomery McFate and Steve Fondacaro, "Reflections on the Human Terrain System During the First Four Years," *Prism* 2, no. 4 (September 2011), 66.

30 *"About tribes alone, we got fifteen totally different answers":* McFate, interview by author, June 30, 2010. "It was a real moment of epiphany to look at that stuff because it really indicated to me that the way the intelligence community works right now in the United States, they are not focused on general social issues or general social structures or phenomena," McFate told me. "They're interested in targets for a lethal or kinetic action. So the information that they have about the society is not a collection requirement, or generally, it hasn't been a collection requirement. If they collect on it at all, it's just . . . kind of secondary, after the fact. . . . The broader notion of strategic intelligence was a concept that was popular in the 1940s and fifties, and to a degree, into the 1960s, but [in 2004, it] had not been really something that many intelligence agencies focused on."

30 *Cultural Preparation of the Environment was an open-source:* Cabayan described Cultural Preparation of the Environment to me this way: "Just picture this in your mind: You've never been to Timbuktu. All of a sudden, you land in Timbuktu. What would you want to know? Where are the hospitals, where are the roads, who are the key people in Timbuktu? Who are the ones who are on my side, who are the ones who are not friendly to me? What's the incidence of IED attacks? That's really what it was. It wasn't for civilians. It was for the military commander in charge so that he or she will absolutely know all the [cultural] information that was acquired, but we also put in the IED attack[s] . . . and it was all there for them and it was searchable, so [if] they wanted to know about all the friendly sheiks, we were supposed to have the sheiks come up with their biographies." Cabayan, interview by author, December 7, 2009. The idea of layering typical intelligence about enemy threats with demographic and cultural information in a single database was what made Cultural Preparation of the Environment unique and potentially useful, because it was becoming clear that threat-specific intelligence wasn't useful on its own, isolated from its political, ethnic, or cultural context. Cabayan

did not use the term *intelligence* in describing Cultural Preparation of the Environment to me, but it is important to note that the project was not envisioned as a way to learn about tribes and culture *in the absence of* other elements of the conflict zone. Conceptually, Cultural Preparation of the Environment resembled tools like the Tactical Ground Reporting System (TIGR), which offers soldiers multilayered maps that include "routes, critical infrastructure, tribal areas and ethnic maps, recent attacks and recent changes in the terrain." "U.S. Army: TIGR Allows Soldiers to 'Be There' Before They Arrive'" http://www.army.mil/article/28700/tigr-allows-soldiers-to-be-there-before-they-arrive/, accessed June 27, 2012. TIGR is now widely used in Afghanistan, "enabling collection and dissemination of fine-grained intelligence on people, places, insurgent activity and understanding the 'human terrain.'" "Defense Update: Extending Intelligence to the Edge," http://defense-update.com/products/t/tigr_141009.html, accessed June 27, 2012. See also James Turner, "Where 2.0: DARPA's TIGR Project Helps Platoons Stay Alive," April 21, 2009, http://radar.oreilly.com/2009/04/where-20-preview---darpas-tige.html, accessed June 27, 2012.

30 *McFate had been intrigued:* McFate, interview by author, June 30, 2010. When McFate read the anthropologist Jeffrey A. Sluka's *Hearts and Minds, Water and Fish: Popular Support for the IRA and INLA in a Northern Irish Ghetto* in graduate school, she told me: "I thought, I can't imagine a more useful book for the British Army. You just gave British intelligence an absolutely staggering amount of information. . . . Inadvertently, you just contributed to the British war effort."

30 *McFate lost no time advancing her view:* McFate, interview by author, June 30, 2010, and "ONR Conference Makes Case for Study of Cultures," *OrigiNatoR,* December 13, 2004. The conference, held in November 2004, drew some 250 people, "more than double the number originally expected, from the services, defense agencies, CIA and DIA, the State Department, and from the staffs of key Congressional committees," the Office of Naval Research newsletter noted. "The more unconventional the adversary, the more we need to understand their society and underlying cultural dynamics," McFate said, according to the newsletter. "To defeat non-Western opponents who are transnational in scope, non-hierarchical in structure, clandestine in their approach, and operate outside of the context of nation-states, we need to improve our capacity to understand foreign cultures and societies." According to one conference participant: "Intelligence analysts don't have time to think—they have become reporters, while tensions between anthropologists and counterintelligence specialists have become unbearable."

30 *The U.S. military and policy community's ethnocentrism:* McFate, "The Military Utility of Understanding Adversary Culture," *Joint Force Quarterly* 38 (July 2005), 42–43, http://www.dtic.mil/doctrine/jel/jfq_pubs/1038.pdf, accessed September 15, 2012.

31 *Coalition forces arrested Iraqis:* David Kilcullen, "Ethics, Politics and Non-State Warfare," *Anthropology Today* 23, no. 3 (June 2007), 20.

31 *Shia Muslims who flew black flags for religious reasons:* McFate, "The Military Utility of Understanding Adversary Culture," 43–44. The Marines were not totally off

base, though they may have relied too heavily on their experience in Falluja, where black flags were an inauspicious sign. "Now at least we knew what the black flags were for," Dexter Filkins wrote "The insurgents had spotted us, and they were signaling their friends to come: Come to the fight. It's here." Filkins, *The Forever War* (New York: Vintage 2008), 190.

31 *She was briefing military officials in Tampa one day in 2005:* McFate, interviews by author, January 28, 2009, and June 30, 2010, and Steve Fondacaro, interview by author, January 28, 2009.

31 *Fondacaro was determined to do whatever it took:* Fondacaro, interviews by author, January 28, 2009, and June 19, 2010.

31 *Born in New York to a mother of Puerto Rican descent:* Unless otherwise noted, biographical information and quotes from Fondacaro in this section are from Fondacaro, interviews by author, June 16 and 19, 2010. See also "IMDb: Phil Fondacaro," http://www.imdb.com/name/nm0284496/, accessed June 28, 2012, and "Sal's Music Instruction: Meet Sal," http://www.salsmusicinstruction.com/Meet_Sal .html, accessed June 18, 2012.

32 *He entered the academy in 1972, toward the end of the Vietnam War:* A year earlier, in 1971, Lieutenant William Calley had been convicted of murdering civilians at My Lai, the *New York Times* had published the Pentagon Papers, and a Harris poll had shown for the first time that most Americans opposed the war. Doug Linder, "An Introduction to the My Lai Courts-Martial," http://law2.umkc.edu/faculty/ projects/ftrials/mylai/Myl_intro.html, accessed July 2, 2012. By 1972, President Richard Nixon had agreed to withdraw seventy thousand troops from Vietnam. Fondacaro recalled that after he and his fellow West Point cadets marched in the Memorial Day parade in New York City during his plebe year, they had to clean the spit off their uniforms. Whether antiwar protesters actually spat on soldiers remains a subject of debate, but other members of Fondacaro's West Point class have also spoken of being subject to intense hostility, including spitting and egg throwing. See Yochi J. Dreazen, "A Class of Generals," *Wall Street Journal,* July 25, 2009. For the controversy over spitting on soldiers, see Jeremy Lembcke, *Spitting Image: Myth, Memory, and the Legacy of Vietnam* (New York: NYU Press, 2000).

32 *The department has long served as an intellectual incubator:* David Cloud and Greg Jaffe, *The Fourth Star: Four Generals and the Epic Struggle for the Future of the United States Army* (New York: Crown, 2009), 53–67. Proponents of counterinsurgency who have taught at Sosh include Andrew Krepinevich, author of *The Army and Vietnam;* John Nagl; and General David Petraeus, who wrote his PhD dissertation while he was an instructor there. See Cloud and Jaffe, *The Fourth Star,* 61–67, and "Center for a New American Security: Dr. John A. Nagl," http://www.cnas.org/nagl, accessed July 2, 2012. For a recent example of Sosh's procounterinsurgency leanings, see Elisabeth Bumiller, "West Point Is Divided on a War Doctrine's Fate," *New York Times,* May 27, 2012.

32 *Fondacaro graduated from West Point in 1976:* For more on the West Point Class of

1976, see Dreazen, "A Class of Generals." For Petraeus, see Cloud and Jaffe, *The Fourth Star,* 18, and Danielle Burton, "10 Things You Didn't Know About David Petraeus," *U.S. News & World Report,* March 27, 2008.

33 *He spent thirteen years there, returning to the States intermittently:* Fondacaro told me that in addition to the Command and General Staff College, he was chosen to attend the School of Advanced Military Studies and later the U.S. Army War College, receiving three master's degrees. The work of the Special Technical Operations Division has included what the military calls "offensive information warfare," such as hacking into the computer and communications networks of American enemies. William M. Arkin, "Phreaking Hacktivists," *Washington Post,* January 18, 1999. "Dozens of special access (or 'black') programs are monitored" at Special Technical Operations, Arkin writes. "These include the United States's own hacking activities; strategic psychological, concealment and deception operations; and 'directed energy warfare.' The latter includes special weapons and capabilities, such as high-powered microwave weapons, that could be used to disable enemy communications, computing, and the production and distribution of electricity." Fondacaro said that the organization's work was very broad, encompassing all government jobs requiring the highest level of classification. In contrast to his time in Korea, he and his colleagues at Special Technical Operations "were very much involved with what was happening in the Middle East," he told me.

33 *He knew that Ho Chi Minh had begged the United States:* For Ho's repeated attempts to interest the Americans in Vietnamese liberation in 1945 and 1946, see Neil Sheehan, *A Bright Shining Lie: John Paul Vann and America in Vietnam* (New York: Vintage, 1989), 146–53: Ho "was not asking for independence, just autonomy. No one from the American delegation or any of the other Allied delegations would receive him [at the Paris Peace Conference of 1945]. Ho discovered that Wilson's self-determination applied only to the Czechs and Poles and other white peoples of Eastern Europe who had been under German and Austro-Hungarian domination, not to the brown and yellow peoples of Asia or to the blacks of Africa. . . . Ho sent Truman and Truman's first secretary of state, James Byrnes, eleven telegrams and letters of appeal over an eighteen-month period after his establishment of a Vietnamese government in Hanoi. None was acknowledged. . . . He offered to turn Vietnam into 'a fertile field for American capital and enterprise.' He hinted that he would give the United States a naval base at Cam Ranh Bay, one of the finest natural deep-water harbors in the world . . . if only the United States would protect the Vietnamese from the French. . . . Ho had been sending his letters and telegrams to a file drawer for historians. The United States had abandoned the Vietnamese and the other peoples of Indochina well before he cited the American Declaration of Independence and the P-38s dipped low over Ba Dinh Square in Hanoi. . . . The State Department classified all of Ho Chi Minh's letters and telegrams and the memorandum of his last conversation with a first secretary at the Paris embassy Top Secret and locked them away. They were not to be published until a quarter of a century later in the Pentagon Papers."

34 *The future soldier he envisioned:* Shinseki did not respond to requests for comment; his support for Fondacaro is based on Fondacaro's account. Fondacaro said he was actually asked to conduct two studies, the first under the auspices of the Army's Training and Doctrine Command, and a second commissioned by Shinseki. See Vernon Loeb, "Army Plans Steps to Heighten 'Warrior Ethos,'" *Washington Post,* September 8, 2003. As Loeb notes, concern over hyperspecialization within the Army intensified after insurgents attacked the 507th Maintenance Company in Nasiriyah, Iraq, in March 2003, killing eleven U.S. soldiers and capturing six, including Private Jessica Lynch. In a more conventional battle, the unit would likely have stayed in the rear, but in Iraq, as the Army was learning, there was no "rear." An Army investigation found that soldiers in the 507th "were unable to defend themselves because their weapons malfunctioned, possibly due to 'inadequate individual maintenance in a desert environment.'" See also "U.S. Army Official Report on 507th Maintenance Co.: An Nasiriyah, Iraq," http://www.why-war .com/files/article07102003a.pdf, accessed July 3, 2012.

35 *But Shinseki was on the wrong side of power:* Eric Schmitt, "Pentagon Contradicts General on Iraq Occupation Force's Size," *New York Times,* February 28, 2003, and Thom Shanker, "New Strategy Vindicates Ex-Army Chief Shinseki," *New York Times,* January 12, 2007.

35 *He blamed his failure to make general on Shinseki's fall:* "The problem was I was the prime guy for the Chief of Staff for the Army when the Secretary of Defense had cut his legs out from underneath him," Fondacaro told me. "So you kind of go down that hole, too. I wasn't going to get any help from Shinseki. I got the nominations, but there was no way I was going to get" promoted to general.

35 *An acquaintance from his Ranger days had been tapped:* Created in October 2003, the Army counter-IED task force evolved into the Joint IED Defeat Organization, or JIEDDO. Votel is now a lieutenant general; in 2011, he was named head of the Joint Special Operations Command. See also Colonel William G. Adamson, U.S. Army, "An Asymmetric Threat Invokes Strategic Leader Initiative: The Joint Improvised Explosive Device Defeat Organization," Industrial College of the Armed Forces, National Defense University, 2007, and Lieutenant Colonel Richard F. Ellis, Major Richard D. Rogers, USAF, and Lieutenant Commander Bryan M. Cochran, U.S. Navy, "Joint Improvised Explosive Device Defeat Organization (JIEDDO): Tactical Successes Mired in Organizational Chaos; Roadblock in the Counter-IED Fight," Joint Forces Staff College, Joint and Combined Warfighting School–Intermediate, Class #07-02, March 13, 2007, http://www.dtic.mil/cgi -bin/GetTRDoc?AD=ADA473109, accessed July 3, 2012.

35 *Votel asked Fondacaro to lead a small group:* The group included "about twenty-four Delta operators, plus Army, Air Force, Navy, Marine, and EOD guys, and we were in direct combat with units, helping them with their training," Fondacaro told me. He learned that commanders were frustrated by massive amounts of information that didn't add up to meaning. "The intel world has oceans of data. This commander needs a glass of water that's specific to time, space, and his mission. That's

his problem. He doesn't have the people that could cull through the ocean to find the drops of water that are relevant to his solution set. And the pathway to that is research."

35 *They ranged from the useless to the bizarre:* Fondacaro, interviews by author, January 28, 2009, and June 19, 2010. The wackiness of early experimental attempts to counter IEDs in Iraq is legendary and well documented. They included harnessing honeybees to the undercarriage of military vehicles so they could use their well-developed scenting organs to sniff out buried bombs. One soldier mounted a toaster on a long pole attached to the front of his Humvee in the hope of triggering a buried bomb's heat sensor before the vehicle passed over it, and a high-powered microwave emitter called BlowTorch was sent back when it didn't work. See Atkinson, "Left of Boom: 'You Can't Armor Your Way out of This Problem,'" *Washington Post,* October 2, 2007. "A review of 70 IED countermeasures found that only half had been tested in the US before being shipped overseas, and that fewer than one-third were evaluated after arriving in the theater," Atkinson wrote.

36 *As he listened to the contractors pitch it:* McFate and Fondacaro, interviews by author, January 28, 2009, and Fondacaro, interview by author, June 19, 2010. McFate did not accompany Cultural Preparation of the Environment into the field for the first time. That job fell to a contractor from the MITR Corporation, a major nonprofit government and defense organization that helped develop it, and Andrea Jackson, who was charged with gathering cultural and demographic information for the database. Jackson worked for the Lincoln Group, the Pentagon contractor best known for planting pro-U.S. news stories in Iraqi media outlets, where they were passed off as independent reporting. The Lincoln Group already had a network of Iraqi employees in Baghdad, some of whom were sent to conduct on-the-ground research in Diyala, which was then loaded onto the Cultural Preparation of the Environment laptop. It remains unclear what the researchers told people from whom they gathered the information for CPE about who they represented and where it would end up. Some observers have also alleged that their data was falsified. Lamb et. al., "Human Terrain Team Performance: An Explanation, draft," forthcoming 2013, 32. For Lincoln's propaganda work, see Mark Mazzetti and Borzou Daragahi, "U.S. Military Covertly Pays to Run Stories in Iraqi Press," *Los Angeles Times,* November 30, 2005; and http://www.democracynow.org/2006/8/21/i _was_a_propaganda_intern_in; http://harpers.org/archive/2006/09/0081195. For Jackson's Lincoln affiliation, see Jackson and McFate, "An Organizational Solution for DOD's Cultural Knowledge Needs," *Military Review,* July–August 2005, and Unclassified Briefing on Cultural Preparation of the Environment, February 2006.

36 *That Arab brides painted their hands with henna before marriage:* Social scientists "love studying . . . marriage practices," Fondacaro told me. "But the commander will say, 'What the fuck? So what?'" Social science alone wasn't enough, he believed. It had to be tailored to the commander's needs.

36 *With violence intensifying in Iraq:* During the 2000 presidential campaign, Bush re-

peatedly stated his belief that the military should not be involved in nation build-ing. "I'm worried about an opponent who uses nation building and the military in the same sentence," he said in November 2000. His public statements began to change as early as 2003, when he told an audience at the American Enterprise In-stitute: "We will remain in Iraq as long as necessary, and not a day more. America has made and kept this kind of commitment before—in the peace that followed a world war. After defeating enemies, we did not leave behind occupying armies, we left constitutions and parliaments. We established an atmosphere of safety, in which responsible, reform-minded local leaders could build lasting institutions of freedom. In societies that once bred fascism and militarism, liberty found a per-manent home." See David E. Sanger, "Rivals Differ on U.S. Role in the World," *New York Times*, October 30, 2000, and Terry M. Neal, "Bush Backs Into Nation Building," *Washington Post*, February 26, 2003.

37 *Given the paltriness of America's civilian:* Budget cuts in the years after the Cold War gutted the State Department and the United States Agency for International Development (USAID), forcing steep reductions in staff. By 2006, civilian agen-cies had received only 1.4 percent of total U.S. funding in Iraq and Afghanistan, "whereas classical counterinsurgency doctrine says that eighty per cent of the ef-fort should be nonmilitary," the journalist George Packer has noted. During Viet-nam, USAID had fifteen thousand employees; by 2006, it had two thousand. "To staff the embassy in Baghdad, the State Department has had to steal officers from other embassies, and the government can't even fill the provincial reconstruction teams it has tried to set up in Iraq and Afghanistan," Packer wrote. "While correct-ing these shortages could not have prevented the deepening disaster in Iraq, they betray the government's priorities." A 2004 attempt by senators Richard Lugar and Joe Biden to set up a nation-building office within the State Department was strongly supported by the military, but the office never gained much traction, receiving only $7 million of the $100 million requested by the administration. Packer, "Knowing the Enemy: Can Social Scientists Redefine the 'War on Ter-ror'?" *New Yorker*, December 18, 2006.

37 *That year, "stability operations":* Department of Defense Directive Number 3000.05, "Military Support for Stability, Security, Transition, and Reconstruction (SSTR) Operations," November 28, 2005. General Colin Powell outlined the so-called Powell Doctrine after the Persian Gulf War, when he was Chairman of the Joint Chiefs of Staff; it was based in part on his experience as a young officer in Viet-nam. In 1992, he presciently suggested that the military should not be given confusing missions—advice that was ignored in Iraq and Afghanistan. "When the political objective is important, clearly defined and understood, when the risks are acceptable, and when the use of force can be effectively combined with diplomatic and economic policies, then clear and unambiguous objectives must be given to the armed forces," Powell wrote. "We owe it to the men and women who go in harm's way to make sure that this is always the case and that their lives are not squandered for unclear purposes. Military men and women recognize

more than most people that not every situation will be crystal clear. We can and do operate in murky, unpredictable circumstances. But we also recognize that military force is not always the right answer. If force is used imprecisely or out of frustration rather than clear analysis, the situation can be made worse." Colin L. Powell, "U.S. Forces: Challenges Ahead," *Foreign Affairs*, Winter 1992–1993, http://www.cfr.org/world/us-forces-challenges-ahead/p7508, accessed July 4, 2012. The so-called Rumsfeld Doctrine, which favored a smaller, faster force with fewer troops and more technology, was also much at play in Iraq and Afghanistan, particularly during the initial invasions. See Julian E. Barnes, "Army Gives Rumsfeld Doctrine a Rewrite," *Los Angeles Times*, November 20, 2006, and Bruce Nussbaum, "It's Time to Shelve the Rumsfeld Doctrine," *BusinessWeek*, April 25, 2004, http://www.businessweek.com/stories/2004-04-25/commentary -its-time-to-shelve-the-rumsfeld-doctrine, accessed July 4, 2012.

37 *In the short term, stability operations would provide security:* Department of Defense Directive 3000.05 (2005), 2.

37 *Commanders were instructed to draft requirements:* Ibid., 9. Commanders were ordered to include information on "key ethnic, cultural, religious, tribal, economic and political relationships, non-military security forces, infrastructure, sanitation and health structure, munitions facilities, border controls, and customs processes" in their intelligence campaign plans.

37 *Intelligence products had to bring together:* According to a later revision of the directive, Department of Defense Instruction, Number 3000.05, "Stability Operations," September 16, 2009, 15. This directive, issued under the signature of Michèle Flournoy, who was until 2012 Obama's procounterinsurgency Undersecretary of Defense for Policy, highlights some ways in which the wars in Iraq and Afghanistan changed and expanded the military's definition of intelligence.

37 *That year, Maxie McFarland:* Maxie McFarland, "Military Cultural Education," *Military Review*, March–April 2005, 62–69.

37 *In McFarland's prose, it became a solid thing:* According to McFarland: "The emerging importance of cultural identity and its inherent frictions make it imperative for soldiers and leaders—military and civilian—to understand societal and cultural norms of populaces in which they operate and function. They must appreciate, understand, and respect those norms and *use them as tools* for shaping operations and the effects they expect to achieve." McFarland, "Military Cultural Education," 62. Emphasis is mine.

37 *McFarland had worked on the counter-IED task force:* McFarland served as a special adviser to retired General Montgomery Meigs, who took over as director of the Joint IED Defeat Task Force in December 2005. The Foreign Military Studies Office, like the Human Terrain System, falls under the intelligence directorate of the Army's Training and Doctrine Command. See Adamson, "An Asymmetric Threat Invokes Strategic Leader Initiative," 48, and http://www.tradoc.army .mil/OrgChart.asp, accessed July 4, 2012.

38 *Kipp saw enough potential in the project to want to keep track of it:* Kipp, interview by author, July 2, 2010. Kipp told me the office had no funding for such an ambitious project, but he agreed to pay Smith's travel costs to attend meetings and get to know the players.

38 *Smith was an ambitious, fast-talking Army reserve captain:* Details of Don Smith's biography and his involvement with the Human Terrain System here and below are from Don Smith, interview by author, February 19, 2013; Jacob Kipp, Lester W. Grau, Karl Prinslow, and Don Smith, "The Human System: A CORDS for the 21st Century," *Military Review,* September–October 2006; and "Speaker Biographies: Rule of Law and Governance as Stabilization Tools," April 16–17, 2008.

38 *he came up with the idea for the program at his kitchen table:* McFate told me that her notion at the time was "kind of vague . . . nothing as specific as HTS," but she told the story as a way of explaining the program's evolution. The same anecdote has been recorded elsewhere: "She wrote on a cocktail napkin: 'How do I make anthropology relevant to the military?'" Noah Shachtman, "Montgomery McFate: Use Anthropology in Military Planning," *Wired,* September 22, 2008. For Fondacaro's claim that it was his idea to embed civilian social scientists with combat units, Fondacaro, interview by author, June 19, 2010, and David Rohde, "Army Enlists Anthropology in War Zones," *New York Times,* October 5, 2007.

38 *McFate had written about the Army's need:* McFate and Jackson, "An Organizational Solution for DOD's Cultural Knowledge Needs," 18–21. McFate and Jackson argued for the creation of a "specialized organization" in the Defense Department that would conduct field research, gather cultural and ethnographic information about far corners of the world, and disseminate it to the U.S. military. Instead of reading nineteenth-century British ethnographies or searching for cultural and demographic information on Google, military staff officers would be able to turn to a group of "social scientists having strong connections to the services and combatant commands." The organization could conduct sociocultural studies on "areas of interest" to the Defense Department and analyze cultural lessons drawn from twenty-first-century Iraq, where the British used cultural knowledge to organize "local councils to co-opt the tribal sheiks in Basra."

38 *After the fall of the Soviet Union, the office had developed:* Karl Prinslow, interview by author, July 12, 2010.

39 *The first was the World Basic Information Library:* Unless otherwise noted, information about the World Basic Information Library in this section is from Prinslow, interview by author, July 12, 2010, and Prinslow, "The World Basic Information Library Program," *Military Intelligence Professional Bulletin,* October–December 2005, 51–53.

39 *A few years later, when the Foreign Military Studies Office's Soviet expert:* Kipp, interview by author, July 2, 2010. The reservist who joined AF1 was Captain Roya Sharifsoltani. See Mike Belt, "Military Veteran: Knowing War Zone's Culture Important,"

*LjWorld.com*, November 16, 2007, http://www2.ljworld.com/news/2007/nov/16/military_veteran_knowing_war_zones_culture_importa/, accessed July 16, 2012.

40 *Since 2005, the Foreign Military Studies Office:* Jerome E. Dobson, "AGS Conducts Fieldwork in Mexico," *Ubique: Notes from the American Geographical Society* 26, no. 1 (February 2006), and "México Indígena: Final Report (Short Version for the Web)," http://uaslp.academia.edu/MiguelRobledo/Papers/1073836/THE_AGS_ BOWMAN_EXPEDITIONS_PROTOTYPE_DIGITAL_GEOGRAPHY_ OF_INDIGENOUS_MEXICO, accessed September 15, 2012.

40 *the project was the brainchild of Jerome E. Dobson:* CV of Jerome E. Dobson, http://www2.ku.edu/~geography/peoplepages/Dobson_D.shtml, accessed July 6, 2012.

40 *Dobson viewed geography as a key source of intelligence:* Jerome E. Dobson, "Foreign Intelligence Is Geography," *Ubique: Notes from the American Geographical Society* 25, no. 1 (March 2005).

40 *In 2006, Dobson and other members:* Jerome E. Dobson, "Fort Leavenworth Hosts AGS Council," *Ubique: Notes from the American Geographic Society* 27, no. 3 (December 2006).

41 *With the Bowman Expeditions, Dobson:* The United States and its allies won the war, but for most Americans, geography was reduced to the study of maps and capitals. Geography lost public support and almost disappeared from academia after World War II, Dobson wrote, in part because a German geographer had served as Hitler's chief geopolitical strategist. In 2006, Dobson wrote of his concern that geography was losing out to cultural anthropology in the contest to influence national policy. He made no secret of his view that geography could and should be used to improve intelligence. The Bowman Expeditions, he wrote, "came about because I, like so many others, am troubled over intelligence failures and bipartisan blunders that lead to conflict. Most of the missing knowledge is not secret, insider information that should be classified. What's missing is open source geography of the type we teach routinely in regional geography courses, and it's based on the type of field-work and data analyses that geographers do routinely in every region on earth. I firmly believe the only remedy is to bring geography back to its rightful place in higher education, science policy, and public policy circles." Later, the American Geographical Society and the Bowman Expedition geographers would seek to dis-tance themselves from the Human Terrain System. In 2009, after a nongovern-mental organization representative and a group of geographers criticized members of the first expedition, México Indígena, for allegedly failing to tell Mexicans whose land they surveyed that the research was funded by the Department of Defense, the Geographical Society wrote: "The program has never requested nor has it re-ceived any funding from the controversial Human Terrain System (HTS) program, whose design differs in crucial ways from our posted guidelines." See Dobson, "Foreign Intelligence Is Geography," 2; "AGS Conducts Fieldwork in Mexico," 2; and "The American Geographical Society's Bowman Expeditions Seek to Improve Geographic Understanding at Home and Abroad: Spotlight on *México Indígena*," http://www.amergeog.org/newsrelease/bowmanPR-en.pdf, accessed July 6, 2012.

41 *Don Smith had met with then-Colonel John W. "Mick" Nicholson:* Smith told me the meeting actually took place in the fall of 2005. Smith, interview by author, February 19, 2013. See also Lamb et al., "Human Terrain Team Performance: An Explanation, draft," forthcoming, 2013, 36.

41 *That summer, Smith and others at the Foreign Military Studies Office:* Prinslow, interview by author, July 12, 2010, and Smith, interview by author, February 19, 2013. Prinslow looked to his World Basic Information Library network for qualified reservists, but the library was never envisioned as an operational group whose members would be sent to a conflict zone. Until then, they had essentially been doing Internet research.

42 *That fall, the men of the Foreign Military Studies Office:* Kipp et al., "The Human System: A CORDS for the 21st Century," 8–15.

42 *In the years when the Human Terrain System was being developed:* Rick Atkinson, "Iraq Will Be Petraeus's Knot to Untie," *Washington Post,* January 7, 2007.

42 *Petraeus saw the move:* Cloud and Jaffe, *The Fourth Star,* 216–17.

42 *Between 2005, when he arrived at Leavenworth:* John A. Nagl, "Foreword to the University of Chicago Press Edition," *The U.S. Army/Marine Corps Counterinsurgency Field Manual* (Chicago: University of Chicago Press, 2007), xiv.

42 *It argued that in this new, old kind of war: The U.S. Army/Marine Corps Counterinsurgency Field Manual,* 39–40.

42 *"Sometimes, the more force is used, the less effective it is":* Ibid., 48–50.

42 *The manual brought together military intellectuals:* Sarah Sewall, "Introduction to the University of Chicago Press Edition: A Radical Field Manual," ibid., xxi, xxv–xxvi.

42 *The manual was a barn burner:* Nagl, "Foreword," ibid., xvii. Copies of the manual were found in Taliban training camps in Pakistan, Nagl notes.

42 *It laid out a plan for winning over Iraqis and Afghans:* In an unprecedented effort to invest American civil society in the strategy, the military invited "journalists, human rights advocates, academics" and others to vet a draft of the manual, Nagl wrote. "James Fallows, of the *Atlantic Monthly,* commented at the end of the conference that he had never seen such an open transfer of ideas in any institution, and stated that the nation would be better for more such exchanges." Conrad Crane, the manual's master conductor, was featured in *Newsweek* as a "Man to Watch" in 2007. Ibid., xvi–xvii. See also Cloud and Jaffe, *The Fourth Star,* 218–20.

43 *This would turn out to be a winning strategy:* When General Stanley McChrystal was asked to assess the Afghan war in 2009, he recruited a team of Washington intellectuals, strategists, and policy makers to help sell his argument back home.

43 *What the manual downplayed:* See *U.S. Army/Marine Corps Counterinsurgency Field Manual,* 174–77. Although the manual does not draw attention to the role of lethal force, General Stanley McChrystal's terrorist-targeting teams were arguably as important to stabilizing Iraq as the development projects and political negotiations undertaken by surge troops. Between the summer of 2010 and the spring

of 2011, at the height of the U.S. counterinsurgency campaign in Afghanistan, Petraeus doubled the number of kill/capture missions in that country. Classical counterinsurgency had been all but abandoned in Afghanistan for lack of political will by mid-2011, but there is no question that the strategy is inherently schizoid in nature. In Afghanistan in 2010, Michael Hastings reported hearing General McChrystal tell a Navy SEAL: "'You better be out there hitting four or five targets tonight. . . . I'm going to have to scold you in the morning for it, though.'" Intelligence gathered in counterinsurgency can help soldiers decide where it is best to build a school, but it also tells them who to kill. If the intelligence is good, it may lead to killing fewer people, supporting the notion that counterinsurgency is a more precise and humane way of war. But if it is flawed, the detentions and killings remain as inhumane as they would be in any conventional fight. See "Iraq After the Surge I: The New Sunni Landscape," International Crisis Group, Middle East Report N°74, April 30, 2008, 2; "Kill/Capture," PBS *Frontline*, http://www.pbs.org/wgbh/pages/frontline/kill-capture/, accessed July 6, 2012, and transcript, http://www.pbs.org/wgbh/pages/frontline/afghanistan-pakistan/kill-capture/transcript/, accessed July 6, 2012; and Michael Hastings, "The Runaway General," *Rolling Stone*, July 8–22, 2010.

43 *Montgomery McFate's articles:* McFate, interview by author, June 30, 2010.

43 *"If you don't get it about this stuff":* General Petraeus, interview by author, October 31, 2010.

44 *McFate's contribution to the manual turned out to be substantial:* The intelligence chapter's lead author was Kyle Teamey, a former Army intelligence captain who had graduated from Dartmouth, served with John Nagl in Iraq, and later helped develop the DARPA intelligence system TIGR. Teamey pulled the chapter together while studying for a master's at the Johns Hopkins School of Advanced International Studies. About thirty-five people contributed to the chapter in some way, he told me, and pointed out McFate's submission on pages 84–100. Teamey, interview by author, August 25, 2010. See also Kyle Teamey and Jonathan Sweet, "Organizing Intelligence for Counterinsurgency," *Military Review*, September–October 2006, 24–29; Mari Maeda, "TIGR: An Introduction," DARPA, March 2010; and "Liquid Light: About Us," http://liquidlightinc.com/about.html#teamey, accessed July 6, 2012.

44 *an active local insurgency led by Jalaluddin Haqqani:* For more on the Haqqanis and their history with the Americans, see Steve Coll, *Ghost Wars* (New York: Penguin Books, 2004), 157; Mark Mazzetti, Scott Shane, and Alissa J. Rubin, "Brutal Haqqani Crime Clan Bedevils U.S. in Afghanistan," *New York Times*, September 24, 2011, http://www.nytimes.com/2011/09/25/world/asia/brutal-haqqani-clan-bedevils-united-states-in-afghanistan.html?_r=1&pagewanted=all; and Dan Froomkin, "Jalaluddin Haqqani, Once CIA's 'Blue-Eyed Boy,' Now Top Scourge for U.S. in Afghanistan," *Huffington Post*, October 7, 2011, http://www.huffingtonpost.com/2011/10/07/haqqani-network-afghanistan_n_987762.html. For Sirajuddin, see http://www.fbi.gov/wanted/terrorinfo/sirajuddin-haqqani/view, accessed August 12, 2012.

44 *Smith left the Human Terrain System:* Smith and Fondacaro disagreed about how to take the project forward. For the initial $20 million from the Joint IED Defeat Organization, McFate and Fondacaro, "Reflections on the Human Terrain System During the First Four Years," 66, and Lamb et al., "Human Terrain Team Performance: An Explanation, draft," forthcoming, 2013, 37.

44 *Fondacaro's old friend Votel:* Lamb et al., "Human Terrain Team Performance: An Explanation, draft," forthcoming, 2013, 41.

44 *It was there, in the fertile bowl-shaped plateau and the mountains:* Coll, *Ghost Wars* (New York: Penguin, 2004), 156–57, and Ahmed Rashid, *Taliban: Islam, Oil, and the New Great Game in Central Asia* (New York: Tauris, 2000), 132.

44 *In 1986, bin Laden had established:* Rashid, *Taliban*, 132, and Coll, *Ghost Wars*, 157.

45 *Years later, he would issue a fatwa from Khost:* Rashid, *Taliban*, 134.

45 *At least twenty-one presumed jihadist volunteers died:* Coll, *Ghost Wars*, 409–11, and Rashid, *Taliban*, 134. For the revival of the Khost training camps, Mark Fineman, Bob Drogin, and Josh Meyer, "Camps Are Rubble but Their Threat Remains," *Los Angeles Times*, December 18, 2001.

45 *Some of the September 11 hijackers trained in Khost:* For a detailed description of Khost as a place whose history "reads like a timeline of the 'global war on terror,'" see Steve Featherstone, "Human Quicksand: For U.S. Army, a Crash Course in Cultural Studies," *Harper's*, September 2008, 61. For Khost as a training ground for U.S. hijackers, see http://www.pbs.org/wgbh/pages/frontline/afghanistan-pakistan/kill-capture/transcript/.

45 *The members of AF1, as the team was known:* Tracy, interviews by author, December 15, 2009, and December 15, 2012.

45 *In one community, Tracy pointed out:* The community with more widows than usual was in Ghazni Province. Tracy, interview by author, December 15, 2012. See also Rohde, "Army Enlists Anthropology in War Zones," and Scott Peterson, "U.S. Army's Strategy in Afghanistan: Better Anthropology," *Christian Science Monitor*, September 7, 2007.

45 *It was a good idea, but one that:* See Mazzetti, Shane, and Rubin, "Brutal Haqqani Crime Clan Bedevils U.S. in Afghanistan."

46 *The Human Terrain Team connected soldiers with local leaders:* Gezari, "The Base, the Mosque and the Olive Trees," Pulitzer Center on Crisis Reporting, February 18, 2010, http://pulitzercenter.org/blog/untold-stories/afghanistan-base-mosque-and-olive-trees, accessed July 6, 2012.

46 *'It may be one less trigger that has to be pulled here':* Peterson, "U.S. Army's Strategy in Afghanistan."

46 *She was 'taking the population and dissecting it':* Ibid.

46 *Colonel Schweitzer would become:* A later iteration of the brigade's Human Terrain Team included Michael Bhatia, a young scholar who had done extensive and im-

pressive research on warring factions and security policy in Afghanistan and was one of the most qualified people ever to deploy with a Human Terrain Team. Bhatia was killed in Khost in 2008. Schweitzer called him "the smartest human being I've ever spoken to in my life." Schweitzer, interview by author, July 14, 2009.

46 *He credited Tracy and her team with reducing:* This was a bit of rhetorical sophistry. To make the statement accurate, Schweitzer would have had to serve two tours in Khost that were identical in every way except for the presence of the Human Terrain Team. A million factors, from weather to political unrest, economic conditions, and the timing of religious holidays, can affect the level of violence, making it all but impossible to attribute such a large reduction in combat operations to a single factor. Tracy agreed that the drop in fighting during her team's tenure in Khost proved only "correlation," not "causality." Tracy, interview by author, December 15, 2012. For Schweitzer's comments, see "Statement of Colonel Martin P. Schweitzer, Commander, 4/82 Airborne Brigade Combat Team, United States Army, Before the House Armed Services Committee, Terrorism & Unconventional Threats Sub-Committee and the Research & Education Sub-Committee of the Science & Technology Committee," 110th Congress, 2nd Session, Hearings on the Role of the Social and Behavioral Sciences in National Security, April 24, 2008.

46 *By the fall of 2007, the Defense Department:* Rohde, "Army Enlists Anthropology in War Zones." McFate says the request to expand came earlier, in the spring of 2007, just as Fondacaro returned from escorting AF1 to Khost. Although Schweitzer's praise for the team clearly could not have impressed the military in February 2007, since he was just beginning to work with them then, his remains one of the clearest and strongest military endorsements the project has received.

*Chapter 3: The Tender Soldier*

47 *In September 2008, Paula Loyd boarded a Chinook:* Loyd and her Human Terrain teammates arrived in Afghanistan on September 20, 2008, and flew out to Maiwand about a week later. Don Ayala, interview by author, August 19, 2009. The description of the landscape is drawn from my notes and photographs during flights from Kandahar to Maiwand in early 2009 and late 2010.

48 *She had spent her early childhood in Alamo Heights:* Gretchen Wiker, interview by author, January 7, 2013; Susanna Barton, interview by author, January 17, 2013; Patty Ward, interviews by author, February 15, 2009, and December 14, 2012. For more on her childhood in Alamo Heights here and below, "Paula Loyd: A Worthwhile Life," self-published memorial book, 2009.

48 *Loyd was an only child:* Her full name was Paula Gene Loyd. She was named after her father and her maternal uncle, Eugene. Patty Ward, interview by author, December 14, 2012. That she became known as a peacemaker, and for the story of her giving toys to her half brother's kids, Paul Loyd, Jr., interview by author, February

15, 2009. "They always fought over toys like starving dogs would over table scraps," Paul Loyd told me of his children. "Paula's first efforts at conflict resolution were with them." For Loyd's father's World War II service, see "Paul Loyd, Sr.: Obituary," *San Antonio Express-News,* http://www.legacy.com/obituaries/sanantonio/obituary.aspx?page=lifestory&pid=142309053. Accessed October 5, 2012.

48 *Loyd's mother sent her to a Montessori school:* "She liked structure: 'This is your job, get it done.' She worked very well under those circumstances," Patty Ward told me. "She had a hard time with Montessori when she was little because this room was real open, and you just had to go pick out and do what you wanted to do." Ward, interviews by author, February 15, 2009, and December 14, 2012.

48 *Later, she would struggle with math:* Stefanie Johnson, one of Loyd's friends from college, noted: "It's no wonder that the woman who could see numbers as people and pluses and minuses as the relationship between them would choose a major that is all about different people in the world. Anthropology was her love." Funeral of Paula Loyd, San Antonio, 2009.

48 *She was quirky and bright, a ravenous reader:* Ward, interview by author, December 14, 2012, and Barton, interview by author, January 17, 2013.

48 *Loyd was different from Barton:* Barton, interview by author, January 17, 2013.

48 *At eight or nine, Loyd and Barton started an animal rescue group:* Ward, interview by author, December 14, 2012.

49 *Loyd's childhood home in Alamo Heights had a broad winding staircase:* Information about Loyd's childhood here and below is from Ward, interview by author, December 14, 2012; Barton, interview by author, January 17, 2013; and Wiker, interview by author, January 7, 2013.

49 *Gretchen Wiker was a recent transplant:* Wiker, interview by author, January 7, 2013.

49 *In some ways, Loyd was a typical preteen girl:* For Loyd's earrings and high '80s style, edgy haircuts, and mall crushes, "Paula Loyd: A Worthwhile Life."

50 *When Loyd was about thirteen, her parents divorced:* "We moved to St. Thomas because she said, 'I want to live somewhere where you're a different color, and see how people treat you.' St. Thomas is 90 percent black." Ward, interview by author, February 15, 2009. That Ward told her, "You're a minority already," Ward, interview by author, December 14, 2012.

50 *"She's basically always been an anthropologist":* Ward, interview by author, February 15, 2009.

51 *It was Ward who made her get out:* Ward, interviews by author, February 15, 2009, and December 14, 2012, and Ward, "Dear Darlin' Daughter," in "Paula Loyd: A Worthwhile Life."

51 *But after two years, Loyd began to worry that the island school:* Ward, interviews by author, February 15, 2009, and December 14, 2012, and "Choate Grad Paula Loyd '90 Passes Away," *The News* (student newspaper of Choate Rosemary Hall), Febru-

ary 20, 2009, http://thenews.choate.edu/archives/2009/02/20/News/Choate_Grad_Paula_Loyd_90_.php, accessed October 5, 2012. See also Farah Stockman, "Anthropologist's War Death Reverberates," *The Boston Globe*, February 12, 2009.

51 *She spent her junior and senior years at Choate Rosemary Hall:* This description of Loyd is from Rafe Sagarin, interview by author, January 7, 2013, and Johnson, funeral address, San Antonio, 2009.

51 *Her teachers noted her hunger for ideas and her gentleness:* "Choate Grad Paula Loyd '90 Passes Away," *The News*, February 20, 2009. The picture of Loyd with the stone lion captures "everything I remember about Paula," Sagarin wrote. "Her wry humor is there, but also her desire to get right down on the same level with everything she interacted with—to be wholly a part of it—which I'm sure is what drove her work in Afghanistan. Most importantly, what comes through in this picture is her fierce inner strength. Paula is a lion."

52 *At Wellesley, Loyd ran along the Charles River:* Johnson, funeral address, San Antonio, 2009, and Johnson, interview by author, June 23, 2010.

52 *At Wellesley, they rowed crew together:* For the crew team waking at 4:30 a.m. to practice, "Varsity Crew," *Legenda: The Wellesley College Yearbook* (1995), 68.

52 *She and Johnson worked together at a student-run coffee shop:* Johnson, funeral address, San Antonio, 2009, and Amanda Beals, "Café Hoop Celebrates 100th Anniversary," *The Wellesley News*, November 24, 1992.

53 *For one of her classes, she was assigned to conduct an ethnography:* Sally Engle Merry, interviews by author, June 7 and 11, 2010.

53 *At Wellesley, Loyd championed human rights:* Johnson, interview by author, June 23, 2010, and Merry, interview by author, June 7, 2010. "Her own politics were quite left," Merry told me. "I followed her activism. She liked to get things stirred up."

53 *Her much older half brother, Paul Loyd, Jr.:* Although Paul Loyd, Jr., described his half-sister as "almost Don Quixote–like," he explained that *dreamer* was not the right word to describe someone as grounded as Loyd. "I don't think she's just Don Quixote tilting at windmills," he told me. "I was what I would call a pragmatist, what are the pros and cons of this thing, and literally calculate my odds of success. That's not what she was about. If the cause is worthy, she's going to take it on, even if the odds are five percent. I don't think that way but she does." Paul Loyd, Jr., interviews by author, February 12 and 15, 2009. For more on Paul Loyd, Jr., see: http://investing.businessweek.com/research/stocks/private/person.asp?personId=222660&privcapId=3051396&previousCapId=4436226&previousTitle=On-TargetSupplies&LogisticsLtd.

53 *He and others were shocked when, upon graduating from Wellesley, she joined the Army:* "I didn't believe her," Paul Loyd told me. "I was blown away. I said, 'You're doing what?'" Paul Loyd, Jr., interview by author, February 15, 2009.

53 *Loyd's decision also surprised Johnson:* Johnson, interview by author, June 23, 2010.

53 *before leaving Wellesley, where she had been:* Loyd's thesis adviser, Sally Engle Merry, recalled that only a few students, perhaps three at most, were selected each year to write an honors thesis in anthropology at Wellesley when she taught there. Merry, interview by author, June 11, 2010.

53 *Her paper clocked in at 181 pages:* Including an extensive bibliography.

53 *Drawing on Marxist and feminist theory, Loyd wrote:* Paula Loyd, "Lesbian Resistance in the Bars of San Antonio, Texas" (bachelor's thesis, Wellesley College, Spring 1995), 10.

54 *"I have found that subordinate groups":* Ibid., 28.

54 *Loyd wrote that she was interested in "the numerous gray areas":* Ibid., 31.

54 *Instead, she enlisted:* Patty Ward, interview by author, December 14, 2012; Paul Loyd, Jr., interview by author, February 15, 2009; and Colonel Steve Walker, funeral address, San Antonio, 2009.

54 *Loyd thrived as an outsider:* "People tried to push her in the Army to go into officer's training, and no doing with her," Ward told me. "She didn't want to be in an office, she wanted to be with the people." Ward, interview by author, February 15, 2009. Said Paul Loyd: "She didn't want to be an officer. She wanted to get down and learn how people work and what made people tick. She's always sort of been for the common guy." Paul Loyd, Jr., interview by author, February 15, 2009.

54 *Soldiers with this job description fix trucks weighing more than five tons;* Loyd's initial classification in the Army was 63S Heavy, according to an Army officer who served with her. The job specifications mentioned here are available online at http://usarmybasic.com/mos/63s-heavy-wheel-vehicle-mechanic and http://www.apd.army.mil/Home/Links/PDFFiles/MOSBook.pdf, accessed October 6, 2012.

54 *Loyd stood five foot six and weighed 120 pounds at most:* Ward, interview by author, February 15, 2009; Barton, interview by author, January 17, 2013; and Walker, funeral address, San Antonio, 2009. "I recall when we took the Army physical fitness test. . . . And Paula gave the men a run for [their] money. . . . There's a men's standard and a women's standard, and I think pretty much she was on the men's standard," Walker said.

54 *Her commanders marveled at the contrast between her flaxen delicacy and her physical toughness:* One officer recalled: "Although she was a petite woman probably not more than a hundred pounds, I marveled when I witnessed Paula, although carrying about thirty-five pounds in her rucksack, was among the top finishers among men and women in a ten-kilometer rucksack march. In sum, I saw Paula as an example of how you cannot judge people by their appearance, and that the boundaries are endless if you're willing to explore them with zest." Walker, funeral address, San Antonio, 2009.

54 *She was sent to Korea, where she lived for a time on a remote outpost ringed with barbed wire:* Paul Loyd, Jr., interview by author, February 15, 2009, and Paul Loyd, Jr., funeral address, San Antonio, 2009. Loyd's letter to her half brother read: "My unit is not

the greatest place for a mechanic. Since it's a Patriot Missile unit, anything related to a missile takes priority. It looks like I'm going to spend a lot of my time over here pulling guard duty. . . . I'll keep you all posted on life here. I live in a two-block area with all the U.S. soldiers, surrounded by barbed wire. People call it a prison camp. . . . After this, I don't need any more character-building life experiences. I'm going to relax and enjoy life when I get out of the Army." The message ended with a smiley face.

55 *After four years, she switched to the reserves:* Ward, interviews by author, February 15, 2009, and December 14, 2012.

55 *In the rarefied atmosphere that nurtures America's policy-making elite:* For her study of Bosnia, Chester Crocker, James R. Schlesinger Professor of Strategic Studies, Edmund A. Walsh School of Foreign Service, Georgetown University, interview by author, June 22, 2010.

55 *Then came the attacks of September 11, 2001, and her reserve unit was called up:* Loyd's unit was called up in August 2002. Ward, interviews by author, February 15, 2009, and December 14, 2012, and Walker, funeral address, San Antonio, 2009.

55 *By now, she had given up fixing trucks in favor of civil affairs:* Loyd received her airborne certification before deploying to Afghanistan. Ward, interview by author, December 14, 2012, and Walker, funeral address, San Antonio, 2009. For more on civil affairs, see "Careers and Jobs: Civil Affairs Specialist (38B)," http://www.goarmy.com/careers-and-jobs/browse-career-and-job-categories/intelligence-and-combat-support/civil-affairs-specialist.html, and "United States Army Civil Affairs and Psychological Operations Command (Airborne)," http://www.usar.army.mil/ourstory/commands/USACAPOC/Pages/Overview.aspx, accessed October 6, 2012.

56 *She had made staff sergeant:* Many details about Loyd's time with the 450th in Afghanistan here and in the paragraphs below are from Mike Rathje, interview by author, January 21, 2013.

56 *'We are screaming into the silence':* Wendy Solomon, "American Women Soldiers Are Opening Afghan Eyes," *The Morning Call,* September 2, 2003.

56 *"They banded together to hide information":* Loyd, "Lesbian Resistance in the Bars of San Antonio, Texas," 20.

57 *At ribbon-cuttings for American-funded schools:* Ibid., and Rathje, interview by author, January 21, 2013.

57 *Afghan men sometimes asked Loyd's translator:* 'They're usually surprised I'm a woman,' Loyd told Solomon in 2003. 'Sometimes I'll be talking to the men in a village and they'll turn to the interpreter and say, 'Is that a man or a woman?' But I haven't had any problems with them. They've all been very nice.' Ibid.

57 *'The fact that I'm a woman':* Ibid.

57 *'They take me for who I am':* Loyd was realistic enough to know that many Afghan men treated her respectfully for their own practical reasons. As a civil affairs sol-

dier, she had access to aid and development funds. "She said, 'Well, mom, I've got the money.'" Ward, interview by author, December 14, 2012.

58 *Loyd understood these concerns:* For Loyd paying the Afghan police directly, Ward, interview by author, December 14, 2012.

59 *Soon she was in Kabul, working for a nongovernmental group:* Ward, interview by author, December 14, 2012.

59 *One winter day, she attended a briefing on the upcoming expansion of NATO forces:* Frank Muggeo, interviews by author, February 2009 and October 18, 2012.

60 *In late 2004, Loyd got a job with the United States Agency for International Development:* She worked for USAID from December 2004 through December 2005. Ward, interview by author, December 14, 2012.

61 *The provincial governor, Delbar Arman:* Information about Arman here and below, Delbar Arman, interview by author, January 14, 2009.

62 *elders covered their faces when they came to meet the governor:* Ibid.

62 *Some woman was sick;* This account of Loyd's evacuation of a pregnant Afghan woman is from ibid.

63 *They tore the building apart.* This story is from U.S. Air Force Colonel Kevin P. McGlaughlin, who got to know Loyd and Arman when he headed the Zabul PRT between 2006 and 2007. McGlaughlin, interview by author, February 20, 2009.

63 *During her year in Zabul, Loyd established a women's tree-planting cooperative.* Ward, interview by author, December 14, 2012. Loyd received a USAID award for her work in Zabul.

63 *She helped return the bodies of development contractors:* Remarks of Paula Loyd, "Stabilization and Reconstruction Operations in Post-Conflict and Crisis Zones: The Challenges of Military and Civilian Cooperation," Woodrow Wilson International Center for Scholars Panel, June 7, 2006. For more on the killings of Chemonics workers in Zabul and Helmand, Golnaz Esfandiari, "Afghanistan: Killings Raise Concerns for Aid Workers' Safety," *Radio Free Europe,* March 20, 2005.

63 *strange women moving around the province:* Walker, funeral address, San Antonio, 2009. "Though the missionaries probably didn't know what she had done, she was their guardian angel that day," a military officer who worked with her recalled.

63 *In 2005, Loyd took a job in Kabul:* For details about Loyd's work with the United Nations, Stacy Crevello, interview by author, December 17, 2012.

64 *she was one of the few people in Afghanistan with whom he could talk openly:* "Paula was very smart, easy to talk to. She spoke military because she'd been in the military. . . . [F]or a guy in my position, she was as close to a peer as I was going to have. . . . I could talk to her normally as opposed to, say, my NCOs and other officers." McGlaughlin, interview by author, February 20, 2009.

64 *Loyd had no problem telling him he was full of shit:* "She was soft and fuzzy but she could be cold and prickly if she wanted to be," McGlaughlin told me. "She was more

than happy to say . . . 'You're full of shit, this is why you're wrong.' She could do what we did because she'd been there, done that, got her T-shirt, but she also saw the bigger picture." Ibid.

64  *Loyd buried their guns in her purse:* "Paula's got this bag the size of Texas, so we deposit our sidearms in the bag, and we blow through the metal detectors and she goes around the metal detectors. There was no way they were going to stop her with that big old smile and blond hair, there was no way they were going to touch her. There we were eating breakfast, armed to the teeth," McGlaughlin recalled. Ibid.

64  *In 2006, Loyd spoke on a panel at the Woodrow Wilson Center:* Remarks of Paula Loyd, "Stabilization and Reconstruction Operations in Post-Conflict and Crisis Zones: The Challenges of Military and Civilian Cooperation."

64  *She was not opposed to the war:* "We need fighting to be done," Loyd said at the Wilson Center. "So when a PRT can work in coordination with an infantry unit to stabilize an area, I think it's really useful." Ibid.

65  *Every American unit and every national force in NATO:* "Every rotation that comes in has to show that they've done something, so they want to put their stamp on something," Loyd said at the Wilson Center. "Sometimes that can be counterproductive to working with the local governments, and working with the national government. They want to put . . . their flag on the project." Ibid.

65  *the U.S. military had shown itself incapable of sustaining long-term relationships:* "The lack of institutional memory is a serious problem," Loyd said. Ibid.

66  *During her time in Zabul:* "When I was in Zabul with USAID at a PRT, I worked with two different Special Forces units," Loyd told the Wilson Center audience. "I found that one was excellent, one was not so excellent. One of the reasons that the group that was not so excellent had some problems is because all of their interpreters were from one tribe. That means that all of their information came from that one tribe. Then we started having problems of certain people getting arrested, that maybe were for more tribal reasons than because they were with the Taliban or al Qaeda . . ." Ibid.

66  *Loyd's lungs had begun to bother her:* Ward, interview by author, December 14, 2012.

67  *They'd dated on and off, but work had kept them apart:* Frank Muggeo, interviews by author, February 2009 and October 18, 2012.

67  *'You'd rather be sitting on a rug talking to elders':* Ward, interviews by author, February 15, 2009, and December 14, 2012. Loyd wanted to get a PhD in Afghan studies, Ward told me, but she needed to work on her language skills, and she knew going back to Afghanistan was the best way to do that.

*Chapter 4: Maiwand*

69  *The Chinook touched down amid a swirl of dirt and stones:* Visual details here and below come from photographs taken by Loyd's teammates, Clint Cooper and Don Ayala,

and from interviews with Ayala, Cooper, and the soldiers and officers of the 2nd Battalion, 2nd Regiment, 1st Infantry Division, known as the 2–2.

69 *It got up near 120 degrees, the heat so oppressive:* For the temperature range, see Ali A. Jalali and Lester W. Grau, "Expeditionary Forces: Superior Technology Defeated— The Battle of Maiwand," *Military Review,* May–June 2001. According to the 2–2's executive officer, Major Cale Brown, who arrived with the first soldiers on August 15, 2008: "It was just bare desert. It was roughing it. It's very hot out here in the summer. It was guys hunkering down underneath the camouflage nets and drinking a whole lot of water, letting the engineers work putting up the initial walls. . . . The sort of rectangular [perimeter of] Hescos, that was the first thing they put up, and then they just pushed up sort of piles of dirt in a triangle around it and that was home sweet home for the first three months." Major Cale Brown, interview by author, March 22, 2009. According to Captain Michael Soyka: "When we first got here it was pretty rough. . . . It was no rocks. We wished there was rocks. It was just sand. We had to bring all that rock in. It was pretty austere. When they first showed up all they did was dig a fighting position, with a shovel, and man their fighting positions and the ground was ours." Soyka, interview by author, March 20, 2009. Captain Trevor Voelkel told me: "[O]ur first time out here was about August 18 of [2008]. . . . Ramrod was in the dust, in the dirt, and that was that." Voelkel, interview by author, March 24, 2009.

69 *The battalion intelligence section consisted:* Cooper, interview by author, April 22, 2010.

70 *Loyd's teammate, Clint Cooper:* Biographical information about Cooper in the first several pages of this chapter comes primarily from my interviews with Cooper, April 20–23, 2010.

70 *His family had lived on Navajo Nation land:* Cooper's father spoke Spanish, having done a Mormon mission in Uruguay and Paraguay. His work for the Bureau of Indian Affairs was an extension of this outreach, but it also connected him to a long and controversial tradition of American ethnography among native peoples. The time Cooper spent on the reservation was formative. Along with his later travels in Germany and elsewhere, his experience among the Navajo was "what got me interested in culture and language," he told me.

70 *They would set up chairs in the gym:* Navajo Lucy Toledo, who attended a boarding school in California in the 1950s, recalled something similar: "Saturday night we had a movie. . . . Do you know what the movie was about? Cowboys and Indians. Cowboys and Indians. Here we're getting all our people killed, and that's the kind of stuff they showed us." Charla Bear, "American Indian Boarding Schools Haunt Many," NPR, May 12, 2008, http://www.npr.org/templates/story/story.php?storyId=16516865, accessed August 17, 2012.

71 *Bosnia wasn't much of a war:* The Bosnian War officially ended with the Dayton Accords in 1995; by the time Cooper arrived, a NATO peacekeeping mission had been in place for seven years.

71 *One man told Cooper he had been forced at gunpoint:* The man refused. "They said, 'Either

you rape your daughter or we're going to kill her or we're going to kill you.' And he knew in his mind that regardless of what he did, his daughter would probably, you know . . . and he didn't do it. And in fact, his daughters disappeared. He never saw them again." Cooper, interview by author, April 20, 2010.

71 *As Cooper listened, he looked into the man's eyes:* "I mean, just watching that kind of pain and suffering in his eyes, you relate to that and you share a little bit of what's going on," Cooper told me. "It's just horrible some of the things that we'd hear." Cooper, interview by author, April 20, 2010.

71 *The National Security Agency was looking for linguists who spoke Pashto and Dari:* Pashto is mainly spoken in Afghanistan's south and east by Pashtuns, members of Afghanistan's largest ethnic group. Dari, which dominates in the north, west, and center of the country, is a cousin of Farsi, or Persian. It has historically been the language of Afghanistan's ruling elite.

73 *"And honestly, a lot of them weren't Taliban":* Cooper, interview by author, April 20, 2010.

73 *With the Taliban out of power and Afghanistan relatively stable:* I witnessed the returning waves of refugees when I was reporting in Afghanistan between 2002 and 2004, and heard often about land disputes then and afterward. Cooper told me: "You know about the blood feuds, and the revenge. You had a huge influx of refugees going out of Afghanistan during the Soviet invasion, and there was, like, seven million refugees that left and, like, a couple of million internally displaced persons. And so once we arrived, all these people are coming, flooding back into the country. Well, you know, the piece of land that you left five or ten years ago, somebody else is now living on it. And so where are you going to go for justice? Are you going to call the police? You have to take care of it yourself. And so that was a convenient way of getting rid of people. Call the coalition, and say your neighbor's Taliban. So we would run into a lot of that."

74 *Cooper learned that the insurgents moved in groups:* Cooper, interview by author, April 20, 2010. "Taliban usually operate in groups," Cooper told me. "They're not from the local area, but they depend on local support. They usually stay on the perimeter of villages and they'll send one or two people into the village to get food or whatever they need, supplies. And then sometimes, if it's a friendly village, they'll actually come in. Sometimes people would send their kids out to serve them because they're obliged to provide for the Taliban. If you don't, there's repercussions. So it's a conflicting situation. When the military says, 'Do they support the Taliban?' Well, yes. Are they bad people? No."

74 *But as he looked at the child lying there wounded:* Cooper, interview by author, April 20, 2010. "When you have a kid laying in front of you and you're interrogating him, it's complicated. He's a Taliban fighter. He fired on American troops. But he's a troubled kid that was indoctrinated and someone gave him an AK-47 and fed him full of lies. Your top priority is still force protection, because you want to protect the soldiers around you. And so you have to manipulate the kid, one way or the other, to get information."

74 *The longer he stayed, the harder it became not to empathize:* Cooper told me: "I could easily relate to what the people were going through, and a lot of times, I saw them more as victims than the evil Taliban fighter or whatever. I mean, they are. They're just victims themselves." Cooper, interview by author, April 20, 2010.

75 *He didn't doubt the worthiness of his mission:* "I definitely learned a lot about culture, a lot about Afghanistan, Afghans, Afghan thinking, and a lot about mind-set and pride. I knew how to push the buttons, so to speak," Cooper told me. "I don't know why, but sometimes I feel guilty for some of those things. I never abused anybody. I never tortured anybody. But I screwed a lot of people." Cooper, interview by author, April 20, 2010.

76 *For a kid raised on cowboys and Indians:* He had expected interrogation to be "just a matter of gathering information and passing it on to where it needed to go." It didn't turn out that way. "I don't think I was expecting the internal struggle or conflict, the whole shaking up of your morals." Cooper, interview by author, April 20, 2010.

76 *Cooper returned from Afghanistan a changed man:* Clint and Kathy Cooper, interviews by author, April 20–22, 2010.

76 *They moved to Sierra Vista, Arizona, at the edge of Fort Huachuca.* Fort Huachuca is home to the Army Intelligence Center, where Cooper worked with HUMINT teams before joining the Human Terrain System.

77 *Coyotes howled at night, rattlesnakes slid:* According to http://www.nnirr.org/drupal/migranttrail, more than six thousand people have died crossing the border since the 1990s. See also Edward Schumacher-Matos, "Immigration Reform Is Within Our Grasp. Meanwhile, People Die," *Washington Post,* July 22, 2010.

77 *He started seeing a counselor:* Kathy Cooper, interview by author, April 22, 2010. When he finally received a diagnosis of post-traumatic stress disorder from a medical professional, "it was almost a relief," he told me. "I finally know what's going on and I can understand what's happening here."

77 *Good experiences, good memories:* "I wanted to sit down and drink tea with them, not talk to them at gunpoint," Cooper told me. Cooper, interview by author, April 22, 2010. According to a study of the Human Terrain System, Cooper was one of several people "attracted [to HTS] by the perception that they could counter-balance previous, more lethal activities by signing up for a program that emphasized non-lethality." Lamb et al., "Human Terrain Team Performance: An Explanation, draft," forthcoming 2013, 165.

77 *Once during his time in Kandahar:* Cooper, interview by author, April 20, 2010. "I thought, man, we are just, like, totally failing as a military. And then I read about the Human Terrain System and I thought, 'That's what I want to do.'" On another occasion, Cooper told me that U.S. troops "weren't connecting the dots. The whole cultural thing was just missing. They were using the wrong kind of interpreters in different areas, and there were a lot of mistakes being made." The

Human Terrain System seemed to be filling "the gap, the thing that the military was missing." Cooper, interview by author, April 22, 2010.

77 *The project hired him immediately:* Technically, Cooper applied to and was hired by the defense contractor BAE, which, along with various subcontractors, employed Human Terrain Team members at that time. Cooper, interview by author, April 22, 2010.

77 *Seven months later, he was in Afghanistan:* Cooper started training in Leavenworth in March 2008 and left for Afghanistan in August, landing in Maiwand in late September.

77 *Someone directed them to a tent with a few cots:* The description of Loyd is from interviews with her teammates and photos taken shortly after their arrival.

78 *Ayala had missed this place:* Unless otherwise noted, biographical details and quotes from Don Ayala in the section below are from Ayala, interviews by author, August 17–19, 2009.

78 *Karzai was a royalist from Kandahar:* "Office of the President, Islamic Republic of Afghanistan: Biography," http://president.gov.af/en/page/1043, accessed August 15, 2012, and Coll, *Ghost Wars,* 285–86.

79 *A relentless diplomat who had been trying:* Karzai's Washington contacts extended back to his days as a press, logistics, and aid worker with the anti-Soviet faction of Sibghatullah Mojaddedi during the jihad of the 1980s. Coll, *Ghost Wars,* 285–86.

79 *In the 1990s, after the Soviets withdrew:* Ibid., 286. For his service under Rabbani, see http://www.pbs.org/newshour/updates/asia/july-dec01/karzai_12-03.html, accessed August 15, 2012.

79 *Fahim had been Massoud's security chief:* Coll, *Ghost Wars,* 286–87 and 461–62. For more on Fahim, see "Center for American Progress: Profiles of Afghan Power Brokers," http://www.americanprogress.org/issues/2009/10/afghan_power_brokers .html/#4, accessed August 15, 2012.

79 *In 1999, appalled:* Some attribute the murder of Karzai's father to the Pakistani intelligence service, the ISI.

79 *Arab bombers posing as journalists assassinated:* Coll, *Ghost Wars,* 582, and John F. Burns, "Afghans, Too, Mark a Day of Disaster: A Hero Was Lost," *New York Times,* September 9, 2002.

79 *The men on the Karzai Protective Detail believed:* "We loved how the villagers and everybody greeted the president," Ayala recalled. "It was very emotional, a very, very proud moment to be a part of this history. . . . He was a good man. He treated people very well and he treated us very well. . . . [T]he guy grew on you. . . . We definitely didn't want to lose him on our watch. . . . You don't want to be part of that; it would be hard to live with. So we took pride, but we ended up liking the man."

80 *He went with Karzai to inaugurate:* Karzai officially reopened the Salang Pass in December 2003 with U.S. ambassador Zalmay Khalilzad, about a month before

Ayala left his job with Karzai's protective detail. See Associated Press, "Vital Tunnel Reopens Between North and South Afghanistan," December 28, 2003, and UNHCR, "Chronology of Events in Afghanistan, December 2003," http://www.unhcr.org/refworld/pdfid/407bdce54.pdf, accessed September 15, 2012.

80 *A natural mentor, he counseled:* See letter of David J. Hazarian, Regional Security Officer, Diplomatic Security Service, U.S. Consulate, Peshawar, Pakistan, and former shift leader of the Karzai Protective Detail, to Judge Claude M. Hilton, filed April 23, 2009, in federal court: "Don exhibited a mature understanding of complicated Afghan cultural sensitivities and treated all those he encountered with respect, dignity and honor. Don was especially effective at dealing with the Afghan members of President Karzai's security detail, the Department of State, and Dyn Corp personnel. They looked up to Don and he responded in kind with professional conduct and insightful mentoring." See also letter of Scott Lynton, former member of the Karzai Protective Detail, to Judge Hilton, April 12, 2009: "He would gain the attention of our Afghani-counter parts [*sic*] (presidential body guards). . . . They were very keen to talk and listen to [Ayala]. He was basically their personal trainer in all issues."

80 *He wrote poetry on his bedroom wall:* Letter of Angelica Ramos, Reuters, to Judge Hilton, April 15, 2009, and letter of Scott Lynton: "He would write his own poetry based on his life experience. He would display his poetry by writing on his room wall."

81 *They called him "Don Juan":* Ayala's radio call sign was "Don Juan." See also letter of Scott Lynton: "When we finished work for the day, we had a bar that we could use to unwind and socialize. There was always a group of working professionals around our operation, the majority of which were females. They would frequent our establishment once or twice a week for cocktails at our bar. This is where I witnessed how Don Juan earned his name and how he could be a true gentleman. He established quality relationships with his female friends and made his sincerity shine. It was almost as if he was a shrink for the women he befriended, trying to understand and appreciate who they were and make them feel better about what ever [*sic*] was troubling them. This was not your typical behavior for contractors on the KPD, especially the single men who were looking for something more than a social drink with the available pretty reporter."

81 *They called him the "Minister of Hugs and Kisses":* Letter of Stephen Hohl, former member of the Karzai Protective Detail, to Judge Hilton, filed April 23, 2009, in federal court; letter of Jeffrey P. Hinton to Judge Hilton, April 15, 2009; and letter of Scott Lynton: "Don would literally give hugs and kisses to our counter parts, which was the traditional cultural showing of appreciation and respect to others. Most of us would decline this gesture for various reasons. Don had no problem expressing his appreciation and compassionate side."

81 *When a friend back home offered:* Letter of Karen Rodriguez to Judge Hilton, March 27, 2009.

81 *He left Afghanistan in 2004 and spent:* Ayala was part of an international team that advised protective services personnel for the Iraqi president and a handful of other top Iraqi officials. Ayala, interview by author, August 19, 2009.

81 *As a research manager, Ayala was taught:* Ayala, interview by author, August 19, 2009. By the "Kevin Bacon game" he meant the idea that there are six degrees of separation between Kevin Bacon and anyone working in Hollywood. The software was known as MAP-HT. It was the first, largely unsuccessful iteration of a program designed to be used by Human Terrain field teams. Ayala liked playing with the software in training but found it useless in the field: "[A]s fast as we were going on patrols, we never really had time to sit there and build a network of people." During my time with Human Terrain Teams in Afghanistan between March 2009 and November 2010, I did not see a single team member use the software. An updated version fielded in 2010 was said to work better, but I found no evidence of anybody using that either. See also Yvette Clinton, Virginia Foran-Cain, Julia Voelker McQuaid, Catherine E. Norman, and William H. Sims, "Congressionally Directed Assessment of the Human Terrain System," Center for Naval Analyses, November 2010, 35–36.

82 *Warren had worked for Blackwater and other:* Mike Warren, interview by author, March 20, 2009. The Kabul to Kandahar road was mainly funded by USAID, but Japan also contributed.

82 *There was a reason that people like Ayala:* Ayala, interview by author, August 18, 2009. The purpose of the Ranger Indoctrination Program was to "weed out the weak," he told me.

82 *What the Army needed, Ayala thought:* During training at Leavenworth, Human Terrain System officials celebrated civilian social scientists as the most important part of the mission. "But in the combat zone, they were not," Ayala said. "They were good. They helped. They wrote good reports. But being in the combat zone, being out in the field itself is a different story. To survive in conflict, you've got to be aware of your surroundings. You got to be aware of what can happen. You got to be aware of the guys you're with, the military, and you got to be in shape to go on foot patrols and stuff like that." Ayala, interviews by author, April 19 and May 4, 2009.

82 *Ayala was no anthropologist, but:* That Ayala did this more than once is evidenced by letters from his supporters to Judge Hilton. In one of our interviews, he recalled a night in Kansas City when he and other Human Terrain trainees went out to a bar, where a man menaced them and Ayala talked him down. "Not to toot my horn, but the things I was going to school for, the ethnography, I put it to work right there and turned him from an enemy to a friendly." Ayala, interview by author, April 17, 2010.

83 *She knew what she was talking about and:* Mike Warren told me: "She was as straight, honest, and sweet as you can get. She could be as stubborn and hardheaded as a mule when she was fighting for something she believed in." Warren, interview by author, March 20, 2009.

83 *She was in excellent physical shape and had village savvy:* Ayala, interview by author, August 19, 2009.

83 *'Make sure you stay next to Don':* Frank Muggeo, sentencing documentary submitted in support of Don Ayala in federal court, 2009. Although Ayala claimed that his job description didn't specifically include protecting his teammates, his experience as a bodyguard made that role natural for him. "Paula trusted Don to protect her out there," Mike Warren told me. Warren, interview by author, March 20, 2009.

83 *The apparent success of the surge in Iraq had vaulted Petraeus:* By the fall of 2008, according to the *Times,* NATO, the U.S. military, and the Bush administration had all undertaken reviews of Afghan strategy. "Defense Secretary Robert M. Gates stressed that while it would be a primary task for General Petraeus to 'keep us on the right path in Iraq,' an immediate challenge was 'bringing coherence to our own strategy' in Afghanistan." Thom Shanker, "Petraeus Steps Into New Role as Head of Central Command," *New York Times,* October 31, 2008.

83 *They urged the recently appointed NATO commander:* Joshua Kucera, "McChrystal Represents a New Direction at the Pentagon and in Afghanistan," *U.S. News & World Report,* May 18, 2009.

83 *But McKiernan was an old-school commander:* McKiernan had already told his superiors that he needed more troops, but they weren't immediately forthcoming. See Charles D. Allen, "Lessons Not Learned: Civil-Military Disconnect in Afghanistan," *Armed Forces Journal,* September 2010, http://www.armedforcesjournal .com/2010/09/4728929, accessed August 16, 2012.

83 *"We can't kill our way to victory":* Mullen made this comment before the House Armed Services Committee on September 10, 2008, just ten days before Ayala and his teammates landed in Kandahar.

83 *The team was attached to an Army unit:* Vanessa M. Gezari, "Rough Terrain," *Washington Post Magazine,* August 30, 2009.

83 *The brigade's other battalions were stationed:* In January 2008, an independent Canadian panel determined that "the most damaging and obvious deficiency in the ISAF mission in Afghanistan is the insufficiency of military forces deployed against insurgents. Therefore, Canada's military mission in Kandahar should be conditionally extended beyond February 2009—*the extension to be expressly contingent on the deployment of additional troops by one or more ISAF countries to Kandahar province.*" (Emphasis is mine.) The deployment of the 2–2 to Maiwand in the summer of 2008 was an attempt to meet Canada's demand for one thousand more troops in Kandahar after no other coalition partners stepped forward, Lieutenant Colonel Dan Hurlbut, the 2–2's commander, told me. "The point of the report and the point of the request was specifically for non-U.S. countries, other coalition partners, to increase their investment . . . in Afghanistan," Hurlbut said. "At the time, for whatever reason, no country said, 'I'll do it.' So the prime minister of Canada went to [President George W. Bush] and said, 'Hey look, these are the things that my country is dealing with politically. The Manley Commission is

being received, these are the requirements . . . and President Bush said, 'Okay, you can have a battalion.'" Hurlbut, interview by author, March 26, 2009. The panel was known as the Manley Commission after its chair, former Canadian cabinet minister John Manley. "The Canadians call us the Manley Battalion," the 2–2's executive officer, Major Cale Brown, told me. "RC South has been the economy of force [theater] for years, and only now people are figuring out that this is the hotbed." Brown, interview by author, March 22, 2009. See Independent Panel on Canada's Future Role in Afghanistan, "Final Report," January 2008, 35, http://publications.gc.ca/collections/collection_2008/dfait-maeci/FR5-20-1-2008E.pdf, accessed August 1, 2012; CanWest News Service, "Troop Shortfall Persists in Afghanistan: Manley," September 11, 2008; and Ian Austen, "Panel Questions Canadian Role in Afghanistan," *New York Times,* January 23, 2008. The rest of the 1st Infantry Division's 3rd Brigade Combat Team was based in Jalalabad with operations in Kunar, Nuristan, Nangarhar, and Laghman.

84 *At first, the Americans thought Maiwand was tame:* This misconception was shared by soldiers of the 2–2 whom I met in Maiwand in 2009 and members of a different unit stationed there in 2010. Said the 2–2's executive officer, Major Cale Brown: "I actually thought it was going to be worse. I thought it was going to be more kinetic, getting shot at more. But I can understand why we don't. There aren't a great number of places to hide around here as opposed to Zhari and Panjwai, where the Canadians get into firefights quite a bit. It's pretty open. Someone shoots at you, you're going to see them and be able to shoot back, and we always have overwhelming firepower." Brown, interview by author, March 22, 2009.

84 *East of the half-built American bases and north:* In a 2001 account of the battle, Ali Jalali, a former colonel in the Afghan army who served as Afghan interior minister in Karzai's government, and Lester Grau of the Foreign Military Studies Office described the British defeat at Maiwand as "one of the major military disasters of the Victorian era." The authors write that, for the British public, the combined impact of the defeat in Maiwand and another loss the previous year in the Zulu wars was similar to what Americans felt after Custer's defeat at Little Big Horn. Jalali and Grau, "Expeditionary Forces: Superior Technology Defeated—The Battle of Maiwand."

84 *"a military rat-trap":* Personal Records of the Kandahar Campaign, by Officers Engaged Therein, edited and annotated with an introduction by Major Waller Ashe (London: David Bogue, 1881), 57. The same British officer described Kushk-i-Nakhud, the Maiwand district center where the American base overlooked the ruins of a British fort, as a place "where a clever and artful enemy knowing the country could give or refuse an attack at discretion. The ground when I saw it last year was cut up with small canals, watercourses, small but frequent stone walls, gardens, vineyards, and ruined houses, affording every facility for a sudden attack, and placing the attacking party, from the scattered nature of these obstacles, on a complete equality with the defenders." *Personal Records,* 56–57.

84 *On a blistering summer day in 1880:* Jalali and Grau, "Expeditionary Forces," and *Personal Records of the Kandahar Campaign*, 71. The British force included 2,599 combat soldiers, six nine-pound cannons, some 3,000 "service and transport personnel," and "[m]ore than 3,000 transport animals—ammunition ponies, mules, donkeys, bullocks and hundreds of camels—[which] were required to move the baggage. The animals required drovers, usually locally contracted Kandaharis. There were many other noncombatants, including cooks, water carriers, tailors, servants and stretcher-bearers." Jalali and Grau, "Expeditionary Forces."

84 *Local volunteers had joined Ayub's forces:* The British also lost some two thousand Afghan forces to Ayub after they mutineed and crossed the Helmand River to join him. *Personal Records,* 48–52, 68–70. For other tribal fighters joining Ayub and details about their weapons as well as the significance of the *ghazis'* white clothes, see Jalali and Grau, "Expeditionary Forces."

84 *By the day of the battle, the Afghans:* Jalali and Grau write that the differential was not so severe, about 5,500 British troops (including Indian and Afghan forces) facing about 8,500 Afghan troops and irregular volunteers loyal to Ayub. But other accounts suggest that the number of Afghan irregular forces was higher. See Sarah Chayes, *The Punishment of Virtue: Inside Afghanistan After the Taliban* (New York: Penguin, 2006), 128.

84 *They hid in shallow wadis, surprising the British: Personal Records,* 74–82. For the story of Malalai, see Jalali and Grau, "Expeditionary Forces," 12. Malalai was killed in the fighting and buried in her native village of Khik, in the northern part of the plain, where a domed shrine stands in her memory. See also "The Second Anglo-Afghan War 1878–1880: Malalai, Afghan Heroine of Maiwand," http://www.garenewing.co.uk/angloafghanwar/biography/malalai.php, accessed August 1, 2012.

85 *The Afghans rolled over the British line like a wave:* Nearly two thousand mostly Indian soldiers on the British side were killed. Those left alive fled in terror toward Kandahar city. Jalali and Grau, "Expeditionary Forces," and *Personal Records,* 78–85. One British officer wrote that the defeat was a result of "the same overweening confidence in our invincibility, the same contempt of an unknown foe, the same attempt at scientific strategy, when the simplest old-fashioned British tactics would have won the day." *Personal Records,* 75.

85 *A century later, a pious peasant arrived:* This account of Omar's early life closely follows Ahmed Rashid's in *Taliban,* 23–25. See also John F. Burns and Steve LeVine, "How Afghans' Stern Rulers Took Hold," *New York Times,* December 31, 1996, and Steve Coll, "Looking for Mullah Omar," *New Yorker,* January 23, 2012. In the lawless era between 1989 and 1996, warring militia commanders killed some forty thousand people in Kabul alone. "Every warlord had a fief, and every fief had its own checkpoint, where neither a man's cash nor his daughter was safe." Filkins, *The Forever War,* 23. See also Chayes, *The Punishment of Virtue,* 70–73. Omar's first companions in his fight against the warlords were his religious students, or Talibs, from which the movement takes its name. Today, Singesar lies in Zhari, a new

district created after the U.S. invasion, but when Omar lived there, Singesar was in Maiwand.

85 *In the beginning, there had been a sense of possibility:* Anyone who spent time in Afghanistan in the early years after the invasion experienced this widespread optimism. Of a moment just before the U.S. invasion Chayes writes that Afghans "were electrified by the belief that, with American help, the nightmare was going to end, and they would at last be able to lay the foundations of the kind of Afghan state they dreamed of: one united under a qualified, responsible government." Immediately after the invasion, Kandahar "shimmered with a breathless hope." Chayes, *The Punishment of Virtue,* 20, 105.

86 *In 2001, the American-supported governor:* Chayes, *The Punishment of Virtue,* 63–68, 73–75, 77, and James Traub, "O Brother, Where Art Thou?" *Foreign Policy,* May 19, 2010: "Like AWK, Sherzai was deeply implicated in the drug trade, had shadowy relations with the insurgents, and ran roughshod over the concerns of Kandaharis, making him a loathed figure. But he had men and trucks at his command and delivered intelligence the Americans trusted." In addition, when I was reporting in Afghanistan in 2002 and 2003, at least one U.S. official, among other sources, discussed Sherzai's ties to the drug trade with me.

86 *Sherzai's chief factotum:* This is based on my own meetings and interviews with Pashtoon in 2003, but Pashtoon's power with the Americans is borne out by other accounts. According to Chayes, Mohammad Akram Khakrezwal, a former police chief in Kandahar and Mazar-i-Sharif, told her: 'The Americans were such amateurs. They were honest to the point of simplemindedness. Anyone Shirzai or his interpreter told them was a Talib, they would take it on faith—and act on the accusation' (77). On Pashtoon's role as Sherzai's "interpreter" and his closeness with the U.S. Special Forces, see Chayes, *The Punishment of Virtue,* 78–79.

86 *But many powerful Afghans and their allies:* Governor Sherzai "applied all of the well-meaning Western aid—lavished on him in his role as a representative of the Afghan government—to the purpose of building up a *personal* power base. . . . Gul Agha Shirzai diverted much of the plunder he extracted from his own province, and much of the subsidy he extracted from international representatives." Chayes, *The Punishment of Virtue,* 169. For the specific targeting of rural people on the outskirts of Kandahar and especially in Maiwand, Hajji Mohammad Ehsan, Maiwand district representative to the Kandahar Provincial Council, interview by author, October 12, 2010.

86 *With the Taliban gone and the soil parched:* Ehsan, interview by author, October 12, 2010. Chayes recounts that after the American invasion, when she was helping to rebuild a village outside Kandahar that had been destroyed by American bombs, she went to Governor Sherzai's office to ask for stone from a quarry he controlled. While there, she saw among the petitioners a "sinewy old man" who tried to get an official's attention by "positively begging—kissing his fingertips and touching them to his own eyes in entreaty—saying he had come three days in a row, please give him his opium back." Chayes, *The Punishment of Virtue,* 165–66. She also mentions

the visit of an Amnesty International delegation "asking a lot of uncomfortable questions about the treatment of prisoners in private jails." Chayes, 167.

86 *Afghans connected to the Kandahar government also ran a kidnapping scheme:* Ehsan, interview by author, October 12, 2010.

87 *The road and its tributaries cut east to west:* Although opium cultivation fluctuates from year to year, it reached a record high in 2008, the year the 2–2 arrived in Maiwand. By 2010, opium production in Helmand had decreased significantly, but the province nevertheless remained Afghanistan's largest opium producer, responsible for 53 percent of the country's total opium cultivation. United Nations Office on Drugs and Crime (UNODC), "Afghanistan Opium Survey 2010: Summary Findings" (September 2010), 10. http://news.bbc.co.uk/2/shared/bsp/hi/pdfs/30_09_10_opiumsurvey.pdf, accessed August 2, 2012.

87 *The U.S. military called it Highway 1:* The United States was the biggest funder of the Kandahar to Herat section of the highway, contributing about $200 million to pave 325 of its 556 kilometers. Saudi Arabia and Japan also contributed about $50 million each to rebuilding this section of the road.

87 *It was so quiet—more truck stop than town, an in-between place:* Lieutenant Kirsten Ouimette, one of the sharpest officers I met in Maiwand in 2010, supplied an apt description of the place: "You're driving down the highway and you stop at a gas station, and there's a little town just to support this one truck stop. That's what this feels like on Highway 1." Ouimette, interview by author, October 2, 2010. Before the arrival of the 2–2, the Americans and their main coalition partners in that area, the Canadians, had paid Maiwand little attention in comparison to places closer to Kandahar city, where fighting was heavier. International troops, mostly Canadians and U.S. Special Forces, had occasionally conducted raids there. Lieutenant Colonel Hurlbut, the battalion commander in Maiwand in 2008 and 2009, described these to me as "either intelligence-driven operations or just because they knew they needed to come out here. They would do very focused, very short-duration operations, but then would go back to wherever they were originally at. So you had this effect of the people not really having faith in the government, not having faith in the coalition, because we weren't there long enough to make any kind of true change." The 2–2, by comparison, wanted to move in and stay. Hurlbut, interview by author, March 26, 2009.

87 *The soldiers of the 2–2 landed:* Major Cale Brown, interview by author, March 22, 2009.

87 *As the first American unit deployed there:* Although the 2–2 was on fifteen-month orders, the battalion got to Maiwand in mid-August and planned to be out of the district by June. Hurlbut, interview by author, March 26, 2009. By the time I got to Maiwand in March 2009, about 700 people lived on Ramrod and a company element of 100 to 130 people lived on each of the smaller bases, Hutal and Terminator. Brown, interview by author, March 22, 2009. The 2–2 was a one-thousand-soldier task force, but because of leave schedules and missions back to Kandahar, it is

unlikely that all of those soldiers were in Maiwand at any one time. Hurlbut, interview by author, March 26, 2009.

88 *That was the vision, at least:* Hurlbut told me: "When we got here, we expected we're going to do one month of driving everywhere for the first time meeting everybody, another month of some security ops where we're going to kill all the bad guys and let 'em know who's in charge of the neighborhood. Do a quarter of building up some government structures so we can get that working and then the last quarter we're going to bring a whole bunch of money in and build roads and projects. Not happening. It took six, seven and a half months for the district leader to start hugging me. That's just one example. So the people I'm not talking to on a weekly basis out there in no-man's-land, their time horizons are much longer than we can conceive of." Hurlbut, interview by author, March 26, 2009. See also Rajiv Chandrasekaran, "Troops Face New Tests in Afghanistan," *Washington Post,* March 15, 2009.

88 *The flat earth over which they sometimes walked:* This description of the bombs is based on my interview with an Explosive Ordnance Device team leader in Panjwaii District, just east of Maiwand, September 24, 2009. In addition to explaining how bombs were made in that part of the country, he showed me the remains of several explosives his team had unearthed in recent months.

88 *Every day, it seemed, someone got hit:* Don Ayala, interview by author, August 19, 2009. Ayala told me that during the time he and his teammates spent in Maiwand, there were "IEDs like crazy every day. The wreckers would have to go pick up one of our vehicles because it was blown on the side of the road every day. We got hit by IEDs every day. Even our wreckers and the sweep team from Darkhorse would go out, and their vehicles would hit an IED."

88 *A Humvee blew up, killing a soldier:* A private was killed and four other soldiers were hurt in the attack on September 4, 2008. The burned lieutenant was Sam Brown, a platoon leader and West Point graduate. Major Trevor Voelkel, interview by author, February 12, 2013, and Jay Kirk, "Burning Man," *GQ,* February 2012.

88 *For a time that fall, more buried bombs:* Brown, interview by author, March 22, 2009: "There was a stretch up through December [2008, when] we were averaging an IED find or an IED strike at least every other day. Significant. We crunched the numbers in December and we were, like, 'We're the most heavily IED'd place in Afghanistan, and not just Afghanistan, but Iraq, too.'" This statistic was widely known in the battalion, and several other soldiers and officers mentioned it to me, including Lieutenant David Ochs, interview by author, April 6, 2009.

88 *Their mission was to win Afghans away from the insurgency:* Ochs, interview by author, April 6, 2009. Observations in this section are based on interviews and patrols with soldiers from the 2–2 in March and April 2009, especially a mission to Zhari on April 6, 2009, when we saw the man cleaning his teeth, glowering and spitting, and overheard insurgents talking about us on the radio.

88 *But Maiwand was so far from being controlled by U.S. forces:* Ayala, interviews by author, May 4 and August 19, 2009.

0

89 *"She didn't necessarily feel that the protection was as good":* Stacy Crevello, interview by author, December 17, 2012. Ayala told me that Loyd agreed that Maiwand was rough and insecure, but that didn't keep her from wanting to be out there. "We did have our disagreements," Ayala told me. "She was so excited about getting projects ready to go for this area, her vision was optimistic, but also very futuristic. I was just a little disappointed with [the 2–2]. They were focused on doing a wheat seed program, and I'm going, 'It's not going to work, this is going to get into the hands of the merchants, who are going to sell it for profit.'" In Ayala's view, "the military need to come [into Maiwand with the] Afghan army, Afghan police, kick out the [Taliban] shadow government, then bring in Human Terrain and civil affairs. But these decisions are made not in the field, but in the Pentagon, back in D.C., where people eat good and sleep warm at night." Ayala, interview by author, May 4, 2009.

89 *She wanted to teach farmers about drip irrigation:* At Loyd's suggestion, the 2–2 was building a sample farm to showcase the results of drip irrigation and other progressive farming methods, Hurlbut told me. Hurlbut, interview by author, March 26, 2009. "She'd been in the country a long time, and she was an absolutely phenomenal asset," Hurlbut told me. "The other thing she brought to the table was the development piece. . . . She opened our eyes to how you [have to] give the people other ideas [about how] to do things."

89 *Don't treat the locals badly:* Ayala told me that the soldiers "were so frustrated that their guys were getting hurt, but they can't find the bad guys. . . . We came up with a solution for these frustrated soldiers and educated them. [We] said, 'Listen, guys, you're not going to see them. They're going to blend in. They're playing the game. They know what your rules of engagement are. They're taking advantage of that.' I said, 'They're going to be right there in broad daylight looking in your eyes with no weapons in their hands. They know that you can't touch them.' But in the meantime, we advised them, 'Do not create more enemies. Don't get frustrated where you're just going to treat everybody like shit.' I go, 'Build rapports. Be patient. They're going to start pointing out to you who the enemy is once they trust you, because they want them out of their villages, because they know it's going to be trouble later on. So build rapports, have patience and they'll give us the enemy.' That's the advice we'd give them. You know we discussed it with Paula, discussed it with Clint." Ayala, interview by author, August 19, 2009.

89 *Tim Gusinov:* Gusinov was born in what is now Azerbaijan but moved to Moscow with his mother when he was a toddler. Unless otherwise noted, quotes and biographical information about him in this section are from Gusinov, interview by author, June 18, 2011.

89 *Trained as an Afghan area specialist and Persian linguist:* At the military academy, Gusinov and other students were assigned to master a pair of languages. His were Farsi, of which Afghan Dari is a dialect, and English. He spent his first tour attached to an Afghan army division in Ghazni and began his second tour with another Afghan unit in Gardez until the Spetsnaz poached him.

90  *When a Human Terrain System recruiter called:* The recruiter was actually from BAE, the defense contractor that handled recruitment and hiring for the Human Terrain System.

90  *Observing that the Americans:* Gusinov, interview by author, June 18, 2011; Hurlbut, interview by author, March 26, 2009; Cooper, interview by author, April 22, 2010.

90  *"He's like a rock star":* When he first met Gusinov, Hurlbut's impression was different: "We're, like, 'Dude, I can tell you're a Soviet by your accent. There is no way we're going to put you in front of any Afghan,'" Hurlbut told me. But Gusinov's Dari and his ease with Afghans ultimately impressed Hurlbut and his fellow officers. Hurlbut, interview by author, March 26, 2009.

90  *Indeed, Gusinov had been trained by the Soviets:* Gusinov's Soviet training prepared him for work as a "linguist-area specialist," a job he described as "much more intel and targeting, especially when you are attached to a Special Forces unit." Gusinov knew that as a member of a Human Terrain Team he wasn't supposed to actively seek out intelligence, but the distinction struck him as theortetical. "On one occasion we captured a young guy who was suspected of putting IEDs on the road, and he was scared to death," Gusinov told me. "He thought he would be killed. And I spoke to him, like, 'Calm down. If you're frank to me I might be able to help you.' And he told me, 'I'm a young man. I want to have nice clothes. I want to have a radio. I want to smoke nice cigarettes. A phone. There are no jobs, and I'm not Taliban but they paid me two thousand Afghani for planting an IED on the road.' . . . I spoke with him when he was back in the base. . . . I was always giving this information or I was even writing a short note to our S2 [intelligence] officer." Gusinov, interview by author, June 18, 2011.

90  *Since they'd met in Kansas:* Cooper, interview by author, April 22, 2010, and Gusinov, interview by author, June 18, 2011. Cooper told me that he and several others, including Loyd, had been so offended by Gusinov's crass comments during training that they had unsuccessfully petitioned program administrators to fire him.

91  *Gusinov thought it was no place for a woman:* Having reported in Maiwand, Kandahar, and other parts of the south since 2003, I disagree with Gusinov. Loyd's Afghan experience had also been primarily in the south, in and around Kandahar after the invasion and later in Zabul before she went to work in Kabul. Don Ayala, who worked with her often, recalled only two occasions out of about twenty interviews they conducted together when he felt moved to step in and stand at her side: one involved an irate village elder; another time, he felt that "some of the males were uncomfortable speaking to her" and "she didn't feel comfortable." But "most of the time, she had people going, people willing to talk to her." Ayala, interview by author, August 19, 2009. Nevertheless, many American troops and even some of Gusinov's fellow Human Terrain teammates shared his view that "Paula was the wrong person in the wrong time and space. Kandahar and Maiwand District is not a place for a lady to go around and ask questions. I understand everything about diversity and equal opportunity," Gusinov told me, "but there are some things that you never ever do in Afghanistan. She would be perfect somewhere up north

with Tajiks, Uzbeks, in Bagram, in Mazar-i-Sharif. In those places she would be absolutely fine." Gusinov, interview by author, June 18, 2011.

91 *His attention was drawn to the edges:* That Gusinov paid special attention to insurgent areas and advised the commander to do so as well, Ayala, interview by author, August 19, 2009, and Gusinov, interview by author, June 18, 2011. For the weapons, supplies, and other paraphernalia found in the Garmabak and Band-i-Timur, Captain Michael Soyka, interview by author, April 5, 2009, and Voelkel, interview by author, February 12, 2013.

91 *When the Maiwand district governor quoted:* Ayala, Cooper, Gusinov, and Warren, "HTT Patrol Report: Maiwand District Governor Meeting," October 25, 2008.

91 *Loyd, Ayala, and Cooper accompanied soldiers:* Ayala, Loyd, and Cooper, "HTT Patrol Report: Kashk E Nokhowd," October 24, 2008, and Loyd, "HTT Patrol Report: USPI Compound," October 26, 2008. USPI is a private security company that was working for the Americans at the time. This report also includes interviews from residential compounds.

91 *Loyd, Ayala, and Cooper lived together:* The description of their working lives in Maiwand in this section is drawn from Ayala, interviews by author, August 19, 2009, and April 17, 2010, and Cooper, interview by author, April 22, 2010.

92 *Understanding the connections:* "Everyone in the villages [was] very standoffish. . . . It would have taken time. You had to build relationships. . . , then start asking personal questions: 'How are you related to this person? Do you know anybody in this village over here? Do you have any family over there?' Once you got to know them, you would have realized if they were telling the truth or not." Ayala, interview by author, August 19, 2009.

93 *They moved between Comanche and Darkhorse:* Ayala, interviews by author, May 4 and August 19, 2009.

93 *Sometimes Loyd asked Cooper:* Cooper, interview by author, April 22, 2010.

93 *A woman gave Loyd her baby to hold:* "HTT Patrol Report: Kashk E Nokhowd," October 24, 2008, includes a photo of Loyd sitting with a group of Afghan women and children and holding a baby. Her popularity among children was legendary among soldiers of the 2–2 and her teammates.

93 *Sometimes the kids were useful:* For Ayala, the incident with the fake name "proved that the adults couldn't be trusted and the kids were very truthful." Ayala, interview by author, August 19, 2009.

93 *Afghan police stationed along the highway:* Ayala, Cooper, Gusinov, and Warren, "HTT Patrol Report: Maiwand District Governor Meeting," October 25, 2008, and Cooper, interview by author, April 22, 2010. Several of the team's reports from this period include accounts of Afghan police corruption. At least one person also complained of Taliban taxes on the roads. See Ayala, Loyd, and Cooper, "HTT Patrol Report: Khaki Chopan," October 27, 2008.

93 *One day in October:* Ayala and Cooper, "HTT Patrol Report: 'Hotel' Police Station," October 26, 2008.

94 *When Loyd's interpreter overheard:* Loyd, "HTT Patrol Report: USPI Compound," October 29, 2008.

94 *A widow told Loyd how much she hated 'the motherfucking Taliban':* Loyd, "HTT Patrol Report: USPI Compound Interviews," October 26, 2008.

94 *She suggested mapping tribal affiliations:* Information in this paragraph comes from Loyd, "HTT Patrol Report: USPI Compound Interviews," October 26, 2008. Loyd wrote: "It would be useful to map tribal affiliations of individual compounds and villages in the AO. The unit would have a better understanding of relationships among the local populace and could utilize this information for COIN operations."

94 *That October, insurgents stopped a bus:* Carlotta Gall and Taimoor Shah, "Taliban Behead 30 Men Pulled from Bus," *New York Times,* October 19, 2008, and Hurlbut, interview by author, March 26, 2009.

94 *An Afghan told the Human Terrain Team:* Ayala, Loyd, and Cooper, "HTT Patrol Report: Khaki Chopan," October 27, 2008. According to Ayala, the checkpoint was never built.

95 *Insurgents taxed villagers and common bandits waited:* On Taliban taxes, see ibid. For the known holdup point where bandits waited, see Ayala, Cooper, Gusinov, and Warren, "HTT Patrol Report: Maiwand District Governor Meeting," October 25, 2008.

96 *The Human Terrain Team met:* Ayala and Cooper, "HTT Patrol Report: Gach Karez Kalay," October 26, 2008.

96 *A man begged the soldiers not to shoot at his sons:* "Another person the HTT members spoke with . . . was worried about being bombed by American airplanes. These two incidences could reflect a general fear of the power/technology of international forces and the potential for civilian casualties. In order to effectively win over the population, the [battalion] needs to reinforce the image of US Forces targeting/attacking [antigovernment forces] but supporting the [Afghan government] and protecting the local populace." Loyd, "HTT Patrol Report: USPI Compound Interviews," October 26, 2008.

96 *told them that he didn't use his kerosene lamp:* Ayala, Loyd, and Cooper, "HTT Patrol Report: Khaki Chopan," October 27, 2008. The team members were apparently unsure of what they had heard: "The interpretation of this statement left much to be desired."

96 *People needed fuel for generators:* Ayala, Loyd, and Cooper, "HTT Patrol Report: Khaki Chopan," October 27, 2008; Ayala and Cooper, "HTT Patrol Report: Gach Karez Kalay," October 26, 2008.

96 *They encouraged soldiers to build trust with locals:* Ayala and Cooper, "HTT Patrol Report: 'Hotel' Police Station," October 26, 2008.

96 *Villagers in Maiwand were poor and would accept help from anybody:* Ibid.

96 *When a man who had lost his foot:* Loyd, "HTT Patrol Report: USPI Compound," October 29, 2008.

96 *That October, Loyd was working on a document:* I obtained three different drafts of this document; it is unclear whether any of them were finished, or if the report were ever distributed to the battalion or sent to the Human Terrain System headquarters in Kansas. I view these drafts as a palimpsest of Loyd's thinking as she puzzled out how best to express her findings to the soldiers.

97 *Part of her job was to make the Americans:* Loyd wrote: "[U]ntil villagers begin to trust the US Forces operating in their area and feel less threatened . . . they are not likely to volunteer much information. It is probably going to take multiple visits, conducted over an extended period of time to gain the trust and confidence of the people. . . . These first engagements should focus on building relationships and trust." Loyd, "Mulik, Malik and Mesheran," draft, October 2008.

97 *Over Loyd's protests, her teammates organized a meeting:* Ayala, interview by author, May 4, 2009; Cooper, interview by author, April 22, 2010; and Gusinov, interview by author, June 18, 2011.

97 *Ahmed Wali was President Hamid Karzai's half brother:* On his alleged drug and CIA connections, see Dexter Filkins, Mark Mazzetti, and James Risen, "Brother of Afghan Leader Said to be Paid by CIA," *New York Times,* October 27, 2009; Simon Tisdall, "Ahmed Wali Karzai, the Corrupt and Lawless Face of Modern Afghanistan," *Guardian,* July 12, 2011; and "Confidential U.S. Diplomatic Cable: Ahmed Wali Karzai and Governor Weesa on Governance in Kandahar," October 3, 2009, via WikiLeaks and published in *New York Times,* http://www.nytimes.com/interactive/2010/11/28/world/20101128-cables-viewer.html?scp=1&sq=memo%20ahmed%20wali%20karzai&st=cse#report/cables-09KABUL3068, accessed August 4, 2012. Wali Karzai denied the CIA payments and links to the drug trade until his death in 2011.

97 *Ayala, Gusinov, and Mike Warren:* Cooper, interview by author, April 22, 2010: "Mike Warren and [the other men on the team were] all excited about, 'We're meeting Wali Karzai.'" Ayala told me: "Wali Karzai, he's a power broker, a strong power broker in the area, and stronger than the government there. And we had some doors open, and we had meetings take place. We met elders, we were invited into villages after that. It didn't matter what other people thought or what allegedly he's done. If he's a big drug lord, he's never been arrested for it, he's never been convicted of it. So everything's a lot of rumors going around. But the thing is, he treated us with respect, we gave him respect. We brought the military to him, he brought other elders from other villages to meet with the military, and it worked out great. So those are things that we made happen out there." Ayala, interview by author, August 17, 2009.

97 *'basically . . . a criminal':* Cooper, interview by author, April 22, 2010.

97 *"She was a little bit idealistic about that":* "She wouldn't go there because he was cor-

rupt. It was against her principles to deal with corrupt officials," Gusinov told me. Gusinov, interview by author, June 18, 2011.

97 *Loyd and Cooper learned about a shopkeepers' organization:* Cooper, interview by author, April 22, 2010.

98 *At least three times, Loyd, Ayala, and Cooper:* For their visits to and impressions of the bazaar, the things they bought, the kids throwing rocks, and Ayala's arm-wrestling match with the Afghan, Ayala, interview by author, August 19, 2009, and Cooper, interviews by author, April 20 and 22, 2010.

98 *Shoppers complained:* "Patrol Report: Today We Went to the Bazaar," draft, November 1, 2008, and Cooper, interview by author, April 22, 2010.

98 *"He said there were no other elders":* Paula Loyd, "HTT Patrol Report," draft, October 31, 2008.

99 *"very cautious":* Citations in this paragraph are from Loyd, "Lesbian Resistance in the Bars of San Antonio, Texas," 11, 14–15.

99 *One Human Terrain draft report that fall recorded a conversation:* "HTT Patrol Report," draft, October 30, 2008.

*Chapter 5: The Anthropology of Us and Them*

101 *T. E. Lawrence's success:* See "Lawrence of Arabia," http://www.pbs.org/lawrence ofarabia/players/lawrence.html, accessed June 8, 2012; and Stephen E. Tabachnick, *The T. E. Lawrence Puzzle* (Athens: University of Georgia Press, 2012), 11, 27, 145, 174, 193–95, 208–15.

101 *"The beginning and ending of the secret":* T. E. Lawrence, "27 Articles," *Arab Bulletin,* August 20, 1917.

102 *Her mother had been the half-Mexican granddaughter:* Unless otherwise noted, quotations and biographical details about McFate in this chapter come from McFate, interviews by author, December 17, 2009, and June 30–July 1, 2010.

103 *At some point, Westerberg . . . got arrested for dealing marijuana:* A letter from an acquaintance of Barney West's notes that he was transferred from San Quentin to the Mendocino State Hospital, where he learned to carve wood: "[A] great doctor in charge. He got Barney interested in wood-carving . . . and his carvings sold very well up there. Today Barney is a very well-known Tiki carver. His place is in Sausalito called: Tiki Junction." "Holly Letters," correspondence of Eleanor Borden, October 23, 1971, with thanks to Victoria Bogdan for sharing these letters.

103 *West told people that he had served:* This is McFate's account. See also Lyle W. Price, "Barney West Famous for Tricky Tikis," Associated Press, December 13, 1965: "West says he was taught by carving masters when he was shipwrecked in the merchant marine for six months in 1943 in the Marquesas Islands, about 800 miles north of Tahiti."

103 *Poynter and West moved to Sausalito:* "He totally capitalized on this crazy story [of his shipwreck in Polynesia] and became, like, the world's most famous tiki carver," McFate told me. McFate, interview by author, December 17, 2009. See also Price, "Barney West Famous for Tricky Tikis," and "Tiki Junction, Sausalito," http://mohurley.blogspot.com/2007/03/tiki-junction-sausalito.html, accessed June 12, 2012. According to Price, West also made tikis for resorts, shopping centers, and a church.

103 *He had found a way to turn mid-twentieth-century America's:* McFate, interview by author, December 17, 2009, and Nina Burleigh, "McFate's Mission," *More*, September, 2007.

103 *The barges had been used to tow ammunition:* Phil Frank, *Houseboats of Sausalito* (Charleston, SC: Arcadia, 2008), 73–76, and Joe Tate, interview by Sara Breselor, July 20, 2012.

104 *Poynter docked her barge in Richardson Bay:* For more on the barge purchase and McFate's early years at Gate 5, Matthew B. Stannard, "Montgomery McFate's Mission: Can One Anthropologist Possibly Steer the Course in Iraq?" *San Francisco Chronicle*, April 29, 2007, and Tate, interview by Sara Breselor, July 20, 2012.

104 *Poynter met McFate's father, Martin Carlough:* Details about Martin Carlough in this section are from McFate, interviews by author, December 17, 2009, and July 1, 2010; Tate, interview by Sara Breselor, July 20, 2012; and Stannard, "Montgomery McFate's Mission."

104 *Although McFate's parents were married briefly:* Stannard quotes McFate on her mother: "Her advice to me when I was a kid was never write anything down, don't leave any records, never trust the government, don't join any organizations. She was a real anarchist." Poynter ultimately relented and let McFate join the Girl Scouts.

105 *Poynter was one of the few houseboat dwellers:* Tate notes that Poynter had a "special deal" with Arques, and that she was more concerned with the respectability of Gate 5 than most residents. See also Frank, *Houseboats of Sausalito*, 74–75.

106 *Poynter, by most conventional definitions a radical:* By McFate's account, Poynter told her neighbors: 'Fuck all of you people. I've been here since 1957. I'd had this boat condemned how many times? I'm all in favor of putting sewage lines in and legal electricity because I want to live in peace and not be subjected to this pressure and insecurity.' McFate, interview by author, December 17, 2009.

106 *The developers declared:* McFate, interview by author, December 17, 2009, and "Gate 5 Survivors," www.gate5survivors.com, accessed July 24, 2012, which includes original news footage of the conflict with the sheriff and the sinking of the Red Barge.

106 *A man known as Teepee Tom:* McFate, interview by author, December 17, 2009, and Tate, interview by Sara Breselor, July 20, 2012.

107 *Meanwhile, a private drama played out on the barge:* For McFate's experience during the houseboat wars and her chaotic homelife, including studying at the bus stop,

McFate, interview by author, December 17, 2009; Burleigh, "McFate's Mission"; and Stannard, "Montgomery McFate's Mission."

107 *She befriended a classmate who lived in Marin City:* McFate, interview by author, December 17, 2009, and "Welcome to Marin City, California," www.marincitygov .org/2.1_history.html, accessed July 24, 2012.

107 *The housing projects of Marin City:* McFate, interview by author, December 17, 2009. Stannard writes: "the white curtains in the bedroom of a Marin City friend seemed to McFate an unimaginable luxury." Stannard, "Montgomery McFate's Mission."

108 *The writer Cintra Wilson:* Unless otherwise noted, quotes from Cintra Wilson in this chapter are from Wilson, interview by author, August 9, 2010.

108 *In her novel:* Cintra Wilson, *Colors Insulting to Nature* (New York: HarperCollins, 2004), 96.

108 *McFate dressed almost entirely in black:* Wilson, interview by author, August 9, 2010. See also Stannard, "Montgomery McFate's Mission": '[W]e called her 'Satan's beekeeper,' Wilson told Stannard. 'She was goth before anybody was goth.'

108 *But she was good at school:* Wilson, interview by author, August 9, 2010, and McFate, interview by author, December 17, 2009. "The only thing that provided order was school, and I was really good at school," McFate told me. "It was a logical system, it was a rational system, like, if you do your homework and you show up to class and you interact and you participate, and you spend a little time working, you're going to get a good grade."

109 *McFate started working when she was fifteen:* Details about McFate's teenaged years, including the deaths of her friends, are from McFate, interview by author, December 17, 2009. See also Stannard, "Montgomery McFate's Mission," and Burleigh, "McFate's Mission." By McFate's account, Elizabeth's death inspired the Jim Carroll song-poem "For Elizabeth"; she felt that his punk anthem "People Who Died" summed up her teenaged experience of loss. See "'For Elizabeth' by Jim Carroll," http://www.youtube.com/watch?v=MpcIYh7sL5Q, accessed July 25, 2012.

109 *She was the first in a series of friends:* In all, three of McFate's boyfriends killed themselves, including one who overdosed on heroin. McFate's friend Sarah Spiegelman was shot on March 17, 1983, in Golden Gate Park by a psychotic man who was infuriated by the sight of Spiegelman, a white woman, out walking with a black man. The case got even stranger when Spiegelman's father shot her murderer in a courtroom in 1986. See Dan Morain, "Court Shooting—Crime Victims Worried: Father's Act Was Understandable but Let the Law Prevail, Some Say," *Los Angeles Times*, April 13, 1986.

109 *Even if they hadn't exactly wanted to die:* McFate, interview by author, December 17, 2009. See also Burleigh, "McFate's Mission": "'After all of those people died, I was like, whoa, this has to end, I can't be involved in this anymore.'"

110 *Actually, Nietzsche famously wrote that hope:* Friedrich Nietzsche, *Human, All Too Human,*

http://www.lexido.com/EBOOK_TEXTS/HUMAN_ALL_TOO_HUMAN_
BOOK_ONE_.aspx?S=71. Accessed March 4, 2013.

110 *When she talked about choosing life over death:* Friedrich Nietzsche, *Twilight of the Idols,*
in *The Portable Nietzsche,* edited and translated by Walter Kaufmann (New York:
Penguin, 1954), 562–63.

110 *Moral dogmatism was "naïve":* Ibid., 490–91.

110 *Like McFate, for whom the realization that different perspectives:* Ibid., 501: "My demand
upon the philosopher is known, that he take his stand *beyond* good and evil and
leave the illusion of moral judgment *beneath* himself." I interpret Nietzsche's "demand" as an injunction to readers in general. McFate told me: "When you're little,
you live in a very circumscribed environment and there is an assumption that reality ends at the borders of your perception. But it's quite a moment when you realize that no, there are multiple realities and everybody in the world has their own,
and it's infinite. In a way, it's kind of what leads to anthropology: the recognition
that your perceived reality in the way in which you organize your experience in
the world is just one possibility among an infinite number of possibilities. And, also
not to judge, because there is no right answer. What worked for my mother and
what worked for the people that I grew up with in that crazy community at Gate 5,
it was their personal choice and it was what they wanted and it was the right thing
for them. It wasn't the only way, and it wasn't the right way." McFate, interview by
author, December 17, 2009.

111 *"One has renounced the great life":* Nietzsche, *Twilight of the Idols,* 465, 489.

111 *For a time, their interest centered on the Donner Party:* McFate, interview by author, December 17, 2009, and "American Experience: The Donner Party," http://www
.pbs.org/wgbh/americanexperience/features/introduction/donner-introduc
tion/, accessed June 13, 2012.

111 *McFate spent two years in community college:* McFate, interviews by author, December 17, 2009, and June 30, 2010; Tate, interview by Sara Breselor, July 20, 2012.
See also Stannard, "Montgomery McFate's Mission," and Burleigh, "McFate's
Mission." Frances Carlough's obituary, *Marin Independent Journal,* September 4,
1985, is at http://www.sfgenealogy.com/boards/mcobits/archive8/9889.html,
accessed July 25, 2012. McFate is identified in the obituary by her nickname,
Mitzy.

112 *Berkeley had a democratic education program:* McFate, interview by author, June 30,
2010, and "DeCal," http://www.decal.org/, accessed June 13, 2012. For more on
"Punks on Film," see "Mitzy," http://www.vicious-world.de/0002.htm, accessed
June 15, 2012.

112 *The morality of the Nazis intrigued McFate less:* "I was more interested in the mechanisms than I was in the moral equation of it," McFate told me. "I was more interested in how [the Nazis] did it, and not trying to make a judgment about the
rightness or wrongness of it, because I think we can all say that it's just flat out
morally wrong."

112 *Liberal Berkeley kids partying on their parents' dime:* McFate, interview by author, June 30, 2010. See also Burleigh, "McFate's Mission": "McFate had little use for students 'living there and taking acid on their parents' money.' . . ."

112 *In Northern Ireland, she visited the Milltown Cemetery:* McFate, interview by author, June 30, 2010.

113 *Back home, she got a job at Chapel of the Chimes:* McFate, interview by author, June 30, 2010. See also "Chapel of the Chimes Oakland: Our History," http://oakland .chapelofthechimes.com/about-us/our-history, accessed July 25, 2012.

113 *Since 1949, the university:* The Human Relations Area Files evolved from the Institute of Human Relations, founded at Yale in 1929. In 1937, "a small group of researchers attempted to design a system for classifying or indexing the cultural, behavioral, and background information on a society," according to the organization's website. The institute tailored its research to the needs of and supplied information to the U.S. military and intelligence communities during and after World War II. David Price, *Anthropological Intelligence: The Deployment and Neglect of American Anthropology in the Second World War* (Durham, NC: Duke University Press, 2008), 91–92; David Price, *Threatening Anthropology: McCarthyism and the FBI's Surveillance of Activist Anthropologists* (Durham, NC: Duke University Press, 2004), 77–78; and "Human Relations Area Files: About HRAF: History & Development," http:// www.yale.edu/hraf/about.htm, accessed June 14, 2012.

113 *"traveler, raconteur, casual pistol-shot":* Thomas Barfield, *The Dictionary of Anthropology* (Oxford: Blackwell, 1997), 170. Evans-Pritchard was a complex figure. John Middleton, his former student, remembered him as much more nuanced and sensitive to the problems of colonialism than Barfield's description suggests. "You've got to remember that when Evans-Pritchard was young, he was a Marxist—probably a parlour one," Middleton said in 1999. "So to accuse him of being a dirty colonialist reptile is silly; he was nothing of the sort. He did accept, I suppose, that the colonial empire was there, and the people on the ground who ran it were usually 'gentlemen.' I think to accuse people like him of consciously abetting a colonial system is naïve and self-serving. . . . I remember being taught by Evans-Pritchard, Fortes, and Forde that our mere presence in another community alters that community, that the community's own members share the task of ethnography with us. . . ." Indeed, Middleton himself appears, by the end of his life, to have grown sharply critical of the imperialism he observed as an officer in the British Army in Africa. "There was a colonial system in power. It was a very unpleasant one and a very immoral one—nobody had any right to rule over and to preach to other people," he said. "But it was there. It doesn't help to shout about it today in order to feel morally superior. . . . The administrators were in the main humane and decent people, but they were caught up in a horrible situation." He also viewed the cultural knowledge gathered by colonial administrators with disdain: "It's comic now when you go back and see how the British misinterpreted what they saw. . . . Looking back, it's antediluvian the views that people had of Africa." Deborah Pellow, "An Interview with John Middleton," *Current Anthropology* 40, no. 2 (April 1999), 220, 228–29.

113 *He led Anuak tribes against the Italians:* Barfield, *The Dictionary of Anthropology*, 170. "As anthropology," Barfield writes, Evans-Pritchard's book on Libya "fails." But as "political manifesto the book worked."

113 *"It helped of course that most of my research":* E. E. Evans-Pritchard, "Some Reminiscences and Reflections on Fieldwork," *Journal of the Anthropological Society of Oxford* 4 (1973), 10–11. Thanks to the anthropologist Tom Fricke for assigning this in his "Almost Ethnography" course at the University of Michigan, which I had the pleasure of auditing as a Knight-Wallace Fellow in 2011.

114 *Instead, a key question of the colonial era absorbed her:* Anthropology of that era "doesn't necessarily decontextualize the society from the position of a British colonial administrator," McFate told me. "He doesn't need to understand the deeper nuances of the penis gourd. He needs to understand how to administer." See also Edward Rice, *Captain Sir Richard Francis Burton: A Biography* (Cambridge, MA: Da Capo Press, 1990), 1–5.

115 *"We say in anthropology":* It's worth noting that even when McFate was in graduate school, some anthropologists were writing about conflict, including Jeffrey A. Sluka, whose book about Northern Ireland she read during her research, and Allen Feldman, whose work she greatly admired. Other anthropologists, however, have also been accused of writing war out of their ethnographies, notably Clifford Geertz. See Price, *Anthropological Intelligence*, xi, 283.

115 *Her first draft, she told me:* "I'm not writing a dissertation to say that the IRA are right or the British are right, so if you sense a kind of moral ambiguity in there, that's because I was undertaking this as a scientific project, not as a moral project," McFate told me. "It's my role to refrain from judgment, to be a cultural relativist, or if I have a [moral] position, not to drag it in, because it's irrelevant to what I'm writing about as science."

115 *whether "good anthropology" might lead to "better killing":* Montgomery Cybele Carlough, "Pax Britannica: British Counterinsurgency in Northern Ireland, 1969–1982" (PhD diss., Yale University, December 1994), 156. "To know is to love," McFate wrote, "but during wartime to know is also to kill."

115 *During her final year there, a friend:* McFate, interview by author, June 30, 2010. See also Burleigh, "McFate's Mission." McFate and Sapone married on New Year's Eve 1997 and divorced in 2010. Sapone declined my request for an interview; my account of their life together is drawn from interviews with McFate.

116 *While Sapone worked, McFate learned to cook:* Montgomery Sapone, "Have Rifle With Scope, Will Travel: The Global Economy of Mercenary Violence," *California Western International Law Journal* 30, no. 1 (Fall 1999), 1–43.

116 *worked for her mother-in-law's company for a time:* McFate, interview by author, June 30, 2010, and James Ridgeway, Daniel Schulman, and David Corn, "There's Something About Mary: Unmasking a Gun Lobby Mole," *Mother Jones*, July 30, 2008. McFate says she only worked for her then mother-in-law's company for eight or nine months while in Germany and after she and Sean returned to the States.

116 *She moved on to the RAND Corporation:* For Mead, Benedict, and the Columbia University Research in Contemporary Cultures project under the auspices of the Office of Naval Research, see "The Institute for Intercultural Studies: Postscript to September 11—What Would Margaret Mead Say?" http://www.interculturalstudies.org/Mead/beeman.html, accessed June 14, 2012. See also Margaret Mead and Rhoda Métraux, eds., *The Study of Culture at a Distance* (New York: Berghahn Books, 2000), and Montgomery McFate, "Anthropology and Counterinsurgency: The Strange Story of their Curious Relationship," *Military Review,* March–April 2005, 32.

117 *She sought out officials working on:* McFate, interview by author, June 30, 2010, and David Kilcullen, interview by author, September 14, 2010.

117 *McFate eventually started a blog:* McFate, interview by author, June 30, 2010. See also Sharon Weinberger, "Do Pentagon Studs Make You Want to Bite Your Fist?" *Wired, Danger Room,* June 17, 2008, http://www.wired.com/dangerroom/2008/06/do-pentagon -stu/, accessed June 15, 2012; and Louisa Kamps, "Army Brat," *Elle,* April 2008.

117 *'I don't have any facts about that':* The commander was General Thomas D. Waldhauser, according to McFate.

117 *Somewhere along the way, she heard Hriar Cabayan's name:* McFate, interviews by author, January 28, 2009, and June 30, 2010, and Hriar Cabayan, interview by author, December 7, 2009.

117 *McFate and Cabayan weren't the only ones:* See, for example, Ike Skelton and Jim Cooper, "You're Not From Around Here, Are You?" *Joint Forces Quarterly,* January 2005.

118 *In 2005, the CIA posted an employment ad:* David Price, "America the Ambivalent," *Anthropology Today* 21, no. 5 (December 2005), and Roberto J. González, "We Must Fight the Militarization of Anthropology," *Chronicle of Higher Education,* February 2, 2007. See also Seymour M. Hersh, "The Gray Zone," *New Yorker,* May 24, 2004.

118 *Anthropologists tend to be overwhelmingly politically liberal:* One 2003 survey found that among anthropologists, Democrats outnumbered Republicans as many as thirty to one. Other studies of social scientists' political leanings have found the imbalance less striking but still significant: "we estimated that the Democratic–Republican ratio for active social-science and humanities faculty nationwide is probably at least 8:1," according to one. In a survey of members of academic anthropological and sociological associations, researchers found that Democrats outnumbered Republicans twenty-one to one. See "Survey Project: Policy Views of Academics: Excel File of the Democrat to Republican Ratios," http://econfaculty.gmu.edu/klein/survey .htm, accessed June 15, 2012; Christopher F. Cardiff and Daniel B. Klein, "Faculty Partisan Affiliations in All Disciplines: A Voter-Registration Study," *Critical Review* 17, nos. 3–4 (2006), 239; and Daniel B. Klein and Charlotta Stern, "Professors and Their Politics: The Policy Views of Social Scientists," *Critical Review* 17, nos. 3–4 (2006), 263–64.

118 *Beginning in 2007, a small group of anthropologists:* For several years, McFate had been publishing articles in military journals about the need for anthropology in contemporary counterinsurgency, including McFate, "Anthropology and Counterinsur-

gency," and McFate, "The Military Utility of Understanding Adversary Culture," *Joint Forces Quarterly* 38 (July 2005). The public exchange between McFate and critical anthropologists began in 2007, with González, "Towards Mercenary Anthropology?" *Anthropology Today* 23, no. 3 (June 2007), 14–19. Responses from McFate and Kilcullen appeared in the same issue of *Anthropology Today*. The Network of Concerned Anthropologists, which believes that "anthropologists should not engage in research and other activities that contribute to counter-insurgency operations in Iraq or in related theaters in the 'war on terror'" and that "anthropologists should refrain from directly assisting the US military in combat, be it through torture, interrogation, or tactical advice," was also born in the summer of 2007. See "Network of Concerned Anthropologists: Download the Pledge," https://sites.google.com/site/concernedanthropologists/, accessed June 15, 2012; and Network of Concerned Anthropologists, *The Counter-Counterinsurgency Manual: Or, Notes on Demilitarizing American Society* (Chicago: Prickly Paradigm Press, 2009), 18.

118 *The first was that deploying social scientists to war zones:* "Because HTS identifies anthropology and anthropologists with U.S. military operations, this identification—given the existing range of globally dispersed understandings of U.S. militarism—may create serious difficulties for, including grave risks to the personal safety of, many non-HTS anthropologists and the people they study." "American Anthropological Association Executive Board Statement on the Human Terrain System Project," http://www.aaanet.org/issues/policy-advocacy/Statement-on-HTS.cfm, accessed June 15, 2012. For specific reference to intelligence work and the danger of anthropologists being viewed as spies, see Andrew Bickford, "Anthropology and HUMINT," Network of Concerned Anthropologists, *The Counter-Counterinsurgency Manual*, 135–51.

118 *that, on principle, anthropology should not be used:* Marshall Sahlins, "Preface," Network of Concerned Anthropologists, *The Counter-Counterinsurgency Manual*, v–vii. See also González, Hugh Gusterson, and David Price, "Introduction: War, Culture, and Counterinsurgency," 8–20, and Greg Feldman, "Radical or Reactionary? The Old Wine in the Counterinsurgency Field Manual's New Flask," *The Counter-Counterinsurgency Manual*, 77–80.

118 *The last, and in some ways the most compelling:* I am paraphrasing the anthropologist Hugh Gusterson here, from the documentary film *Human Terrain*, produced and directed by James Der Derian, David Udris, and Michael Udris (2010): "Most anthropologists these days see culture as something that's fluid, that's contested, it's constantly changing, it's very difficult to define. So there used to be a time in the fifties when academic anthropologists thought that you could write a sort of cultural grammar book. They thought of culture as being like a language, and you could write the semantics and the grammatical rules of a culture. You'll find very few respected academic anthropologists who would subscribe to that theory today. *So what we do is we tell interesting stories from the field to each other, we try and tell very complicated, multilayered, partly contradictory stories about those stories, to show how different people within a culture might interpret an event or an interaction somewhat differently, and how cultural*

*meanings are constantly on the move.* Now I think the reason the Pentagon has become interested in culture is that they subscribe to that 1950s version of culture. If culture is complex, multilayered, and contradictory, it's really not much use to them. They want culture in the wallet, right, that you can put in a wallet-size card. They want culture that you can put into a computer program. So the irony is, I think, that the military is interested in a version of culture that doesn't exist." (Emphasis is mine.) For the statement that "anthropology is not predictive," I am drawing on Rob Albro, interview by author, September 1, 2010, and Clifford Geertz, *The Interpretation of Cultures* (New York: Basic Books, 1973), 26.

119 *"The questions they are asking":* Kerry Fosher, interview by author, February 24, 2013.

119 *"Of all the modern social sciences":* Edward Said, "Introduction," in Rudyard Kipling, *Kim* (Middlesex: Penguin, 1987), 32–33.

119 *Colonel Creighton, the ethnographer and spymaster:* Kipling, *Kim*, 166–67.

119 *Claude Lévi-Strauss wrote that anthropology:* Claude Lévi-Strauss, "Anthropology: Its Achievement and Future," *Current Anthropology* 7, no. 2 (1966), 126.

120 *Around the time that McFate and others:* Packer writes that Kilcullen studied "political anthropology." Kilcullen told me that in Australia, this is closer to the American discipline of political science than to cultural anthropology, but that he relied on a "qualitative, interpretive" methodology similar to that used by anthropologists when researching his dissertation. His doctorate is actually in politics. Kilcullen, interview by author, September 14, 2010. See also Packer, "Knowing the Enemy"; "Center for a New American Security: Dr. David Kilcullen," http://www.cnas .org/kilcullen, accessed June 16, 2012; "The University of New South Wales: UNS Works," http://www.unsworks.UNSunsw.edu.au/primo_library/libweb/action/ dlDisplay.do?vid=UNSWORKS&docId=unsworks_3240, accessed June 16, 2012; and González, "Towards Mercenary Anthropology?," 14.

120 *In 2006, he wrote a tip list:* Kilcullen, "Twenty-Eight Articles: Fundamentals of Company-level Counterinsurgency," Edition 1, March 2006. The list was initially circulated by email and later published in *Military Review,* May–June 2006, 103–18. See also Packer, "Knowing the Enemy." For the allusion to Lawrence, Kilcullen, interview by author, September 14, 2010, and Lawrence, "27 Articles."

120 *"Know the people, the topography, economy":* Kilcullen, "Twenty-Eight Articles," 103. For a discussion of Kilcullen, Lawrence, and the ramifications for the contemporary debate, see González, "Towards Mercenary Anthropology?," 14–19, and Kilcullen, "Ethics, Politics and Non-State Warfare," *Anthropology Today* 23, no. 3 (June 2007), 20.

120 *"Remain in touch with your leader as constantly":* Lawrence, "27 Articles."

120 *When the anthropologist Clifford Geertz:* I was led to Geertz's description of "rapport" in Bali by its mention in David B. Edwards, "Counterinsurgency as a Cultural System," *Small Wars Journal,* December 27, 2010. Edwards, an anthropologist who has worked extensively among Afghans, cites Geertz to make a different point

about his own fieldwork. See Clifford Geertz, "Deep Play: Notes on the Balinese Cockfight," in *The Interpretation of Cultures*, 412–16.

121 *But Geertz's aim and the ultimate product:* Ibid., 416–17. The difference between intelligence work and anthropology begins with "rapport," which in anthropology cannot be engineered or forced. For intelligence soldiers and interrogators, the relationship is transactional. Not so with anthropology, or not so simply. "Fieldwork is always and inevitably an exercise in hope over experience, the hope being that you can pass through the barrier of culture and language to feel and understand what the world looks like for someone from some place else, which experience tells you rarely if ever happens," writes Edwards. While intelligence gathering and anthropology may look alike, and while anthropology and archeology have often served as covers for spying, their inner workings are fundamentally different. And yet, not even this settles the question, for the spy can never escape the basic humanness of his encounter with his source, and the more skilled he is, the less he wants to escape it. The relationship between a spy and his "asset" is "the most intense personal relationship in one's life, more intense even than with one's spouse," retired CIA agent Glenn Carle writes. "I cannot state forcefully enough how crucial it is in an interrogation, when developing an asset—when establishing any textured and worthy human relation—to sustain and foster the other person's honor, sense of personal independence and control, integrity, and trust. . . . Perversely, interrogation and treason, like love, rest upon personal bonds and trust." Although McFate often downplayed or elided entirely the differences between ethnography and intelligence, other practitioners, like Kilcullen, felt differently. "Intelligence officers in a counterinsurgency environment are engaged in something that's very akin to ethnography, but it's not the same thing," Kilcullen told me. Edwards, "Counterinsurgency as a Cultural System," 6; Glenn L. Carle, *The Interrogator: An Education* (New York: Nation Books, 2011), 76, 233–34; Kilcullen, interview by author, September 14, 2010.

121 *The nineteenth-century Bureau of Ethnology:* Dustin M. Wax, "The Uses of Anthropology in the Insurgent Age," in *Anthropology and Global Counterinsurgency*, edited by John D. Kelly, Beatrice Jauregui, Sean T. Mitchell, and Jeremy Walton (Chicago: University of Chicago Press, 2010), 153–55.

121 *Early American military leaders also sought:* As Patrick Porter writes in his excellent study of the Western obsession with Eastern ways of war: "Paradoxically, war can drive cultures closer together." Porter, *Military Orientalism: Eastern War Through Western Eyes* (New York: Columbia University Press, 2009), 33.

121 *But the settlers took far more than they gave:* In tracing the history of the U.S. military's use of sociocultural knowledge, the authors of one study of the Human Terrain System write of nineteenth-century General George Crook's fascination with and "respect for" his Apache enemies. But Crook's methods were far from friendly. He believed that "the ultimate weapon against the nomadic Native Americans was cultural. By enticing them into a pastoral and monetary economy that diminished their poverty it was also possible to destroy their ability to sustain decentralized

and autonomous operations indefinitely." Lamb et al., "Human Terrain Team Performance: An Explanation, draft," forthcoming 2013, 11.

121 *Under the management of the U.S. government:* Beginning in the 1870s and continuing well into the twentieth century, Indian children were taken from their families and sent to boarding schools run by the Bureau of Indian Affairs, where they were abused, forbidden to speak their native languages, and systematically robbed of their cultural heritage. See Bear, "American Indian Boarding Schools Haunt Many."

121 *In 1919, the celebrated:* Franz Boas, "Scientists as Spies," *Nation,* December 20, 1919.

122 *The American Anthropological Association:* "Boas did not call for anthropologists to contribute their linguistic skills, field-research abilities, and cultural knowledge to the production of propaganda to the war," Price writes, "but his students did." It is worth noting that Mead, Benedict, and Bateson each contributed in different ways to Allied efforts during World War II and to American war-related efforts afterward. It is also true that, as Price notes, Boas "did not argue that science must not be used for harm during times of warfare. He did not argue that using anthropological skills and knowledge for purposes of warfare was wrong. He did not argue that anthropologists should never work for military and intelligence agencies in any professional capacity." In a largely ceremonial act that nonetheless indicates how times have changed, the American Anthropological Association repealed Boas's censure in 2005. See Price, *Anthropological Intelligence,* 13–22, and "From the Archives: Editorial Note," *Anthropology Today* 21, no. 3 (June 2005), 27.

122 *In 1941, the AAA passed a resolution:* "Report: Proceedings of the American Anthropological Association for the Year Ending December, 1941," *American Anthropologist* 44, no. 2 (April–June 1942), 281–93, quoted in Price, *Anthropological Intelligence,* 23.

122 *More than half the anthropologists:* Price, *Anthropological Intelligence,* 37.

122 *They wrote handbooks for soldiers:* Ralph L. Beals, F. L. W. Richardson, Julian H. Steward, Jr., and Joseph E. Weckler, "Anthropology During the War and After," Memorandum Prepared by the Committee on War Service of Anthropologists, Division of the Anthropology and Psychology National Research Council, March 10, 1943, cited in Price, *Anthropological Intelligence,* 26.

122 *They worked in military intelligence and at internment camps:* Price, *Anthropological Intelligence,* xvii, 37–42, 153.

122 *Although some anthropologists expressed doubts:* Virginia Yans-McLaughlin, "Mead, Bateson and 'Hitler's Peculiar Makeup'—Applying Anthropology in an Era of Appeasement," *History of Anthropology Newsletter* 13, no. 1 (1986), 3–8, quoted in Price, *Anthropological Intelligence,* 35–36.

122 *Vietnam changed everything:* Seymour J. Deitchman charts this change in his fascinating account of the U.S. government's attempts to apply social science to defense and foreign policy problems in the 1960s. Seymour J. Deitchman, *The Best-Laid Schemes: A Tale of Social Research and Bureaucracy* (Cambridge, MA: MIT Press, 1976), especially 37, 66, 137.

122 *In 1965, Project Camelot:* Ibid., 116, 139–67, 255–87. Deitchman notes that Camelot's original conception would have taken it beyond Latin America to study coups and uprisings in Iran, Egypt, Korea, and elsewhere (145). See also *The Rise and Fall of Project Camelot: Studies in the Relationship Between Social Science and Practical Politics,* edited by Irving Louis Horowitz (Cambridge, MA: MIT Press, 1967), 3–5, 11–17, 47–49.

122 *develop "a general social systems model":* From the description of Project Camelot sent to social scientists by the Office of the Director of the Special Operations Research Office of American University, quoted in Horowitz, *The Rise and Fall of Project Camelot,* 4–5. Deitchman, then special assistant (counterinsurgency) in the Defense Department's Office of the Director of Defense Research and Engineering, writes that when he saw those words on the Camelot task statement after the scandal exploded, "I knew that the whole idea of doing research in Latin America was in trouble, and possibly dead." Deitchman, *The Best-Laid Schemes,* 159.

122 *What they really wanted was to win the Cold War:* The rationale for Camelot and related research is laid out most clearly in two government reports quoted in Deitchman: "Behavioral Sciences and the National Security," Report No. 4, prepared for the Subcommittee on International Organizations and Movements of the Committee on Foreign Affairs, House of Representatives, December 6, 1965; and Ithiel de Sola Pool et al., "Social Science Research and National Security," Research Group in Psychology and the Social Sciences, Smithsonian Institution, March 5, 1963. See Deitchman, *The Best-Laid Schemes,* 23–24, 29–35.

123 *But before the project even got off the ground:* Horowitz, *The Rise and Fall of Project Camelot,* 11–13. That Camelot exploded in Chile is ironic, as Horowitz points out, because Chile was never among the countries proposed for study by Camelot researchers (see also Deitchman, *The Best-Laid Schemes,* 157). Nutini was a former citizen of Chile, but he was neither an employee nor a staff member of Project Camelot when he made his 1965 visit. He was essentially freelancing. He had been assigned a small task by the Project, but he "somehow managed to convey the impression of being a direct official of Project Camelot and of having the authority to make proposals to prospective Chilean participants." Horowitz, *The Rise and Fall of Project Camelot,* 12.

123 *If the U.S. military wanted social scientists:* Horowitz, *The Rise and Fall of Project Camelot,* 13–14, and Deitchman, *The Best-Laid Schemes,* 156–59, 192–93, 225–54.

123 *A key lesson of Camelot:* Horowitz, *The Rise and Fall of Project Camelot,* 16–19, and Deitchman, *The Best-Laid Schemes,* 165–68. "On the one hand, the DOD was condemned for trying to learn something about its task, since if it tried to do so this implied it was seeking control of foreign policy," Deitchman writes. "On the other hand, the military were condemned for being insensitive to the nuances of international affairs and diplomacy. Either way, the DOD was out of line." Deitchman, *The Best-Laid Schemes,* 166. That this State-Defense conflict began to be noticed around the time of Vietnam, with what Horowitz calls "the rise of ambiguous politicomilitary conflicts . . . in contrast to the more precise and diplomatically

controlled 'classical' world wars," is not surprising. The same frustrations have been echoed by soldiers, marines, and senior military officers in Afghanistan, as have concerns that the growing strength of the military threatens civilian control over American foreign policy.

123 *"The story of Project Camelot":* Horowitz, *The Rise and Fall of Project Camelot,* 40.

123 *Camelot—admittedly suspect, ethically problematic:* This is borne out by the accounts of Deitchman and Horowitz. See also George R. Lucas, *Anthropologists at Arms* (Lanham, MD: AltaMira Press, 2009), 60–62.

123 *Perhaps its most significant negative outcome:* Horowitz, *The Rise and Fall of Project Camelot,* 23.

124 *They were united, he wrote:* Ibid., 6–7, 33.

124 *The blowup that ended Camelot did little to resolve:* Ibid., 35.

124 *A few years later, in 1970, a group of students:* Eric R. Wolf and Joseph G. Jorgensen, "Anthropology on the Warpath in Thailand," *New York Review of Books,* November 19, 1970.

124 *Social scientists had been asked to supply:* Ibid. Few of the "entry spaces" on the dummy "Village Tribal Data Card" the anthropologists found in the files left room for "the kind of information normally collected by anthropologists or data which could be kept anonymous," Wolf and Jorgensen note. For a U.S. government perspective, see Deitchman, *The Best-Laid Schemes,* 300–306.

124 *The purloined documents revealed:* Wolf and Jorgensen, "Anthropology on the Warpath in Thailand." The problem of never knowing exactly how information gathered under government or military auspices may be used would crop up again for the Human Terrain System, since most of the project's reports on Afghanistan were stored in a classified database accessible to anyone with a Secret clearance. For Steve Fondacaro, the Human Terrain System's program manager, the standard to which Wolf, Jorgensen, and other anthropologists aspired was "ridiculous." "You can't produce any information that could not possibly be used for harm," he told me. "For the anthropologists to say that they have never produced any information that has resulted in harm is a lie." Fondacaro was right, but his assertion also created a helpful layer of plausible deniability between the Human Terrain System's management and the use of its products by intelligence operatives and others. "I can only speak for what I control," Fondacaro told me. Steve Fondacaro, interview by author, June 16, 2010.

125 *"disengage itself from its connection with colonial aims":* Wolf and Jorgensen, "Anthropology on the Warpath in Thailand." See also McFate, "Anthropology and Counterinsurgency," 36–37.

125 *McFate had studied anthropology at a university:* McFate, interview by author, June 30, 2010. "Younger faculty members who were educated in the seventies and eighties have a really different viewpoint," McFate told me. "I come from a very conservative tradition in anthropology. . . . That's a different intellectual genealogy than most people have."

125 *wasn't "supposed to be making moral arguments":* McFate, interview by author, June 30, 2010.

125 *In 2007, the American Anthropological Association:* American Anthropological Association, "Executive Board Statement on the Human Terrain System Project."

125 *Paula Loyd's college anthropology professor:* Sally Engle Merry, interview by author, June 7, 2010, and Stefanie Johnson, interview by author, June 23, 2010.

126 *"It's a really hard question":* Merry, interviews by author, June 7 and June 11, 2010.


*Chapter 6: Hearts and Minds*

127 *Back in Maiwand, Don Ayala had just put a bullet:* This chapter is based on interviews with Don Ayala; Clint Cooper; the Afghan interpreter known as Jack Bauer; and soldiers of the 2nd Battalion, 2nd Regiment, of the Army's 1st Infantry Division. I have also relied on federal court records and the U.S. Army Criminal Investigation Command's report on the events of November 4, 2008.

127 *He turned away. 'Oh fuck!' he said:* "I turned away and said, 'Oh fuck.'" Justin Skotnicki, interview by author, March 24, 2009. The word is repeated here because an Afghan policeman told me that he heard a soldier repeat it at least six times in the moments after Abdul Salam was shot. It seems likely these are two versions of the same event. Amir Mohammad, interview by author, January 19, 2009.

127 *'Are you serious?' Pathak yelled:* "I yelled at him for doing it and asked him for his weapons. . . . I asked 'Are you serious?' And he answered, 'Yes, I am.'" U.S. Army Report of Investigation 08-CID369–43873–5H1.

127 *Ayala handed Pathak his rifle and pistol:* "I relieved him of his weapons and immediately sent him away from the scene . . . ," Pathak told Army investigators, adding that Ayala "turned [his weapons] over willingly and without reservation." Another soldier recalled Pathak's demeanor: "He was just like 'damn it.' That's basically how everybody was." Soldiers' statements, Army investigation, and statement of Lieutenant Matthew Pathak, November 4, 2008, filed in federal court, May 1, 2009.

128 *'I just shot the guy,' Ayala said:* Cooper, interview by author, April 22, 2010; Ayala, interview by author, August 19, 2009; and Cooper statement to Army investigators. A soldier recalled of Ayala: "When he came closer I could hear him saying how he 'fucked up' and 'I killed him' to [Cooper]. . . . [Ayala] was distressed, like he was rambling more than actually saying it to someone. Walking around like he'd fucked up."

128 *'You did the right thing,' Cooper told him:* "Of course I had no idea about the flex cuffs or any of that stuff," Cooper told me. "I just thought that he shot the guy while he was running away. And if I would have known the circumstances, maybe I would have said the same thing. I probably would have. But I definitely tried to assure him, or comfort him." Cooper, interview by author, April 22, 2010. According to

Ayala, he was the one comforting Cooper: "Clint gave me a big hug and he was crying, really crying. He lost it. And I felt bad for him, because I knew he had PTSD, he had a pretty bad case of it, and I knew this just triggered it." Ayala, interview by author, August 19, 2009.

128 *'Clint, don't leave me':* "She kept calling my name and she begged me not to leave and to stay with her to the hospital. I promised Paula that I would stay with her no matter what it took to do so. . . . An Afghan national police truck pulled up and we loaded Paula into the back on an old mattress. I looked back at [Ayala] and that was the last time I saw him." Cooper statement to Army investigators. Additional details in this paragraph are from interviews with Cooper and Ayala and soldiers' statements to Army investigators.

128 *'I can't tell,'* he told her haltingly: Cooper, interview by author, April 22, 2010.

128 *third-degree burns covered 60 to 70 percent of her body:* Statement of the platoon medic to Army investigators and Army medics in Maiwand, interview by author, March 24, 2009.

128 *'Call Frank,' she said:* This and other details below are from Cooper, interview by author, April 22, 2010. In his statement to Army investigators, Cooper made it sound as if this exchange happened while Loyd was still on the ground in Chehel Gazi, but he later told me that he believed she told him these things when they were in the aid station on the American base.

129 *'They're taking us to FOB Bastion':* Cooper, interview by author, April 22, 2010, and Cooper statement to Army investigators.

129 *At 2 a.m. at Fort Benning, the phone rang:* Frank Muggeo, interview by author, October 18, 2012, and Cooper, interviews by author, April 19–22, 2010.

130 *Cooper was afraid to see Muggeo:* Cooper was and remains guilt-ridden. He told Army investigators: "Paula's safety was always our number one concern. We felt a huge responsibility to protect her. We let her down." Cooper, interviews by author, April 19–22, 2010, and Cooper statement, Army investigation.

131 *White bandages hid Loyd's body:* Cooper, interview by author, April 22, 2010.

131 *The soldiers didn't know if he was nuts or what:* "We had to sit him down and pull security on him because we didn't know if he was crazy or not," a soldier told Army investigators. Another soldier recalled: "He sat quietly, Indian style against the wall, with someone watching him. At one point he got up to walk around and the individual watching him asked him to sit down. Mr. [Ayala] asked if the individual was there to watch him. The individual asked what Mr. [Ayala] thought, and he said yeah and sat down."

131 *'Why you killed that person?':* Details in this paragraph are from Jack Bauer, interview by author, September 23, 2010.

132 *'Everything's going to be okay,' one told him:* Ayala, interview by author, August 19, 2009.

132 *As he watched armed escorts lead Ayala off:* Ayala looked "bewildered," Warren told me.

"His face, the way he moved. He was almost in a daze." Mike Warren, interview by author, March 20, 2009.

132 *They took Ayala for a physical exam:* Ayala, August 19, 2009, and soldiers' statements to Army investigators.

132 *They . . . studiously avoided discussing what had happened that day:* "While I was pulling guard [Mr. Ayala] didn't really talk about what happened much, but when he did I would quickly change the subject to avoid Depressing [sic] or distressing him," one soldier told Army investigators. "Other than that, we only had very few other conversations consisting of football and women and that's pretty much it."

133 *'I was thinking I saw Paula and thought fuck this guy':* Ayala, statement to Army investigators, November 4, 2008. On the way to the detention facility, one soldier recalled, Ayala "asked numerous times why he was being held against his will. He was also asking to speak to a lawyer, his boss, or someone in charge." Mike Warren, Ayala's friend and team leader, didn't help the situation. When an Army investigator advised him that Ayala was being held pending an investigation of Salam's death, Warren "said if Mr. [Ayala] had not been detained . . . he would have flown Mr. [Ayala] out of the country. After a brief pause, Mr. [Warren] said he was joking."

133 *After three days, they cuffed Ayala:* Many details about Ayala's detention here and below are from Ayala, interview by author, August 19, 2009.

133 *They had been sent to do jobs they hadn't been trained to do:* "Just seeing the morale of the troops out there, not knowing, 'What are we here for? We can't go out and fight anybody. We go out there and try to protect them and we're getting killed left and right. It doesn't make sense.'" Ayala, interview by author, August 18, 2009.

133 *Ayala read about McCain's time as a prisoner of war in North Vietnam:* "When I was on the *Forrestal,* every man in my squadron had thought Washington's air war plans were senseless," McCain wrote. "It's hard to get a sense that you are advancing the war effort when you are prevented from doing anything more than bouncing the rubble of an utterly insignificant target. . . . We could see SAMs being transported to firing sites and put into place, but we couldn't do anything about them because we were forbidden to bomb SAM sites unless they were firing on us. Even then, it was often an open question whether we could retaliate or not." John McCain with Mark Salter, *Faith of My Fathers: A Family Memoir* (New York: Random House, 1999), 184–85.

133 *How similar that war had been to this one:* "One thing I did learn from it was . . . when the politicians get involved with war, it creates casualties." Ayala, interview by author, August 19, 2009.

133 *American soldiers in Afghanistan watched their buddies get killed:* "We should be responsible by sending men into war and supporting them and protecting them. Not just send them in and say, 'Okay, well, you guys can't shoot until they kill three or four of us, maybe,'" Ayala told me. The turn toward counterinsurgency in Afghanistan, with its emphasis on protecting civilians, was spelled out in a NATO-ISAF tacti-

cal directive issued shortly after Ayala's arrest: "In order to minimize death or injury of innocent civilians in escalation of force engagements, Commanders are to set conditions through the employment of techniques and procedures and, most importantly, the training of forces to minimize the need to resort to deadly force. Signals, signs, general and specific warnings (visual and audible) must be unambiguous and repeated to ensure the safety of innocent civilians." Ayala, interview by author, August 19, 2009, and "Tactical Directive," Headquarters, International Security Assistance Force, Kabul, December 30, 2008.

134 *It was an impossible conflict:* "You really wonder, who is the enemy? Nobody knows who the enemy is. Everybody can call it the Taliban. But they can be local villagers who are not Taliban, they're just anti-American. . . . The Taliban takes credit for it, but who knows? You never know who the enemy is." Ayala, interview by author, August 18, 2009.

134 *their intelligence was often flawed:* For one devastating account, Kate Clark, "The Takhar Attack: Targeted Killings and the Parallel Worlds of US Intelligence and Afghanistan," *Afghanistan Analysts Network,* http://www.humansecuritygateway.com/documents/AAN-Takhar-Attack-Targeted-Killings-US-Afghan-Intel.pdf, accessed March 4, 2013. Afghan civilian deaths from U.S. and NATO air strikes nearly tripled between 2006 and 2007, from 116 to 321. The United Nations found that 167 civilians were killed and 40 hurt in NATO aerial attacks between January and June 2011; another 127 were killed and 49 hurt in the first half of 2012. Human Rights Watch, "'Troops in Contact': Airstrikes and Civilian Deaths in Afghanistan," 2008, and "Afghanistan Mid-Year Report 2012: Protection of Civilians in Armed Conflict," United Nations Assistance Mission in Afghanistan and UNHCR, Kabul, July 2012, 35.

134 *In August 2008, a coalition air strike in the western village of Azizabad:* Carlotta Gall, "Evidence Points to Civilian Toll in Afghan Raid," *New York Times,* September 7, 2008.

134 *Then-Secretary of Defense Robert Gates flew to Kabul:* "U.S. Apologizes for Afghan Civilian Deaths," CNN, September 17, 2008.

134 *General McKiernan, declared reducing civilian casualties "of paramount importance":* "Tactical Directive," Headquarters, International Security Assistance Force, Kabul, December 30, 2008.

135 *He cried on TV:* See Jason Straziuso, "Tearful Karzai Says Afghan Children Are Dying from Terrorism and NATO Bombs," Associated Press, December 20, 2006.

135 *U.S. aircraft had bombed a wedding party north of Kandahar:* Abdul Waheed Wafa and Mark McDonald, "Deadly U.S. Airstrike Said to Hit Afghan Wedding Party," *New York Times,* November 5, 2008, and "Afghanistan: US Missile Strike Kills 37 Civilians," Jason Straziuso, Associated Press, November 7, 2008. Fox put the number of dead at forty, including twenty-three children. "U.S. Strike Reportedly Kills 40 at Afghanistan Wedding," FOXNews.com, November 5, 2008.

135 *the prevailing Afghan narrative of an arrogant foreign occupation that valued Afghan lives cheaply:*

"It was right in the middle of all these civilians getting killed," Ayala recalled. "So the military had to tiptoe through this process and do the right thing, say, 'Hey, we're doing what we can to prosecute our soldiers.' But you never see the pilots getting prosecuted when they drop a bomb and kill twenty-seven, twenty-eight kids, children, wives and husbands, you know?" His Army lawyer advised him that the military had to "placate the Afghan government here," and that Ayala could "be a sacrifice." Ayala, interview by author, August 19, 2009.

135 *Ayala knew that he would be accused of betraying his mission:* "I know people are going to judge me, saying, 'Well, [we] could have got a lot of information.' And what was anybody going to do with that information? You tell me. How many guys have died there and nothing has happened?" Ayala, interview by author, August 19, 2009.

135 *more than one thousand men had escaped from the main prison in Kandahar:* The Sarposa prison break occurred in June 2008. Candace Rondeaux and Javed Hamdard, "Taliban Seizes Seven Afghan Villages," *Washington Post,* June 17, 2008.

136 *almost certainly with help from inside:* "As is to be expected in Afghanistan, a degree of insider involvement is likely." Captain Nils N. French, "The Sarposa Prison Break," *Canadian Army Journal* 11.2 (Summer 2008), 8.

136 *But rushing aid and development into Maiwand was getting soldiers killed:* Soldiers in Maiwand "were just being told to accomplish the wheat seed program. Support USAID! And in the meantime they're losing tons of vehicles to IEDs and stuff like that." Ayala, interview by author, August 18, 2009.

136 *The U.S. military was building a new office for the district governor:* In March 2009, Lieutenant Colonel Dan Hurlbut, the 2–2 battalion commander in Maiwand, told me that the Americans hoped to move the Maiwand district governor out of his current office and into a new one. The new district center became a project for each successive U.S. unit based there. By the time I visited Maiwand again in fall 2010, it had been built, but the governor rarely used it. "There's trash everywhere and they don't like working there because there's no electricity, no plumbing," Lieutenant Kirsten Ouimette told me. "So the [district governor] prefers working at the old district center. Even though it's a little bit crummier, it has trees and flowers and grass and it's beautiful and that's a status symbol. So we're working hard to get them all this stuff so that it'll become a new district center and that's good. But at the same time, it's just, like, ridiculous when they have this old district center we could have just refurbished." For this and other details about the new district center's lack of plumbing, police chipping holes in the walls, and officials asking for big-screen TVs, Ouimette, interview by author, October 2, 2010.

136 *American commanders seemed more interested in winning awards and promotions:* "Everybody was there just to check the box," Ayala told me. " 'Okay, we're going to be here for this long, let's just do this, do that, and then we can go check the box and we can go home and get awards for it and medals. We're officers, we can write that up and give each other medals for doing what we did out there.' But what did you actually do? Build a FOB? What did you do? . . . There was no stability. We got to

have security out there, and that wasn't accomplished." Ayala, interview by author, August 18, 2009.

137 *"It's not what you can do for the people":* Ayala, interview by author, August 18, 2009.

137 *maybe the only difference one man could make:* "It was a way that I can make a difference in this war, because it's not fair that they get to do all the killing, and nobody gets to kill back," Ayala told me. "All these soldiers are out there not knowing what they're doing or why they're doing it." Ayala, interview by author, August 19, 2009.

137 *"Fuck this Muslim shit":* Ayala, interview by author, August 19, 2009.

138 *Outraged at how the Army was treating his friend:* Mike Warren, interview by author, March 20, 2009.

138 *It was the same law used to charge Blackwater security guards:* U.S. Department of Justice, "Five Blackwater Employees Indicted on Manslaughter and Weapons Charges for Fatal Nisur Square Shooting in Iraq," http://www.justice.gov/opa/pr/2008/December/08-nsd-1068.html, accessed March 9, 2013.

139 *Strategic Analysis, the defense contractor that had employed him:* A letter arrived at his home in New Orleans, terminating his employment. Ayala, interview by author, August 19, 2009.

139 *In late November, military police escorted him:* The account of Ayala's trip back to the States below is from ibid.

139 *His longtime girlfriend, Andi Santwier:* Santwier, correspondence, February 2, 2013, and Ayala, interview by author, August 19, 2009.

139 *He had lost twelve pounds:* Ibid.

140 *Someone brought Star Wars books:* Frank Muggeo, interview by author, October 18, 2012.

140 *Muggeo wanted to do something:* Ibid.

140 *she contracted pneumonia and needed a ventilator to breathe:* For some details about Loyd's condition as well as the cause and manner of her death, Army investigation.

140 *some sights can permanently disorder your mind:* Patty Ward, letter to Judge Claude M. Hilton, and Ward, interview by author, December 14, 2012.

141 *The next day in Maiwand, a man on a motorcycle:* When I met the interpreter Jack Bauer, he showed me shrapnel scars in his neck and leg from the bombing; his close friend and bunk mate, an interpreter named Niazi, was killed that day. In addition to the dead, fifty-three Americans and Afghans were wounded. "You can look at that as it's one hundred meters outside the base and we don't go there," Captain Trevor Voelkel, the company commander overseeing that part of the district, told me. "But because of the environment and there's just hundreds of people everywhere, unless you seal it off like an airport and search every single individual and every single shop, that suicide bomber threat is very real, and we've gotten a lot of information, intelligence that they're walking around or they're out there. So the benefit of the gains of going there don't really [justify] the risk of another

suicide attack. And therefore, right now, those risks are greater than we are willing to accept for the benefit that we're going to get by just going and talking to
shop owners." The small firebase near the district center, known during Loyd and
Ayala's time there as FOB Hutal, was renamed Combat Outpost Rath after Staff
Sergeant Joshua L. Rath, twenty-two, of Decatur, Alabama, one of the soldiers
killed in the January attack. Voelkel, interview by author, March 24, 2009; Jack
Bauer, interview by author, September 23, 2010; and Vanessa M. Gezari, "Death
on Film," Pulitzer Center on Crisis Reporting, April 3, 2009.

*Chapter 7: Crime and Punishment*

143 *The federal public defender came to see Don Ayala:* This chapter is based on federal court
records, interviews, and the U.S. Army Criminal Investigation Command's report
on the events of November 4, 2008. Nachmanoff and Ayala had spoken on the
phone while Ayala was being held in Afghanistan; they met in person for the first
time the Sunday he returned to the States. Ayala, interview by author, August 19,
2009.

143 *He was fresh off a Supreme Court victory:* The case, *Kimbrough v. United States,* centered
on the latitude granted judges to depart from federal sentencing guidelines in
drug cases involving crack cocaine, the possession and sale of which is punished
much more harshly than that of powder cocaine. Nachmanoff represented Der-
rick Kimbrough, an African-American Gulf War veteran convicted of dealing
crack, who had been sentenced to fifteen years in prison when the guidelines called
for nineteen to twenty-two years. In December 2007, the Supreme Court ruled
in Kimbrough's favor. Bill Mears, "Justices: Judges Can Slash Crack Sentences,"
CNN, December 10, 2007.

144 *to escape the possibility of a life sentence:* "Statement of Facts," *United States of America
v. Don Michael Ayala,* February 3, 2009, and Ayala, interview by author, August 19,
2009.

144 *"Anyone possessing a shred of compassion":* Letter of Lieutenant Colonel David C.
Thomas to Judge Hilton, March 20, 2009.

144 *Had he shot the man while he was running:* This, at least, was Nachmanoff's view.

145 *The wife of one of Ayala's fellow Karzai bodyguards:* The two paragraphs below are
based on letters to Judge Hilton from Jeannie Thorpe; Christopher Castruita, Sr.;
Greg Lapin; Rodger Kenneth Garrett; Glenn Rodriguez; Randall S. Houghton;
Jack Heany; and Scott A. Monaco, filed April 23, 2009, in federal court; some
details are drawn from a sentencing documentary filed in support of Ayala.

145 *The most powerful letter came from Paula Loyd's mother:* Patty Ward, letter to Judge Hilton, April 11, 2009.

146 *"upon heat of passion and without malice":* "Statement of Facts," *United States of America
v. Don Michael Ayala,* February 3, 2009.

146 *Ayala spent two ten-hour days:* Ayala, interview by author, August 17, 2009.

146 *Figley taught at Tulane University's Graduate School of Social Work:* CV of Charles R. Figley, PhD, filed in federal court, May 1, 2009. Figley coedited *Combat Stress Injury: Theory, Research, and Management* (New York: Routledge, 2007). For his work with the Navy and Marine Corps, Nachmanoff, *United States of America v. Don Michael Ayala,* "Transcript of Sentencing before the Honorable Claude M. Hilton, U.S. District Judge," May 8, 2009.

146 *Figley prepared a report based on his conversations with Ayala:* "Dr. Figley concluded that, without knowing it, Mr. Ayala was vulnerable to errors in judgment under combat conditions." "Defendant's Position with Regard to Sentencing Factors," filed May 1, 2009, 5–6.

147 *Ayala had told Figley about his childhood in Whittier:* Unless otherwise noted, the account of Ayala's childhood below is based on my interviews with Ayala, August 17–19, 2009.

147 *Ayala and his brothers played baseball, football:* Letter of Dean M. Ayala to Judge Hilton, filed May 1, 2009.

147 *He and his friends banded together, joining a neighborhood gang called Sunrise:* For more on Sunrise: http://www.topix.net/forum/city/west-whittier-los-nietos-ca/TF57AEI 5NFH1GO886/p5; http://www.streetgangs.com/hispanic/whittier; and http://lang.sgvtribune.com/socal/gangs/articles/sgvnp1_ganglist.asp, accessed March 9, 2013.

147 *fighting had been the way he survived:* After the incident in junior high, he told me: "Now fighting was a way of life, and I fought a lot. I fought a lot as a young kid, young boy. I'd say about once a week."

147 *Ayala pitched all through Little League:* Ayala's active role in sports and his drawing skills are mentioned in Castruita's letter to Judge Hilton, April 2, 2009.

148 *After high school, he enrolled at a local community college:* ". . . he was attending Rio Hondo Junior College near our home and then all of a sudden he decided to enlist in the US Army." David Ayala, Sr., and Frances Ayala, letter to Judge Hilton, March 17, 2009.

149 *Ayala excelled at basic training as he never had in high school:* "I, his father, warned and challenged him that he might not be able to cope with military service especially if a ranking soldier of small stature started yelling orders directly to his face. . . . Don proved us wrong. He did handle it well and became the 'top trooper' in his basic training group in Fort Benning, Georgia." Ibid.

150 *Ayala's unit was sent to Grenada to stop the Soviet Union from gaining a new strategic foothold:* The account of Operation Urgent Fury is from Ayala, interview by author, August 18, 2009, and "Operation Urgent Fury: The Invasion of Grenada, October 1983," http://www.history.army.mil/html/books/grenada/urgent_fury.pdf, accessed March 5, 2013.

151 *he joined the 12th Special Forces Group in Los Alamitos:* Details of Ayala's Special Forces

affiliations and activities are from Ayala, interview by author, August 18, 2009, and Thomas, letter to Judge Hilton, March 20, 2009.

151 *A Special Forces buddy had started a company:* The company was Delta Investigations. Scott Guffey, interview by author, February 23, 2013.

152 *It was DynCorp, the private security company hired to protect Hamid Karzai:* For DynCorp, Inc., being hired to take over Karzai's protective detail in 2002, Jonathan D. Tepperman, "Can Mercenaries Protect Hamid Karzai?" *New Republic,* November 18, 2002.

152 *nearly twice what he had been paid in Afghanistan:* Ayala recalled that he was being paid about $15,000 a month in Afghanistan by that time. In Iraq, at least initially, he worked for Triple Canopy.

153 *When Ayala shot Abdul Salam, Warren told me:* Mike Warren, conversation, March 2009. See also letter of Michael J. Warren to Judge Hilton: "Don was extremely protective of Paula, I have no doubt that what happened to her, he blames himself and that guilt consumed him at the time of the shooting."

154 *that Paula Loyd's death was a "tragedy":* Nachmanoff, "Transcript of Sentencing," May 8, 2009.

154 *For manslaughter, the guidelines recommended six to eight years:* Based on a number of factors, a probation officer calculated that the sentencing guidelines in Ayala's case called for seventy-eight to ninety-seven months' imprisonment, or six to eight years.

154 *Nachmanoff was asking the judge not to imprison Ayala at all:* "A just punishment would be probation," Nachmanoff told the judge.

154 *Most voluntary manslaughter cases involve fights:* "In 1997, the United States Sentencing Commission established the Manslaughter Working Group, which presented its report to the Commission in December of that year," Nachmanoff wrote. "The group analyzed three years of Commission monitoring data, including 54 of the 60 federal voluntary manslaughter cases reported for fiscal years 1994, 1995, and 1996. Data derived from this study revealed that 82% of the voluntary manslaughter cases between these dates were the results of fights. Native Americans comprised 68% of the defendants, and family members and friends accounted for more than 50% of the victims. Alcohol was involved in roughly 50% of the cases. Needless to say, the present case does not fall within these typical fact patterns that reflect that most federal manslaughter cases occur on federal Native American reservations and/or between family members or friends." "Defendant's Position with Regard to Sentencing Factors," 17, and Nachmanoff, "Transcript of Sentencing."

154 *The struggle to subdue the Afghan had been "very violent":* Statement of Justin Skotnicki to Army investigators, "Defendant's Position with Regard to Sentencing Factors," 5.

155 *Salam could be seen to pose a continuing threat:* At least one soldier told Army investigators that he "believed Mr. SALAM was still a threat even though his hands were

secured behind his back. Mr. SALAM had attacked Miss LOYD causing serious injuries, gave them a hard fight to get him down and was still resisting attempts to detain him by moving his body from side to side and kicking at them prior to being shot." That Salam might have still been a danger "by possibly being armed with some type of self-explosive device," "Defendant's Position with Regard to Sentencing Factors," 20.

155 *A victim's behavior . . . is an important factor in manslaughter sentencing:* "Defendant's Position with Regard to Sentencing Factors," 15.

155 *"the kind of provocation that I think this court has never seen":* Nachmanoff, "Transcript of Sentencing."

155 *Her assault was "a terrorist act":* Nachmanoff, "Transcript of Sentencing." For a detailed analysis of the Taliban's "claim of responsibility," see Chapter 9.

155 *an "outstanding individual, a hero . . . who's dedicated his adult life to public service:* Nachmanoff, "Transcript of Sentencing."

155 *If Ayala's friends and relatives were surprised that he had killed the Afghan:* Ayala "always seemed calm under pressure," his teammate Clint Cooper told Army investigators. Asked what he thought should happen to Ayala, Cooper said: "It's hard for somebody who was not there to understand the emotion behind something like this; I mean the attack on Paula. We were all very close. . . . I think [Ayala] has paid a pretty high price and will continue to pay for the rest of his life."

155 *Ayala routinely scolded them for "morbid jokes":* Statements of Lieutenant Matthew Pathak and Staff Sergeant Steven Anthony Smith, filed in federal court, May 1, 2009.

155 *A manslaughter sentence can be reduced if the defendant can prove he was "suffering from a diminished capacity":* "At the instant that Mr. Ayala learned of Salam's despicable attack on Ms. Loyd, Mr. Ayala was primed to pull the trigger without regard for the consequences," Nachmanoff and his co-counsel, Richard H. McWilliams, wrote. "The convergence of these prior stress injuries and the horror of learning about the nature and the brutality of the attack upon his friend created a rare 'perfect storm' of conditions, causing Mr. Ayala to abandon his years of discipline and to make the wrong choice." This and other references to the Figley report in this paragraph are from "Defendant's Position with Regard to Sentencing Factors," 23–25.

156 *Ayala had already been severely punished:* Nachmanoff, "Transcript of Sentencing."

156 *a moving sentencing documentary in which Loyd's boyfriend, Frank Muggeo:* "Sometimes it seems like we're forgetting that Paula was the victim," Muggeo said in the documentary. "I don't forget that. Her mother doesn't forget that. And each time something happens to me or to her mother or to Don, it's like they keep winning. And I don't want them to win anymore."

157 *Rich was a veteran himself—a retired Marine general:* Nachmanoff was born in 1968. Rich was an infantry company commander at Gio Linh in 1967 and took his

LSATs in Da Nang. In September 1988, he was promoted to brigadier general and became director of the Judge Advocate Division. Lieutenant Colonel Gary D. Solis, U.S. Marine Corps, *Marines and Military Law in Vietnam: Trial by Fire* (Washington: History and Museums Division Headquarters, U.S. Marine Corps, 1989), 86–87.

157 *"Ms. Loyd and her friends and supporters and family deserve all of our sympathy"*: This and other quotes from Rich in this section are from "Transcript of Sentencing."

158 *"It was an execution"*: *United States of America v. Don Michael Ayala*, "Government's Sentencing Memorandum," May 8, 2009, 2.

158 *"We know much about Paula Loyd and the defendant"*: "Government's Sentencing Memorandum," 3.

159 *"he was a 'frequent stranger' in the village where he died"*: This detail is from Lieutenant Pathak's statement to Army investigators.

159 *"We know nothing at all about what caused him to torch Paula Loyd"*: "Government's Sentencing Memorandum," 3.

159 *A few days before the sentencing, the government had entered fifteen photographs into evidence:* "Addendum to the Government's Sentencing Memorandum," filed May 4, 2009, by Michael E. Rich, Assistant United States Attorney, United States District Court for the Eastern District of Virginia, Alexandria Division.

159 *"The day of November 4, 2008, I wish it never occurred"*: Ayala, "Transcript of Sentencing."

159 *One photograph showed Salam's forearm bearing a rudimentary tattoo of his name:* Abdul Salam might also be translated "Servant of the Peaceful One," "Servant of the All-Peacable." *Salam* means "peace" in Arabic, but it is also one of the names of Allah, so possibly: "God's Servant."

160 *"You can't forget that this didn't occur here on the streets"*: Hilton, "Transcript of Sentencing."

*Chapter 8: Good Intentions*

161 *Paula Loyd had been the third:* Eight months measures the time from May 2008, when Michael Bhatia was killed, until Loyd died of her wounds in January 2009.

161 *The previous May, a brilliant thirty-one-year-old:* For more on Michael Bhatia, see Adam Geller, "'Professor' Pays a Heavy Price," Associated Press, March 15, 2009, and "Marshall Scholarships: 2001 Marshall Scholar Michael Bhatia," http://www.marshallscholarship.org/about/michael, accessed July 16, 2012.

162 *A month later, Nicole Suveges:* Ovetta Wiggins, "Johns Hopkins Grad Student Dies in Iraq," *Washington Post*, June 27, 2008, and "American Grad Student Dies in Iraq," CNN, June 26, 2008.

162 *By the fall of 2008, reports of trouble:* Geller's story mentions that Bhatia and his team-

mates hung articles sent by colleagues in Fort Leavenworth on their office wall in Khost: "Critics were not letting up in their condemnation of the Human Terrain project. The team kept score, posting what they considered the most outrageously off-base characterizations of their work. 'Mercenary anthropologists,' one critic called them. 'The Army's new secret weapon,' another said." Geller, "'Professor' Pays a Heavy Price."

162 *It emerged that among the Human Terrain social scientists deployed to Iraq:* Dan Ephron and Sylvia Spring, "A Gun in One Hand, a Pen in the Other," *Newsweek,* April 21, 2008. The story notes that of nineteen Human Terrain Team members operating on five teams in Iraq at the time, "fewer than a handful can be described loosely as Middle East experts, and only three speak Arabic."

162 *In Afghanistan, a Human Terrain Team leader:* "Memorandum for Commander, Task Force Gladiator, Bagram Airfield: Battalion Commander's Investigation of Congressional Inquiry on Behalf of Dr. Marilyn Dudley-Flores," March 29, 2009. The investigation started in response to an inquiry from Dudley-Flores's congressional representative, California Democrat Lynn Woolsey, through whose office Dudley-Flores had filed a formal complaint. The executive summary, forwarded to Woolsey's office four months later, found that Dudley-Flores and her female colleagues were subject to "an egregious example of hostile work environment," but it also noted "sufficient evidence" to support Dudley-Flores's teammates' allegations that she "systematically exaggerated her civilian and military experience and personal connections to famous people." The military officers who conducted the investigation were clearly flummoxed by the Human Terrain Analysis Team's dysfunction and lack of professionalism. "In this case," military officials wrote, "poor and unverified credentials, and exaggerations of pertinent experience on the part of team members contributed to a toxic environment" in which the team, "rather than being an enabler, actually became a distraction from the CJTF-101 mission." Thanks to John Stanton for sharing these documents with me. See also Stanton, "Death Threat Tarnishes U.S. Army Human Terrain System," February 26, 2009, http://zeroanthropology.net/2009/02/26/some-breaking-news-on-the-human-terrain-system-death-threats/, accessed September 16, 2012.

162 *The military asked that the team leader:* Cover letter from Lieutenant Colonel David L. Dellinger to Congresswoman Lynn Woolsey, April 26, 2009. The team leader, Milan Sturgis, and his colleagues, were contractors, not DOD civilians. They were dismissed from their contracts with HTS, a Human Terrain System official said, but another contractor promptly rehired them, which meant they simply moved to other jobs within the program. To observers, it looked like impunity. "You fuck up, you move up," Major Robert Holbert, who worked in the program's training directorate, told me. "They all kept working for HTS." Holbert, interview by author, August 9, 2012.

162 *Meanwhile, the United States was planning to send more troops:* The 2009 expansion raised the Pentagon's requested number of Human Terrain Teams in Afghanistan from six to thirteen. See Gezari, "Rough Terrain."

162  *The training consisted:* My description of training is based on visits to Leavenworth to observe Human Terrain System training in February and December 2009 as well as interviews with dozens of program administrators, staff, and Human Terrain System field team members.

163  *several weeks known as "immersion":* The Afghan "immersion" course in Omaha was up and running when Loyd and Cooper did their training in 2008, but the Iraq immersion program didn't really get off the ground until late 2008 or early 2009, according to Holbert, who was the Human Terrain System's primary coordinator for Afghan and Iraqi immersion courses and academic outreach during that period. The Human Terrain System assigned incoming trainees to learn about one country or the other depending on where it intended to send them, but the decision sometimes had little to do with the skills they already possessed. One trainee who spoke Dari quit in disgust after failing to convince program administrators to send him to a part of Afghanistan where Dari is prevalent; instead, he was sent to Helmand, where the main language is Pashto. The unpredictability of military deployments also meant that things could change at the last minute, that people trained for Iraq could be sent to Afghanistan and vice versa. Finally, most team members were not told exactly where they would be sent (to which province or geographic area) until very late in their training. Iraq and Afghanistan are extremely complex and vary greatly from place to place, so the lack of geographic specificity made it nearly impossible for team members to research their areas ahead of time and led to intense frustration among those who took the job seriously.

163  *The Human Terrain System's press handler:* Lieutenant George Mace, interview by author, February 18, 2009.

164  *Fort Leavenworth is home to mid-career master's programs:* The Command and General Staff College, which Army majors attend before being promoted to lieutenant colonel, is at Fort Leavenworth, as is the School of Advanced Military Studies, which offers "a second year of intermediate, master's-level education," and several other advanced military schools. When General Petraeus was named commander of the Combined Arms Center at Fort Leavenworth, he "wasn't entirely sure what his new command even did," Cloud and Jaffe write. "Digging into the Internet, he learned that he'd have responsibility for running the Army's nationwide network of training centers and schools. He would also oversee the drafting of Army doctrine." Cloud and Jaffe, *The Fourth Star,* 216–18. See also "School of Advanced Military Studies Reflects and Looks Forward After 25 Years," http://usacac.army.mil/cac2/cgsc/Events/SAMS25th/index.asp, accessed July 17, 2012; "Command and General Staff School," http://usacac.army.mil/cac2/cgsc/cgss/index.asp, accessed July 17, 2012; and "Combined Arms Center—Overview," http://usacac.army.mil/CAC2/overview.asp, accessed July 17, 2012.

164  *They included a former soldier who spoke Dari:* The trainees were Joe Stringer, Cas Dunlap, Mary Thompson, Steve Lacy, AnnaMaria Cardinalli, and a cultural anthropologist who asked not to be identified.

164 *Weston Resolve was an elaborate game:* Holbert, interviews by author, February 25, 2009, and August 19, 2012.

165 *"I've lived in Leavenworth my whole life":* Interview with Lindsay Driscoll, twenty-two, of Leavenworth County, Kansas, by Human Terrain trainee Joe Stringer, February 25, 2009.

166 *One of the few Human Terrain social scientists:* Ted Callahan, "Ein Ethnologe im Krieg," *GEO,* May 5, 2010, 51–70. The article ran in German; I am quoting from the pre-publication final draft that Callahan submitted in English, with many thanks to Callahan for sharing this with me.

166 *found their training in Kansas disappointing:* Ayala, interview by author, August 19, 2009, and Clint Cooper, interview by author, April 22, 2010. "I think it was a waste of time for the most part," Cooper said of his training in Leavenworth. "I might sound arrogant, but there wasn't much they had to teach me. And Paula and everybody else felt the same way. The things they were teaching, like MAP-HT and military rank structure, things like that were just kind of useless. . . . It was nice to go to Omaha and talk a little about culture [and] language with the Afghans. . . . And they had a couple of HTS people that came back, and they talked to us a little bit, and they told us some of their experiences in the field. But even that, we could see that they weren't necessarily doing things how we wanted to do things, or how they should be done."

166 *Ayala in particular:* Ayala, interview by author, August 19, 2009. "I was hoping to learn more," Ayala told me. "But . . . I saw a lot of flaws in this training program. They had all the right classes but . . . there were days we showed up at training [and] they said, 'Have a reading day, because the instructor is not going to be here.' The schedules were conflicting, so we had a lot of downtime because they just weren't organized. And it was a new program so you got to give them the benefit of the doubt on that. But time after time, you would try to see development, it wasn't happening. And the biggest discouragement was the quality of people that were in there."

166 *Like many former soldiers, he viewed:* "Those people who were opposed to it had no knowledge of what takes place in a combat zone and they had no knowledge on the concept of the mission itself," Ayala told me. "My concern wasn't what the anthropology community thought. I think it's for each individual what they want to do with their lives." He continued: "If I was an anthropologist, it [wouldn't] matter what I was providing, it [would matter] how could I be helping the situation. I think they should have looked at it that way instead of saying, 'It's unethical.' What's unethical about it? You can help save lives." Ayala, interview by author, August 19, 2009.

166 *understood that his job was to take photographs:* Ayala, interview by author, August 19, 2009. Ayala told me: "They tried to appease the anthropology community and the [American Anthropological Association] that, 'Let's not use the word *intel.* We're not here to provide intel.' But that's all it is."

167 *Bhatia and Suveges had been killed while Ayala was in training:* Ayala, interview by author, May 4, 2009.

167 *"that touchy-feely thing that no one understood":* Cas Dunlap, interview by author, August 23, 2012.

167 *"If you go into a totally unknown area":* Holbert, interview by author, August 19, 2012.

168 *trainees got no operational security training in Kansas:* For the lack of firearms training and other practical preparation for a conflict zone, Ayala, interviews by author, May 4 and August 19, 2009. The Human Terrain System training regimen has since been revised, and prospective field team members now spend nine weeks at Fort Polk, Louisiana, "where they are trained in basic combat techniques, life on a Forward Operating Base and Combat Outpost, and other necessities for living and operating in a war zone." Lamb et al., "Human Terrain Team Performance: An Explanation, draft," forthcoming 2013, 20, and Steve Lacy, interview by author, December 2, 2012.

168 *"As a member of a 5-person":* "BAE Systems: Human Terrain System," recruiting pamphlet, November 3, 2008. The brochure also emphasizes the "positive, lasting impact" that Human Terrain Team members can have by helping to create an "unclassified" database that will be "easily accessible to organizations and individuals involved in stability operations." Though program administrators often referenced such a database, I saw no evidence of it during the time I spent with Human Terrain Teams in Afghanistan between early 2009 and the end of 2010; instead, they stored their reports on a secret system accessible to members of the military and others with a government-issued clearance.

168 *gave their Human Terrain Team members guns:* John Green and Sonya Brown, interviews by author, January 21, 30, and 31, 2010. When he resigned from the Human Terrain System in 2009, anthropology grad student Ted Callahan noted among his concerns the "[c]omplete lack of tactical training (to include weapons training), which puts HTS personnel and the military units supporting them at greater risk." Callahan, "HTS Assessment," correspondence. On the issue of firearms training, Callahan wrote: "HTS needs to confront the issue of weapons. Most participants will opt to be armed in Afghanistan, yet HTS irresponsibly shifts the burden to the host [brigade] of ensuring that HTS personnel are qualified to carry a weapon. This allows management to dodge the tricky (for some) ethical issue of civilian academics being armed by saying that it is 'an individual decision.' However, in many cases, the [brigade] will assume that HTS personnel are qualified to be issued a weapon, without independently verifying it. At a minimum, training should involve basic weapons handling, shooting, and maintenance, for both the M9 [pistol] and the M4 [rifle]."

168 *When Ayala completed his training:* Ayala, interviews by author, May 4 and August 19, 2009. "I thought it was very fraudulent," Ayala told me. "It was a liability. . . . We all said, 'One day this will come back and bite them in the butt.'"

168 *On my first morning there:* Interview with an anthropologist who asked to be identified

only as "Dr. Wilson," February 24, 2009. Wilson subsequently quit the program. He later rejoined and was severely wounded when a buried bomb exploded beneath him during a patrol in southern Afghanistan.

168 *When we met again many months later:* Dr. Wilson, interview by author, September 25, 2009.

169 *The team had been reconstituted:* Karl Slaikeu, interview by author, March 21, 2009; Stephen James "Banger" Lang, interview by author, March 22, 2009; and "Spen," interview by author, April 2, 2009. For Slaikeu and Lang having never been to Afghanistan, see Gezari, "Rough Terrain." For Slaikeu taking Loyd's place on the team and Lang taking Ayala's, Slaikeu, interview by author, April 7, 2009.

169 *The psychologist was a tall man with wire-rimmed glasses:* Slaikeu was six foot three. For this and other elements of his appearance, see Gezari, "Rough Terrain." By the time Slaikeu arrived in Afghanistan, he told me that he had been thinking about the "oil spot" theory of spreading security in a conflict zone "for years." During his Human Terrain training at Fort Leavenworth, he was "delighted to find" that this approach was a key counterinsurgency technique, and he latched on to it. At the Joint Readiness Training Center at Fort Polk, Louisiana, ahead of his deployment, Slaikeu's obsession with the "oil spot" approach prompted colleagues to start calling him "Oil Spot Spock." By the time he landed in Maiwand, he had drafted the better part of a paper on the strategy's utility in Afghanistan. "It was rather bold of me to think of writing such a paper so early in the game," Slaikeu told me self-deprecatingly, but I saw little evidence that being in Afghanistan significantly changed his view of what was needed there. His embrace of the "oil spot" approach, like so many initiatives proposed by newcomers seeking to make their mark on the war, seemed aimed at impressing higher-ups rather than addressing the very complicated problems Afghans faced in Maiwand. Slaikeu, interview by author, April 7, 2009.

169 *One afternoon, I watched as he tried to convince:* Meeting with Slaikeu, Lang, Canadian CMIC officers, and USAID representative Brian Felakos, March 23, 2009.

169 *Later, I asked one of the Canadians:* A Canadian soldier who asked not to be identified, interview by author, March 23, 2009.

170 *Slaikeu had been issued an assault rifle:* Slaikeu, interviews by author, March 21 and April 7, 2009. "There was no weapons training," Slaikeu told me. "There was no operational security training." His teammate, Lang, agreed: "We had no weapons training in the program, and no discussions about operational security, no discussions about many different things." Lang, interview by author, April 8, 2009. Said a third team member: "We were told we were going to get weapons training. . . . But as it turns out, we did not get any weapons training. It was optional. I think some companies would give a five-hundred-dollar reimbursement for . . . like, a Saturday-afternoon or maybe a two-day shooting course for five hundred dollars . . . which is better than nothing, but come on." "Spen," interview by author, April 2, 2009.

170 *The former Marine who had replaced Ayala went by the nickname Banger:* Observation and conversation with Lang, March and April 2009.

170 *Early in my visit, when I was just getting to know the Human Terrain Team members:* The barbecue took place on March 21, 2009. See Vanessa Gezari, "Kill the Goat," Pulitzer Center on Crisis Reporting, April 1, 2009, http://pulitzercenter.org/blog/untold-stories/kill-goat, accessed July 19, 2012.

170 *He had grown up on a farm in Iowa:* Lang, interview by author, March 22, 2009.

170 *The commander came from Logar, near Kabul:* Lieutenant Abdul Saboor, interview by author, March 21, 2009.

171 *Hazaras have long occupied the lowest rung:* See, for example, Thomas Barfield, *Afghanistan: A Cultural and Political History* (Princeton, NJ: Princeton University Press, 2010), 17–27.

172 *A year later, after a lengthy deployment:* Lang, correspondence, July 12, 2010. *Pashto* is the language spoken by members of the *Pashtun* ethnic group.

172 *A more culturally knowledgeable member of AF4:* "Spen," interview by author, April 2, 2009. Although Spen's familiarity with the region meant that he operated like a social scientist on the team, he was technically a Human Terrain Analyst, as Cooper had been. Like other Human Terrain Team members, he had found the training "tremendously lacking." Among his concerns was the absence of any physical fitness test for deploying team members, and in this he was not alone. "There are people in this program who are going to put people's sons and daughters in danger because they're too slow, they're too old, or too fat to be out embedded with a group of soldiers. I think [physical fitness] should be part of the hiring process," Spen told me.

172 *By far the most serious problem, in his view:* Ibid.

173 *"Wadaregah, motherfucker!":* Notes from a patrol with soldiers of the 2–2, March 21, 2009.

173 *Like the original members of AF4, many were paid very well:* The $250,000–$350,000 figure is based on interviews and published accounts, but in reality the number may have been even higher. The BAE program manager for the Human Terrain System told the Center for Naval Analyses that under the contractor system, "a Senior Social Scientist with 1 year of field research experience could make $390K–$420K with differentials and overtime. . . . As government employees, he estimates they would get about $200K–$250K with differentials and overtime." The study also notes that Department of Army Civilians were subject to a "pay cap which limited total pay, overtime and comp time to $234,000 per year." Salaries varied depending on which contractor the team members worked for, but Karen Clark, the program's chief of staff during this period, confirmed the range cited here. Clinton et al., "Congressionally Directed Assessment of the Human Terrain System," 88, 142; Gezari, "Rough Terrain"; and Hugh Gusterson, "Do Professional Ethics Matter in War?" *Bulletin of the Atomic Scientists,* March 4, 2010.

173 *But in early 2009, the Human Terrain System:* Steve Fondacaro, interview by author, June 16, 2010, and Campbell Robertson and Stephen Farrell, "Pact, Approved in Iraq, Sets Time for U.S. Pullout," *New York Times,* November 16, 2008. For specific consequences for Human Terrain System field team members of Iraqi descent, who would have had to disclose the location of any relatives living in Iraq, putting them at risk, see Clinton et al., "Congressionally Directed Assessment of the Human Terrain System," 141. For changes contractors faced under the agreement, see "New Status of Forces Agreement Subjects Government Contractors to Iraqi Law," http://www.gibsondunn.com/publications/pages/NewStatusofForcesAgreementSubjects GovernmentContractorstoIraqiLaw.aspx, accessed July 20, 2012.

173 *An official from the Army's Training and Doctrine Command emailed:* "Memorandum: Offer/Acceptance of Employment as Human Terrain Analyst GG-12," Robert Reuss, Defense Intelligence Senior Leader, Assistant Deputy Chief of Staff, G-2, Headquarters United States Army Training and Doctrine Command, February 9, 2009. This deadline may have been extended—the Center for Naval Analyses study says team members were given a month. Clinton et al., "Congressionally Directed Assessment of the Human Terrain System," 141.

174 *About a third of the project's field team members quit in disgust:* Noah Shachtman, "Mass Exodus from 'Human Terrain' Program; At Least One Third Quits," *Wired: Danger Room,* http://www.wired.com/dangerroom/2009/04/htts-quit/, accessed July 25, 2012. See also Clinton et al., "Congressionally Directed Assessment of the Human Terrain System," 76.

174 *In the spring of 2009, the Obama administration:* "Obama's Strategy for Afghanistan and Pakistan, March 2009," remarks by President Barack Obama, March 27, 2009, http://www.cfr.org/pakistan/obamas-strategy-afghanistan-pakistan-march -2009/p18952?breadcrumb=%2Fpublication%2Fby_type%2Fessential_docu ment, accessed July 20, 2012.

174 *Obama had already agreed to send 21,000 more troops:* Obama, "Obama's Strategy for Afghanistan and Pakistan, March 2009," remarks, March 27, 2009, http:// www.cfr.org/pakistan/obamas-strategy-afghanistan-pakistan-march-2009/p189 52?breadcrumb=%2Fpublication%2Fby_type%2Fessential_document, accessed July 20, 2012. For the total number of U.S. troops in Afghanistan being more than 60,000 after the addition, see Karen DeYoung, "Obama Announces Strategy for Afghanistan, Pakistan," *The Washington Post,* March 28, 2009. Nine months later, after General Stanley McChrystal took command, the president would approve an additional "surge" force of 30,000 troops, bringing the total number of forces in Afghanistan to more than 100,000 by the summer of 2010. Eric Schmitt, "Obama Issues Order for More Troops in Afghanistan," *New York Times,* November 30, 2009. See also "Remarks by the President in Address to the Nation on the Way Forward in Afghanistan and Pakistan," December 1, 2009, http://www.whitehouse.gov/the-press-office/remarks-president-address-nation-way-forward -afghanistan-and-pakistan, accessed July 20, 2012.

174 *Training for Afghan security forces:* See Obama's March 27, 2009, speech and "White

Paper of the Interagency Policy Group's Report on U.S. Policy toward Afghanistan and Pakistan," Spring 2009, http://www.cfr.org/pakistan/white-paper-interagency-policy-groups-report-us-policy-toward-afghanistan-pakistan/p18959, accessed July 20, 2012.

175 *As one year slipped into the next:* A kitchen fire can be tackled with a small extinguisher, General Stanley McChrystal told Congress that year, but a house fire requires bigger guns. "In Afghanistan, the insurgency grew as they recovered after 2001," McChrystal told the House Armed Services Committee. "Their shadow governance, their presence among the people, was not met by increases in Afghan national security force strength levels or in coalition forces. So what I'm saying is, we lagged behind that." Remarks by General Stanley McChrystal before the House Armed Services Committee, December 8, 2009, http://www.isaf.nato.int/article/transcripts/transcript-u.s.-house-armed-services-committee-hearing-on-afghanistan.html, accessed July 20, 2012.

175 *By 2009, even pro-Western Afghans:* Vanessa M. Gezari, "The Secret Alliance," *New Republic,* August 19, 2011.

175 *That summer, then–Secretary of Defense Robert Gates fired the commander:* "Officials said it appeared that General McKiernan was the first general to be dismissed from command of a theater of combat since Douglas MacArthur during the Korean War." See Yochi J. Dreazen and Peter Spiegel, "U.S. Fires Afghan War Chief," *Wall Street Journal,* May 12, 2009, and Chandrasekaran, *Little America,* 53.

175 *McKiernan was said to be too plodding:* That the war was profoundly underresourced is clear from Obama's March 2009 remarks on the strategy, McChrystal's assessment, and from dozens of other official and press accounts. McKiernan had been asking for more troops in Afghanistan for months before Obama took office, but President George W. Bush declined to act on the request in the final days of his second term, leaving the decision to Obama. See Chandrasekaran, *Little America,* 50.

175 *General Stanley McChrystal, then director:* Between 2006 and 2008, McChrystal commanded the Joint Special Operations Command and Joint Special Operations Command Forward. Much of the command's work during that time involved targeting high-level insurgents in Iraq, and McChrystal was sometimes personally involved in the raids. Forces under McChrystal's command were credited with capturing Saddam Hussein and finding and killing Abu Mussab al-Zarqawi. See "Biography of General Stanley McChrystal," Council on Foreign Relations, http://www.cfr.org/afghanistan/biography-general-stanley-mcchrystal/p19396, accessed July 20, 2012; and "In Hunt for Terrorists in Iraq, General Is No Armchair Warrior," *Washington Times,* October 2, 2006.

177 *"All ISAF personnel must show respect":* McChrystal's exhortation may seem obvious, but it is hard to convey how earth-shattering it was for an American commanding general in Afghanistan to write these words in an official document that was leaked to the *Washington Post's* Bob Woodward, albeit in the eighth year of the war.

177 *A small number of British forces:* This is based on interviews with marines during a three-week trip to Helmand in September 2009, especially members of the 1st Battalion, 5th Marines, in Nawa. See also Chandrasekaran, *Little America,* 45–46, 48–50.

177 *The team's leader was Steve Lacy:* Lacy had been a captain when I met him in Leavenworth. By the time I saw him in Afghanistan, he had been promoted to major.

177 *Camp Leatherneck occupied an expanse of fine sand and rock:* The Desert of Death, or Dasht-e-Margo in Pashto. See Kristina Toderich and Tsuneo Tsukatani, "Water/Pasture Assessment of Registan Desert (Kandahar and Helmand Provinces)," Discussion Paper No. 606, Kier Discussion Paper Series, Kyoto Institute of Economic Research, October 2005, http://www.kier.kyoto-u.ac.jp/DP/DP606.pdf, accessed July 20, 2012; and Declan Walsh, "Desert of Death Takes Its Toll on Beleaguered Troops," *Guardian,* July 7, 2006.

178 *AF6 had been sent to Helmand too early:* Dunlap, interview by author, August 23, 2012.

178 *Dunlap flew north to Bagram:* Ibid.

178 *The Marines disliked the idea:* The concept of a Marine Female Engagement Team, known as a FET, was still germinating. Some Marine officers looked at the women on the Human Terrain Team and assumed it was just another version of the FET. They figured both teams would serve the same purpose: to reach out to Afghan women, provide medical and other services, and gather whatever intelligence they could about local politics and the insurgency.

178 *Unable to conduct the village and area assessments:* AnnaMaria Cardinalli, "Pashtun Sexuality," Human Terrain Team (HTT) AF6, Research update and Findings, 2009, and Dunlap, interview by author, August 23, 2012. For years in various parts of the country, night letters had supported a highly effective insurgent campaign to intimidate local people into resisting the advances of NATO forces and the fledgling Afghan government. Dunlap showed the British how to craft responses that would appeal to Afghans' concerns for local sovereignty, their hatred of Pakistanis, and their adherence to central tenets of *Pashtunwali,* the traditional code of the Afghan south. Dunlap, "Shabnamah 1SEP09 Babaji wNotes," a sample coalition night letter to be distributed in Babaji to counter Taliban propaganda, correspondence. For background on the use of night letters in Afghanistan, see "Lessons in Terror: Attacks on Education in Afghanistan," Human Rights Watch, July 2006, http://www.hrw.org/sites/default/files/reports/afghanistan0706.pdf, accessed August 20, 2012. See also Declan Walsh, "'Night Letters' from the Taliban Threaten Afghan Democracy," *Observer,* September 18, 2004.

179 *They worked because they belonged to the place:* Dunlap told me that the term *night letter* (*shabnameh* in Persian) was used to refer to the resistance tactic of large groups of people standing on rooftops at night yelling "Allah-ho-Akbar," or "God is great," as a means of protest. Afghans did this during the war against the Soviets; it was also a hallmark of the Iranian Revolution in 1979. The concept of *shabnameh* resurfaced in Iran during the antigovernment uprisings of 2009 and 2010. Dunlap,

interview by author, August 23, 2012, and "The Iranian Night Letter," http://theiraniannightletter.blogspot.com, accessed January 10, 2013.

179 *A few days after I arrived at Leatherneck:* The patrol took place on September 4, 2009.

179 *She had grown up in New Mexico:* Cardinalli, interview by author, February 24, 2009, and "AnnaMaria," http://annamaria.ws/bio.htm, accessed July 23, 2012.

179 *At Notre Dame, she had written a PhD dissertation:* Cardinalli, interview by author, February 24, 2009, and AnnaMaria Cardinalli-Padilla, *"El Llanto:* A Liturgical Journey into the Identity and Theology of the Northern New Mexican Penitentes and Their Spiritual Siblings" (PhD diss., University of Notre Dame, April 2004).

179 *When hijacked planes hit New York and Washington:* Cardinalli, interview by author, February 24, 2009.

179 *had written that the "secrecy":* Cardinalli-Padilla, *"El Llanto,"* 7.

179 *Later, she would describe her dissertation:* Dr. AnnaMaria Cardinalli, "Cardinalli Resume July 09."

180 *"Being an activist type, I had a lot of preconceptions":* Cardinalli, interview by author, February 24, 2009.

180 *It had grown out of a medical mission:* Cardinalli, "Human Terrain Team (HTT) AF-6 Patrol Report and Findings," September 4, 2009; Captain Jennifer Gregoire, "Mission Summary," on the August 19, 2009, FET and MEDCAP mission to Settlement 1; and Cardinalli, "Human Terrain Team (HTT) AF-6 Patrol Report and Findings," August 18, 2009.

180 *When the Navy doctor had finished:* "Women would not respond to questions regarding community issues, even when such questions were framed by HTT as simply an inquiry into their personal opinions and experiences," she wrote in her patrol report. "When pressed . . . interviewees said simply, 'We are not comfortable answering any questions.'" Cardinalli, "Human Terrain Team (HTT) AF-6 Patrol Report and Findings," August 18, 2009.

180 *But this concern struck Cardinalli:* Ibid.

181 *She had no medical training:* Like others on her team, Cardinalli had taken part in a brief combat lifesaving course during her Human Terrain System training cycle. I have taken two similar courses myself, but I am profoundly unqualified to hand out medicine to Afghans.

181 *He later told me he was from Nad Ali:* Also known as Nad-i-Ali.

186 *The Afghans were growing vegetables in the sewage runoff from the nearby military bases:* Marine Lieutenant Colonel Christopher Naler made a reference to the runoff during a briefing to the Marine commander, General Larry Nicholson, on September 13, 2009: "They're all competing, quite frankly now for the same fertilizer, and that is commonly referred to as shit creek coming out of Bastion. That is what is fueling their agrarian society all the way down the central wadi."

187 *AF7 had arrived at the beginning of a long-awaited troop surge:* In Helmand and most of the south, the Afghan postal service hadn't worked in any dependable way since before the civil war. "Night letters," however, are mentioned with some frequency in press accounts.

187 *Cardinalli had handed out Icy Hot:* Afghanistan had the second-highest maternal mortality rate according to United Nations figures issued in 2008 and 2009. Sayed Salahuddin, "Maternal Mortality Rate High in Afghanistan: UN," http://in.reuters.com/article/2009/01/26/afghan-mortality-idINISL40747920090126, accessed July 23, 2012. The number has since declined; see "Efforts Intensify to Reach MDGs on Maternal Health," United Nations Assistance Mission in Afghanistan, April 11, 2012, http://unama.unmissions.org/Default.aspx?tabid=12254&ctl=Details&mid=15756&ItemID=33617&language=en-US, accessed July 23, 2012.

187 *Their commander, Lieutenant Colonel Bill McCollough:* McCollough commanded the 1st Battalion, 5th Marines, in Nawa. The area was repeatedly held up by the military as a shining example of what good counterinsurgency tactics could accomplish. See Gezari, "Talking to the Enemy: How One Company of Marines Is Helping to Bring Afghan Insurgents Home," *Slate,* October 16, 2009.

188 *They landed 180 times in thirty-seven countries:* U.S. Marine Corps, *Small Wars Manual* (Washington, DC: U.S. Government Printing Office, 1940), 2–7.

188 *A Marine Corps intelligence officer had to know the enemy:* Ibid., 19.

188 *That is a much broader definition of intelligence:* The Army's definition of intelligence has been evolving these last few years as a result of its involvement in Iraq and Afghanistan. A comparison between the 2004 and 2010 versions of Army intelligence doctrine is illuminating. The 2004 edition of *U.S. Army Field Manual 2-0: Intelligence* describes intelligence as a means of combating threats within a commander's battlespace and is overwhelmingly focused on the enemy. The word *enemy* occurs 242 times in the 2004 manual, compared with only 130 times in the 2010 version. Although both manuals state that a key purpose of intelligence is to drive a commander's "decisionmaking," the 2010 manual devotes considerable attention to "civil considerations" as a key aspect of understanding the battlefield. In the 2004 version, relatively little attention is paid to "open source intelligence" (OSINT), which receives its own chapter in the 2010 update. This addition to the concept of intelligence coincided with the advent of the Human Terrain System and similar initiatives, and Steve Fondacaro and others at the Human Terrain System have argued that the program played an important role in forcing the Army to revise and broaden its definition of intelligence. The only mentions of "culture" in the 2004 manual come in subsections on intelligence support to psychological operations, linguistics, and stability operations. In the section on stability operations, which gives the fullest treatment of the importance of culture, only one sentence is devoted to the consequences of failing to understand it: "A lack of knowledge

concerning local politics, customs, and culture could lead to US actions which attack inappropriate targets or which may offend or cause mistrust among the local population." In the 2010 revision, by contrast, the word *culture* occurs more than twenty times in the context of culture as an important element of the population or the Army itself (compared with only five occurrences in the 2004 edition). "Culture is a key factor in understanding the local population," the 2010 manual states. *"Cultural awareness has become an increasingly important competency for intelligence Soldiers.* Culture is the shared beliefs, values, customs, behaviors, and artifacts members of a society use to cope with the world and each other. . . . Understanding other cultures applies to all operations, not only those dominated by stability." (Emphasis is mine.) In the 2010 manual, the sentence about the consequence of failing to understand cultural variables has been expanded to read: "A lack of knowledge concerning insurgents, local politics, customs, and culture as well as how to differentiate between local combatants, often leads to U.S. actions that can result in unintended and disadvantageous consequences—such as attacking unsuitable targets or offending or causing mistrust among the local population. This lack of knowledge could potentially threaten mission accomplishment." *U.S. Army Field Manual 2-0: Intelligence,* May 17, 2004, and *U.S. Army Field Manual 2-0: Intelligence,* March 23, 2010.

188 *A few months before my visit to Helmand:* Major Ben Connable, U.S. Marine Corps, "All Our Eggs in a Broken Basket: How the Human Terrain System Is Undermining Sustainable Military Cultural Competence," *Military Review,* March–April 2009, 57–64.

190 *Cardinalli's report on homosexuality among Pashtun men:* A Marine intelligence sergeant in Helmand, Afghanistan, interview by author, September 20, 2009.

190 *That fall, a Marine officer asked Lacy:* Lacy, interview by author, November 18, 2009.

190 *In a September 30 field report, Lacy detailed:* Lacy, "Human Terrain Team (AF6) INTSUM 30 September 2009 Re: Marjeh."

191 *This was not the sort of cultural information:* Phoenix was a Vietnam War–era intelligence program focused on understanding the social and political organization of the Viet Cong, with the aim of killing and capturing its leaders and sympathizers. See among others Nathan Hodge, *Armed Humanitarians: The Rise of the Nation Builders* (New York: Bloomsbury, 2010), 125–28.

191 *"They have a hard time, any of these guys":* Lacy, interview by author, November 18, 2009. The Marine colonel who supervised the Human Terrain Team was so impressed by what Lacy was able to gather from the Afghan police sergeant and other internally displaced Afghans in Lashkar Gah that "he said, 'Stop what you're doing. I want you to do this. Because even our intel guys can't get good information about this place,'" Lacy told me. "That's part of what [the colonel] liked so much about it, it was stuff he could use for operations. . . . This whole idea in the program is that we're going to make this huge distinction with intel, not intel, blah, blah, blah, but the lines are so blurred. I'm one of the few people

that openly calls it 'open-source intelligence.' HTS just freaks out when you use the term *intel* because they think it's a bad word, or it's going to frighten away their PhDs, and I don't care. If that frightens them away, then they shouldn't be here."

191 *By late 2009, the American Anthropological Association:* American Anthropological Association Commission on the Engagement of Anthropology with the Security and Intelligence Communities (CEAUSSIC), "Final Report on the Army's Human Terrain System Proof of Concept Program," October 14, 2009, 49–51.

191 *a number of anthropologists in good standing:* See "Moving Forward with the CEAUSSIC: Ethics Casebook: What is the Casebook, and Why Now?" http://blog.aaanet .org/2010/01/27/ceaussic-ethics-casebook/, accessed September 5, 2012.

191 *It wasn't working for the military:* "As a security paradigm may come to modify or even replace the older one of [*sic*] developed during the Cold War, the question of engagement, non-engagement, or even anti-anti-engagement which the Commission began by taking up will seem even more naive than it does now," the CEAUSSIC members wrote. "The challenge will increasingly be to define ethically defensible research in complex environments of collaboration." AAA Commission on the Engagement of Anthropology with the Security and Intelligence Communities, "Final Report," November 4, 2007, 8.

191 *Rob Albro, an anthropologist at American University:* Rob Albro, interview by author, December 4, 2009. "In a very real sense, our reluctance to engage with institutions that make us uncomfortable—military or corporate—means that anthropologists are missing an opportunity to educate policymakers about how our discipline has evolved," Albro and his colleagues had written. "Final Report," 2007, 22.

192 *The Human Terrain System lied:* Fondacaro told me that he didn't identify what the Human Terrain System did as "intelligence" because the "social science community" believed intelligence was "anything that helps the Army kill people better. . . . I want us in the Department of Defense to see intelligence as something that's greater-expanded, that captures HTS. . . . *I think intelligence has become more like Human Terrain. I think we've driven that.*" Fondacaro, interview by author, June 16, 2010; emphasis is mine.

192 *Within a few months of my visit to Helmand:* "L—— Formal Performance Counseling, 17 February 2010"; "Developmental Counseling Form for ——," U.S. Army Training and Doctrine Command, October 15, 2009; and "Request for Termination of ——; Based on Poor Performance and Lack of Professionalism," Program Manager Forward, Afghanistan.

192 *One of her teammates, a Vietnam veteran, was sent home:* A Human Terrain System official, interview by author, March 24, 2010.

192 *By February 2010, the Marine colonel:* Email correspondence between a Marine officer and a Human Terrain System official, February 18, 2010. I focus on the dysfunction in Helmand because those teams stood at the heart of the U.S. military effort in Afghanistan in 2009 and 2010, and because I spent time with many of their

members. Such antics were not confined to Helmand. During some twelve weeks I spent with Human Terrain Teams in Afghanistan between the spring of 2009 and the fall of 2010, I also met a handful of smart, hardworking people who managed to commit useful acts of cultural and political analysis and avoid being strangled by the bureaucracy.

193 *Soon after, the military wanted twenty-six teams:* McFate, interview by author, June 30, 2010. Other quotes from McFate in this paragraph come from the same interview.

193 *The first is its frankness:* The paper begins: "Conducting military operations in a low-intensity conflict without ethnographic and cultural intelligence is like building a house without using your thumbs: it is a wasteful, clumsy, and unnecessarily slow process at best, with a high probability for frustration and failure." Kipp et al., "The Human System: A CORDS for the 21st Century," 8. The word *intelligence* appears twelve times in the paper, while the word *anthropologist* is used only three times.

194 *As the people who ultimately ran the Human Terrain System:* The program's job descriptions would change significantly as it evolved. For a full accounting, see Clinton et al., "Congressionally Directed Assessment of the Human Terrain System," 76–85. As McFate told me: "Ideally you'd like everyone to have served in a military unit, have a PhD in the social sciences, speak the local language, and have [done] fieldwork in that particular place. If you were waiting for those people to knock on your door, we would still be waiting, because there are just not enough of them in the U.S., especially given the fact that Afghanistan and Iraq have been more or less closed to researchers for decades now. *So the goal was never actually to just look for people who had experience as social scientists working in those domains, 'cause you're simply not going to find them.*" McFate, interview by author, January 28, 2009. Emphasis is mine.

194 *The article was not shy about the need for intelligence skills:* Kipp, interview by author, July 2, 2010. "Our original idea—it didn't prove feasible—was to use reservists with the language and anthropological skills," Kipp told me. "And my vision was flawed here, because I figured we'd get time to do a small test concept and it wouldn't grow [so] much. . . . I did not anticipate when I wrote that article that we would do the surge and create the immediate demand that we did. . . . My vision was what we'd done with Foreign Area Officers, which was to get them area background, deep language." Kipp is a historian, and the prominence of anthropology in the Human Terrain System had not been his idea. That was McFate's contribution, he told me, but Kipp seemed to understand the potential conflicts better than she did. "Montgomery is a hybrid," Kipp told me. "She's a lawyer and an anthropologist. She's never taught anthropology at a university. She was not particularly sensitive to academic turf. And an anthropologist who has done thorough research has certain things he's saying, 'I'm not doing.'"

194 *During his fourth rotation in late 2009:* Colonel Mike Howard, interview by author, December 20, 2009.

195 *In January 2010, Flynn published a paper:* Major General Michael T. Flynn, Captain

Matt Pottinger, and Paul Batchelor, "Fixing Intel: A Blueprint for Making Intelligence Relevant in Afghanistan," Center for a New American Security, January 2010, 4–17. One would think it would have been harder for the Human Terrain System to deny its role in the intelligence cycle when the top intelligence officer in Afghanistan exhorted analysts to gather information from Human Terrain Teams, yet the program's official position did not immediately change.

195 *More than eight years into the war:* Ibid., 7.

195 *Human Terrain Teams could help solve these problems:* Flynn, interview by author, January 16, 2010. This dissonance—between what senior officers saw or said they saw in the Human Terrain Teams and what I and other observers saw on the ground—is borne out by the Center for Naval Analyses report, which found that brigade commanders and other "customers" of the program, "including those most critical of HTS, indicated that HTS teams are performing a vital function" and "contend that even if only a few of the teams are successful, the good work that the successful teams do is so important that it makes the whole enterprise worthwhile." Clinton et al., "Congressionally Directed Assessment of the Human Terrain System," 103, and Lamb et al., "Human Terrain Team Performance: An Explanation, draft," forthcoming 2013.

196 *McFate and Fondacaro had told me that their recruitment:* Fondacaro, interview by author, June 16, 2010. The Army's Training and Doctrine Command had a broad contract with BAE, and because the Human Terrain System fell under the intelligence section of that command, the program was stuck with BAE as a hiring contractor, Fondacaro told me. "We were constantly forced into an omnibus contract that exclusively favored BAE, and we were unable to get quality performance standards out of the contract," he said. "I get an eighty-six-year-old Iraqi guy. He's eighty-six years old and he's never used a computer in his life. And he's showing up as a team member. He can barely walk! And I'm saying, 'Oh my God, take this guy away from here, you're wasting our time.' Then I'm told by TRADOC I have to write a statement stating why he doesn't fit. I've got a woman who shows up and it turns out she's got pornographic pictures on the Internet of herself. There's a guy who shows up, he looks very good, he's an Iraqi . . . and we discover he has prior service with the Iraqi intelligence service. This individual was not picked up in the clearance process. We had to bring him back to the U.S. His clearance was being handled by another agency that wasn't talking to our agency." In December 2010, Fondacaro told *Wired*'s *Danger Room* blog that "[t]hirty to forty percent of the people [in the Human Terrain System] were not qualified." Spencer Ackerman, "Hundreds in Army Social Science Unqualified, Former Boss Says," *Wired: Danger Room,* December 21, 2010, http://www.wired.com/dangerroom/2010/12/human-terrain-unqualified/, accessed July 25, 2012.

196 *Convinced that the project's failures stemmed:* There is evidence that Fondacaro and McFate were correct about the BAE contract, and that ultimate responsibility for many of the program's shortcomings lay with the Army's Training and Doctrine

Command. In 2009, citing "anecdotal evidence indicating problems with management and resourcing" in the Human Terrain System, the House Armed Services Committee asked the Defense Department to conduct an independent assessment of the program. The assessment, undertaken by the Center for Naval Analyses and published in the fall of 2010, paints a picture of TRADOC as understaffed and uncooperative, and suggests that "some of these unresolved issues may require a reassessment of where the HTS program resides. . . . [T]here may be a lack of TRADOC institutional commitment to making HTS a success." The report notes that TRADOC's contract with BAE, worth $380 million, included few protections for the government, and that it was renewed in 2009, despite Fondacaro's complaints. Human Terrain Team members were hired on the basis of a phone or online interview, and BAE's rejection rate was remarkably low. In fiscal year 2009, more than half of those who applied for a job on a Human Terrain Team got one; the following year, some 40 percent did. While some were removed during training, many stayed on, for there were no tests or other measures of competency during the program's four-and-a-half-month training period. BAE, for its part, complained that the program didn't give its contractors enough lead time to find qualified recruits. An in-person interview with potential recruits would have tested "the candidate's ability to interact with people—likely an important attribute for someone going to a foreign country and attempting to 'map' the human terrain," the authors of the study noted dryly. But BAE estimated that such an interview would cost about one thousand dollars more per candidate and the contractor "had no incentive to spend the additional money." The authors of the study were not able to look at the contract, but they noted that it apparently contained no "penalties for providing substandard recruits or incentives for providing good recruits. The government seems to have to take whatever BAE provides. . . . In our judgment, the contract needs to be modified to provide more protection for the government." Moreover, the study finds significant grounds that TRADOC did not properly review or oversee its contract with BAE. Unsurprisingly, the study found that the Human Terrain System suffered from crippling attrition rates and that "many of the currently deployed HTS personnel are underqualified for their jobs." Clinton et al., "Congressionally Directed Assessment of the Human Terrain System," 3, 6, 86–93, 106–9, 135–37.

196 *"Steve has the attitude that":* McFate, interview by author, June 30, 2010.

197 *Overselling is pretty much required:* Despite the findings of the Center for Naval Analyses, the Human Terrain System successfully graduated from its experimental "Proof of Concept" phase to program status, gaining its own line item in the fiscal 2011 defense budget, where it is listed as a "Military Intelligence Program." See Department of the Army, "Fiscal Year 2011 Budget Estimates: Volume 1, Operation and Maintenance, Army," February 2010, 31, 108. And this from the HTS website: "In OCT 2010, the Army funded the HTS enduring (force generation) capability starting in the FY 11-15 POM (base budget)," http://humanterrainsystem.army.mil/htsFAQ.aspx.

197 *"The problem with the Human Terrain System"*: Fondacaro, interview by author, June 19, 2010.

197 *"American lives have become intertwined"*: Horowitz, *The Rise and Fall of Project Camelot*, 3.

197 *By 2012, the Human Terrain System had cost*: Steve Lacy, "Propping Open the Door: The Argument for Permanent Integration of Population-Centric Intelligence to Understand the Human Terrain," Master's Thesis, National Intelligence University, 2012, 58. This figure does not include start-up funding. The actual amount spent on the program is likely considerably higher.

198 *Fondacaro was no longer in charge by then:* The Human Terrain System was "a foreign policy implementation tool," Fondacaro told me. Fondacaro, interview by author, June 19, 2010.

*Chapter 9: The Devil You Don't Know*

199 *It seemed obvious to everyone back home that the Taliban had killed Paula Loyd:* Clint Cooper, Loyd's teammate, took this view, and his was one of the earliest and most persuasive accounts of the motivations behind the attack. "I know Paula was targeted because she was a woman, because she was obviously a well educated woman and a person of some importance," he told Army investigators. "Other women in the Bazaar always wore the full head to toe coverings usually associated with more radical forms of Islam. Although Paula always kept herself covered she stood out and represented to the Taliban everything they were trying to suppress. They could easily have taken anyone of us, but in a cowardly act they targeted a person who was very obviously engaged in humanitarian work. She wore no uniform. I have worked with many people down range, but never have I met someone more purely motivated than her. She wanted to make a difference. In a way she did. She will never be forgotten." Cooper statement, U.S. Army Report of Investigation 08-CID369-43873-5H1.

199 *"Paula Loyd, in our estimation based on the facts that we have"*: Steve Fondacaro, interview by author, January 28, 2009.

200 *What he knew was that Loyd's killer was not from Maiwand:* "We haven't been able to trace him identitywise," Fondacaro told me, "only we know that he's not from the area, and that's a specific choice by these people, because if he doesn't survive, if he's known by people, people will come and say, 'Oh, I know him, he's Akhmar and he's associated with . . . et cetera, et cetera.'" Fondacaro was mistaken. The eventuality he described—that Salam would be identified by local people—was exactly what had happened.

200 *"You know there are a lot of kids in Afghanistan"*: McFate and Fondacaro, interview by author, January 28, 2009.

200 *When it was over, the boy told the soldiers he had seen the man around:* "A child in the house my [platoon] cleared knew the man as a frequent stranger in the village, and gave

his name the same name tattooed on the man's forearm." Statement of Lieutenant Matthew Pathak to Army investigators.

201 *a* New York Times *reporter had been kidnapped:* David Rohde was kidnapped on November 10, 2008, after heading off to interview a Taliban commander in Logar Province south of Kabul. "Times Reporter Escapes Taliban After 7 Months," *New York Times,* June 20, 2009.

202 *the Kandahar office of the Afghan government reconciliation commission:* The program, one of many largely unsuccessful attempts by the Afghan government and the international community to reintegrate Taliban fighters, was Proceay Takhim-e Solh, known as PTS or Peace Through Strength. Candace Rondeaux, correspondence, September 15, 2012, and "Talking About Talks: Toward a Political Settlement in Afghanistan," International Crisis Group, Asia Report N°221, March 26, 2012, 17.

202 *The government had promised to help support former fighters and protect them:* "Now in the suburbs and villages, on every side of the city center, there is the influence of Taliban, and because of that, people are scared, and they cannot come for reconciliation," Lalai told us. "We promised the people that if they had problems with the Taliban afterward, we will come and help you—I even promised this. We could not keep the promise. These people, especially high-profile people, sometimes had problems, and they should have government security, but we have not been able to provide it." Hajji Agha Lalai Dastagiri, interview by author, January 19, 2009.

203 *a new, more extreme brand of Taliban were targeting aid workers:* See Marc Kaufman, "Rising Violence Hurts Afghanistan Aid Work," *Washington Post,* February 9, 2003, and Gezari, "Hostilities Threaten U.S. Effort to Rebuild Kandahar," *Chicago Tribune,* February 20, 2003.

203 *Then came the assassinations:* Among the most prominent victims of these attacks was veteran police chief Mohammad Akram Khakrezwal, who was killed in a suicide attack in 2005, but this trend began much earlier. Gezari, "Afghans Now Focus of Taliban Violence," *Chicago Tribune,* October 10, 2003, and Carlotta Gall, "Afghan Mosque Attack Seen as Effort to Hinder Political Process," *New York Times,* June 8, 2005.

203 *He said he had heard about Salam's attack on the American woman:* Speech attributed to Hajji Sadoo Khan here and below is from Sadoo Khan, interview by author, January 19, 2009.

204 *For as long as most people could remember, he had lived with his father, Mohammad Umar, near the highway in Chehel Gazi:* When I asked Mike Warren, Loyd's team leader, where Salam was from, he concurred with the elders: "He's from the village right there." Warren, interview by author, March 20, 2009.

204 *Salam's family owned a tractor:* The family had bought it the previous year with borrowed money, the elders told me. The account of the stolen tractor is from Sadoo Khan and Qala Khan, interviews by author, January 19, 2009.

205 *'What bad work you have done!'*: Qala Khan, interview by author, January 19, 2009.

205 *'I was arrested by the Taliban and I was beaten'*: "He disappeared," Qala Khan said. "And we thought that people were talking that, 'Oh, this poor man was kidnapped by robbers and he was disappeared for two days. Two nights.' After two nights, he showed up, and said, 'I was arrested by Taliban and I was beaten and they have tied my hands.'" Ibid.

205 *'Who did this?' they asked each other:* Qala Khan gave this account of what had happened in the bazaar that day, which was remarkably accurate given that he hadn't actually witnessed the attack himself: "Everyone knows in that area about the incident. We are going to that mosque and we are praying. In that street where the mosque is, [Abdul Salam] was coming and he had this petrol and a lighter with him. And he was stopped by the translator of the American woman and asked if he can talk. And he was laughing with them, he said, 'Okay, I'm talking with you.' At that moment, he poured the petrol on her and ignite with the lighter and he ran away. And . . . when he ran away, at the end of the street, there were other foreigners, and they killed him. . . . They arrested him alive and later they killed him. . . . The local people come and start asking and talking about this incident, 'Who done this? This was done by the son of Mohammad Umar, Salam. He was arrested a few days ago by Taliban.' And some people say, 'Okay, the Taliban had told him that if you don't do work for us, we will kill you.'"

205 *In Afghanistan, hard facts are exceedingly difficult to come by:* For more on the fluidity of information in Afghanistan, see Gezari, "Can Afghanistan Really Develop a Free Press?" *Slate*, March 26, 2004; Gezari, "Journalism in an Oral Culture: From Homer's *Odyssey* to Tolo TV," Pulitzer Center on Crisis Reporting, November 11, 2010; and Gezari, "Crossfire in Kandahar," *Columbia Journalism Review*, January/February 2011.

206 *Bride burning persists in India:* See, for instance, Rahul Bedi, "Indian Dowry Deaths on the Rise," *Telegraph*, February 27, 2012.

206 *immolation is a known form of domestic abuse in Pakistan:* Parveen Azam Ali and Maria Irma Bustamante Gavino, "Violence against Women in Pakistan: A Framework for Analysis," *Journal of Pakistan Medical Association* 58, no. 4 (April 2008): "According to a survey conducted on 1,000 women in Punjab, 35% of the women admitted in the hospitals reported being beaten by their husbands. The survey reported that on an average, at least two women were burned every day in domestic violence incidents and approximately 70 to 90% of women experience spousal abuse. In 1998, 282 burn cases of women were reported in only one province of the country. Out of the reported cases, 65% died of their injuries."

206 *Instead, Afghan women mostly set fire to themselves:* Fire as a mode of attack against women in Afghanistan is rare, but not unheard of. Self-immolation, however, is a significant public health problem. See Rheana Murray, "Self-Immolation Among Afghan Women Rises as UN Pushes Country to Take Action Against Violent

Crimes," *Daily News,* December 13, 2012, and Alissa J. Rubin, "For Afghan Wives, a Desperate, Fiery Way Out," *New York Times,* November 7, 2010.

206 *Lighters bearing English lettering:* Salam's lighter was recovered and photographed by Army investigators.

207 *an Afghan man swung an axe into the head:* "Axe Attack Was an Ambush, Canadian Military Says," CBC News, March 5, 2006, http://www.cbc.ca/news/world/story/2006/03/04/canada-afghanistan060304.html, accessed March 6, 2013.

207 *The medic remembered this detail because the boy wore a skullcap:* Statement of a platoon medic to Army investigators.

207 *another Afghan had been trying to hurry the kids along:* "There was a headmaster that came out and was signing [to the kids], 'Leave the soldiers alone, get in school.' But we were handing out pencils and pens and that was a big distraction. That's why there are so many kids around." Cooper, interview by author, April 22, 2010.

207 *Even an American staff sergeant had tried to disperse the kids:* Statement of a staff sergeant to Army investigators.

207 *Abdul Salam was known as an oddball and an annoyance in the village:* Hajji Mohammad Ehsan, Maiwand district representative to the Kandahar Provincial Council, interview by author, October 12, 2010.

207 *"They were working all the time":* Qala Khan, interview by author, January 19, 2009.

208 *after Salam's death, the Taliban sent a message to Salam's father:* Sadoo Khan, interview by author, January 19, 2009.

208 *Salam must have known they would kill him:* As one soldier told Army investigators: "There's really no where [sic] to avoid people because it's so narrow and there's a creek. There's no where [sic] you can run to try and get away."

208 *Sadoo Khan and Qala Khan condemned Salam's crime in the strongest terms:* Loyd's attacker didn't "have the right to do such kind of thing as he has done," Sadoo Khan told me. "This was a woman. Why did he do that with a woman?" In fact, "the people in the area don't like [Abdul Salam's] family anymore because they have committed a big mistake to attack a woman." As Qala Khan put it: "Traditionally the law is that if someone [kills] our women . . . of course we are executing them. Those who are killing our daughters or sisters or mothers. So if we are killing other people's daughters or sisters, of course we must also blame ourselves, and we must suffer the punishment."

208 *In Kandahar, men sprayed acid at Afghan girls:* Men doused girls going to Mirwais School in Kandahar with acid on November 12, 2008, just days after the attack on Loyd. Dexter Filkins, "Afghan Girls, Scarred by Acid, Defy Terror, Embracing School," *New York Times,* January 13, 2009.

209 *it is also true that many Afghans would consider attacking a woman . . . more egregious than attacking a man:* "Traditionally, women in our society are more protected than men," Sadoo Khan told me. My experience as a foreign woman in Afghanistan bears this out. While the situation is much more complicated for Afghan women, being

322

a foreign woman has won me special protection from Afghans far more often than it has drawn threats. Sadoo Khan, interview by author, January 19, 2009.

209 *they would not attack a convoy with a woman in it:* "It has a very deep roots in our culture," Sadoo Khan told me. "[There is] an area called Dera [in Maiwand]. Dera was the place where the robbers were coming and waiting for convoys to rob. And even if they were spending, like, two or three, four or five nights, when the convoy would come and pass them, if in this convoy there was a woman, they would say, 'Okay, in the convoy there is woman, because of that woman, don't touch it, don't rob it.'" Ibid.

209 *A female American lieutenant . . . was stunned when he told her that she was the daughter of a whore:* Lieutenant Kirsten Ouimette, interview by author, October 2, 2010.

209 *In at least one case, insurgents even threatened to burn a teacher's daughter:* Rachel Reid, "Who Benefits from Taliban Revisionism?" *Guardian,* January 21, 2011.

210 *Afghans who lived "independently" and clung to their culture:* Specifically, "that the woman has to be protected and the woman has to have value." Sadoo Khan, interview by author, January 19, 2009.

210 *"We are not blaming the Americans for what they have done":* Qala Khan, interview by author, January 19, 2009.

211 *Amir Mohammad worked as a police officer in Maiwand:* Amir Mohammad's account of the events of November 4, 2008, is from Mohammad, interview by author, January 19, 2009.

211 *He had also said something about having epilepsy:* Statement of the interpreter known as Tom Cruise to Army investigators.

211 *"epilepsy" is what they call it when the spirits seize you:* See, for example, M. Miles, "Epilepsy in the Afghan Village," *Disability World,* no. 9, July–August 2001. According to one group of doctors: "People report a high burden of mental disorders and seek refuge to traditional shrines or self medication with psychopharmacological drugs." http://www.ayubmed.edu.pk/JAMC/PAST/14-4/Peter.htm, accessed March 6, 2013.

212 *he was still trying to erase it from his memory:* Skotnicki told me the shooting was "just one of those things I try to forget." Skotnicki, interview by author, March 24, 2009.

212 *Salam's father and brother had arrived with a group of villagers to collect his body:* Amir Mohammad, interview by author, January 19, 2009. That the body was kept overnight at the district center and not released to his family until the following morning is also noted in the Army investigation.

212 *Salam's brother yelled and cursed the police:* This account is from Amir Mohammad, interview by author, January 19, 2009.

213 *the Taliban had issued a statement saying that children had poured fuel on a female foreign soldier:* According to Reuters, the original statement was posted on the Taliban website, but I have been unable to find it. The quote given here is from "U.S. Civilian Kills

Afghan After Fire Attack," Reuters, November 4, 2008, http://www.reuters.com/article/2008/11/04/us-afghan-violence-idUSTRE4A34MW20081104, accessed March 6, 2013.

214 *He went by the name Al Fathy, an Arabic nom de guerre:* Al Fathy, interview by Muhib Habibi with author, March 29, 2009.

215 *Amir Mohammad, didn't believe that Salam was crazy:* Neither, incidentally, did Jack Bauer. "I don't know," Jack told me. "If he is crazy, he is talking, like, thirty-five, thirty minutes with Paula. I never seen him [act] crazy [while] talking to her." Jack Bauer, interview by author, September 23, 2010.

215 *The Afghan police investigation had yielded little of interest:* "The investigation that we did, we did not find out any kind of activities Abdul Salam was doing before, except that he was a poor man and he was working for his family." Amir Mohammad, interview by author, January 19, 2009.

215 *Agents from the Army's Criminal Investigation Division had arrived in Maiwand:* The Army investigators gathered a good deal of crime scene evidence, but by the time they got to Maiwand, the flex cuffs that had restrained Abdul Salam were gone. They had either been thrown in the trash by mistake or purposefully removed, perhaps in an effort to spare Ayala from blame, according to the Army investigation.

216 *"maintain good relations with the officials he dealt with constantly":* Army investigation.

216 *It was a clear, warm, windless day when Lieutenant Pathak took them out there:* Details about the weather on November 5, the cleaned-up death scene, the burn marks on the ground, and the grass come from the description of the scene in the Army investigative report. Of the place where Salam had been killed, the investigators wrote: "There were no stains associated with heavy blood flow. Several feet away there was miscellaneous trash in the drainage trench."

216 *"She had a disproportionate effect on a lot of people":* Hurlbut, interview by author, March 26, 2009.

217 *"They asked us, 'Please don't kill the family'":* "When we went and talked to all the leaders, we had a little shura, and we brought in all the elders. . . . and [the district governor] just let them have it. And the one question they had was, 'We would ask that you don't wipe out the family.' . . . They asked us, 'Please don't kill the family.' And we're, like, is that an option? We're, like, what are you talking about? And that was all they wanted to talk about for twenty minutes, 'Are you going to kill the family?' And, 'We'll take care of it.' I was, like, 'You don't need to kill anybody. No one needs to kill anybody. Enough dying's happened.'" Hurlbut, interview by author, March 26, 2009.

217 *Salam was not a hard-core militant:* "Often the Taliban use mentally challenged people to do their dirty work, whether it's a small kid at the age of ten detonating himself, or this guy," Hurlbut told me. "He was definitely mentally disturbed. We found out after the fact that he was not a Taliban sympathizer but became a Taliban agent provocateur kind of guy, that they just churned up, got high on, I think he was high on drugs and then did the thing. Why they were targeting Paula, if they were

targeting Paula, remains to be seen." After Salam was killed, the soldiers checked him against their biometric data system and found that he was "not on any watch list," according to the Army investigation.

217 *Salam, he told me, had been known around Chehel Gazi as "the village wacko":* Warren, interview by author, March 20, 2009.

217 *"He didn't have Taliban connections":* Ibid.

218 *"People were just making a joke of him because he was an abnormal person":* Hajji Moham-mad Ehsan, interview by author, October 12, 2010.

218 *Abdul Salam had been about twenty-five years old:* This and other details below are from Mohammad Umar, interview by Muhib Habibi with author, March 29, 2009.

*Epilogue*

221 *news that a group of soldiers recently stationed there had been accused of killing Afghan civilians:* The week I landed in Maiwand, the free copies of *Stars and Stripes* piled around Ramrod carried a story about allegations that a handful of American soldiers had killed three unarmed Afghan civilians between January and May 2010 while they were stationed in Maiwand. The soldiers, known as the "kill team," belonged to the 5th Stryker Brigade of the 2nd Infantry Division headquartered at Joint Base Lewis-McChord in Washington State. Four are now in prison for their crimes, including Staff Sergeant Calvin Gibbs, the ringleader, who was sentenced to life for the three murders, and Specialist Jeremy Morlock, who is serving twenty-four years for his role in the killings. See Megan McCloskey, "A Question of Account-ability: Worst U.S. War Crimes Case to Emerge from Afghanistan Leaves Some Asking: Where Was the Leadership?" *Stars and Stripes*, October 5, 2010; Adam Ash-ton, "Army Sergeant Is Sentenced to Life in Murders of Afghan Civilians," *Stars and Stripes*, November 11, 2011; Mark Boal, "The Kill Team: How U.S. Soldiers in Afghanistan Murdered Innocent Civilians," *Rolling Stone*, March 27, 2011; and Luke Mogelson, "A Beast in the Heart of Every Fighting Man," *New York Times Magazine*, April 27, 2011.

222 *Abdul Salam's brother was named Omar Bank:* Hajji Lala, interview by author, October 10, 2010.

222 *He griped that the Americans took his intelligence informants for granted:* Lala said that the Americans had asked for help locating a Taliban prison in Maiwand. He had contacted an informant, who found the prison. The Americans took aerial photo-graphs and paid the informant two thousand Afghanis, about forty dollars. "They came . . . and said to me, 'Take this, this is for the informant.' And I said, 'Please be kind, keep your money in your pockets.' It's a shame and it's a joke and it's disrespect," Lala told me. "This man, three days, four days, he was riding on a motorbike with his own expenses and he was looking for a Taliban prison for us, and he put his life in danger, and you are giving two thousand Afghanis. I'll give something to him from my own money."

325

223 *He had met with her the day before she was attacked:* "One day before the incident, she came to me and we had a meeting and she told me, 'When will we have the next meeting in the FOB?' I told her that I'm going to Kandahar today, when I return back I will see you. But after that she just went to the next village near the district office, and a man by the name of Salam, he came and he threw petrol on her and she was burned by that. She was alive in the beginning and after two months, she passed away."

223 *Lala and the Americans arrested Bank:* They picked him up on November 5, 2010. For this and the additional details below, Lieutenant Roy Ragsdale, 3rd Squadron, 2nd Cavalry Regiment, correspondence, March 11, 2011.

224 *Lieutenant Colonel Bryan Denny, acknowledged that there was much he didn't know:* Lieutenant Colonel Bryan Denny, commander, 3rd Squadron, 2nd Cavalry Regiment, interview by author, October 8, 2010.

224 *to train the local Afghan army unit so his men wouldn't have to come back:* "To me, winning means being able to turn Maiwand over to my Afghan army battalion counterparts," Denny told me. "Winning for me means no American having to come here again."

224 *the project had come under scrutiny from Congress:* The result was the Center for Naval Analyses study previously cited. See "National Defense Authorization Act for Fiscal Year 2010, Report of the Committee on Armed Services, House of Representatives, on H.R. 2647," 154–55, http://www.gpo.gov/fdsys/pkg/CRPT -111hrpt166/pdf/CRPT-111hrpt166.pdf, accessed March 6, 2013.

224 *it suffered from inadequate government oversight, an overreliance on unaccountable contractors:* The Army's Training and Doctrine Command initiated an investigation of the Human Terrain System in March 2010 to look into an array of allegations of impropriety ranging from sexual harassment to fraud. Department of the Army, Headquarters United States Army Training and Doctrine Command, "Appointment of Investigating Officer for an Informal Investigation," March 5, 2010, obtained under the Freedom of Information Act. The results noted here are from "Findings and Recommendations, AR 15–6 Investigation Concerning Human Terrain System (HTS) Project Inspector General Complaints," 1–3, and attached memorandum of Lieutenant General John E. Sterling, Jr., Deputy Commanding General/Chief of Staff.

224 *faced with a mess it had helped to create:* Before becoming head of the Human Terrain System, Hamilton was the deputy chief of staff for intelligence at the Army's Training and Doctrine Command. Jim Hodges, "Cover Story: U.S. Army's Human Terrain Experts May Help Defuse Future Conflicts," *DefenseNews,* March 22, 2012.

224 *"He was right to a degree," the official told me:* A TRADOC official, interview by author, July 1, 2010.

225 *"I want to retire to obscurity and raise llamas":* McFate, interview by author, July 1, 2010.

225 *Clint Cooper had returned to Afghanistan briefly after Loyd's attack:* Cooper, interviews by author, April 19–22, 2010, and January 15, 2013.

225 *Don Ayala had gone home to New Orleans and returned to painting:* Ayala, interview by author, January 4, 2013.

226 *"Your daughter was a remarkable public servant":* Letter of Secretary of State Hillary Rodham Clinton to Patricia Ward, June 1, 2010.

# INDEX

Abu Ghraib abuses, 118
Adamson, Bill, 29
Afghanistan, Afghans, 32, 69–99, 120,
  123, 125, 167–95, 197, 243*n*, 257*n*
  agriculture in, 11, 47, 56, 86–87, 89,
    92, 94, 170, 174–75, 182, 185–86,
    188, 190, 274*n*, 312*n*
  Abdul Salam and, 133–35, 137, 204,
    206–8, 216
  Ayala and, 127, 131–39, 152, 158
  bombings in, 27, 35, 64, 75–76, 88,
    127, 131–39, 141, 144–47, 153–62,
    169, 186, 190, 201, 208, 210, 223,
    240*n*, 271*n*, 273*n*, 275*n*, 294*n*,
    296*n*–98*n*, 307*n*
  Canada and, 84, 169–70, 207,
    268*n*–69*n*, 272*n*
  casualties in, 14, 26, 35, 59–60, 63,
    65, 74, 76, 84, 88–89, 96, 133–36,
    139, 141, 161–62, 167–68, 202–3,
    221, 270*n*, 273*n*, 294*n*–98*n*, 307*n*,
    325*n*–26*n*

children in, 7–8, 11–13, 19, 57, 60,
  74–75, 80, 85, 87, 93, 95, 98–99,
  134–35, 156–57, 182–85, 187, 207,
  213–14, 222, 232*n*–34*n*, 263*n*,
  276*n*, 296*n*, 322*n*
civil war in, 26, 174–75, 313*n*
Cooper's interrogation of detainees in,
  72–77, 263*n*–64*n*
corruption in, 7, 21, 58, 86, 93, 96, 137,
  174–75, 203, 237*n*, 276*n*
counterinsurgency in, 1–2, 10, 42–43,
  83, 134, 136, 174–76, 187–89, 238*n*,
  249*n*, 253*n*, 294*n*–95*n*, 307*n*
cultural intelligence and, 2–3, 10, 31,
  41, 165, 171–73, 175–77, 187–88,
  190–92, 195, 198
difficulty in finding hard facts in, 205–6
drug trade in, 7, 11, 86–87, 91, 97,
  174–75, 203–4, 271*n*–72*n*, 278*n*
education in, 7, 11, 14–15, 56–57,
  61–62, 65, 80, 88, 95, 98, 136, 185,
  191, 209, 232*n*, 234*n*, 322*n*

Afghanistan, Afghans (*cont.*)
 ethnic groups in, 171–72, 182, 184, 226
 Great Britain and, 84, 177–78, 186–87, 190, 192, 209, 269*n*–70*n*, 311*n*
 health care in, 56–57, 180–87, 311*n*–12*n*
 HTS and, 1–3, 7, 10–11, 40, 44–46, 77, 81–83, 89–96, 99, 138, 161–65, 167–73, 177–87, 189–95, 199–200, 225, 255*n*, 267*n*–68*n*, 275*n*, 291*n*, 303*n*–4*n*, 306*n*, 311*n*–12*n*, 315–17*n*
 immolations in, 127–28, 130, 135, 206, 208–9
 insurgency in, 10, 12–13, 25, 44–46, 58–59, 62, 65–66, 72, 74–76, 83, 86–88, 90, 94–96, 130, 134–36, 174–77, 186, 190–91, 195, 199–203, 209–10, 213–14, 216–17, 221–22, 268*n*, 271*n*, 273*n*, 276*n*, 310*n*–11*n*
 Karzai's treatment of, 79–80, 265*n*
 lack of U.S. expertise on, 173–75
 languages spoken in, 6, 72, 74–75, 90, 163–64, 172–73, 184, 188, 263*n*, 304*n*
 Loyd's military career and, 56–59, 259*n*–61*n*
 McChrystal's assessment of, 176–77, 252*n*, 310*n*
 male-on-male affection in, 81, 266*n*, 273*n*
 marriages in, 58, 206, 209
 misogyny in, 199, 206, 208–10, 322*n*
 NATO and, 59, 64–65, 83, 87, 134–35, 175–77, 179, 187, 190, 294*n*–95*n*, 311*n*
 need for cooperation between military and civilian workers in, 64–66, 261*n*
 Pakistani border with, 44, 60, 87
 PRTs in, 58–64, 261*n*
 reconciliation commission of, 202–3, 211, 320*n*
 refugees and, 73–74, 95, 186, 210, 263*n*
 religion in, 7–8, 210
 Soviet war in, 7, 24–25, 31, 44, 61, 79, 85, 89–91, 171–72, 210, 238*n*, 263*n*, 311*n*

 Taliban and, 7, 9, 26, 59, 73–74, 76, 78–79, 83, 85–86, 88, 91, 93–96, 99, 134–37, 172, 174–75, 177, 179, 188, 190, 199–210, 213–14, 216–18, 222, 224, 261*n*, 263*n*–64*n*, 295*n*, 311*n*, 319*n*–21*n*, 323*n*–25*n*
 U.S. troop commitments in, 1, 10, 25, 174, 177, 187, 309*n*–10*n*, 316*n*
 U.S. war in, 25–26, 39, 43, 66, 72, 74, 76, 78, 82–87, 90, 106, 118, 133–37, 151, 169, 174–77, 182, 195, 202–3, 208, 210, 241*n*, 248*n*–49*n*, 252*n*–53*n*, 271*n*–72*n*, 275*n*, 277*n*–78*n*, 297*n*, 309*n*–10*n*, 315*n*–16*n*
 U.S. withdrawal from, 224, 326*n*
 weather in, 69, 78, 84, 263*n*
 women and girls in, 6–7, 12, 17, 56–59, 62–63, 80–81, 84–85, 91, 93–94, 136, 171–72, 177–87, 190, 192, 199–200, 206, 208–10, 220, 226, 234*n*, 259*n*, 266*n*, 270*n*, 275*n*, 296*n*, 311*n*–12*n*, 319*n*–23*n*
Afghanistan Independent Human Rights Commission, 161
Africa, 113, 245*n*, 283*n*
agriculture:
 in Afghanistan, 11, 47, 56, 86–87, 89, 92, 94, 170, 174–75, 182, 185–86, 188, 190, 274*n*, 312*n*
 HTS and, 89, 92
 Maiwand and, 86–87, 94
Agriculture Department, U.S., 58, 60
Ahmadullah, Hajji (Hajji Lala), 221–23, 325*n*
Air Force, U.S., 39, 64, 246*n*
Albro, Rob, 191–92, 315*n*
Al Fathy, 214–15
Al Qaeda, 26, 177, 186, 261*n*
American Anthropological Association (AAA), 118, 122, 125, 191, 291*n*, 315*n*
American Enterprise Institute, 248*n*
American Geographical Society, 40, 251*n*
anthropology, 34, 39, 82, 110–26, 251*n*, 315*n*
 in Bali, 120–21
 colonialism and, 119, 125, 283*n*–84*n*

comparisons between intelligence and, 30, 121–22, 288n–89n
counterinsurgencies and, 118–19, 124–25, 286n–87n
cultural intelligence and, 2–3, 29–31, 192, 243n
HTS and, 1–2, 10, 41, 45–46, 101–2, 125, 164, 166, 168, 191, 194, 198, 286n, 303n, 305n–6n
Iraq and, 29–31, 37, 118
Lévi-Strauss on, 119–20
Loyd and, 7, 50, 53–54, 56, 125, 256n, 258n
McFate and, 29–31, 43, 101, 105, 112–18, 125–26, 250n, 282n, 284n–86n, 291n, 316n
politics and, 114, 118, 125, 240n, 285n, 287n
war and, 101, 110–11, 115, 118, 121–22, 125–26, 289n
*Arab Mind, The* (Patai), 118
Arabs, Arabic, 31, 45, 79, 81, 164, 189, 194, 214, 240n, 303n
and cultural intelligence in Iraq, 36, 247n
and Grau's trip to Iraq, 39–40
Lawrence and, 101, 120–21
Arkin, William M., 245n
Arman, Delbar, 61–63
army, Afghan, 12, 223–24, 269n, 274n
U.S. withdrawal and, 224, 326n
Army, U.S., 30, 40, 105, 118, 130, 134, 188, 209, 298n
and attack on Loyd, 16–21, 129, 132, 235n–36n, 293n
and Ayala's arrest and imprisonment, 132, 138, 293n–94n
Ayala's career in, 6, 78, 80, 82–83, 144–45, 149–51, 160, 166, 299n
Ayala's sentencing and, 154–55, 158–59
Chehel Gazi patrols and, 6–11, 13–19, 207, 232n–35n
Cooper's career in, 70–73, 262n–63n
cultural intelligence and, 2, 6, 28, 37–39, 41, 102, 165, 173, 192, 194–95, 241n
Culture Center of, 172, 225
Fondacaro and, 31–35, 44

Foreign Military Studies Office and, 25, 37–38, 238n
Forward Operating Base Ramrod and, 69, 93, 262n
and Grau's trip to Iraq, 39–40
Grenada and, 150–51
HTS and, 2–3, 10, 24, 38, 41, 45–46, 77, 83, 92–93, 97, 124, 162–65, 168, 170, 173–74, 177, 187, 193–94, 224–25, 234n–35n, 303n, 308n, 313n–14n, 317n–18n, 326n
IED attacks and, 27–28, 35, 75–76, 246n–47n
intelligence defined by, 249n, 313n–14n
interpreters used by, 11, 16, 234n
Iraq and, 23–24, 27–28, 37, 239n, 246n–47n
and Jack Bauer's monitoring of insurgents, 12–13
Joint IED Defeat Organization (JIEDDO) and, 35–37, 43, 246n, 249n, 254n
Loyd's career in, 7, 53–60, 82–83, 258n–61n
McFate and, 29, 31, 116
Maiwand and, 5–7, 9, 87–88, 90, 92, 94, 97, 207, 224, 232n, 235n, 272n–74n
Project Camelot and, 122–24
and revision of counterinsurgency doctrine, 42–43, 252n–53n
Salam and, 20, 131–33, 135, 137, 154–55, 158–59, 206–8, 211–12, 215–17, 236n–37n, 292n, 300n–301n, 319n–320n, 343n–25n
technology and, 239n
Vietnam War and, 23, 32, 244n
World Basic Information Library and, 39, 252n
Army, U.S., units of:
2nd Battalion, 2nd Regiment, 1st Infantry Division (2–2), 5, 83–84, 87, 90, 134, 155, 216, 262n, 268n–59n, 272n–74n, 276n, 296n
4th Mechanized Infantry Division, 239n
5th Stryker Brigade, 2nd Infantry Division, 325n
10th Mountain Division, 41

Army, U.S., units of (*cont.*)
  82nd Airborne Division, 44, 149
  101st Airborne Division, 38, 42, 162
  450th Civil Affairs Battalion, 56, 259*n*
  507th Maintenance Company, 246*n*
  Air Defense Artillery, 116
  Central Command, 10
  Comanche Company, 5–6, 11, 15–18, 93, 141, 235*n*
  Criminal Investigation Division, 139, 159, 215–16, 324*n*
  Darkhorse Company, 93, 273*n*
  Rangers, 6, 31, 33, 35, 82, 150–51
  Special Forces, 24, 34, 45, 55, 59, 66, 72, 74–75, 77, 80, 83, 86, 144–45, 151, 156–57, 162, 261*n*, 271*n*–72*n*
  Special Operations, 35, 55, 151, 175
  Special Technical Operations, 33, 245*n*
  Training and Doctrine Command (TRADOC), 35, 37–38, 46, 173, 196, 224–25, 246*n*, 317*n*–18*n*, 326*n*
Atkinson, Rick, 240*n*, 247*n*
Ayala, Don, 78–83, 131–39, 143–60, 292*n*–303*n*, 324*n*
  Afghan police and, 21, 237*n*
  on anthropology, 305*n*
  artistic talent of, 80–81, 147–48, 225
  and attack on Loyd, 16, 19–22, 127–28, 131–33, 146, 237*n*
  bodyguard career of, 6, 78–81, 92, 136–38, 145, 152–53, 155, 265*n*–68*n*
  Chehel Gazi patrol and, 6–9, 11, 16, 19, 232*n*, 235*n*
  childhood and adolescence of, 145, 147–49
  and civilian casualties in Afghanistan, 134–35
  criminal charges against, 138–39, 143
  cultural intelligence and, 91–93
  education of, 147–48, 151
  HTS and, 6–8, 11, 81–82, 88–89, 91–94, 98, 135, 137–39, 162, 166–70, 234*n*, 236*n*, 255*n*, 267*n*–68*n*, 274*n*, 277*n*, 298*n*, 305*n*–6*n*

injuries of, 149, 155
  interpreters used by, 11–12
  on Karzai's treatment of Afghans, 79–80, 265*n*
  letters from supporters of, 144–46, 156–57
  and Loyd, 8, 18, 82–83, 92, 153, 157, 236*n*, 268*n*, 300*n*
  Maiwand and, 23, 82, 88–89, 91–94, 97–98, 127–28, 131, 133, 135, 137, 153, 156, 159, 221, 273*n*–74*n*
  mentoring skills of, 80–81, 137–38
  military career of, 6, 78, 80, 82–83, 144–45, 149–51, 160, 166, 299*n*
  nicknames of, 81, 266*n*
  physical appearance of, 6, 20, 132, 139, 153, 232*n*
  physical fitness of, 147–49
  probation of, 160, 225
  and Salam, 19–22, 127–28, 131–39, 144–47, 153–60, 212, 219–20, 236*n*–37*n*, 292*n*–94*n*, 301*n*
  sentencing of, 144, 146, 153–60, 300*n*
  144, 146, 154–56, 225
  and Sunrise, 147–49, 152–53
Ayub Khan, 84, 270*n*
Azizabad, bombing of, 134

backtracking, 241*n*
BAE Systems, 168, 196, 265*n*, 275*n*, 306*n*, 308*n*, 317*n*–18*n*
Baghdad, 29, 64, 81, 139, 152, 162, 247*n*
  IED attacks and, 27, 35–36
Bagram, Bagram Air Base, 73, 276*n*
  Ayala's imprisonment at, 133, 138
  HTS and, 138, 162, 178
Bali, 120–21
Band-i-Timur, 91, 276*n*
Banger (Stephen James Lang), 170–72, 307*n*
Bank, Omar, 221–23
Barfield, Thomas, 283*n*
Barton, Susanna, 48–49
Bastion, Camp, 129, 178, 312*n*

Bateson, Gregory, 122, 289*n*
Bauer, Jack (interpreter), 11–18
  and attack on Loyd, 16–18, 20–22
  background of, 12, 234*n*
  Chehel Gazi patrol and, 13–14, 16–17,
    207, 234*n*–35*n*
  injuries of, 141, 297*n*
  Salam and, 13–16, 21–22, 131–32,
    159, 236*n*–37*n*
Bedouin women, 56–57
Benedict, Ruth, 117, 122, 291*n*
Berkeley, University of California at,
  111–14
Bhatia, Michael, 161–62, 167–68,
  254*n*–55*n*, 302*n*–3*n*
Biden, Joe, 248*n*
bin Laden, Osama, 27, 44–45, 55
Blackwater, 82, 139
blood feuds, 240*n*, 263*n*
Boas, Franz, 121–22, 289*n*
bombs, bombers, bombings, 13, 19, 45,
  79, 277*n*
  in Afghanistan, 27, 35, 64, 75–76, 88,
    127, 131–39, 141, 144–47, 153–62,
    169, 186, 190, 201, 208, 210, 223,
    240*n*, 271*n*, 273*n*, 275*n*, 294*n*,
    296*n*–98*n*, 307*n*
  insurgent social networks and,
    27–28
  in Iraq, 2, 26–28, 35–37, 88, 162,
    240*n*–41*n*, 246*n*–47*n*, 249*n*, 273*n*
  Maiwand and, 14, 88, 90, 94, 96,
    99, 141, 201, 210, 221–23, 273*n*,
    297*n*–98*n*
  and need for cooperation between
    military and civilian workers,
    65–66
  suicide, 6, 19, 141, 208, 214, 232*n*,
    297*n*–98*n*, 320*n*
  *see also* improvised explosive devices
Bosnian War, 55, 71, 73, 238*n*, 262*n*
Bowman Expeditions, 40–41, 251*n*
Brooke Army Medical Center, 130–31,
  140
Brown, Cale, 262*n*, 269*n*, 272*n*–73*n*
Brown, Sam, 273*n*
Brun, Djeens, 235*n*
Bureau of Ethnology, 121
Bureau of Indian Affairs, 70, 262*n*
Burton, Sir Richard, 114

Bush, George W., 43, 118, 268*n*–69*n*,
  310*n*
  and nation building in Iraq, 36–37,
    247*n*–48*n*
Buzkashi, 80

Cabayan, Hriar "Doc," 28–30
  background of, 28, 241*n*
  cultural intelligence and, 29–30,
    241*n*–43*n*
  IED attacks and, 28, 240*n*–42*n*
  McFate and, 29–30, 117
Callahan, Ted, 306*n*
Camelot, Project, 122–24, 197, 290*n*–91*n*
Canadians:
  in Afghanistan, 84, 169–70, 207,
    268*n*–69*n*, 272*n*
  HTS and, 169–70
Cardinalli, AnnaMaria:
  education and background of,
    179–80
  HTS and, 177–87, 190, 312*n*
Carle, Glenn, 288*n*
Carlough, Martin, 104, 107
Center for Naval Analyses, 308*n*,
  317*n*–18*n*
Central Intelligence Agency (CIA),
  24–25, 29, 40, 44–45, 97, 116, 118,
  243*n*, 288*n*
Chayes, Sarah, 271*n*–72*n*
Chehel Gazi:
  attack on Loyd in, 16–22, 127–28,
    235*n*–37*n*
  bazaar near, 7–9, 11, 13–15, 206, 232*n*,
    279*n*, 319*n*
  Jack Bauer and, 13–14, 16–17
  meaning of name of, 9
  physical appearance, 8–9
  Salam and, 13–16, 204–6, 208,
    217
  U.S. military patrols in, 6–11, 13–19,
    207, 232*n*–35*n*, 293*n*
Chile, 123–24, 290*n*
Choate Rosemary Hall, 51–52, 226
Clark, Karen, 308*n*
Clinton, Bill, 45
Clinton, Hillary Rodham, 52, 226
Cloud, David, 304*n*
Coburn, Noah, 240*n*
cockfights, 121

Cold War, 2, 24, 33, 123, 150, 198, 238*n*, 241*n*, 248*n*, 315*n*
Colonialism, 30
  anthropology and, 119, 125, 283*n*–84*n*
  of British, 113–14, 283*n*–84*n*
*Colors Insulting to Nature* (Wilson), 108
combat-stress related injuries, 76–77, 146–47, 155–56, 264*n*, 293*n*, 301*n*
Commission on the Engagement of Anthropology with the Security and Intelligence Communities (CEAUSSIC), 315*n*
Congress, U.S., 24, 35, 83, 123, 193, 224, 243*n*, 310*n*, 318*n*
Connable, Ben, 189
Cooper, Clint, 70–77, 132, 279*n*
  and attack on Loyd, 16–21, 127–31, 236*n*, 292*n*–93*n*
  Chehel Gazi patrol and, 6–8, 10–11, 13–18, 232*n*, 234*n*–35*n*, 292*n*–92*n*
  childhood and adolescence of, 70–71, 76
  cultural intelligence and, 91, 225
  education of, 70, 72
  foreign language skills of, 6, 13, 70–75, 130
  HTS and, 2, 6–8, 10–11, 77, 91–93, 97–98, 162, 166, 169, 172, 200, 225, 264*n*–65*n*, 275*n*, 304*n*–5*n*, 308*n*
  and IED attacks in Afghanistan, 75–76
  illnesses and injuries of, 72, 76–77, 129, 264*n*
  intelligence and, 72, 75–77, 263*n*–64*n*
  interpreters used by, 11–12
  as interrogator, 72–77, 263*n*–64*n*
  and Loyd, 8, 16–21, 127–31, 200, 236*n*, 234*n*–35*n*, 319*n*
  Maiwand and, 7, 13–14, 23, 91–92, 97–99, 127–29, 221, 232*n*, 235*n*, 265*n*
  military career of, 70–73, 262*n*–63*n*
  physical appearance of, 6, 232*n*
  religious beliefs of, 18, 70, 77, 91
  Salam and, 13–15, 128, 292*n*–93*n*, 301*n*
  Taliban and, 73–76, 263*n*–64*n*
Cooper, Kathy, 70–71, 76–77

counterinsurgency, 46, 120, 138, 241*n*, 288*n*, 313*n*
  in Afghanistan, 1–2, 10, 42–43, 83, 134, 136, 174–76, 187–89, 238*n*, 249*n*, 253*n*, 294*n*–95*n*, 307*n*
  anthropology and, 118–19, 124–25, 286*n*–87*n*
  intelligence and, 10, 43–44, 253*n*
  Iraq and, 2, 10, 42–43, 252*n*
  Maiwand and, 87–88
  and Obama, 174
  Petraeus and, 10, 42–43, 253*n*
  research in Thailand on, 124–25
  revision of doctrine of, 42–44, 252*n*–53*n*
  Sosh and, 32, 244*n*
Crook, George, 288*n*
Cruise, Tom (interpreter), 11, 22, 211, 237*n*
cultural intelligence, 249*n*, 277*n*, 313*n*–14*n*
  Afghanistan and, 2–3, 10, 31, 41, 165, 171–73, 175–77, 187–88, 190–92, 195, 198
  Army and, 2, 6, 28, 37–39, 41, 102, 165, 173, 192, 194–95, 241*n*
  colonialism and, 30, 283*n*
  counterinsurgency and, 10, 43–44, 241*n*
  geography and, 40–41
  Gusinov and, 90–91
  HTS and, 6, 10, 41, 46, 91–93, 96, 165–66, 171–73, 190–92, 194, 225, 305*n*
  insurgents and, 28, 36, 195, 241*n*, 244*n*
  and invasion of Marja, 190–91
  Iraq and, 10, 29–31, 35–38, 117, 165, 244*n*, 246*n*–48*n*, 250*n*
  Kipp and, 238*n*, 250*n*, 316*n*
  McFarland on, 37–38, 249*n*
  McFate and, 29–31, 35–36, 43–44, 102, 117, 242*n*–44*n*, 250*n*
  technology and, 24–25, 29, 238*n*–39*n*
  war and, 1–3, 118, 125–26
Cultural Preparation of the Environment (CPE), 29–30, 36, 38, 117–18, 241*n*–43*n*, 247*n*
Custer, John, 241*n*

Dari, 72, 90, 263$n$, 276$n$, 274$n$–75$n$,
  304$n$
  HTS training and, 163–64
Defense Department, U.S. (DOD), 34,
  72, 134, 175, 241$n$, 245$n$–47$n$,
  274$n$
  anthropology and, 117, 287$n$
  cultural intelligence and, 29, 247$n$,
    250$n$
  HTS and, 24, 46, 162, 164, 173, 193,
    196–98, 251$n$, 303$n$, 315$n$,
    318$n$
  Iraq and, 27–28, 35, 249$n$, 268$n$
  Project Camelot and, 123, 290$n$–91$n$
  Special Technical Operations Division
    of, 33, 245$n$
Deitchman, Seymour J., 289$n$–90$n$
Democrats, 285$n$
demographics, 30, 36, 166, 192, 242$n$,
  247$n$, 250$n$
Denny, Bryan, 224, 326$n$
Diyala Province (Iraq), 29–30, 247$n$
Dobson, Jerome E., 40–41, 251$n$
Dudley-Flores, Marilyn, 303$n$
Dunlap, Cas, 177–79, 187, 190,
  311$n$–12$n$
DynCorp, 152, 266$n$

economics, economy, 9, 39, 65, 97, 120,
  188, 197, 203, 255$n$
  Afghan civil war and, 174–75
  counterinsurgencies and, 124–25,
    174
  cultural intelligence and, 30, 195
  Iraq and, 30, 37, 248$n$–49$n$
Edwards, David B., 287$n$–88$n$
Egypt, 56, 105
Ehsan, Hajji Mohammad, 86, 217–18
espionage, 114, 118–21, 123, 167,
  288$n$
ethnography, ethnology, 53, 113, 124,
  171, 179, 262$n$, 267$n$, 283$n$–84$n$
  cultural intelligence and, 242$n$–43$n$,
    250$n$
  HTS and, 45, 81, 163, 166–67
  intelligence and, 120, 288$n$,
    316$n$–17$n$
  Vietnam War and, 30–31
  windshield, 166
Evans-Pritchard, E. E., 113, 283$n$

Fahim, Mohammad, 79
*Faith of My Fathers* (McCain with
  Salter), 133, 294$n$
Fallows, James, 252$n$
Falluja, 187, 244$n$
Farsi, 184, 263$n$, 274$n$
Faulkner, William, 79
Federal Bureau of Investigation (FBI),
  164, 177
Feldman, Allen, 284$n$
Figley, Charles, 146–47, 155–57, 299$n$,
  301$n$
Flo (interpreter), 181–85
Flournoy, Michèle, 249$n$
Flynn, Mike, 195–96, 317$n$
"Fog and Friction of Technology, The"
  (Kipp and Grau), 239$n$
Fondacaro, Steve, 31–38, 319$n$
  education of, 31–33, 244$n$–45$n$
  HTS and, 38, 44, 46, 124, 193,
    195–98, 200, 224, 247$n$, 250$n$,
    254$n$–55$n$, 291$n$, 313$n$, 315$n$,
    317$n$–18$n$
  and IED attacks in Iraq, 35–37,
    246$n$–47$n$
  intelligence and, 36, 38, 247$n$, 313$n$,
    315$n$, 317$n$
  Korean tour of, 33–34, 245$n$
  and McFate, 31, 35
  Pentagon tour of, 33, 245$n$
  on soldiers of future, 34–35,
    246$n$
  on U.S. policy failures, 33–34
  Vietnam and, 32–34, 244$n$
Foreign Military Studies Office, 24–25,
  37–41, 193–94
  Grau and, 25, 40, 238$n$, 269$n$
  HTS and, 38, 41, 193
  technology and, 25, 39
foreign policy, 174, 197, 289$n$
  Ayala's mentoring skills and,
    137–38
  Fondacaro on, 33–34
  Project Camelot and, 122, 290$n$–91$n$
Fort Benning, Ga., 67, 129, 140,
  299$n$
Fort Leavenworth, Kans., *see*
  Leavenworth, Fort Leavenworth,
  Kans.
Fosher, Kerry, 119

Galtung, Johan, 123
Gardez, 78, 274*n*
Garmabak Pass, 91, 276*n*
Gate 5, 104–8, 282*n*
Gates, Robert, 134, 175, 268*n*
Geertz, Clifford, 120–21, 284*n*,
    287*n*–88*n*
Geller, Adam, 303*n*
geography, 40–41, 251*n*, 304*n*
Germany, 49, 64, 115–16, 121, 129–30,
    262*n*
  Cooper's adolescence in, 70–71
  geography and, 251*n*
  Nazis and, 112, 282*n*
*ghazis,* 84
Ghazni, 78, 136, 274*n*
Gibbs, Calvin, 325*n*
González, Roberto J., 118
Grau, Lester W., 270*n*
  Foreign Military Studies Office and,
    25, 40, 238*n*, 269*n*
  Soviet-Afghan War and, 25,
    238*n*
  technology and, 25, 38, 239*n*
  trip to Iraq of, 39–40
gray literature, 39
Great Britain, 72, 112–17, 129, 243*n*
  Afghanistan and, 84, 177–78, 186–87,
    190, 192, 209, 269*n*–70*n*, 311*n*
  Arabs and, 101, 120
  colonialism of, 113–14, 283*n*–84*n*
  cultural intelligence and, 30,
    250*n*
  HTS and, 178, 187, 190, 192
  IRA and, 30, 112, 284*n*
  Maiwand and, 84–85, 269*n*–70*n*
  night letters and, 311*n*
Great Game, 84, 119
Grenada, 33, 150–51
gunfire, celebratory, 36
Gusinov, Tim, 97
  cultural intelligence and, 90–91
  foreign language skills of, 90,
    274*n*–75*n*
  HTS and, 89–92, 274*n*–76*n*
  IEDs and, 275*n*
  and Loyd, 90–91
  Maiwand and, 90–91, 275*n*
  Soviet-Afghan War and, 89–91
Gusterson, Hugh, 286*n*

Habibi, Muhib, 201–2, 218
hand signals, 31
Haqqani, Jalaluddin, 44–46
Harvard University, 29, 115
Hastings, Michael, 253*n*
Hazaras, 171–72, 226
health care, 80, 91, 249*n*
  HTS missions and, 180–87,
    311*n*–12*n*
  Loyd and, 56–57, 62, 130–31, 140,
    146
Hekmatyar, Gulbuddin, 61, 78
Helmand, 56, 87, 95, 97, 129, 177–90,
    272*n*, 313*n*
  HTS and, 177–87, 190, 192–93, 304*n*,
    315*n*–16*n*
  Marines in, 177–78, 186–88, 190,
    192–93
Helmand River, 84, 187, 270*n*
Herat, 87, 95, 272*n*
Highway 1, 82, 87, 267*n*, 272*n*
Hilton, Claude M., 159–60, 266*n*–67*n*
hippies, 51, 105, 108, 112
Hitler, Adolf, 251*n*
Ho Chi Minh, 33–34, 245*n*
Holbert, Robert, 163, 167–68,
    303*n*–4*n*
Horowitz, Irving Louis, 123–24, 197,
    290*n*–91*n*
houseboats, houseboat communities,
    104–8, 111–12, 280*n*–82*n*
Howard, Mike, 194–95
humanitarian aid, 10, 37, 63–66, 72, 167,
    192, 197, 203
  in Afghanistan, 64–66, 261*n*
  Loyd and, 55, 261*n*, 319*n*
  in Maiwand, 88, 136 PRTs and,
    58–59
Human Relations Area Files, 113, 283*n*
*Human Terrain,* 286*n*–87*n*
Human Terrain System (HTS),
    Human Terrain Teams (HTTs),
    38–42, 161–74, 232*n*–36*n*, 251*n*,
    274*n*–78*n*, 288*n*, 313*n*
  AF1, 45–46, 255*n*
  AF4, 83, 89, 169–70, 172
  AF6, 177–78, 180, 189–90
  AF7, 186–87
  Afghanistan and, 1–3, 7, 10–11, 40,
    44–46, 77, 81–83, 89–96, 99, 138,

161–65, 167–73, 177–87, 189–95, 199–200, 225, 255n, 267n–68n, 275n, 291n, 303n–4n, 306n, 311n–12n, 315n–17n
alleged improprieties of, 162, 224, 256, 326n
anthropology and, 1–2, 10, 41, 45–46, 101–2, 125, 164, 166, 168, 191, 194, 198, 286n, 303n, 305n–6n
arguments among members of, 166–67
Ayala and, 6–8, 11, 78, 81–82, 88–89, 91–94, 98, 135, 137–39, 162, 166–70, 234n, 236n, 255n, 267n–68n, 274n, 277n, 298n, 305n–6n
Cardinalli and, 177–86, 190, 312n
casualties among social scientists in, 161–62, 167–69
Chehel Gazi patrol and, 6–11, 13–18, 232n, 235n
Cooper and, 2, 6–8, 10–11, 77, 91–93, 97–98, 162, 166, 169, 172, 200, 225, 264n–65n, 275n, 304n–5n, 308n
counterinsurgency and, 10, 46
criticisms and disappointment with, 125, 165–66, 172–73, 189, 191–93, 195–97, 286n, 303n, 305n–8n, 317n–18n
cultural intelligence and, 6, 10, 41, 46, 91–93, 96, 165–66, 171–73, 190–92, 194, 225, 305n
culturally conscious war and, 1–3
Dunlap and, 177–79, 187, 190, 311n
evolution of, 24, 102, 247n, 249n–50n, 316n
finances of, 2, 41, 46, 197–98, 254n, 318n
firing members of, 192, 195–96
growth of, 46, 193, 196
Gusinov and, 89–92, 274n–76n
investigations of, 162, 224, 256, 326n
and invasion of Marja, 190–91
Iraq and, 2, 24, 81–82, 162–65, 167–68, 173–74, 194, 303n–4n, 309n, 316n–17n
in Khost, 44–46, 162, 195, 255n, 303n

Lacy and, 177–78, 186, 190–91, 314n–15n
Leatherneck and, 177–80, 186, 189, 192
Loyd and, 1–3, 7–8, 10–11, 77–78, 83, 88, 90–98, 125, 161–62, 167–69, 199–200, 214, 217, 235n, 255n, 275n–78n, 298n, 304n–5n, 320n
McFate and, 38, 101–2, 120, 124, 193, 196–97, 224–25, 250n, 255n, 316n–18n
Maiwand and, 23, 82–83, 85, 88–98, 169, 172, 178, 223–24, 255n, 265n
management and administration of, 38, 44, 46, 167, 173, 192–96, 198, 200, 224–25, 291n, 303n–4n, 308n, 317n–18n
medical missions and, 180–87, 311n–12n
mission and goals of, 77, 81–82, 89, 91, 166–68, 189–90, 193, 250n, 317n
origins of, 2, 23–24, 38, 241n
overhaul of, 224–25
pay and benefits of members of, 173–74, 224, 308n
praise for, 194–96, 314n, 317n
precursors of, 38–41
Salam and, 21, 135, 236n
security of, 12, 95, 168–70, 233n, 235n, 268n, 286n, 294n, 306n–7n
staffing and hiring practices of, 41, 44, 194, 196, 264n, 275n, 303n, 306n, 308n, 316n–18n
training of, 46, 81–82, 90–92, 162–68, 172–73, 177–78, 181, 183, 193, 265n, 267n, 275n, 303n–8n, 312n, 318n
Warren and, 82, 89, 92, 278n, 320n
Weston Resolve and, 163–65
Hurlbut, Dan, 268n–69n, 272n–75n, 296n
Loyd's death and, 216–17
Maiwand and, 90, 272n–73n
Salam and, 217, 324n–25n
Hussein, Saddam, 26, 310n
Hutal, Forward Operating Base, 272n, 298n

IED Blitz, 240*n*–41*n*
imperialism, 2, 59, 114, 122–23, 283*n*
improvised explosive devices (IEDs),
    239*n*–42*n*
  in Afghanistan, 27, 35, 75–76, 161–62,
    223, 240*n*, 273*n*, 275*n*, 296*n*
  cultural intelligence and, 28, 241*n*–42*n*
  in Iraq, 2, 26–28, 35–37, 240*n*–41*n*,
    246*n*–47*n*, 249*n*, 273*n*
India, 84, 206, 270*n*
infrastructure, 39, 62, 243*n*, 249*n*
  Highway 1 and, 82, 87, 267*n*, 272*n*
  Maiwand and, 88, 273*n*
Institute of Human Relations, 283*n*
insurgents, insurgencies, insurgency, 106,
    120, 167, 314*n*
  in Afghanistan, 10, 12–13, 25, 44–46,
    58–59, 62, 65–66, 72, 74–76, 83,
    86–88, 90, 94–96, 130, 134–36,
    174–77, 186, 190–91, 195, 199–203,
    209–10, 213–14, 216–17, 221–22,
    268*n*, 271*n*, 273*n*, 276*n*, 310*n*–11*n*
  Cooper and, 72, 74–75
  cultural intelligence and, 28, 36, 195,
    241*n*, 244*n*
  escape from Kandahar prison of,
    135–36
  IED attacks and, 27, 76
  and invasion of Marja, 190–91
  in Iraq, 25, 27, 36, 152, 176, 246*n*,
    310*n*
  in Khost, 44–46
  Jack Bauer's monitoring of, 12–13
  Loyd's death and, 199–200, 206–7,
    214, 216–17, 219
  Maiwand and, 12, 87–88, 90–91,
    94–96, 201, 210, 221–22
  Project Camelot and, 122–23
  Salam and, 135, 202, 219, 222
  social networks of, 27–28, 241*n*
  tools of convenience in attacks of,
    206–7
  *see also* Taliban
intelligence, 69, 90, 113, 116, 134,
    163, 176, 188–91, 222–23, 239*n*,
    241*n*–43*n*
  Cardinalli and, 179–80
  comparisons between anthropology
    and, 30, 121–22, 288*n*–89*n*
  Cooper and, 71–72, 75–77, 263*n*–64*n*

counterinsurgency and, 10, 43–44,
    253*n*
  cultural, *see* cultural intelligence
  defined by Army, 249*n*, 313*n*–14*n*
  ethnography and, 120, 288*n*,
    316*n*–17*n*
  HTS and, 2, 41, 92, 94–95, 166–67,
    189, 194–95, 275*n*, 291*n*,
    313*n*–15*n*, 317*n*
  Iraq and, 37, 180, 241*n*
  Maiwand and, 94, 272*n*
  open-source, 30, 39, 190, 241*n*–42*n*,
    251*n*, 313*n*, 315*n*
International Committee of the Red
    Cross, 58–59
International Security Assistance
    Force (ISAF), 176–77, 190, 268*n*,
    294*n*–95*n*
Internet, 116, 178, 252*n*, 304*n*, 317*n*
Iran, 31, 87, 95, 179, 311*n*–12*n*
  Afghan refugees in, 73, 210
Iraq, 9, 23–32, 44, 91, 123, 188–89,
    242*n*
  anthropology and, 29–31, 37, 118
  Ayala's work in, 81, 137, 144, 152
  bombings in, 2, 26–28, 35–37, 88,
    162, 240*n*–41*n*, 246*n*–47*n*, 249*n*,
    273*n*
  casualties in, 27, 31, 35, 139, 162,
    167–68, 246*n*, 310*n*
  counterinsurgency and, 2, 10, 42–43,
    252*n*
  cultural intelligence and, 10, 29–31,
    35–38, 117, 165, 246*n*–48*n*, 250*n*
  Grau's trip to, 39–40
  HTS and, 2, 24, 81–82, 162–65,
    167–68, 173–74, 194, 303*n*–4*n*,
    309*n*, 316*n*–17*n*
  insurgency in, 25, 27, 36, 152, 176,
    246*n*, 310*n*
  intelligence and, 37, 180, 241*n*
  Kuwait and, 23, 31
  Petraeus and, 42, 83, 120, 268*n*
  technology and, 26–27, 35, 239*n*, 248*n*
  terrorist-targeting teams in, 176, 252*n*,
    310*n*
  U.S. budget cuts and, 248*n*,
    250*n*
  U.S. nation building in, 36–37, 197,
    248*n*

U.S. stability operations and, 37, 248*n*, 252*n*
U.S. troop commitments in, 10, 83, 252*n*
U.S. wars in, 23–24, 26–29, 37–39, 43, 83, 118, 175–76, 194, 239*n*, 241*n*, 246*n*–49*n*, 268*n*, 298*n*, 313*n*
women in, 36, 40, 189, 248*n*
Irbil, 152
Irish Republican Army (IRA), 30, 112–14, 284*n*
Islam, 43, 45, 71, 80, 91, 116, 120, 137, 163, 179, 188, 191, 215, 243*n*–44*n*, 321*n*
extremists and, 210, 319*n*
HTS and, 46, 81

Jack Bauer, *see* Bauer, Jack
Jackson, Andrea, 247*n*, 250*n*
Jaffe, Greg, 304*n*
Jalali, Ali Ahmad, 270*n*
Johnson, Stefanie, 52–53, 125, 256*n*
Joint IED Defeat Organization (JIEDDO) and, 35–37, 43, 246*n*, 249*n*, 254*n*
Jorgensen, Joseph, 125, 291*n*
Justice Department, U.S., 143

Kabul, 12, 59–61, 161, 170–72, 192, 234*n*, 275*n*
Ayala and, 78, 80–81, 138
highway between Kandahar and, 82, 267*n*
Karzai and, 78–81
smog and overcrowding in, 66
violence in, 64, 240*n*, 270*n*
Kandahar, 12, 15, 60, 62, 77, 82–87, 134–38, 211, 223, 226, 233*n*, 263*n*, 267*n*–73*n*, 326*n*
acid attacks on girls in, 208–10
axe attack in, 207
and British defeat in Maiwand, 269*n*–70*n*
Canadians in, 84, 268*n*, 272*n*
casualties and, 134–35
highway between Kabul and, 82, 267*n*
HTS and, 1, 83, 178, 255*n*, 268*n*
insurgents in, 87, 135–36, 203, 271*n*

Karzais and, 78–79, 97
Loyd's military career and, 7, 56, 59
Provincial Council of, 217–18
Salam and, 200–202, 215–18
U.S. occupation of, 5, 55
and U.S. war in Afghanistan, 86, 271*n*
Kandahar Airfield, 47, 56, 91, 201, 234*n*
Ayala's imprisonment at, 132–33
and Cooper's interrogation of Afghan detainees, 72–73, 75–76
Kansas, 83, 164–65, 278*n*
Karzai, Ahmed Wali, 97, 216–17, 278*n*
Karzai, Hamid, 61, 79–80, 97, 216, 265*n*
Ayala and, 6, 78–82, 92, 136–38, 145, 152, 265*n*–66*n*
background of, 78–79
and casualties in Afghanistan, 134–35
Taliban and, 78–79, 95, 202
Khakrezwal, Mohammad Akram, 271*n*, 323*n*
Khik, 270*n*
Khost, 44–46, 162, 195, 255*n*, 303*n*
Kilcullen, David, 117, 120, 287*n*–88*n*
*Kimbrough v. United States*, 298*n*
Kipling, Rudyard, 119
Kipp, Jacob W.:
cultural intelligence and, 238*n*, 250*n*, 316*n*
Foreign Military Studies Office and, 25, 194, 238*n*
HTS and, 194, 316*n*
Soviet-Afghan War and, 238*n*
technology and, 25, 38, 239*n*
Koran, 91
Korea, South, 63
Fondacaro's tour in, 33–34, 245*n*
Loyd's tour in, 54–55, 258*n*–59*n*
Korean War, 32, 310*n*
Kuchis, 182
Kunar, 83–84
Kurdistan, 152
Kushk-i-Nakhud, 84, 269*n*
Kuwait, 23, 31, 139

Lacy, Steve, 177–78, 186, 190–91,
  314*n*–15*n*
Lala, Hajji (Hajji Ahmadullah), 221–23,
  325*n*
Lalai Dastagiri, Hajji Agha, 202,
  320*n*
Landing, the, 163–66, 168–69
Lang, Stephen James "Banger," 170–72,
  307*n*
Lashkar Gah, 183, 190, 314*n*
  HTS and, 178–79
Latin America, 102, 122–24, 162
Lawrence, T. E., 101, 120–21
Leatherneck, Camp, 177–80, 186, 189,
  192
Leavenworth, Fort Leavenworth, Kans.,
  25, 303*n*–4*n*
  HTS training in, 81–82, 90–92,
    162–65, 167–68, 177–78, 265*n*,
    307*n*
  Petraeus's command at, 40, 42, 304*n*
  Weston Resolve and, 164–65
Lévi-Strauss, Claude, 119–20
liberals, liberalism, 43, 112, 163
  anthropology and, 118, 285*n*
Libya, 113
Lincoln Group, 247*n*
Little Big Horn, battle of, 269*n*
Lockheed Martin, 72–73
Loeb, Vernon, 246*n*
London, 114, 116, 143
Los Angeles, Calif., 78, 147, 151,
  181
Loyd, Paul, Jr., 48, 53, 55, 156, 160,
  255*n*–59*n*
Loyd, Paul, Sr., 48–50
Loyd, Paula Gene, 47–67, 72
  Afghan children and, 7–8, 11–12, 57,
    60
  and Afghan women and girls, 56–58,
    62–63, 93–94, 226
  animal rescue group of, 48–49
  anthropology and, 7, 50, 53–54, 56,
    125, 256*n*, 258*n*
  and Arman, 61–63
  Army enlistment of, 53–54
  attack on, 16–22, 127–33, 135–37, 140,
    144, 146, 153, 155, 161, 169, 204–6,
    208–9, 211–14, 216–19, 235*n*–37*n*,
    293*n*, 301*n*, 321*n*–22*n*, 326*n*

and Ayala, 8, 18, 82–83, 92, 131, 133,
  153, 154–60, 268*n*, 300*n*
  on Bedouin women, 56–57
  Chehel Gazi patrol and, 7–8, 10–11,
    13–18, 207, 232*n*–34*n*, 293*n*
  childhood and adolescence of, 48–51,
    54, 256*n*
  cultural intelligence and, 2, 91, 96,
    277*n*
  education of, 1–2, 7, 48–49, 51–56,
    59–60, 99, 125, 256*n*, 258*n*,
    261*n*
  honors thesis of, 53–54, 99, 258*n*
  HTS and, 1–3, 7–8, 10–11, 77–78, 83,
    88, 90–98, 125, 161–62, 167–69,
    199–200, 214, 217, 235*n*, 255*n*,
    275*n*–78*n*, 298*n*, 304*n*–5*n*,
    320*n*
  idealism of, 7, 53, 59, 97, 257*n*
  interpreters used by, 11–14, 16, 94,
    96–97, 259*n*
  legacy of, 226
  Maiwand and, 7, 13, 23, 83, 85, 89,
    91–98, 127–29, 131–32, 145, 200,
    215, 217, 221, 274*n*–76*n*
  medical treatment of, 130–31, 140,
    146
  military career of, 7, 53–60, 82–83,
    258*n*–61*n*
  Muggeo's relationship with, 59–60,
    64, 66–67, 83, 128–31, 156–57
  naming of, 255*n*
  and NATO forces in Afghanistan,
    59, 64
  and need for cooperation between
    military and civilian workers, 64–66,
    261*n*
  on the partially veiled and partially
    open, 99
  as peacemaker, 48, 255*n*–56*n*
  physical appearance of, 7–8, 16–18,
    48, 50–52, 54, 57, 59–60, 64–65, 69,
    128, 130, 140–41, 199–200, 214,
    232*n*–33*n*, 236*n*, 256*n*, 258*n*, 261*n*
  physical fitness of, 52, 54, 60, 83,
    258*n*
  PRTs and, 58–64, 261*n*
  at Ramrod, 69–70, 132
  and Research Triangle Institute
    International, 66–67

and Salam, 127, 133, 137, 144, 146, 154–55, 157, 301*n*
Wilson Center appearance of, 64–66, 261*n*
in Zabul, 60–64, 66, 96–97, 161, 261*n*
Lugar, Richard, 248*n*

McCain, John, 133, 294*n*
McCarthy, Bob, 181
McChrystal, Stanley, 32, 175–77, 195, 309*n*
Afghanistan war assessment of, 176–77, 252*n*, 310*n*
on cultural intelligence, 176–77
McCollough, Bill, 187–88, 313*n*
Mace, George, 163
McFarland, Maxie, 37–38, 238*n*, 249*n*
McFate, Montgomery Carlough, 101–18, 200, 279*n*–86*n*
anthropology and, 29–31, 43, 101, 105, 112–18, 125–26, 250*n*, 282*n*, 284*n*–86*n*, 291*n*, 316*n*
childhood and adolescence of, 104–10, 112, 126, 282*n*
cultural intelligence and, 29–31, 35–36, 43–44, 102, 117, 242*n*–44*n*, 250*n*
education of, 29–30, 107–9, 111–16, 120, 125, 280*n*–81*n*, 284*n*
heritage of, 102–4
houseboats and, 104–8, 111–12, 280*n*–82*n*
HTS and, 38, 101–2, 120, 124, 193, 196–97, 224–25, 250*n*, 255*n*, 316*n*–17*n*
intelligence and, 120, 242*n*, 288*n*
marriage of, 115–17
mother of, 102–9, 111–12, 280*n*
ONR and, 29, 116–17, 243*n*
physical appearance of, 29, 108, 112
research on Northern Ireland of, 112–14, 116, 284*n*
and revision of counterinsurgency doctrine, 43–44, 253*n*
survival instincts of, 110–11
on war, 107, 112, 114–16, 118
and Wilson, 108–9, 196–97
McGlaughlin, Kevin P., 260*n*–61*n*

McKiernan, David, 83, 134, 268*n*
firing of, 175, 310*n*
McWilliams, Richard H., 301*n*
Maiwand, 82–99, 172–73, 203–11, 213–18, 220–24, 232*n*–35*n*, 269*n*–76*n*, 296*n*, 307*n*
Amir Mohammad and, 211, 215
Army and, 5–7, 9, 87–88, 90, 92, 94, 97, 207, 224, 232*n*, 235*n*, 272*n*–74*n*
and attack on Loyd, 127–29, 213–14
Ayala and, 23, 82, 88–89, 91–94, 97–98, 127–28, 131, 133, 135, 137, 153, 156, 159, 221, 273*n*–74*n*
bandits in, 95–96, 209, 323*n*
bazaar in, 97–98, 141, 200, 207–8, 214, 218, 232*n*, 319*n*, 321*n*
bombings and, 14, 88, 90, 94, 96, 99, 141, 201, 210, 221–23, 273*n*, 297*n*–98*n*
children in, 95, 98–99
drug trade and, 86, 91
education in, 95, 98
Great Britain and, 84–85, 269*n*–70*n*
HTS and, 23, 82–83, 85, 88–98, 169, 172, 178, 223–24, 255*n*, 265*n*
Hajji Lala and, 221–23, 325*n*
humanitarian aid in, 88, 136
insurgency and, 12, 87–88, 90–91, 94–96, 201, 210, 221–22
Loyd and, 7, 13, 23, 83, 85, 89, 91–98, 127–29, 131–32, 145, 200, 213–14, 215, 217, 221, 274*n*–76*n*
opposition to U.S. presence in, 14, 235*n*
prices of commodities in, 7, 13–14, 98, 232*n*
Salam and, 128, 200–201, 204–7, 215, 217–18, 220, 223, 324*n*
soldiers accused of killing civilians in, 221, 325*n*
Taliban and, 14, 85–86, 88, 91, 93–96, 99, 201, 214, 235*n*, 270*n*–71*n*
women in, 209, 275*n*, 322*n*–23*n*
Malalai, 84–85, 209, 270*n*
*malik*, Malik system, 96, 98–99
Maliki, Nouri al-, 81, 137
Manley Commission, 268*n*–69*n*

Manslaughter Working Group, 300$n$
Marine Corps, U.S., 24, 34, 82, 102, 104,
    119, 146, 246$n$, 312$n$
    counterinsurgency and, 42–43,
        187–89, 313$n$
    cultural intelligence and, 31, 117,
        187–88, 190–92, 241$n$, 243$n$–44$n$
    in Helmand, 177–78, 186–88, 190,
        192–93
    HTS and, 10, 169–70, 177–78,
        180–81, 187, 189–93, 196, 311$n$,
        314$n$
    and invasion of Marja, 187, 190–91
    medical missions and, 180–84, 186,
        311$n$
Marine Corps, U.S., units of:
    1st Battalion, 5th Marines, 311$n$, 313$n$
    2nd Marine Expeditionary Brigade,
        190
    Female Engagement Team (FET),
        177, 311$n$
    Fox Company, 179, 181, 186
    Judge Advocate Division, 157, 302$n$
Marja, invasion of, 187, 190–91
Marxists, Marxism, 53–54, 283$n$
Massoud, Ahmed Shah, 79
Mazar-i-Sharif, 234$n$, 271$n$, 276$n$
Mead, Margaret, 103, 117, 122, 289$n$
media, 80, 108, 123, 135–36, 247$n$, 313$n$,
    323$n$–24$n$
    HTS and, 46, 163, 168, 183, 191
    Loyd and, 54, 57, 324$n$
    and revision of counterinsurgency
        doctrine, 43, 252$n$
    Salam and, 200–201, 218
Merry, Sally Engle, 53, 258$n$
Mexicans, Mexico, 39, 102, 147, 251$n$
México Indígena, 251$n$
Middle East, 71, 83, 101, 241$n$, 245$n$,
    303$n$
Middleton, John, 113, 283$n$
Military Extraterritorial Jurisdiction Act,
    138–39
Military Review, 193–94
militias, 25–26, 85, 174, 203, 270$n$
    Karzai and, 78–79
Milošević, Slobodan, 71
misogyny, 199, 206, 208–10, 321$n$–22$n$
Mission Essential Personnel (MEP),
    234$n$

MITR Corporation, 247$n$
Mohammad, Amir, 211–13, 215, 292$n$,
    324$n$
Mohammad Zahir Shah, King of
    Afghanistan, 80
Morlock, Jeremy, 325$n$
Mormons, 18, 70, 181, 262$n$
Muggeo, Frank:
    Ayala's sentencing and, 156–57
    and Loyd, 59–60, 64, 66–67, 83,
        128–31, 140, 156–57, 301$n$
    and Salam, 303$n$–4$n$
mujaheddin, 202, 214
    Soviet-Afghan War and, 24–25, 85,
        90, 171–72
Mullen, Mike, 83

Nachmanoff, Michael, 143–46, 225,
    298$n$, 300$n$–302$n$
    Ayala's sentencing and, 154–58,
        160
    and letters from supporters of Ayala,
        144–45
    and shooting of Salam, 154–55, 301$n$
Nad Ali, 182
Nagl, John A., 252$n$–53$n$
Najibullah, Mohammad, 85
Naler, Christopher, 312$n$
National Security Agency, U.S., 71–72
Native Americans, 102, 162, 262$n$,
    300$n$
    and comparisons between
        anthropology and intelligence, 121,
        288$n$–89$n$
    and Cooper's childhood and
        adolescence, 70, 76
Navajo Nation, 70, 262$n$
Navy, U.S., 29, 103, 117, 133, 146, 180,
    225, 246$n$, 253$n$
Nawa, 188, 311$n$, 315$n$
Nazis, 112, 282$n$
Network of Concerned Anthropologists,
    286$n$
New Orleans, La., 80, 102, 139, 144–47,
    225
New York, 31, 179, 244$n$
Nicholson, John W. "Mick," 41, 44
Nietzsche, Friedrich, 110–11, 282$n$
night letters, 179, 187, 190, 311$n$,
    313$n$

Nixon, Richard, 32, 244*n*
nongovernmental organizations, 59,
    63–65, 165, 251*n*
Noorzai, 96, 98–99
North Atlantic Treaty Organization
    (NATO), 59–60, 71, 195, 215,
    234*n*
  Afghanistan and, 59, 64–65, 83, 87,
    134–35, 175–77, 179, 187, 190,
    294*n*–95*n*, 311*n*
  ISAF of, 176–77, 190, 268*n*,
    294*n*–95*n*
  McChrystal and, 176–77
  night letters and, 179, 187, 311*n*
Northern Ireland, 112–14, 116,
    284*n*
Nutini, Hugo G., 123, 290*n*

Obama, Barack, 1, 9, 134–35, 174, 249*n*,
    309*n*–10*n*
Office of Naval Research (ONR):
  cultural intelligence and, 29,
    243*n*
  McFate and, 29, 116–17, 243*n*
Office of Strategic Services (OSS), 40,
    122
oil spot theory, 307*n*
Omaha, Neb., 163, 304*n*–5*n*
Omar, Mullah Muhammad, 79, 85, 202,
    270*n*–71*n*
open-source intelligence, 30, 39, 190,
    241*n*–42*n*, 251*n*, 313*n*, 315*n*
Ouimette, Kirsten, 272*n*, 296*n*

Packer, George, 248*n*, 287*n*
Pakistan, Pakistanis, 15, 67, 174, 204,
    225, 240*n*, 311*n*
  Afghan border with, 44, 60, 87
  Afghan refugees in, 73, 95, 210
  and Cooper, 73, 75
  immolations in, 206, 321*n*–22*n*
  Karzai and, 79, 265*n*
  Taliban and, 61, 79, 86, 202–3, 210
Panjwai, 269*n*
Pashto, 172–73, 184, 188, 194, 263*n*,
    304*n*, 308*n*
  Cooper's knowledge of, 6, 13, 72,
    74–75
Pashtuns, 11, 73, 170, 172, 184, 200–201,
    263*n*, 308*n*

Pashtunwali, 188, 311*n*
Patai, Raphael, 118
Pathak, Matthew, 17
  HTS and, 232*n*, 234*n*–35*n*
  Salam and, 20, 127, 155, 159, 216,
    236*n*, 292*n*, 320*n*
Peace Through Strength (Proceay
    Takhim-e-Solh), 202–3, 211,
    320*n*
Penitentes, 179–80
Pentagon, *see* Defense Department, U.S.
Pentagon Papers, 244*n*, 245*n*
Persian Gulf War, 38, 248*n*, 298*n*
Petraeus, David Howell, 32, 195
  counterinsurgency and, 10, 42–43,
    252*n*
  cultural intelligence and, 40–41,
    43–44
  Fort Leavenworth command of, 40,
    42–43, 304*n*
  Iraq and, 42, 83, 120, 268*n*
Phoenix Program, 191, 314*n*
police, 54, 106–8, 121, 132, 145, 149
police, Afghan, 12, 76, 190, 263*n*, 271*n*,
    274*n*, 320*n*
  and attack on Loyd, 127–28, 136,
    293*n*
  Chehel Gazi patrol and, 8–9, 13
  corruption of, 21, 58, 93, 96, 237*n*,
    276*n*
  HTS and, 21, 92–93, 314*n*
  Maiwand and, 13, 93–96, 221–23
  Salam and, 21, 211–13, 215–17, 219,
    221, 292*n*, 324*n*
  Taliban and, 95, 203
politics, 39, 54–55, 133, 188, 193, 249*n*,
    314*n*
  Afghanistan and, 55, 61, 74, 79, 96–97,
    135, 137, 201, 203, 240*n*, 253*n*,
    268*n*, 316*n*
  anthropology and, 114, 118, 125,
    240*n*, 285*n*, 287*n*
  Cooper and, 71, 74
  counterinsurgencies and, 10, 43,
    124–25, 253*n*
  cultural intelligence and, 10, 30, 192,
    242*n*
  HTS and, 81–82, 88–89, 163, 168–69,
    255*n*
  IRA and, 113–14

politics (*cont.*)
Iraq and, 30, 35, 37
McFate and, 105, 112
Maiwand and, 14, 87–88, 94, 97
and need for cooperation between
military and civilian workers,
65–66
Project Camelot and, 122–23
PRTs and, 58–59
Salam and, 134, 207, 216–17
Polynesia, 103, 280*n*
postcolonialism, 198
Post-traumatic Stress Disorder (PTSD),
76–77, 146–47, 155–56, 264*n*, 293*n*,
301*n*
Powell Doctrine, 37, 241*n*, 248*n*–49*n*
Poynter, Frances, 102–9, 111–12, 280*n*
Price, David, 118, 289*n*
Prinslow, Karl, 252*n*
Provincial Reconstruction Teams (PRTs),
248*n*
Loyd and, 58–64, 261*n*
in Zabul, 60–64

Qala Khan, Hajji, 204–5
Salam and, 205, 207–8, 210, 213,
321*n*–22*n*
Qalat, 60, 62

Ramirez, Mequilita, 102
Ramrod, Forward Operating Base, 93,
132, 172, 221, 272*n*, 325*n*–26*n*
physical appearance of, 69–70,
262*n*
RAND Corporation, 116–17
rapport, 121, 287*n*–88*n*
Rath, Joshua L., 298*n*
Rathje, Mike, 56–57
Republicans, 285*n*
Research Triangle Institute International,
66–67
Reuters, 323*n*–24*n*
Rich, Michael:
Ayala's sentencing and, 156–59
military career of, 157, 301*n*–2*n*
and Salam, 157–59
Riefenstahl, Leni, 112
Rohde, David, 320
Route Irish, 152
Rumsfeld, Donald, 35, 249*n*

Sabari, 162
Sadoo Khan, Hajji, 203–5
on bandits in Maiwand, 209, 323*n*
on independent Afghans vs. slaves,
210
Salam and, 203–4, 208, 213, 322*n*–23*n*
and story of stolen tractor, 208
on women, 209, 322*n*–23*n*
Sagarin, Rafe, 51, 257*n*
Said, Edward, 119
St. Thomas, 51, 54, 129, 256*n*
Salam, Abdul, 13–16, 199–208, 210–23,
319*n*–26*n*
alleged mental illness of, 22, 211–15,
217–19, 222, 324*n*
arson in history of, 218–19
attempted escape of, 208
and Ayala, 146, 154–55, 157–59
brother of, 204, 210, 212–13, 215,
218–23
capture of, 19–22, 211–12, 236*n*–37*n*,
301*n*, 321*n*
childhood of, 204, 218
Ehsan on, 217–18
emotions of, 213, 215
employment of, 14–15, 204, 207, 215,
218–20, 324*n*
father of, 204–5, 207–8, 212–13,
218–20, 321*n*
Loyd attacked by, 16, 204–6, 211–13,
217–19, 321*n*–22*n*, 326*n*
Qala Khan and, 205, 207–8, 210, 213,
321*n*–22*n*
release of body of, 215–16, 323*n*
Sadoo Khan and, 203–4, 208, 213,
322*n*–23*n*
shooting of, 22, 127–28, 131–39,
144–47, 153–60, 206, 208, 210, 212,
215–16, 219–20, 237*n*, 292*n*–94*n*,
301*n*, 321*n*, 324*n*–25*n*
story of stolen tractor of, 204, 208,
215, 219–20
as symbol, 223
Taliban and, 204–5, 207–8, 214–15,
217–19, 222, 321*n*, 324*n*
Salang Tunnel, 80, 265*n*–66*n*
San Antonio, Tex., 48, 50, 130
Santwier, Andi, 78, 80, 139, 225
Ayala's sentencing and, 153–54,
160

*Sanusi of Cyrenaica, The*
  (Evans-Pritchard), 113
Sapone, Sean, 115–17
Scales, Robert H., 28
Schweitzer, Martin "Marty," 45–46, 194,
  254*n*–55*n*
September 11th, 24–25, 30, 39, 43, 55,
  71, 78–79, 144, 151, 175, 179,
  241*n*
Settlement 1, 180–86
Sewall, Sarah, 42
Sherzai, Abdul Razik, 216–17
Sherzai, Gul Agha, 86, 216, 271*n*
Shiites, Shia, 31, 180, 243*n*–44*n*
Shinseki, Eric, 34–35, 246*n*
Singesar, 85, 270*n*–71*n*
Skotnicki, Justin, 19, 21, 127, 212, 236*n*,
  237*n*
Slaikeu, Karl, 169–70, 307*n*
Sluka, Jeffrey A., 284*n*
Smith, Don, 38, 41, 44, 250*n*, 252*n*,
  254*n*
Solomon, Wendy, 259*n*
Sosh, 32, 244*n*
Soviet-Afghan War, 7, 31, 44, 61, 79,
  210, 263*n*, 311*n*
  Grau and, 25, 238*n*
  Gusinov and, 89–91
  Mujaheddin and, 24–25, 85, 90,
   171–72
Soviet Union, 60, 79
  fall of, 23, 38, 238*n*
  Foreign Military Studies Office and,
   25, 238*n*
  and Gusinov's move to U.S., 89–90
Soyka, Michael, 262*n*
Special Operations Research Office
  (SORO), 123
Spen (HTS analyst), 172–73, 307*n*–8*n*
State Department, U.S., 66, 120, 145,
  198, 226, 243*n*, 245*n*, 248*n*
  Karzai's bodyguard detail and, 78, 152,
   266*n*
  Project Camelot and, 123, 290*n*–91*n*
  PRTs and, 58, 60, 64
Status of Forces Agreement, 173
structural functionalism, 114
Sturgis, Milan, 303*n*
Sudan, 113
Sunrise, 147–49

Supreme Court, U.S., 143, 298*n*
Suveges, Nicole, 162, 167–68

Tactical Ground Reporting System
  (TIGR), 243*n*, 253*n*
Tajiks, 78–79, 170, 276*n*
Taliban, 237*n*, 273*n*–76*n*
  Afghanistan and, 7, 9, 26, 59, 73–74,
   76, 78–79, 83, 85–86, 88, 91, 93–96,
   99, 134–37, 172, 174–75, 177, 179,
   188, 190, 199–210, 213–14, 216–18,
   222, 224, 261*n*, 263*n*–64*n*, 295*n*,
   311*n*, 319*n*–21*n*, 323*n*–25*n*
  Arman and, 61–62
  assassination campaigns of, 203,
   320*n*
  Cooper and, 73–76, 263*n*–64*n*
  fall of, 55, 73, 78–79, 86, 175
  HTS and, 83, 94
  Jack Bauer and, 12–13, 234*n*
  Karzai and, 78–79, 95, 202
  Loyd's death and, 155, 199–200,
   204, 206, 213–14, 216–17, 319*n*,
   323*n*–25*n*
  Maiwand, 14, 85–86, 88, 91, 93–96,
   99, 201, 214, 235*n*, 270*n*–71*n*
  night letters and, 179, 311*n*
  origins of, 85, 270*n*
  Pakistan and, 61, 79, 86, 202–3, 210
  reintegration of, 174, 202, 320*n*
  Salam and, 204–5, 207–8, 214–15,
   217–19, 222, 321*n*, 324*n*
  in Zabul, 62–63
Teamey, Kyle, 253*n*
Team Spirit, 33
technology, 23–27, 39
  cultural intelligence and, 24–25, 29,
   238*n*–39*n*
  Grau and, 25, 38, 239*n*
  Iraq and, 26–27, 35, 239*n*, 248*n*
  and U.S. war in Afghanistan, 26, 249*n*,
   277*n*
terrorists, terrorism, 3, 45, 66, 110, 118,
  155, 164, 233*n*
  Ayala's sentencing and, 157–58
  IRA and, 112–13
  on September 11th, 24–25, 30, 39, 43,
   55, 71, 78–79, 144, 151, 175, 179,
   241*n*
  targeting of, 10, 176, 252*n*–53*n*, 310*n*

Thailand, 124–25
Toledo, Lucy, 264*n*
Tom Cruise, 11, 22, 211, 237*n*
Tracy (HTS social scientist), 45–46, 255*n*
Trader Vic's, 103
tribes, tribal systems, 34, 56, 81, 94–97,
   116, 124, 137, 216
   cultural intelligence and, 3, 10, 29–31,
      242*n*–43*n*, 249*n*, 277*n*
   HTS and, 45–46, 88–89, 91
   Karzai and, 78–79
   in Maiwand, 88–89, 91, 94–96, 99
   and need for cooperation between
      military and civilian workers, 65–66,
      261*n*
   and U.S. war in Afghanistan, 26, 86
Truman, Harry, 245*n*
*Twilight of the Idols* (Nietzsche), 110

Umar, Mohammad (Salam's father),
   204–5, 207–8, 212–13, 218–20,
   321*n*
   on Ayala, 219–20
   on son's history of arson, 218–19
   on story of stolen tractor, 219–20
United Nations, 7, 26, 113
   Afghanistan and, 63–65, 134, 295*n*,
      313*n*
United States Agency for International
   Development (USAID), 169, 248*n*,
   296*n*
   and Loyd, 56, 60, 161, 261*n*
   and PRTs, 58, 60, 64
*U.S. Army Field Manual 2–0*, 314*n*
*U.S. Army/Marine Corps
   Counterinsurgency Field Manual*,
   42–44, 252*n*–53*n*
United States Sentencing Commission,
   300*n*
Urgent Fury, Operation, 33, 151
use-of-force continuum, 138

Vietnam, Vietnam War, 2, 23–25, 41, 58,
   122, 133, 157, 192, 248*n*, 290*n*–91*n*,
   294*n*
   ethnography and, 30–31
   Fondacaro and, 32–34, 244*n*
   France and, 34, 245*n*
   opposition to, 32, 124, 244*n*
   Phoenix Program and, 191, 314*n*

villages, villagers, 65, 74, 109, 124, 175,
   79, 182, 202, 237*n*, 263*n*, 271*n*,
   276*n*–78*n*
   in Bali, 120–21
   cultural intelligence and, 3, 195, 277*n*
   HTS and, 81, 92–96
   Loyd's military career and, 56, 259*n*
   Maiwand and, 95–96, 98–99, 215–16,
      235*n*
   Salam and, 206, 215–16, 319*n*–20*n*
   Zabul and, 61–63
violence, 205, 214
   combat-stress related injuries and,
      146–47, 155
   HTS Khost mission and, 46, 255*n*
   Kabul and, 64, 240*n*, 270*n*
   Kandahar and, 55, 86, 207–10
   Salam and, 154–56, 223
   *see also* bombs, bombers, bombing
Voelkel, Trevor, 262*n*, 297*n*–98*n*
Votel, Joseph, 35–36, 44, 246*n*

Walker, Steve, 258*n*, 260*n*
Ward, Patty (Loyd's mother):
   and attack on daughter, 129–30
   Ayala's sentencing and, 156–57, 160
   and daughter's childhood and
      adolescence, 48–51, 54
   daughter's death and, 141, 156–57
   daughter's education and, 48, 53, 256*n*,
      261*n*
   daughter's legacy and, 226
   daughter's medical treatment and, 140,
      146
   daughter's military career and, 258*n*,
      260*n*
   letter in support of Ayala by, 145–46
   and shooting of Salam, 132, 146,
      301*n*
Warren, Mike, 97, 267*n*
   and Ayala's arrest and imprisonment,
      138, 294*n*
   HTS and, 82, 89, 92, 278*n*, 320*n*
   Salam and, 153, 217, 294*n*, 320*n*
Washington, D.C., 55, 64, 116–17, 139,
   163, 179, 274*n*
Wellesley College, 1, 7, 52–53, 56, 99,
   226, 258*n*
Westerberg, Cecil (Barney West), 103–5,
   279*n*

Weston Resolve, 163–65
West Point, 31–32, 45, 244*n*–45*n*, 273*n*
Wiker, Gretchen, 49
Wilson, Cintra, 108–9, 196–97
Wilson, Dr. (alias), 307
Wilson, Woodrow, 40, 245*n*
Wolf, Eric, 125, 291*n*
women:
 Bedouin, 56–57
 FET and, 177, 311*n*
 in Iraq, 36, 40, 189, 248*n*
 Loyd and, 56–58, 62–63, 93–94,
  226
 in Maiwand, 209, 275*n*, 322*n*–23*n*
 marriages and, 36, 56–58, 206, 209,
  247*n*
 misogyny and, 199, 206, 208–10,
  321*n*–22*n*
 Sadoo Khan on, 209, 322*n*–23*n*
 *see also under* Afghanistan

Woodrow Wilson Center, 64–66, 261*n*
World Basic Information Library, 39–40,
 252*n*
World War I, 40, 121–22, 241*n*
World War II, 48, 103–4, 107, 113, 241*n*,
 283*n*
 anthropology and, 122, 289*n*
 geography and, 40, 251*n*

Yale University, 113–14

Zabul, 226
 Arman and, 61–62
 Loyd in, 60–64, 66, 96–97, 161,
  261*n*
 PRT in, 60–64
Zadran, 45–46
Zhari, 269*n*–71*n*, 273*n*
Zinni, Anthony, 24
Zulu wars, 269*n*

# ABOUT THE AUTHOR

**Vanessa M. Gezari** has been writing about Afghanistan since 2002. Her reporting from four continents, nine countries, and many corners of the United States has appeared in *The Washington Post, The New Republic, Slate,* and others. A 2012 Knight-Wallace Fellow, she is the James Madison Visiting Professor on First Amendment Issues at the Columbia Journalism School. This is her first book.